Also by Garland A. Haas

Jimmy Carter and the Politics of Frustration
(McFarland, 1992)

The Politics of Disintegration

The Politics
of Disintegration

*Political Party Decay
in the United States,
1840 to 1900*

by Garland A. Haas

McFarland & Company, Inc., Publishers
Jefferson, North Carolina, and London

This book is dedicated to Pauline (especially)
and to Judith and Joseph
for reasons they are well aware of

British Library Cataloguing-in-Publication data are available

Library of Congress Cataloguing-in-Publication Data

Haas, Garland A., 1919–
    The politics of disintegration : political party decay in the
United States, 1840–1900 / by Garland A. Haas.
        p.   cm.
    Includes bibliographical references and index.
    ISBN 0-89950-983-5 (lib. bdg. : 50# alk. paper) ∞
    1. Political parties—United States—History—19th century.
    2. United States—Politics and government—19th century.   I. Title.
JK2261.H23   1994
324.273'09—dc20   94-21678
                                                                    CIP

Manufactured in the United States of America

McFarland & Company, Inc., Publishers
  Box 611, Jefferson, North Carolina 28640

Contents

Prologue

In 1840 William Henry Harrison, a Whig, was elected to be the ninth president of the United States. His election ended the reign of the Jacksonian Democratic Party and brought the emerging Whig Party to power in the national government. Harrison's election also signaled the completion of a national two-party system in which the Whigs and Democrats would confront each other on more or less even terms in every region and in every state of the country.

With the election of Harrison, the act of political party creation in America was generally complete. Processes for organizing voters, nominating candidates, and conducting campaigns had been regularized. The party constituencies were well on the way to being defined, party administration–congressional relations clarified, and the role of public opinion and the press in politics formalized.

The completion of a national two-party system was a remarkable achievement. Yet the two-party system failed to survive. Almost immediately it began to disintegrate under the impact of such sectional conflicts as tariff reform, patronage abuse, and especially slavery, which — as the "unspoken issue" already had a long history of provoking sectional conflict — emerged as the central political issue in the 1840s and 1850s. Eventually, as the result of subsequent slavery-related political developments — the repeal of the Missouri Compromise by the Kansas-Nebraska Act of 1854, the Dred Scott decision, John Brown's raid at Harper's Ferry, and the birth of the Republican Party (a purely sectional party), all of which increased tensions between the North and the South — the national parties died, to be replaced by sectional parties.

Thus, the American two-party system, which had begun as an instrument of national unity, by the onset of the Civil War had become the servant of sectional interests. Then, after the compromise of 1877, the Republican and Democratic parties quickly became the servants of special interests as they fought fiercely over patronage and the welfare of the wealthy. The result was the absence of genuine issues in politics and the neglect of the problems of the disadvantaged. Dissension rather than unity came to characterize the conduct of the parties in the decade before the turn of the century.

This volume is not intended as a general history of American political parties from the Civil War to the turn of the century. Rather, the aim has been to sketch the main outlines of political development in the period and to answer certain basic questions about those parties. What were the social, economic, and political forces which shaped them? Who were the people who did the job of organizing and office seeking? What have been some of the key issues which have provided the foci of political conventions and campaigns? And, of course, many more similar questions. Considerable attention is devoted to such things as the humor of American politics, views of national political leaders on the role of political parties in the American governmental system, and the development of the national organization of the major parties. Considerable attention is also directed to the personalities of the people and the philosophies of the parties, which provide the historical milieu in which the American political parties developed during the post–Civil War period.

This brief account of the decline of American political parties is one of the fruits of "giving" a survey course in American political history to undergraduate and graduate students for more than three decades. During that time I worked through a considerable number of primary and secondary sources. Many of these sources are included in the bibliography — although the listing, at best, is a hopelessly stingy acknowledgment of my debt to these predecessors and contemporaries.

What I have written is really the result of the efforts of several people to whom I owe a deep debt of gratitude: my wife, Pauline, who offered unflagging encouragement; Homer Cunningham, my colleague and friend, who read the full manuscript and made helpful suggestions for revision; and Gail Fielding, the "Inter-Library Loan Lady" at the Whitworth College library who, through her computer, made the resources of the universe available to me. Of course, any errors of fact or interpretation are mine.

GARLAND A. HAAS
Spokane, Washington
Spring 1994

1. The Whigs
Compromisers of American Politics

On March 4, 1841, Martin Van Buren yielded the presidency of the United States to William Henry Harrison. At 68 Harrison was the oldest president to be inaugurated until Ronald Reagan in 1981. In his meandering, two-hour inaugural address, delivered hatless and coatless on a frigid and stormy day, the new president made it clear that he believed that Jackson had misused the executive authority and promised that he would not interfere with the affairs of Congress. Harrison's attitude pleased the Whig leaders who had their fill of what they called the "executive usurpation" of Jackson. (As he spoke bone-chilled politicians roamed around the platform stamping their feet to get the blood running.)

Although the Whigs had succeeded in electing their candidate, at the core they were a hopelessly divided party. Henry Clay and Daniel Webster, the real leaders of the Whig Party, regarded Harrison, the ostensible leader of the party, as little more than an impressive figurehead. Trouble was visible on the horizon. Clay had been offered any place in the cabinet to which he might aspire, but declined to accept a cabinet post because he preferred to remain in the Senate, where, as Senate majority leader, he would mastermind the legislative program in Congress. The president, the brash Kentuckian was sure, would dutifully sign the bills so passed. He was quite willing to be the power beside the throne.

The Whigs had hardly tasted power before they experienced a real calamity. Thirty-two days after he took the oath of office, "Old Tip" was dead as a result of pneumonia incurred, it was said, when reading his inaugural address into the teeth of a cruel northeast wind. John Tyler, the vice president, insisted that he be sworn in as president and not merely be, as the Constitution implies, a vice president "acting" as president.[1]

Trouble between Tyler and Clay broke into the open within a month. When Congress met in the special session called by Harrison at Clay's behest for early June 1841, Clay was ready with an elaborate legislative program which he called his "general orders to Congress" (essentially the key features of his American system). It included the repeal of the Democrats' Independent Treasury Act and the establishment of a third bank of the United States; and high tariffs and the distribution to the states of the proceeds from the sale of public lands. Although Clay's program was completely in accord with the principles of the National Republicans in the Whig Party, it ignored almost completely the states' rights adherents among the Whigs. It also revealed Clay's intention to brush aside the president (now Tyler) whom he chose to regard only as a sort of regent.[2] It was inevitable that Clay's nationalistic program would meet with a cold reception at the White House.

Tyler refused to be bullied by Clay into the role which Harrison had been willing to accept. The Whigs soon found that they could not draft a tariff or bank bill acceptable to President Tyler. In August 1841, when Congress passed a bill creating a new bank, he flatly vetoed it. Although the Clay men drenched the president with invective, Tyler dug in his heels. As he saw it, no commitment on the crucial issues of the tariff and the bank had been made by him or the Whig Party in the campaign, and so he felt that he was as free to oppose the measures as Clay was to support them.

The infuriated Whigs now rallied wholeheartedly to Clay's side. Hundreds of letters were received by the president threatening him with assassination. "The fires of a thousand effigies," Tyler wrote afterward, "lighted the streets of the various cities." "Indignation meetings were everywhere held; . . . and a universal roar of Whig vengeance was heard in every blast." The Richmond *Whig* called Tyler "a vast nightmare over the Republic." The pro–Clay *Lexington Intelligencer* (Kentucky) was quoted as saying: "If a God-directed thunderbolt were to strike and annihilate the traitor all would say that 'Heaven is just.'"

In September 1841, Clay, now thoroughly frustrated, hatched a curious but ill-fated scheme to force Tyler out of office. He persuaded the members of the cabinet to resign suddenly and without previous warning one Saturday afternoon (September 11). Since Congress was to adjourn at noon Monday, he reasoned that Tyler in the interim would be unable to form a new cabinet. Since the vacancies would occur while Congress was in session, they could not be filled without senatorial approval and the president, since he could not carry on the government without a cabinet, would be driven to resign.

However, Daniel Webster, who had accepted the post of secretary of state after Clay turned it down, refused to go along with the plan. With Webster's aid Tyler had no trouble in patching up a cabinet which the Senate quickly confirmed. Clay's plan to destroy Tyler's cabinet had put Webster in an awkward, not to say embarrassing dilemma. If he held on to his place in the cabinet he could be charged with party irregularity, but he also realized that if he resigned he might lose a good chance to succeed

Tyler in the presidency. He had a certain reluctance to have it appear that Clay could tell him what to do. Fortunately for Webster, he had entered upon sensitive diplomatic negotiations with the British minister regarding the U.S.–Canada border, which gave him an excellent excuse to remain in the cabinet. His negotiation with the British resulted in the highly popular treaty which became known as the Webster-Ashburton Treaty. Once the treaty was ratified Webster resigned, fearful that a longer stay in Tyler's cabinet would hurt him with the Whigs.

The Tariff Issue

The issue of the tariff had been a difficult and persistent problem for the political parties right from the beginning of the American nation. Once the Constitution had been ratified, presidential and congressional elections held, and a new government under George Washington, the new president, established, it soon became obvious that one of the new government's most pressing needs was for money to cover its day-to-day expenses.

The Tariff Act of 1789. James Madison, then a Congressman from Virginia, proposed that the necessary funds be raised by means of a modest tariff bill which he submitted to the House of Representatives. Under the bill, which was entitled "An Act for the Encouragement and Protection of Manufactures," a flat tax (or tariff) of 5 percent was levied on all goods entering the United States, which afforded a measure of protection for American producers. Despite the low rate, the Southern spokesmen complained that they had little to gain from the tariff since it discriminated against the agricultural South which consumed more imported merchandise than did the North where domestic manufactured goods were relatively advanced. If protection were continued, they observed, the role of the South in the new government would be to provide revenue to be spent in building up Northern manufactures and shipping. Even so, under the leadership of John C. Calhoun, of South Carolina, they generally supported the measure and on July 4, 1789, the first tariff went into effect.

The Tariff of 1816. However, since it failed to produce the needed revenues, by 1812 the Tariff Law of 1789 had been amended upward to a level of about 12.5 percent. These duties were doubled during the War of 1812, but with the understanding that they should be dropped to the normal peacetime level a year after the war's close. It became clear soon after the war was over that the peacetime duties were not high enough to keep out foreign goods, which after 1815 glutted the American market. As American infant industries, ranging from the textile mills of New England to the iron foundries of Pittsburgh, closed their doors, American manufacturers raised a hue and cry for tariff protection which would check the inflow of English goods until they could get firmly on their feet. In short order such a bill, to be known as the Tariff of 1816, was introduced. Almost unseen, the emphasis on the tariff had shifted from that of raising revenue to that of protecting the war-spawned and highly vulnerable American industries.

The battle in Congress over the tariff reflected North-South sectional crosscurrents. Calhoun led the forces in support of the tariff because at that time he believed that South Carolina, possessing many streams where water power could be developed, could grow into a Southern manufacturing center with the whole Southern interior as a market. The opposition to the tariff was led by Daniel Webster who, speaking for the shippers of his New Hampshire district, eloquently opposed the act's highly protective rates. "He was not in haste," Webster said, "to see Sheffields and Birminghams in America." He would rue the day when the great mass of American laborers would "immerse themselves in close and unwholesome workshops": when they would "open their ears in dust, and smoke, and steam to the perpetual whirl of spools. Despite Webster's opposition, the new tariff received support from every section of the country.

The Tariff of 1824. But the demand for protectionism persisted and the Tariff of 1824, enacted while President James Monroe was still in office, included protection for cotton textiles, raw wool, hemp, iron, and other commodities. The New Englanders in Congress were fairly evenly divided. But the middle states and the West and Southwest strongly favored it, and they overcame the almost complete opposition of the South.

As it turned out, the fears of the South were justified. Following the passage of the Tariff of 1824, the price of cotton started on a long, steady, decline — a decline that hit South Carolina planters with exceptional force. In 1825 the South Carolina legislature adopted strong resolutions condemning the tariff and asserting that tariff acts for the protection of domestic manufacturing were unconstitutional. The Southerners who had supported the earlier (1816) law were coming to realize that the protective policy harmed their section.

The Tariff of Abominations, 1828. At this point Senator Martin Van Buren of New York and the group of Jacksonians who dominated the House Committee on Manufactures, took a hand. They knew that Jackson, in order to be elected in 1828, had to win support from the South, which opposed the protective tariff, and the Northeast and Southwest where a strong majority favored it. Before the election of 1828 they had worked out what they thought was a foolproof scheme to present their candidate to the North as favoring a high tariff, and to the South as an opponent of this policy. They devised a tariff bill which set such high rates on raw materials that Northern manufacturers were expected to join shippers and Southern planters in opposing the measure. Amendments making the tariff more palatable to manufacturers were to be defeated, thus Jacksonians could pose in the North as friendly to a high tariff, and in the South as its adversary. If President John Quincy Adams signed the bill he would alienate the South and strain his own credibility, and if he vetoed it he would antagonize both agrarian and manufacturing interests in the rest of the country. Either way, the crucial middle states would be drawn into the Jacksonians' camp. As it turned out the scheme failed to work, for enough Northern support for the bill was obtained to enact the tariff, even though it was not to the immediate advantage of that region.

When President Adams signed the tariff, Southern hotheads promptly branded it the "Tariff of Abominations." Boycotts of Northern manufacturers and farmers suddenly became fashionable. Some Southerners took to wearing ill-fitting homespun garments, untaxed by the Yankee tariff. Many refused to eat Irish potatoes since they were grown in the North.

The South Carolina Exposition and Protest. In 1829 the legislature of South Carolina published its famous *Exposition and Protest* (written in 1828 by Calhoun while he was running for reelection to the vice presidency) which declared that the federal government's taxing power could be used constitutionally only for the raising of revenue; any protection in a tariff law must be incidental. Hence the tariff of 1828 and the whole protective system that it represented were in flagrant violation of the Constitution.

In a message to Congress on December 6, 1831, President Jackson recommended that the tariff be revised downward from the level to which the "Tariff of Abominations" had boosted it in 1828. On July 14, 1832, Congress passed a tariff bill that conceded little to the Southern demands for lower duties. The South Carolina members of Congress reported to their constituents that high protection was now a fixed federal policy and that no relief could be expected from Washington. South Carolina now braced itself for drastic action. Nullifiers and Unionists clashed head-on in the state election of 1832. To nullify or not to nullify—that was the issue. The "Nullies" won an overwhelming victory over the Unionist Party, securing more than a two-thirds majority in the state legislature.

Without delay, the newly elected legislature called for the election of delegates to a state convention. When the convention met in November 1832, a few days after Jackson's reelection, it was completely in the hands of the nullifiers. The delegates, by an overwhelming majority, declared the tariffs of 1828 and 1832 "null, void and no law, binding upon this State, its officers or citizens." It threatened secession from the Union should Congress pass any law for the employment of force against the state.

An angry President Jackson reacted vigorously. On December 10, in a "proclamation to the People of South Carolina," the president warned that the laws of the United States compelled him to meet treason with force and appealed to the people of the state to reassert their allegiance to the Union. He issued orders for appropriate disposition of troops and requested additional powers for the collection of duties.

The Tariff Act of 1833. In the end Congress adopted a policy combining concession with force. Early in 1833 Henry Clay introduced a compromise tariff, worked out in consultation with Calhoun, which provided that all duties in excess of 20 percent of the value of the goods imported were to be reduced by easy stages so that by 1842 the duties on all articles would reach the level of the moderate tariff of 1816. On March 1, 1833, Congress passed the compromise tariff.

The new tariff bill aroused bitterness in Daniel Webster and other advocates of protection, but it pleased the South and especially South Carolina. It also received support from moderates who wished to conciliate the palmetto state. Since the new measure effected an easing of tensions, it won for Clay the name of "Great Pacificator" and increased his popularity with the South.

When the news came out that the new tariff law had been passed, the South Carolina convention reassembled and repealed the nullification ordinance.

Once John Tyler became president in 1841, as we have seen, he and the Clayite Whigs had serious disagreements over the tariff issue. Under the terms of a Distribution-Preemption Act pushed through Congress by Clay in 1841, 10 percent of the revenues obtained from the sale of public land were to be returned to the state in whose boundaries the land lay; the rest was to be distributed among the states in proportion to their population. The distribution of the proceeds from the public land sales would bolster the sagging finances of the states, many of which were staggering under debt burdens too heavy for them in a period of hard times.

However, President Tyler, who was anxious to meet the demands of Southerners who feared that depletion of the treasury as a result of distribution would provide a good argument for the supporters of a high tariff, insisted upon and secured from Clay an amendment pledging that if the tariff schedules should ever exceed the 20 percent maximum provided for by the Compromise Tariff of 1833, the distribution of land revenues to the states would cease. Clay apparently assumed that he could later induce Congress to strike out the amendment, but in this he failed.

The Tariff Act of 1842. In June 1842 Congress passed a temporary tariff measure which raised the tariff rate above the 20 percent level and explicitly repealed the distribution limitation provided for in Clay's Distribution-Preemption Act of 1841, and it was promptly vetoed by President Tyler. If the bill passed, the president said, the government "would not only have to lay additional taxes, but would also have to borrow money to meet pressing demands." Such a proceeding he regarded "as highly impolitic, if not unconstitutional."

After the veto the Whig leaders and the Whig press raised a savage outcry against President Tyler, charging him with treason against his party.

Despite all the noise made by them, the Whigs in Congress realized that they dared not return to their constituents without having enacted some kind of revenue measure. It was estimated that the deficit in the federal treasury at the end of 1841 would be more than $11 million. If this deficit was to be wiped away and the budget balanced, an increase in revenues of some kind would have to be made. So they pushed through a tariff measure in 1842 which raised duties up to the high levels of 1832 — that is, to about 40 percent — and was thus decidedly protective in character. Although Tyler still held antitariff views, the government's need for revenue was imperative, so he swallowed his objections and signed the measure thus reneging on the promise made to the South in 1833 to reduce tariffs to 20 percent in ten years. The Southerners were enraged and one South Carolina group wished to nullify it or even secede from the Union. But Calhoun was playing a higher stakes game and he cooled the hotheads.

Before the tariff bill finally passed, Clay retired from the Senate in disgust to rest and to consolidate the Whig forces in preparation for 1844. When he bid his farewell to his Senate colleagues, Clay's devoted friend and fellow Kentuckian John Crittenden wrote that it was "something like the soul's quitting the body." The gallant Kentuckian's followers, determined to right the wrong of Tyler's "treachery," began to prepare for 1844 with almost fanatical zeal.

Meanwhile, the Whig leaders succeeded in getting through the House of Representatives, by a narrow majority, a series of resolutions that severely arraigned Tyler for his misdeeds. Finally, in 1843 at a caucus of some 50 or more Whig members of Congress, Tyler was drummed out of the party which had elected him (and to which he had never really belonged). Henceforth, Tyler ("the accident of accidents") was a president without a party. When an epidemic of influenza swept over the country that winter, the Whig press was quick to name it "the Tyler Grippe."[3]

The Twin Issues of Texas and Slavery

The Development of Slavery as an Issue. In the early years of the nation, chattel slavery in the United States was no great problem. It had existed all across colonial America, but had died out in the North simply because it did not pay. Soon after the Revolution most Americans, North and South, considered that eventually it would go out of existence everywhere. However, that attitude changed in 1793, after Eli Whitney invented a gin capable ot separating the lint from the seeds of the upland, short-stapled cotton, which gave immediate commercial value to that variety. Overnight, the South's economy and attitude toward slavery was irrevocably altered. Soon, cotton was being sown and harvested in the South on an unprecedented scale. As the world's textile mills gobbled up everything Southern cotton planters could produce, they looked westward for new land to open to cotton cultivation. At the same time, slavery was given a new lease on life and the value of black slaves to work the crop skyrocketed. The slavery issue was born.

Although there were serious differences between the various parties, almost certainly, without slavery, the problems between those groups could have been worked out by the ordinary give-and-take of politics; with slavery they became insoluble. It was the issue that could not be compromised, that made men so angry they did not want to compromise. Yet, men of goodwill from both sides tried.

The Missouri Compromise. The slavery issue was injected into national politics for the first time in 1818 when the application of Missouri for statehood reopened the controversy over slavery. When the question of admitting Missouri came up, it happened that, more or less by accident, a balance between slave and free states had been established with 11 each. Missouri would have made the twelfth slave state.

Debate had scarcely begun on Missouri's statehood petition when Representative James Tallmadge, a relatively unknown congressman from upstate New York, threw a bombshell into the proceedings by proposing an amendment to the enabling bill prohibiting the further importation of slaves into the state and requiring that all children born of slaves in Missouri be freed at the age of 25.

Southerners clearly saw in the Tallmadge Amendment an ominous threat to the sectional balance. If approved, the amendment would ensure the North a majority in both houses of Congress and open the way to sectional legislation that would harm the South. The South felt that its only chance for equality in the federal government rested in the control of the Senate where representation was not based on population. By 1820 the population north of the Ohio River was over 5 million as compared with less than 4.5 million to the south. Since five slaves counted as three people in the apportioning of representatives among the states, the North now had 105 members in the House of Representatives to 81 for the South. Yet in the Senate, with 11 states free and 11 slave, the Southerners had maintained equality. They were, therefore, in a good position to thwart any Northern effort to interfere with the expansion of slavery, and they did not want to lose this veto.

After bitter debate the Tallmadge Amendment passed the House of Representatives by a vote of 97–56, but was promptly rejected by the Senate where a few Northern senators joined with their Southern colleagues to defeat it 22–16. The public was also agitated over the issue. Both houses were deluged with petitions for and against the amendment. To the relief of nearly everyone, the problem was settled peacefully when Massachusetts announced her willingness to give up the territory of Maine which was ready for statehood. Henry Clay and the other compromise-minded senators, in a series of measures known as the "Missouri Compromise," arranged for the preservation of the balance of power in the Senate by admitting Missouri as a slave state and Maine as a free one. The Missouri Compromise also provided that slavery should be excluded from all the Louisiana Purchase territory north of latitude 36 degrees 30 minutes except in Missouri itself. The South and Southwest voted solidly for the compromise, while the Northwest, despite the large number of settlers from the South, voted generally with the Northeast. A political North and a political South had begun to develop.

The country accepted the compromise with relief, the people supposing the compromise had ended the controversy. However, most far-thinking observers knew that the vigor of American society, ever pushing westward, meant that the sectional balance could not last. Dour John Quincy Adams, who, as president, would inherit the problem, wrote that he considered the debate over the compromise nothing less than a mere preamble — "a title page to a great, tragic volume."

Adams was right. The Missouri Compromise of 1820 took the slavery issue out of politics for only a very short time. From the 1830s on the issue grew larger and more portentous as the Northern abolitionists assailed the "peculiar institution" of the South with ever-increasing zeal.

The Issue of Texas

The issue of slavery was projected onto the national political scene by the developments taking place in Texas. By the early 1830s more that 20,000 citizens of the United States with nearly 2,000 slaves had become residents of Texas, at that time a province of Mexico. Most of them came from Tennessee, Mississippi, and Louisiana. For the most part they were law-abiding, God-fearing, hardworking farmers seeking the fertile delta soil along the Gulf coast, but some of them had left the "states" only one or two jumps ahead of the sheriff — the initials "GTT" carved on the doorpost of a shack was a message to relatives and friends that the carver was in trouble with the law and so had "Gone to Texas."

Annexation of the "Lone Star Republic" was favored by the South. Four or five large slave states could be carved out of this vast domain to offset those likely to be admitted from the free territories of the Northwest. The movement for expansion was also supported by expansionists who regarded it as the nation's destiny to occupy the whole continent.

The North, however, generally opposed the admission of Texas because slavery was permitted there. In 1836 Benjamin Lundy, the Quaker abolitionist, had published a pamphlet called "The War in Texas: A Crusade Against the Government Set on Foot by Slaveholders," in which he claimed that the Texas revolution was plotted by a Southern proslavery conspiracy. At the same time a growing number of Northerners openly denounced slavery in Congress and elsewhere, and expressed moral indignation over its possible extension. In 1833 Henry Clay, though himself a slaveholder who advocated gradual emancipation, had told the Senate that slavery was "the darkest spot in the map of our country," and four years later termed the institution "a curse to the master; a wrong, a grievous wrong, to the slave."⁴ John Quincy Adams, although a fervent continentalist, denounced slavery on the floor of the House of Representatives in a speech which, at the rate of an hour a day, took three weeks to deliver. A declaration by Mexico that annexation of Texas would be considered an act of war was another deterring factor.

Although President Jackson himself wanted Texas and had tried to purchase the territory from Mexico, he was in no hurry to raise the issue of annexation because he knew that to do so would touch off the whole explosive issue of slavery at a time when he was trying to engineer the election of Martin Van Buren. But after Van Buren had been elected, Jackson recognized the independence of Texas, the day before he left office in 1837.

For his part, Van Buren, when he became president, displayed so little interest in the addition of Texas to the Union that the Texans turned to Great Britain as a friend in time of need. Steps were taken to negotiate a treaty with Great Britain. An independent Texas served British interest perfectly, for it could provide an alternative supply of cotton and also a market for manufactures unfettered by tariffs. However, one of the terms the British insisted upon was that Texas should renounce slavery. This the planters could not accept. To the slaveholding interests of the South, the very worst thing that could happen would be a nonslave republic, which, as a next-door neighbor, could serve as a sanctuary for fugitive slaves. So, they started pressing for immediate annexation.

Tyler's Texas Treaty. President Tyler, who was strongly in favor of acquiring Texas despite what he knew to be the almost inevitable cost in sectional conflict, made the issue his own after his dispute with the Whigs. By reopening the issue of Texas, which his precedessors had deliberately avoided, Tyler introduced the issue which would eventually almost destroy the nation and its political party system.

The resignation from the cabinet of Webster, who was against annexation, and the appointment of Abel P. Upshur of Virginia to head the State Department gave Tyler a secretary of state who was also enthusiastically in favor of the acquisition of Texas. Upshur negotiated a treaty of annexation in February 1844, but before Upshur had signed it he was killed in an accident on the battleship USS *Princeton.* Tyler then brought back Calhoun, an ardent expansionist, as secretary of state, to put Texas into the Union, and to get "Tyler too" the Democratic (not the Whig) nomination — his enemies charged—for the presidency in 1844. On April 12, 1844, a treaty of annexation was agreed upon by the representatives of the two republics just as the political parties were tuning up for the presidential elections to be held in the fall of that year.

On June 8, 1844, before the 1844 campaigns were well under way, the Texas Treaty came before the Senate. A letter from Calhoun to the British minister justifying annexation as a step in protecting slavery so outraged the senators that it was defeated by a vote of 35–16. Although, generally speaking, the North opposed and the South favored annexation (although only 16 out of 26 Southen senators voted for the treaty), the vote was generally on partisan rather than sectional grounds. Henry Clay, who was almost certain to be the Whig nominee for president, had come out against annexation, and so the Whigs both in the North and the South opposed it; only one Whig, a Southerner, voted for the treaty.

The Election of 1844

To stop the slavery question from growing into an issue that they did not want, Clay and former President Van Buren—who most people assumed would be the Democratic Party candidate since he already had a majority of the delegates to the upcoming Democratic national convention pledged to him—made an agreement not to make it an issue. On the morning of April 27, 1844, a week before the Whig convention and a month before the Democrats were to meet, there appeared in the morning *National Intelligencer* a letter from Clay, and in the afternoon *Boston Globe* a reply from Van Buren, both opposing the annexation of Texas. The annexation of Texas was clearly constitutional, Van Buren said, but "inexpedient" at this time. It would, he argued, lead to war with Mexico, and would be a further provocation of sectional bitterness between North and South.

Although Van Buren did not mention slavery in this letter, no one doubted that behind his opposition to the treaty was opposition to the further extension of slavery, and the South quickly and accurately sensed it. Van Buren's opponents were delighted with the letter. They had practically given up all hope of preventing his nomination. However, the publication of Van Buren's reply severely weakened his popularity throughout the whole country. Almost at once, Van Buren's supporters began to drop away. Some of his delegates resigned; others declared his position absolutely contrary to the known wishes of their states and that they would oppose his nomination. Andrew Jackson, distressed by Van Buren's letter, began to look around for another candidate. He eventually settled on James K. Polk of Tennessee, then a strong contender for the second place on the ticket.

The Whig Convention, 1844. The Whig convention met in Baltimore on May 1 in an atmosphere of harmony and jubilation. Clay sticks, clay hats, Ashland coats, and boxes of live coons, symbols of "the old coon," Clay himself, were to be seen everywhere. Clay was easily the most popular man in the country. Everywhere state legislatures, state conventions, public dinners, and mass meetings had demanded that Clay be made the party's candidate. Even Webster had declined a nomination from New Hampshire and General Winfield Scott had retired in Clay's favor when named by a Whig meeting in Pennsylvania.

In a one-day session the delegates nominated Clay by acclamation. Senator Theodore Frelinghuysen of New Jersey, who had been active in Protestant evangelical movements such as the American Bible Society and foreign missions, was named as the vice presidential nominee. However, Freylinghuysen's known association with nativist movements would weaken Whig appeal to Irish Catholics. It was not clear how much, however, since these foreign-born voters were usually Democrats.[5]

The Whig platform, the first one the party ever had, was brief (fewer than 100 words) and somewhat ambiguous. It declared that "the name of Henry Clay needs no eulogy. The brightest pages of the country's history are identified with the principles which he has upheld, as its darkest and more disastrous pages are with every material departure in our public policy from those principles." It also included a summary of "all the great principles of the Whig Party — principles inseparable from the public honor and prosperity." These were said to be:

> A well-regulated currency; a tariff for revenue to defray the necessary expenses of the government, and discriminating with special reference to the protection of the domestic labor of the country; the distribution of the proceeds of the sale of public lands; a single term for the presidency; a reform of executive usurpation; and generally, such an administration of the country as shall impart to every branch of the public service the greatest practicable efficiency, controlled by a well-regulated and wise economy.[6]

There was no mention of the U.S. bank, slavery, or Texas and no plank on foreign policy; nor was immigration mentioned. To all appearances the Whig Party was going into the campaign enthusiastically united behind its magnetic chieftain. At the same time their opponents were in serious discord and had become discouraged. It looked at long last as if the ambitious but often frustrated "old prince" Henry Clay would be the next president of the United States.

Although couriers sped to Washington with the news of Clay's nomination by the Whigs by every available means of conveyance, they got there too late. Samuel Morse's new "lightning wire" had beaten them by more than an hour.

The Democratic Convention, 1844. The Democrats gathered in convention in the Baltimore Odd Fellows Hall ("the proper place for them," said the Whigs) on May 27 in an atmosphere of bitterness and suspicion. Present were 266 delegates representing every state except South Carolina. The embittered Van Burenites came to the convention in force, determined to purge the party of its corrupt and traitorous elements and to vindicate their leader by triumphantly renominating him. The conservatives were just as determined to eliminate Van Buren and his "impracticables" once and for all.[7]

Van Buren appeared to have the nomination in his pocket, despite the defections from his ranks as a result of his letter on Texas annexation. Fourteen state conventions, four congressional district conventions, and one state legislative caucus had instructed their delegates to support the former president for a third nomination. His committed votes came to 159; more than enough to secure the nomination for "The Red Fox of Kinderhook" unless the two-thirds rule were again adopted. This rule had been adopted at the first Democratic national convention in 1832, and subsequenlty applied in 1836 but not in 1840. Senator Robert J. Walker of Mississippi, moved readoption of the rule, stressing that the two-thirds rule assured a "Democratic majority," which a mere majority did not — a strategy Walker, in alliance with Calhoun, had devised for denying Van Buren renomination.

On the first ballot Van Buren received 146 of 266 votes, a majority of 13. Six succeeding ballots saw Van Buren's votes fall off and showed that no one could command a two-thirds majority. Van Buren thus became the first Democratic presidential candidate to secure a majority vote in the convention and fail to get the necessary two-thirds.[8]

The first convention deadlock was at hand. It was broken the next day when James K. Polk of Tennessee was offered as a compromise presidential nominee. Polk, his friends pointed out, was "right" on Texas (for annexation), he was an ideal compromise man, and he was not big enough to excite animosity. He had the blessing of the Van Buren supporters. Furthermore, Jackson approved of him. The thing to do was to take Polk for the sake of "unity and harmony." When New York was reached on the ninth roll call, the chairman of the delegation, former Attorney General Benjamin Butler, who had cried when Van Buren lost the nomination, read a letter purportedly from Van Buren authorizing Butler to withdraw his name if it seemed in the interest of "harmony" to do so. He thereupon cast New York's vote for Polk. This was the signal for a mad rush to the Polk bandwagon, as delegation after delegation cast or "corrected" their votes to nominate Polk unanimously, the first "dark horse" in American political history.[9]

When the news of the nomination of Polk was flashed over the newfangled magnetic telegraph which Samuel Morse had just installed between the convention hall in Baltimore and the capitol in Washington it was received with dismay and with overtones of disgust. "Polk! Great God, what a nomination!" the Whig governor of Kentucky wrote to James Buchanan; and a Louisiana senator remarked in disbelief: "I can hardly believe such a ridiculous thing." For their part, Whigs across the nation celebrated the event with music:

> Ha, ha, ha, what a nominee,
> Is old Jem Polk of Tinnessee![10]

Even though Polk is remembered as the first dark-horse presidential candidate, the term is valid only in the sense that he had not been considered for the nomination before the Democratic convention. He was far from a political unknown in 1844. Born in North Carolina, he had moved to Tennessee as a young man and soon became a successful lawyer and planter. He entered politics as a Jacksonian Democrat and served seven terms in the House of Representatives (two as Speaker) and one term as governor of Tennessee. In 1836 Polk had demonstrated his loyalty to the Democratic Party by refusing to leave the party to support an old friend and fellow Tennessean, Judge Hugh L. White, for president. This regularity was a great recommendation of Polk to the Democratic convention in 1844.

To soothe the wounded feelings of Van Buren's adherents, the Democratic leaders nominated his close personal and political friend and fellow expansionist, Senator Silas Wright of New York, for the vice presidency. However, Wright declined to run, notifying the delegates by telegraph that "he did not propose to ride behind on the black pony [slavery] at the funeral of his slaughtered friend, Mr. Van Buren."[11] The delegates then picked George M. Dallas of Pennsylvania (Senator Walker's brother-in-law) for the second place on the ticket. Dallas would give the ticket strength in the large and crucial keystone state. Polk unwisely announced in his letter of acceptance that he would enter the office with "the settled purpose of not being a candidate for reelection."[12]

Before adjourning, the Democrats adopted a remarkable resolution which came out solidly for expansion, demanding that Texas be reannexed and that all of Oregon be reoccupied. By the use of the prefix "re" the effort was made to remove from a policy of expansion the taint of imperialism, the implication being that the United States was only trying to regain territory which it had formerly held. This plank, the Democrats hoped, would appeal to the Western farmers who wanted Oregon and the Southern planters who longed for Texas, without exposing the party to the charge of favoring one section above another. Nevertheless, it was apparent that effectual control of the Democratic Party was passing into Southern hands. There was a tragic significance in one departure from tradition: the platform did not, as it always had prior to this time, include Jefferson's words in the Declaration of Independence that all men are created equal.

The "Tyler and Texas" Convention, 1844. On the same day in the same city (Baltimore) an unofficial "Tyler and Texas" nominating convention was held. It was thought that overtures from the Democrats to Tyler would be forthcoming and the place and time had been arranged so that acceptance could be prompt and easy. When nothing was heard from the Democrats, Tyler was nominated unanimously on a platform of immediate annexation of Texas.

Tyler's nomination threatened to split the expansionist vote; but old Andrew Jackson, who had nothing but contempt for "Tiler," wrote him a letter professing "real regard" for him and praising his "good since and patriotism." This, together with a little flattery from Polk, convinced the president that Polk's election was the only hope of immediate annexation and that he should withdraw. So Tyler did this in August and announced his support of Polk.

The Liberty Party

In November 1839, when the movement for the annexation of Texas had gathered some headway, a small group of abolitionists led by James G. Birney, the executive secretary of the American Antislavery Society at New York, a former Alabama slaveholder turned abolitionist, met in convention at Warsaw, New York, where they adopted a resolution stating that in their judgment "every consideration of duty and expediency which ought to control the action of Christian freemen requires the abolitionists of the United States to organize a distinct and independent political party, embracing all the necessary means of nominating candidates and sustaining them by public suffrage."[13] The convention then proceeded to name Birney for the presidency and Francis Lemoyne of Pennsylvania for the vice presidency. Birney would not accept the nomination until he was convinced that neither major party would meet the slavery issue. Lemoyne also refused the dubious honor.

When the Whigs and the Democrats, with Harrison and Van Buren as their nominees, evaded the issue of slavery in 1839, a second antislavery convention met at Albany in April 1840. One hundred and twenty-one delegates from New York and New England renominated Birney with Thomas Earle of Pennsylvania as his running mate. The delegates adopted the name Liberty Party to be their official name. This time Birney agreed to run.

The Liberty Party's platform remained little changed throughout its existence. Although the new party did not call for outright abolition — admitting that the national government had no control over slavery in the states — it did call for "free soil" in the territories. It also promised action on the state level wherever it could organize and succeed in elections. The party

pledged itself to foster the commercial interests of the free states and break
the Southern control over the national economy.[14]

Although the Liberty Party had won only a tiny vote (about 7,000) in
its first presidential venture in 1840, the members had been encouraged by
the success of Liberty candidates in state elections in several key Northern
states where it hoped to swing the balance of power. (In New York the
abolitionists had risen from 2,808 votes in 1840 to 16,275 in 1843, and in
Ohio during the same period from 903 to 7,480.) On August 30, 1843, 18
months before the election, about 148 delegates from 12 states, including
all of the free states except New Hampshire, met in convention at Buffalo,
New York, and nominated Birney, now a Michigan resident, for president
with Thomas Morris of Ohio as his running mate.

The delegates adopted a platform largely written by Salmon P. Chase
of Ohio which discussed only one issue—slavery. However, it hedged
somewhat on outright abolition, a position which many of the members
were insisting upon, and merely demanded "the absolute and unqualified
divorce of the general government from slavery."[15] The Liberty platform
did not specifically mention Texas, because when it was adopted the issue
had not yet become prominent.

When Texas did become a major issue, the Liberty Party recognized
that it was in a difficult position. A heavy third-party vote might reduce
the Whig vote in the doubtful Northern states and elect expansionist Polk
over Clay who was committed against Texas.[16]

The Campaign of 1844. The campaign in 1844 was an intense electoral
campaign that put much stress on parades, mass meetings, and slogans.[17]
The Democrats dubbed Polk "Young Hickory" to capitalize on his close
friendship with Andrew Jackson, and passed out Hickory "polkers" with
which to "polk" Whigs. As they marched they shouted "All of Oregon or
None," "Fifty-Four Forty or Fight" and "Polk, Dallas, and Texas" in the
South, and "Polk, Dallas, and the Tariff of 1842" in the protectionist areas
of the North. Much was made of Clay's gambling, drinking, profanity, and
duels. A particularly shocking piece of propaganda was entitled "Henry
Clay's Moral Fitness for the Presidency Tested by the Decalogue" in which
the Democrats avowed that the Kentuckian had systematically violated all
of the Ten Commandments. The voters were warned:

> Christian Voters!
> Read, Pause, and Reflect!
> Mr. Clay's
> Moral Character.[18]

The Whigs countered with such slogans as "Hooray for Clay" and
"Polk, Slavery, and Texas" or "Clay, Union, and Liberty," and chanted
songs about the lack of qualification for high office of "Polk the Plodder"

in comparison to the obvious presidential (leadership) qualities of the gallant "Harry of the West." In the protectionist states Polk was denounced as a free trader. Whig stump speakers belittled the Democratic candidate by repeating the question many Americans asked just after his nomination: "Who is James K. Polk?" The Northern Whigs emphasized Polk's status as a slave owner. He was an *ultra* slaveholder, they said, who had recently purchased a large plantation in Mississippi, "*stocked* it with negroes," and "had gone into it *up to his ears.*"

In his campaign Clay attempted to talk about the traditional principles and measures of the Whig Party.[19] However, the old Whig principles no longer interested the people and it soon became apparent that Texas was what they wanted to hear about. In the South fiery orators demanded Texas so vehemently, threatening a Southern convention, nullification, and even secession, that Clay trimmed his sails on Texas in two "Alabama letters" written to an Alabama newspaper and in a letter published in the *National Intelligencer* in September. He would welcome the annexation of Texas, he said, if it could be accomplished without war and upon "just and fair terms," and under circumstances such that "slavery ought not to affect the question one way or another." This was probably a fatal mistake. The South did not want annexation at just some possible time and the North could imagine no situation in which the Texas question could be settled without any reference to slavery. One of Clay's Northern friends summed up the Whig dilemma well when he exclaimed in disgust that what the Whig Party needed was a candidate who could neither read nor write.[20]

The Outcome, 1844. Polk's popular vote was 1,339,000 to Clay's 1,300,000; his electoral vote was 170 to 105 for Clay, a popular vote margin of less than 40,000 votes. Birney, the Liberty Party candidate, received only 62,300 votes (about 2 percent) more than 25 percent (16,000) of which were cast in western New York State. Since Polk carried the empire state by only a plurality of 5,106, if half of that state's Liberty Party vote had gone to Clay he would have carried the state's 36 votes and would have been elected 143 to 141. Ironically, by giving this indirect aid to Polk, the Liberty Party, the bitterest of all of them against slavery, helped elect Polk and thereby contributed to the annexation of Texas as a slave state, to which they were violently opposed.[21]

Clay was totally dismayed at his defeat. Horace Greeley explained that it was the Liberty Party vote in New York State which defeated Clay, but the *New York Herald* said it was his (actually Polk's) stand on Texas. Clay, however, later expressed the view that his loss could be attributed in large measure to the foreign-born vote in New York City where there had been an illegal registration of thousands of Irish and German newcomers by the Democrats. He had, he said, "no doubt of the greatness of the evil of this constant manufacture of American citizens out of foreign emigrants."[22]

Polk's election inspired a popular new "Polka," which the Whigs described as "one step forward and two steps back." But Whig pessimism was ill-founded, for Polk emerged as a strong chief executive.

The Annexation of Texas. President Tyler regarded Polk's election as a referendum on the Texas question and immediately demanded that the lone star republic be offered admission into the Union by a congressional joint resolution, an action which requires only a simple majority of both houses.[23] Since the voters had just elected Polk, who had campaigned on this very platform, Congress could hardly refuse Tyler's demand, and on March 1, 1845, only three days before Tyler left the White House, the resolution passed with a whoop. Tyler signed the fateful measure. Texas promptly accepted the terms and on December 29, 1845, became the twenty-eighth state in the Union.

The Administration of James K. Polk

When he took office, President Polk was approaching 50. His forceful inaugural address, delivered on a dark, rainy day to what John Quincy Adams described as "a large assemblage of umbrellas," was Jeffersonian in tone and spirit. It coupled the "support of state governments in all their rights" with the "preservation of general government in its whole constitutional vigor." It condemned attempted exercise by states of powers not reserved to them equally with usurpation of federal powers. "Not in the ruins of the Union," the president said, "would our people find happiness." He described that it was his duty to assert and maintain by all constitutional means the right of the United States to that portion of the territory which was beyond the Rocky Mountains. Our title to the country of the Oregon was "clear and unquestionable," and already the people were preparing to perfect that title by occupying it with their wives and children.[24]

In making his cabinet selections, Polk tried unsuccessfully to satisfy the friends of Van Buren. The first offer of a place in the cabinet was made to Silas Wright, Van Buren's New York colleague, who was asked to become secretary of the treasury. Wright declined on the ground that he had been elected governor of New York on a pledge that he would serve if elected. Benjamin F. Butler, another Van Burenite, was offered the portfolio of war, which he declined because he considered it an inferior position. Polk then unwisely offered the War Department to William L. Marcy, the leader of the rival New York Democratic faction, who accepted and proceeded to deal out federal patronage in accordance with his well-known maxim: "To the victor belongs the spoils." James Buchanan of Pennsylvania became secretary of state and Senator R.J. Walker was appointed secretary of the treasury.

Polk's cabinet appointments antagonized the still angry Van Buren supporters. They were especially incensed at the appointment of Walker, who had spun the "vile intrigue" that defeated their favorite at the Baltimore convention, to the patronage-rich treasury post.

Polk approached the job he called "no bed of roses" with intense single-mindedness from his first day in office. (John Quincy Adams testified that Polk "worked like a galley slave.") He had four great objects in view: a reduction of the Whig-inspired tariff of 1842; the establishment of an independent treasury system to regulate the national finances; the peaceful settlement of the Oregon question; and the acquisition of California. Before he left office, Polk achieved every single feature of his domestic program.

The Tariff Issue

The Walker Tariff, 1846. When Polk became president he was determined to do something about the protectionist Whig Tariff of 1842. In his first message to Congress in 1845, Polk characterized it as "so framed that much the greatest burden which it imposes is thrown on labor and the poorer classes, who are least able to bear it, while it protects capital and exempts the rich from paying their just proportion of the taxation required to support the government."

President Polk's secretary of the treasury Robert J. Walker, who was deeply impressed with the success Great Britain was having in abandoning protection, devised a tariff-for-revenue measure which reduced the average rates of the tariff which Henry Clay had persuaded President Tyler to accept in 1842 from about 32 percent to 25 percent—enough to delight the South. With the strong support of low-tariff Southerners, Walker lobbied the measure through the Democratic Congress, though not without the customary opposition from the Whigs, especially in New England and the middle states, who complained loudly that it was a "free trade, cotton planter's" tariff which would ruin American manufacturing by lowering the rates of wages, throwing thousands out of employment, inducing general disaster and incalculable individual suffering, lessening the value of property, depreciating the value of agricultural products, checking public and private improvements, and plunging the states into the "inky pot of repudiation."[25] The Walker Tariff, as it came to be known, passed the House of Representatives by a comfortable margin. However, in the Senate, Vice President Dallas cast the deciding vote in a tied ballot—and thereby jeopardized his political chances in his home state of Pennsylvania where, because of the local iron industries, even democrats were protectionists. It was signed by President Poly July 30, 1846.

But these prophets of doom were way off the mark. Despite its low rates, the Walker Tariff proved to be an excellent revenue measure, producing on an average nearly 40 percent greater receipts than the Whig Tariff of 1842, largely because it was followed by boom times and heavy imports. The iron industry, far from being ruined by the Walker Tariff, actually found new business. The textile industry, moreover, was exporting its products to the whole world. Whig "calamity howlers" gave up in despair; the tariff issue disappeared from the political agenda — at least for a time.

The Issue of Expansion

Oregon. As we have already seen in the campaign of 1844, the expansionists had made the annexation of Texas more acceptable to Northern voters by linking it with the acquisition of Oregon.

Until the 1830s Americans had displayed little interest in the Oregon Territory, and only a few enthusiasts, mostly land providers and Indian mission societies, kept the issue before the public. American statesmen had never thought of laying claim to all of the Oregon country. From the time of James Monroe, every administration had offered the forty-ninth parallel to Great Britain as a dividing line, and Polk renewed this offer in July 1845. The British envoy at Washington refused it and the offer was withdrawn. The extreme expansionists soon demanded that the United States acquire all of Oregon. The Democrats, as we have seen, converted this claim into an effective campaign slogan in the election of 1844: "Fifty-Four Forty or Fight" (40° 40').[26]

For a number of reasons, President Polk felt it unwise to break openly with Great Britain. Most importantly, he realized that to demand all of Oregon probably would mean war with England, a reckless move as long as war with Mexico over Texas was threatened. When Britain offered to compromise by expanding the forty-ninth parallel to the Pacific as the northern boundary of the United States, the president "reluctantly" concluded a treaty which reached the Senate in June 1846. Although a number of Western senators who had taken "Fifty-Four Forty or Fight" seriously voted against the treaty, the Senate approved it after only three days of consideration. One major reason Polk and the Senate were so willing to compromise was the fact that war with Mexico had begun some six weeks earlier. American territory for the first time faced the Pacific, a fact of momentous importance.

California. Although California was not a major issue in the 1844 presidential campaign, soon after the election it began to be coupled in the public mind with Oregon. Numerous Americans, President Polk among them, had long coveted its verdant valleys, and especially the splendid harbor of San Francisco. In October 1845 the president appointed as his special agent Thomas O. Larkin, an American residing in California, instructing him confidentially to inform the Californians that if they "should desire to unite their destiny with ours, they will be received as brethren."

In the summer of 1846, while General Zachary Taylor was invading northern Mexico, the War Department sent Colonel Stephen W. Kearney to lead a column into the provinces of New Mexico and California. Kearney soon captured the adobe town — "mud town," as they called it — of Santa Fe, without firing a shot. Thereupon, he announced that New Mexico was now annexed by the United States, and after setting up a government he pressed on to California. When Kearney arrived in December 1846, he found the conquest of California all but completed. The American settlers had risen in the "Bear Flag Revolt" and had already cut off the tenuous authority of the Mexican government.

The Mexican War

President Polk, when he learned that Mexican forces had crossed the Rio Grande River, informed Congress on May 9, 1846, that war existed by the act of Mexico itself. On May 13 the Democratic Congress declared war by a vote of 40–2 in the Senate and 174–4 in the House. Under protest, most of the Whigs voted for war even though they thought Polk had intentionally provoked it. However, they knew if they voted against the declaration of war they would be accused of indifference to the fate of heroic American soldiers who had only defended themselves when attacked, and possibly even of disloyalty to the United States.

Polk hoped to fight the war with bipartisan support, but this was not to be. Clay, Webster, and the other antislavery Whigs in Congress — dubbed "Mexican Whigs" — did not hesitate to use their newspapers and speeches in Congress to denounce the president as "Polk the Mendacious," an evil man willing to wage war in order to get California. In New England, where many Whigs looked upon annexation of Texas and the Mexican War as another drive by the Southern planters for more slave territory, opposition to "Mr. Polk's War" was almost as widespread as it had been to "Mr. Madison's War" in 1812. As James Russell Lowell had Hosea Biglow fret in his Yankee dialect in the *Biglow Papers:*

> They jest want this Californy
> So's to lug new slave-states in
> To abuse ye, an' scorn ye,
> An' to plunder ye like sin.[27]

The president could not even rely on a united Democratic Party. He was opposed by the Van Buren men who supported the war on patriotic grounds but viewed it as a tactical mistake. They were well aware that victorious Whig generals made good presidential timber, and that both Winfield Scott, the commanding general in Washington, and Zachary Taylor, the commander in the field, were Whigs. The pessimism of the Van

Burenites was justified. No sooner had Zachary Taylor won his first battles in May 1846 than Whig managers began to see in him another military leader whom they could expect to lead them to political victory. The general, was, in fact, highly "available"[28] as a candidate.

General Scott actually appeared to be more of a threat to the Democrats than Taylor, since he had political ambitions and numerous assets which could be exploited politically (as well as some liabilities which could be glossed over). Scott was a handsome giant of a man standing nearly 6.5 feet tall. He was also intelligent, even-tempered, and cultivated, if somewhat punctilious and pompous. He had earned the nickname of "Old Fuss and Feathers" because of his strict discipline and resplendent uniforms (it was said that Scott looked, even in peacetime, "like Mars going into battle"). In addition, Scott had barely missed securing the Whig nomination for president in 1840.

President Polk undertook to offset this Whig advantage by appointing a number of Democratic ("political") generals, hoping that from their number would emerge one with enough valor to rival Scott and Taylor. William O. Butler of Kentucky was made a major general and Joseph Lane of Indiana, James Shields of Illinois, Gideon J. Pillow of Tennessee, John A. Quitman of Mississippi, Franklin Pierce of New Hampshire, and Caleb Cushing of Massachusetts became brigadiers.

The Slavery Issue Continued

The Wilmot Proviso, 1846. Scarcely had the Mexican War begun when the prospect of acquiring more territory started a controversy in Congress over the extension of slavery. The portentous question quickly arose — would the new lands be slave or free?

In a special message to Congress delivered about 12 weeks after the beginning of the Mexican War, the president asked Congress for a secret appropriation of $2 million "for the purpose of settling our differences with Mexico." This money was to be used, the message said, "to pay a fair equivalent for any concession . . . made by Mexico" in the adjustment of the Mexican-American boundary." A Democratic congressman from North Carolina promptly introduced a bill to appropriate the sum mentioned.

As Congress neared adjournment,[29] David Wilmot, an obscure antislavery Democratic representative from Pennsylvania, thereupon introduced an amendment to the "Two Million Bill" which provided that "neither slavery nor involuntary servitude should ever exist" in any territory acquired from Mexico through the use of the money. The introduction of the proviso by a Democrat rather than a Whig clearly indicated that sectional issues were cutting across party lines. Wilmot had also raised the dread issue of slavery extension that was to dominate American politics for years to come. "As if by magic," commented the *Boston Whig*, "it brought to a head the great question that is about to divide the American people."

Immediately, fierce sectional bitterness flared up. In Congress hot-headed Southerners threatened secession if Wilmot's Proviso was adopted. The proviso, they argued, was the supreme act of injustice. The Southern states were furnishing 75 percent of the volunteer soldiers who were fighting the war; should they and their belongings be barred from the land won by their valor and blood? Furthermore, if slavery were excluded from the Mexican cession, the political balance between the North and the South would be upset to the disadvantage of the South.

Wilmot's Proviso passed the House by a vote of 87-64. Northern Whigs lined up with antislavery Democrats in pushing it through the House. However, the Senate, where Northerners and Southerners were equal in number, refused to consider it in the summer of 1846.

The Congressional Elections of 1846. Meanwhile, in the fall of 1846 the Whigs did so well in the races for congressional seats that they took control of the House of Representatives away from the Democrats. The voters had taken revenge on the Democrats and on old members of Congress for an unpopular war. Abraham Lincoln was a new Whig member from Illinois. It began to look as though 1848 would be a Whig year.

When the new Congress assembled in December 1846, the Wilmot Proviso was reintroduced and John C. Calhoun answered it by introducing a series of resolutions in the Senate asserting that the territories were the common property of all the states; that Congress had no power to deprive the citizens of any state of their right to migrate to the territories with their property, including slaves; and that only when a territory was ready for statehood could it constitutionally prohibit slavery. Calhoun's position, therefore, was that *all* the territories must be open to slavery — which made even the Missouri Compromise unconstitutional. Most Northerners considered this idea as repulsive as Southerners found the Wilmot Proviso. The resolutions were never acted upon — Calhoun really didn't expect them to be — but his doctrine of noninterference rapidly gained favor in the South.

The Northern Whigs called for the proviso in more stringent form in 1847, and demanded that slavery be positively forbidden in any territory secured from Mexico, except for Texas. The prohibition was approved by the House but was defeated in the Senate by a vote of 31-21. Even though it created conflict, the Whigs did not let it die. By tacking a Wilmot Proviso on to every measure for the organization or acquisition of new territory, they kept the issue alive and kept the Democrats wrangling among themselves. The proviso soon became a tenet of political faith which split parties, churches, and the people.

Finally, after months of debate, the House defeated the proviso and

Polk's appropriation bill passed without the amendment in March 1847. Despite its defeat, however, the proviso remained a burning issue in political circles for months to come. The *Savannah Georgian* accurately foretold the future: "The only great question before the country . . . is the Wilmot Proviso. This question will enter into the next Presidential canvass, and exert a controlling influence upon the result."[30]

During the long debate over the Wilmot Proviso several solutions to the problem of slavery in the territories were advanced. One, based on the theory that Congress could legislate for the territories, called for the extension of the line of the Missouri Compromise to the Pacific. This proposal had the support of President Polk and a majority of Southerners, although it would not have preserved the balance between free and slave states. However, most Northerners would no longer agree to the reservation of any new territory for slavery.

Another possibility, advocated by Senator Lewis Cass of Michigan, rested upon the principle of "popular sovereignty" — contemptuously called "squatter sovereignty" by Calhoun — which called for organizing new territories without mention of slavery, thus leaving it to the local settlers to determine whether or not they wanted slavery. Maintaining that settlers in territories were as capable of self-government as citizens of states, Cass proposed that they should decide for themselves whether to have slavery. "Popular sovereignty" thus had the superficial merits of appearing to be democratic and of enabling the members of Congress to escape the responsibility of deciding the question themselves. In addition, it was designed to remove the slavery issue from Congress and from national politics.[31] Because it renounced the Wilmot Proviso and endorsed congressional noninterference, many Southerners would accept popular sovereignty as a viable solution. Finally, there were those who would leave the question of the legality of slave property in the territories to the Supreme Court.

The Election of 1848

As the presidential campaign of 1848 commenced, the issue of expansion of slavery into new territories was agitating the whole country and dividing both major parties. In state after state the Whigs were increasingly referring to themselves as either "Cotton Whigs" or "Conscience Whigs." The former, numbering men like Abbot Lawrence, Nathan Appleton, and Robert C. Winthrop of Massachusetts, were criticized for ignoring the slavery issue because of their close financial and political connections with the cotton growers of the South. The "Conscience Whigs," including Charles Francis Adams, Henry Wilson, and Charles Allen, emphasized the immoral character of slavery and demanded that the Whig Party take a stand against it.

Early in the Polk administration the Democrats also began to split up into "Barnburners" — so called because they were said to be so eager to rid the Democratic Party of its proslavery elements that they were willing to "burn down the barn to expel the rats" — and pro-Polk "Hunkers" — the conservative party regulars — who so "hunkered" (that is, hungered) for the patronage jobs that Polk and his Southern supporters could bestow, that they were willing to support the expansion of slavery.

Leading the pro-Van Buren Barnburners were men like Silas Wright (who had refused the vice presidential nomination in 1844), until he died suddenly and unexpectedly of a heart attack in August 1847, Benjamin F. Butler, Senator John A. Dix, Azariah C. Flagg, "Prince John" Van Buren — the flamboyant and politically ambitious second son of the ex-president — and Samuel J. Tilden. The chief leaders of the Hunkers were William L. Marcy and Daniel C. Dickinson.

These factions were particularly contentious in the 1848 Democratic national convention. Utterly exhausted from the labors of his strenuous administration, Polk did not seek renomination. He was ill during the latter part of his presidency, and his health absolutely forbade his being a candidate again. Although Polk had avowed at the time of his nomination that he would be a one-term president, no other personage had been built up to take his place.

On the eve of the 1848 convention there were a number of aspirants for the Democratic presidential nomination. Martin Van Buren and James Buchanan had support, as did Levi Woodbury of New Hampshire — a Supreme Court justice with longtime experience in high Democratic positions.

However, the most active aspirant for the Democratic nomination was Lewis Cass, the aging and sour-visaged senator from Michigan. Cass did not have much to offer the party along political or personal lines. He had served as secretary of war under presidents Jackson and Van Buren, and for 18 years as governor of Michigan Territory and as a U.S. senator from Michigan.

A firm expansionist, Cass had strongly favored the annexation of Texas, demanded that the United States take *all* of Oregon, and had eagerly pushed the war with Mexico. Like many Northern Democrats, he had been an early supporter of the Wilmot Proviso. Yet when that measure began to threaten a party schism, he abandoned it in the interest of unity and political expediency.[32] Also, Cass was the first major figure in national politics to broach the idea of "popular sovereignty," although he did not really care, as he made clear, whether slavery was "voted up or down." He just wanted to get the issue out of national politics so that the territories could be organized and the nation's expansion of settlements could continue.

Cass's support was not overwhelming. Despite the fact, as Gideon Welles pointed out, that Cass had a "good deal of ability and tact," was a tolerable debater, and elegant writer, and had received some experience as a statesman, he had few partisans in Congress. Also, he was more than somewhat pompous. Cass's numerous enemies dubbed him "General Gass." A current rhyme proclaimed:

> And he who still for Cass can be
> He is a Cass without the C.[33]

The Democratic Party Convention, 1848. The fifth Democratic National Convention met in Baltimore on May 22, 1848. Every state was represented. New York had two contesting delegations, the pro–Polk Hunkers, led by Marcy and Dickinson, and the pro–Van Buren Barnburners, led by Dix, Tilden, and John Van Buren. After a bitter floor fight, the convention voted to seat both New York delegations and let them share the empire state's votes. This arrangement satisfied neither of the contesting delegations and each announced that it would take no further part in the convention. New York was thus left unrepresented. The two-thirds rule was adopted which gave the anti–Cass delegates some slim hope of stopping the Michigan politician.

Only three names were placed in nomination: Cass, Buchanan, and Woodbury. When the convention chose Cass on the fourth ballot, the enraged Barnburners dramatically stalked out of the convention, displaying a wrath so lurid, according to one observer "that the delegates from the black states" were frightened "almost out of their wits."[34] More ominously, they carried off with them the 36 New York electoral votes by which the Democrats were destined to lose the election. William O. Butler from the slave state of Kentucky, one of Polk's major generals and an avowed opponent of the Wilmot Proviso, was chosen for second place over a military colleague, General John A. Quitman of Mississippi.

The Democratic platform was purposely vague. It was, in general, a strong endorsement of the Polk administration, although, somewhat ironically, few delegates would have voted to renominate Polk. The slavery plank effectively dodged the issue of slavery in the territories. It repeated the planks from its 1840 and 1844 platforms which said that Congress could not interfere with slavery in the states, but it said nothing about extension, the only real issue of the day.[35] Every attempt to commit the party to the Wilmot Proviso was shouted down. An effort by William L. Yancey of Alabama to get acceptance of the idea that the "doctrine of noninterference with the rights of property in the states or in the territories" was the "true republican doctrine" was also defeated.[36]

The Cass nomination was generally approved by the Democrats of the

West. The *Cleveland Plain Dealer* greeted the news in big, bold, headlines proclaiming "The Great West Triumphant" and the *Illinois State Register* reported that "no nomination" had ever been "hailed . . . with more cordial and genuine joy and enthusiasm." However, the antislavery Democrats were unhappy about both candidate and platform. Many began talking about running a separate ticket.

The Whig Party Convention, 1848. In 1848 Henry Clay wanted the Whig nomination in the worst way. He was old (past 70) and he bore the onus of a fourth defeat in 1844. Daniel Webster also wanted the nomination; his chance was now or never. In reality, neither Clay nor Webster was being seriously considered for the nomination by the leaders of the Whig Party who wanted a candidate that could win. They were well aware of what a military career had done for William Henry Harrison. The Mexican War offered the Whigs in 1848 a choice between two popular generals, Zachary Taylor and Winfield Scott. Between the two, Taylor appeared to have the most support (neither Clay nor Webster had a military record).

Zachary Taylor was a Virginian by birth—the last president born before the enactment of the Constitution—but he grew to manhood in frontier Kentucky. As a young lieutenant in the U.S. Army (but not a West Pointer), he had fought with vigor in the War of 1812, the Black Hawk War, and the Seminole War, as well as in the war with Mexico. Taylor's spectacular victories over Mexican forces at Palo Alto, Resaca de la Palma, Monterrey, and Buena Vista, when his troops routed the largest army that American troops had ever met, caught the imagination of the American people. To the Whig leaders, the appeal of the newly acclaimed "Hero of Buena Vista" became almost irresistible. The prevailing wisdom was that "Old Zach" would be elected president in 1848 by "spontaneous combustion."

Yet, many Whigs were appalled by the prospect of Taylor's nomination. For one thing the 64-year-old general did not look presidential. He was a thick-set man with stubby legs and heavy brows contracted into a perpetual frown. He stuttered and squinted, had practically no formal education, and was incapable of delivering even a passable political speech. Further, he knew nothing of politics. He had made the army his whole life; although eligible to vote for four decades, he had never cast a ballot. He had no views on domestic or foreign policies. When asked for his opinions on the bank and the tariff, he replied bluntly that he had "had no time to investigate" those questions. Even Daniel Webster had called him "an illiterate frontier colonel" and warned that there were thousands of Whigs "who will not vote for a candidate brought forward only because of his successful fighting in the war against Mexico." In addition, many Whigs were concerned that Taylor was a Louisiana sugar planter and owner of several hundred slaves.[37] Yet the general opposed the extreme proslavery doctrine of Calhoun and of his own son-in-law, Jefferson Davis of Mississippi. He therefore was not in favor of yielding to the South on the slavery issue. Any hint of secession aroused in him violent antagonism, and he let it be known that an effort in that direction would be met by a boldness like that shown by Jackson in the Nullification Crisis.

One of Taylor's strong assets was that he resembled Jackson in a number of ways. Like Jackson, he was extremely popular with his troops who called him affectionately "Old Rough and Ready" because of his iron constitution and incredibly unsoldierly appearance. Taylor had directed Mexican War battles while sitting astride his favorite horse, knock-kneed "Old Whitey," wearing a private's uniform and an old oilcloth cap and looking more like a farmer than a soldier. (Democrats preferred to think that "economical, comical Old Zach" was merely too stingy to buy a decent uniform.) Also, like Jackson, he was basically a Westerner rather than a Southerner.[38]

On June 7, 1848, a few days after the Democrats nominated Cass, the Whigs met in Philadelphia with delegates from every state present. Five names were placed before the convention: Taylor, Clay, Judge McLean, Webster, and Clayton. McLean immediately withdrew. Taylor led throughout the balloting and received the nomination on the fourth round. The only real opposition came from Northern groups who did not relish a Southern, slaveholding candidate who was not only noncommittal about slavery but was not too sure he was a Whig.[39]

Abbott Lawrence of Massachusetts, a "Cotton Whig" and an active Taylor supporter, was the favorite for vice president. However, as Taylor was a Southern slave owner and Lawrence a wealthy cotton mill owner, the anti–Taylor Conscience Whigs protested that "King Cotton" should not have both ends of the ticket. The vice presidency was then offered to Daniel Webster who declined. "No thank you," he said, "I do not propose to be buried until I am really dead and in my coffin."[40] He, of course, had no way of knowing that the death of the president in a little more than a year would have put him in the White House.

Finally, portly, round-faced Millard Fillmore of New York was selected to be Taylor's running mate, even though little was known about him. However, no one really cared much that little was known about him. He had good "New York" credentials. Born in a rural New York log cabin, his family had apprenticed him to a wool carder as a young man. He soon tired of that hard and dirty work and sought a more genteel education. However, by the time he showed up for his first day of regular school he was 19 years old. He quickly fell in love with the teacher, and with her help he bought his freedom and married her. He eventually studied law, went to live in Buffalo, New York, and became a fairly successful lawyer.

Fillmore got excited about politics around 1827, when the Anti-Masons came along, and, with the help of Thurlow Weed, went to the New York State Assembly in 1828 as an Anti-Mason. When that party folded, he secured election to Congress as an anti–Jackson Whig. Leaving Congress in 1842, with the support of the Clay faction he was nominated for governor of New York in 1844 after he lost the nomination for the vice presidency. When he was defeated in the fall election, he retired to his law practice.[41]

The Whigs dodged the slavery issue. A resolution endorsing the Wilmot Proviso was tabled by a large majority so that it was impossible to know where the party stood on the most important issue — that of the extension of slavery. In the end the Whigs issued a platform which confined itself to defending Taylor in saying that, had he voted in 1844, he would have voted the Whig ticket.

Taylor's nomination brought to a head a long-festering schism in Northern Whiggery. Horace Greeley went back to New York, making no effort to disguise his unhappiness over what he termed the "Slaughterhouse Convention" (because of its alleged slaughter of Whig principles and of anyone devoted to these principles) and its "impossible nomination." He soon began publication of *That Same Coon*, a paper which came out frankly in favor of Henry Clay as an independent candidate.

The Free Soilers Emerge

The slavery question was too deep-seated to be ignored, and the attempts of the Democrats and Whigs to evade it led to the formation of a third party, the Free Soil Party. The seceding Barnburners, returning to New York, held a mass meeting in the City Hall Square at which the Democratic ticket, the party, and the platform were all denounced. An address written by Samuel J. Tilden "calling independent Democrats to action," was read and a Barnburner or Free Soil convention was called for in Utica, New York, on June 22. When it assembled delegates from New York, Massachusetts, Connecticut, Ohio, Illinois, and Wisconsin were in attendance.

The Utica convention was presided over by Colonel Samuel Young who set the tone by declaiming "if the convention does its duty a clap of thunder in November will make the propagandists of slavery shake like Belshazzar."[42] A long letter from ex–President Van Buren was read explicitly declaring against Cass, the Democratic candidate. If there were no other candidates but General Taylor (the Whig nominee) he would not vote at all. The delegates promptly nominated Van Buren as the Free Soil candidate for president, much against his will and in spite of his protest. Senator Henry Dodge of Wisconsin was named for the second place. A week after his nomination, of which he was never officially informed, Dodge declined the honor, announcing that he would support Cass.

The Free Soil Convention, 1848. Before the major party conventions the Liberty Party had held a convention in November 1847, at which time it had nominated the fiery John Parker Hale of New Hampshire — who was not really a Liberty Man but an antislavery Democrat — and Leicester King of Ohio. Hale's nomination was received in the West with favor but aroused much discontent in the East, however, and when the Barnburners "took their walk" out of the Democratic Party, the leaders of the Liberty Party decided that a union between them and the Barnburners should be effected. This was done by issuing a call for a national convention representing all the antislavery elements.

Fifteen thousand fervent delegates from 18 states, including 3 border states (Virginia, Maryland, and Delaware) assembled on a sweltering day in August 1848 at Buffalo, New York, in a huge, broiling hot tent in the city park. Antislavery men of every stripe were there, including New York Barnburners, such as Samuel J. Tilden and David Dudley Field; the Conscience Whigs, such as Charles Francis Adams; the Liberty Men, Salmon P. Chase, Henry B. Stanton, and Joshua Leavitt, the editor of the *Emancipator;* and even some "soft" Hunkers. Several black delegates, including Frederick Douglass, were also present.[43] Meanwhile, an "executive committee" of 465 met in a nearby church to do the real work.

A Free Soil Party was formed. The resolutions, composed by Chase, announced the principle that: "There must be no more compromises with slavery and if made they must be repealed. We inscribe on our banner, Free Soil, Free Speech, Free Labor, and Free Men, and under it we will fight on and fight ever until a triumphant victory shall reward our exertions."[44] In a bid for the support of Eastern laborers as well as Western farmers, the platform supported free homesteads and national improvement of rivers and harbors, early payment of the public debt, and a tariff for revenue only. The delegates ratified the platform with a roar of approval which "could have been heard in every part of Buffalo."

Van Buren was chosen as the new party's standard-bearer on the first ballot by a vote of 244 against 183 for John P. Hale, who had been nominated by the Liberty Party in October 1847, but with Van Buren's nomination he withdrew from the race. For vice president the Free Soilers selected Charles Francis Adams, a longtime political and personal foe of Van Buren. It was an exceedingly curious combination as William Lloyd Garrison, the extreme abolitionist, pointed out: "When Van Buren and Charles Francis Adams combine, the Revolution has at last begun."[45]

The "mass convention" in the park approved the ticket with a deafening acclamation; then in a tumultuous din it adjourned to march through the streets of Buffalo with torches flaring and drums beating, behind a banner that succinctly summarized its campaign position:

'87 and '48
JEFFERSON AND VAN BUREN
No Compromise[46]

The First Women's Rights Convention, 1848. Another convention held in the fall of 1848 was the "Women's Rights" convention at Seneca Falls, New York, under the energetic efforts of Mrs. Lucretia Mott, a demure Quaker preacher of Philadelphia, and Mrs. Elizabeth Cady Stanton of Seneca Falls, an abolitionist's wife and a mother of seven.[47] The 250 delegates adopted a Declaration of Women's Independence modeled on the great document of 1776 and beginning: "We hold these truths to be self-evident: that all *men and women* are created equal." Besides demanding "the institution of a new government" by means of the repeal of all discriminatory laws, and the end of masculine monopoly of trades, professions, and business, the convention asserted that it was the duty of the women of the country "to secure to themselves their sacred right to the elective franchise." Not surprisingly, the Seneca Falls meeting was the object of scorn and denunciation from the press and pulpit.[48]

The 1848 Campaign. The 1848 election itself aroused little popular enthusiasm. Whig campaign literature and oratory expounded the personal foibles of Cass and Polk — although the Whigs were careful to avoid attacking "Mr. Polk's War" lest it reflect unfavorably on their candidate's role in it. Since little was known of Taylor's views, the Whigs were able to offer him to voters in different sections according to which posture would draw the most support. In the South they pointed out that "Old Rough and Ready" was a Louisiana slaveholder; Northern voters heard that Taylor was friendly to the Wilmot Proviso. The general's admirers sloganized his remark, allegedly uttered during the Battle of Buena Vista, "General Taylor never surrenders."[49] The "General's Boys" rallied the faithful:

> Rough and Ready is the man
> That all good Whigs delight in;
> He's just the sort for President,
> And "a" the man for fighting.
> They raise the song, the States along,
> From Maine to Loosiana.
> We've got "the coon" that sealed the doom,
> Of Polk and Santa Anna.[50]

Sheet music of the day stressed the general's career.[51]

However, the general's opponents insisted that Taylor was a "military autocrat," who would adopt a bellicose foreign policy if he became president to satisfy his lust for martial glory. Moreover, his only qualifications for the highest office in the land, they insisted, consisted of "sleeping forty years in the woods and cultivating moss on the calves of his legs."

Cass, the Whigs charged on the other hand, was a windbag – a "mountain of evil" who had "surrendered himself unconditionally to the South" and was therefore "odious to all friends of the Wilmot Proviso." By nominating Cass "the Convention has given to the republic . . . a candidate . . . who has solemnly proclaimed, as his, a principle which allows the South the option of making every new territory hereafter to come into the Union a slave state without allowing any opposite equal privilege to the North."[52]

The Democrats also were forced to run two very different campaigns. In the South they emphasized Cass's pledge to veto the proviso should Congress ever pass it. In the North they stressed other issues but argued, when forced, that a territorial decision on slavery would result in free soil as surely as congressional prohibition and without threatening the bonds of the Union.

The deeply disappointed Henry Clay retired to Ashland, his Lexington estate, where he remained in seclusion throughout the campaign. All appeals for him to proclaim his approval of Taylor's nomination to help the Whigs reunite their party were returned with decided and bitter refusals. As for Webster, after much obvious hesitation, he gave Taylor a token endorsement. Only late in the campaign did he make speeches for the ticket.

The major parties did not ignore the Free Soil Party as they had the Liberty Party. Bitter personal attacks were launched against Van Buren and Adams and their supporters. Van Buren was charged with being an "apostate" – the leader of the fiends of disunion who would rather rule in hell than serve in heaven – a "traitor," a "hypocrite," a "sorehead," an "ingrate," an "assassin," and the "Judas Iscariot of the nineteenth century." It was charged that he was supported by radical, agrarian Locofocos whose principles were "at war with the safety of . . . civil and religious institutions – fanatics . . . who were willing and ready to let down the flood gates of anarchy and misrule whenever they secured power."[53] A particularly effective piece of Democratic propaganda was an eight-page pamphlet which contained a compilation of nasty things Adams had said about Van Buren when they had been political foes instead of bedfellows.[54]

Of the three parties, the Free Soilers displayed by far the most enthusiasm in their campaigning. A favorite Free Soil campaign song went:

> Come, ye hardy sons of toil,
> And cast your ballot for Free Soil;
> He who'd vote for Zacky Taylor,
> Needs a keeper or a jailor.
>
> And he who still for Cass can be,
> He is a Cass without the C;
> The Man on whom we love to look,
> Is Martin Van Buren of Kinderhook.[55]

The Democrats responded with the following:

> Awake, old spirit of the past —
> Awake, and put thy armor on —
> Nail Freedom's ensign to the mast,
> Nor falter till the fight is won.
>
> Heed not disunion's croaking voice,
> Expose each dark and damning plan;
> Elect the leader of your choice —
> The gallant Cass of Michigan.[56]

James Russell Lowell's "Hosea Biglow" could not hide his disappointment over Van Buren:

> I used to vote for Martin,
>   but I swan I'm clean disgusted —
> He ain't the man that I can say
>   is fittin' to be trusted,
> He ain't half antislav'ry 'nough,
>   nor I ain't sure, es some be,
> He's go in for abolishin'
>   the Deestrick o' Columby.[57]

The Free Soil Press. In support of Van Buren's candidacy, numerous free soil journals sprang up all over the North. Gamaliel Bailey's *National Era*, established in 1847 by the abolitionist American and Foreign Antislavery Society, quickly established itself as the leading and most popular liberty paper in the country. Other important free soil papers were the *Boston Republican* and Walt Whitman's *Weekly Freeman*. Also, many established presses endorsed the Free Soil ticket. Probably the most influential of these were William Cullen Bryant's *New York Evening Post* and the *Albany Evening Atlas*, edited by James M. French and William Cassidy.

The Outcome, 1848. On November 7, Zachary Taylor won the election in a close race. Thirty states — half slave and half free — participated in the election, the first presidential election to be held on the same day everywhere. The voter turnout was light. Taylor received a popular vote of 1,360,000 and 163 electoral votes to Cass's 1,221,000 and 127. Taylor won 8 slave states and the important Northern states of New York, Pennsylvania, and Massachusetts. Cass carried all of the Midwest and 7 slave states. As with the Whigs, Democratic losses were greatest in the North.[58]

The most noteworthy aspect of the 1848 election was the size of Van Buren's Free Soil vote. Although the ex-president's party had entered the campaign only three months before the election, he polled an impressive 291,000 votes, about 10 percent of the total and nearly five times as many votes as Birney had won in 1844. Van Buren's vote exceeded that of Cass in three states: Vermont, Massachusetts, and New York. Ironically, Kinderhook, Columbia County, New York, went for Old Rough and Ready.[59]

As in the election of 1844, the vote of New York was the deciding factor. The division in the Democratic ranks enabled the Whigs to carry that state and thereby to elect Taylor and Fillmore. The antislavery Barnburner Democrats of New York, who gave Van Buren 40 percent of his total vote, were thus the decisive factors in the defeat of the Democratic ticket, and the election of a Southern slaveholder to the presidency.[60]

Though he accomplished his major aims and led the nation through a great war with large acquisitions of territory, Polk was amazingly unpopular at the close of his term. Exhausted from overwork, he returned to his home in Nashville. When an epidemic of cholera swept the South, Polk was among its casualties. He died on June 15, 1849, at the early age of 53, only three months after he left office.[61]

The Administration of Zachary Taylor

Zachary Taylor, as president, quickly became enbroiled in the issue that haunted the country — slavery.[62] Political problems arising in the far West demanded immediate action by Congress. New Mexico was in need of a territorial government. The Mormons in Utah had organized a government for the new state of Deseret, elected Brigham Young as governor, and applied for admission into the Union as a free state. However, the problem of greatest urgency had arisen in connection with California.

In January 1848, nine days before the signing of the Treaty of Guadalupe Hidalgo ending the Mexican War, gold was found on one of the tributaries of the Sacramento River. "Forty-niners" were soon pouring into the valleys of California singing "O Susannah," and shouting "Gold! Gold! Gold!"

When Congress met in November 1848, immediately after Taylor's election, it admitted the state of Wisconsin, which made the North and South evenly balanced in the Senate. However, it provided no government for California, New Mexico, or Utah. Oregon had been organized in 1848 as a territory without any stipulation as to slavery, which meant that the government of the territory would be on an antislavery basis. The debates in Congress showed that there was going to be a bitter struggle over California, New Mexico, and Utah.

By the time that President Taylor took office in 1849, California was petitioning for statehood (without slavery) and New Mexico was demanding territorial government. The petitions were favored by Taylor, who hoped to take California and New Mexico into the Union unconditionally and without direction from Congress, thereby avoiding the whole problem of slavery in the territories for the time being. In a message to Congress he recommended the admission of California and New Mexico under conditions that would allow each to make its own determination whether or not to admit slavery. Taylor's proposal in substance would represent a Free Soil victory, since the proposed states seemed fairly certain to be free states. The president's plan had the support of most Northern Whigs, but it provoked hot words from Southern Democrats and Southern Whigs.

California accepted this hint eagerly. By the time the new Congress assembled in December 1849 California had written a constitution which prohibited slavery, organized a state government, and was sending two senators eastward, one of whom was John C. Fremont, Missouri Senator Thomas Hart Benton's son-in-law, together with two representatives. Also, Utah's constitution as the state of Deseret was on its way.

The issue of slavery was rapidly approaching a climax as the Thirty-First Congress convened in December 1849. The hotheaded extremists were there: Salmon P. Chase of Ohio, William H. Seward of New York, and Charles Sumner of Massachusetts for the North; John C. Calhoun, Jefferson Davis of Mississippi, and Alexander H. Stephens and Robert Toombs of Georgia for the South. Fortunately for the United States, the Congress contained wiser and cooler men, "the Union Savers," Henry Clay and Daniel Webster.

Controversy over slavery was so acute in the House of Representatives that for three hectic weeks the House could not organize because no Speaker could be elected. House rules called for a majority decision, but there was no majority. Amid taunts, jeers, and catcalls the representatives from the free and from the slave states hurled taunts and threats at one another, leading one member to complain: "On the whole, a seat in Congress is a most undesirable possession." However, on the sixty-third ballot Howell Cobb, a Georgia Democrat, defeated the scholarly Robert Winthrop of Boston, Massachusetts, the Speaker of the Thirtieth Congress, by the close vote of 102–99 with most of the Free Soilers voting for David Wilmot (which made Cobb a minority Speaker). However, when Cobb named the committees' personnel the Democratic Party found itself in control of both House and Senate organizations.

Slavery, in its various aspects, cropped up almost daily in speeches made in both houses. Southerners in Congress were soon speaking rather freely of disunion. On one occasion, when Toombs of Georgia threatened secession, the Southern members cheered him with vigor and abandon. Until this time Congress had managed to maintain a balance of slave and free states in the Senate, and they could count on that body to defeat any legislation hostile to the South. Now, no slave territory was awaiting admission to statehood. Instead, Minnesota was clamoring to be admitted as a free state, and if California and New Mexico were also brought in as the president proposed, the handwriting on the wall would be clear. Southerners could foresee the day when their section would be at the mercy of a government controlled by unsympathetic Northerners. If California's action was approved by Congress it might become a precedent for the rest of the Mexican cession; at best it would eliminate the possibility of extending the Missouri Compromise line to the Pacific since California straddled that line.

In October 1849 a state convention in Mississippi issued a call for an all-Southern convention to meet in Nashville in June 1850 to work out a united Southern position. It seemed certain that secession would be discussed. In the face of the growing secessionist talk, President Taylor made it clear in his message to Congress in December 1849 that disunionists would receive no comfort from him. He threatened to take the field and hang all those captured in rebellion "with as little mercy as he had hanged deserters and spies in Mexico." However, the president had no constructive proposals to offer. In a message to Congress he simply advised that body to avoid "exciting topics of sectional character" — this at a time when senators and representatives carried Bowie knives and Colt revolvers. Clearly, the South had no intention of allowing California to enter the Union as a free state unless it received important concessions in return.

The Compromise of 1850

Into this feverish atmosphere Henry Clay came forward on January 29, 1850, with an elaborate compromise which he hoped would restore the "peace, concord, and harmony of the Union." Despite his age (he was now 73), Clay's mind was still sharp; his silvery voice, though racked by a serious cough, could still hold an audience captive.

The essential provisions of the compromise which Clay proposed were as follows: that California should be admitted as a state without slavery; that territorial governments should be established in New Mexico and Utah without restrictions upon slavery; that the slave-trade but not slavery was to be prohibited in the District of Columbia; that a more effective fugitive slave law should be enacted; and that Congress should have no power to interfere with the slave trade among the slaveholding states.

A few days after offering his resolutions (February 5, 1850), Clay appeared on the floor of the crowded, red-carpeted Senate chamber to speak passionately for his beloved Union. He urged the North to be magnanimous and the South to banish thoughts of disunion. Could not both sections be satisfied, he pleaded, with the gains they would make under his proposals? "You have got what is worth more than a thousand Wilmot Provisos," Clay pointed out to his Northern colleagues. "You have nature on your side." He warned Southerners that they would gain nothing and lose a great deal by secession — that secession was certain to lead to "furious, bloody, implacable, exterminating" civil war.

Clay was followed a month later (March 4) by Calhoun, so ill that he grimly sat in his seat while his carefully prepared speech was read for him by a colleague, Senator James Mason of Virginia. However, it quickly became clear that Calhoun's speech was no plea for compromise. Clay's proposals, he said, did not go far enough in recognizing the rights of the South. The Union, he said, could be saved — not by compromise by the weaker party but by concessions from the stronger. The North, he said, must demonstrate a willingness to return to the South her runaway slaves; stop the slavery agitation; allow the South an equal share in the public domain; and consent to an amendment to the Constitution which would restore the political equilibrium. Otherwise, he urged, "let the states . . . agree to separate and part in peace."[63] Calhoun's speech was recognized immediately as an argument for secession; nothing could satisfy the South Carolinian except abject surrender by the North.

Three days later Daniel Webster took the floor. Contrary to the expectations of the antislavery group, his famous "Seventh of March Address" was a plea for compromise. When he rose he declared he came to speak "Not as a Massachusetts man, not as a Northern man, but as an American." Though strongly opposed to the extension of slavery, Webster put aside that feeling out of devotion to the Union and gave full support to Clay's proposed compromise.

Like Clay, Webster acknowledged that the South had just cause for complaining about the North's refusal to return fugitive slaves and insisted that the South was right in demanding a more stringent fugitive slave law. New Mexico and California he insisted would in all likelihood be free by "an ordinance of nature." He saw no reason, therefore, of needlessly antagonizing the South by proposing legislation to exclude slavery from these territories. In closing, Webster ridiculed the possibility of "peaceful secession." The Union could not be sundered without bloodshed. "Peaceful secession!" Webster exclaimed, "Heaven forbid! Where is the flag of the republic to remain? Where is the eagle still to tower?" Webster closed with poetry's tribute to his great love," Union":

> Now the broad shield complete, the artist crowned
>   with his last hand and poured the ocean round;
> In living silver seemed the wares to roll,
>   And beat the buckler berge, and bound the whole.[64]

As he knew it would, Webster's speech in support of the compromise and the Fugitive Slave Act brought down on his head the bitter criticism of outraged antislavery men in the Northeast. Ralph Waldo Emerson accused Webster of believing that "government exists for the protection of property," and abolitionist Theodore Parker compared him to Benedict Arnold, selling his soul for Southern support for the presidency. John Greenleaf Whittier, the Quaker poet laureate of the abolitionists, called him "Ichabod" and wrote with words filled with remorse:

> All else is gone; from those great eyes
> The soul has fled:
> When faith is lost, when honor dies,
> The man is dead![65]

To the antislavery group in the North the godlike Daniel had now become anathema. In 1851 the Massachusetts legislature delivered a stern rebuke to Webster by electing Charles Sumner, a radical Free Soiler and enemy of the compromise, to the U.S. Senate. Sumner's election was little noticed at the time, but it soon came to have a tremendous significance.[66]

William H. Seward, the slight and weak-voiced freshman Whig senator from New York, spoke ably for many of the younger Northern radicals in denouncing compromise as "radically wrong and essentially vicious." There was only one way to end antislavery agitation, he said, and that was by "yielding to the progress of emancipation." Despite the constitutional obligation to return the fugitive slaves, there was a "higher law" than the Constitution, Seward proclaimed, the law of God which required men to oppose slavery, implying that the advocates of a righteous cause need not be deterred by constitutional niceties.

The fate of the compromise was still very much in doubt when President Taylor died unexpectedly a few days after taking part in a Fourth of July celebration of the building of the Washington monument, after only 18 months in office. He was succeeded by the far less engaging Millard Fillmore, who, although a moderate antislavery man like Clay, thought the issue should be settled by compromise and not by force.[67]

When Clay, exhausted by his labors, temporarily left the capital for a rest, the young, dynamic Democrat Senator Stephen A. Douglas of Illinois took charge of the efforts to pass the compromise measures. Under the "Little Giant's" leadership, Clay's resolutions were taken up one by one and passed. By September 5 the six measures that collectively became known as the Compromise of 1850 were approved. Fillmore gladly signed them all.[68] With the adoption of the Compromise of 1850, the nation breathed a sigh of heartfelt relief. Celebrations were held throughout the country. In the nation's capitol the event was celebrated with bonfires, parades, singing in the streets, and cannon salutes. Hundreds of newspapers, North and South, gave the compromise editorial approval. Before the Thirty-First Congress adjourned, Clay secured the signatures of 40 members to a pledge that they would support no man for public office who refused to abide by the "the final settlement."

Calhoun died before the debate was finished on the compromise, still doubting that "two peoples so different and hostile" could "exist together in one common union." His final benediction were the sad words: "The South! The South! God knows what will become of her." Clay did not live much longer. He spent the summer of 1851 at Ashland making a will and providing for the disposition of his estate and the freeing of his slaves. He returned to Washington in the fall but answered only the first Senate roll call.

The Fugitive Slave Law. In accordance with the promise of the Compromise of 1850 that the Fugitive Slave Act of 1793 would be amended and strengthened, Congress passed and President Fillmore signed the Fugitive Slave Law of 1850, which permitted slave owners to seize blacks in the North as fugitives without process of law and for their return to their owners. It soon became known as the "Bloodhound Bill" and the "Man Stealing Law." Ralph Waldo Emerson called it a "filthy enactment," and pledged: "I will not obey it, by God." Horace Greeley despised the Fugitive Slave Law and was unreconciled. "Is there any use in throwing up rockets to warn the willfully blind?" he chided the Democratic "doughfaces" who had engineered its passage. That the people of the North who opposed slavery on moral grounds did not cooperate in the enforcement of the Fugitive Slave Act is beyond question. Between 1855 and 1859 Connecticut, Rhode Island, Massachusetts, Michigan, Maine, Ohio, and Wisconsin passed "personal liberty" laws deliberately intended to hamper the recovery of runaways. In some states it became next to impossible to enforce the Fugitive Slave Act. These laws revealed the strength of Northern fears of the slave power. To the South, they were outrageous signs of bad faith.

The Election of 1852

The race for the presidency in 1852 began as early as the spring of 1851. The most active and energetic aspirant for the Democratic nomination was Stephen A. Douglas, the 38-year-old junior senator from Illinois.[69]

Douglas was born in Vermont in 1813 but moved to Illinois when he was barely 20 years old. There he was soon deep in Democratic politics. From 1835 to 1843 he held a succession of state offices; then he was elected to Congress where he served two terms. In 1847 he was chosen U.S. senator and he soon won a national reputation. Douglas was a man with a large head, a mighty voice, and very short legs, which gained him the title of the "Little Giant" (he stood only 5 feet 4 inches). Others called him "the steam engine in britches." Douglas loved the rough-and-tumble life of politics. "I live with my Constituents," he once boasted, "Drink with them, lodge with them, pray with them, laugh, hunt, dance, and work with them. I eat their corn dodgers and fried bacon and sleep two in a bed with them."[70]

There were many obstacles in the way for Douglas. He had no machine, and various organizations outside his state opposed him for his apparent lack of concern for the moral aspects of slavery. Moreover, his preconvention support outside Illinois was destroyed by his excessive attacks on his political opponents for the nomination. He expressed open contempt for James Buchanan, and said of Lewis Cass, who had served in the diplomatic corps, that his "reputation was beyond the C." While Douglas's characterizations of Cass were accurate as well as amusing, they did not add to his political strength. His foes soon began to combine against him. But Douglas went after the nomination with tooth and toenail. He traveled about the country buttonholing local bigwigs and making speeches pledging himself anew to the compromise measures which he had helped frame.

Cass, the logical candidate of the Democrats, had been defeated in 1848 because of the defection of the Free Soilers. But with the return of Van Buren and the Barnburners to the Democratic fold, that rift in the Democratic Party now appeared to be healed. The party leaders in the Northwest, an area which was still wedded to Cass, were arguing that it would only be fair to give him this opportunity for vindication. Others were not so sure. His support of the compromise as a whole had estranged some Southern Democrats without winning broad Northern endorsement. His supporters, though numerous, were widely scattered, and he lacked any significant nucleus. As no large state delegation favored his candidacy he could scarcely emerge as a leader around whom the party could rally and win in 1852. Also, he was an "Old Fogey" — nearly 70, obese, and inactive. It was doubtful that Cass could win even with a united party.

James Buchanan of Pennsylvania and William L. Marcy of New York were also eager for the nomination. But both men were also over 60 years old.

The Democratic Convention, 1852. The Democratic National Convention convened at Baltimore on June 1, 1852. The delegates quickly fell into a deadlock among the supporters of Cass and Douglas, the two popular sovereignty advocates, and Buchanan, who had heavy support from the Southern delegates. On the thirty-fifth ballot the Virginia delegation introduced a new name — Franklin Pierce of New Hampshire — after assurances that the New Englander was solidly in favor of the 1820 compromise line. North Carolina started the stampede to Pierce on the forty-ninth ballot when an obscure delegate made an electrifying speech and cast all the Tarheel votes for the lawyer from Concord.[71] Senator William R. King of Alabama, president pro tempore of the Senate, a red-wig-wearing mediocrity, was chosen for vice president although he was dying of tuberculosis at age 66.

The platform adroitly avoided trouble on the compromise by failing to proclaim its finality. "The Democratic Party of the Union," it said, "will abide by, and adhere to, a faithful execution of the acts known as the 'compromise' measures settled by the last Congress and will resist all attempts at renewing in Congress or out of it, the agitation of the slavery question." The plank dealing with the compromise was read and reread amid great enthusiasm and long-continued applause.[72]

Franklin Pierce was the darkest of dark horses – few of the delegates had even heard of him before the convention. He had begun his public career in the New Hampshire legislature in 1829. Elected to Congress in 1833, he was a strong Jackson Democrat active in opposition to internal improvements and all antislavery measures. He was promoted to the Senate in 1837. However, bourbon and branch water became a problem for Pierce in Washington and in 1842 he resigned his seat in Congress. As soon as the Mexican War was declared he enlisted as a private. Commissioned as a colonel and later as a brigadier general, he served with distinction.

The nomination of the handsome, engaging, well-spoken, 47-year-old nonentity was well received by the Democrats. In the words of Allan Nevins, a majority of the Democratic Party "accepted the new leader joyously. Since he had not been sufficiently in public life to make enemies and his deeper convictions were a mystery, every faction and section felt that it could gamble on him."[73]

The Whig Convention, 1852. Things looked very bright for the Whigs in 1852. Theirs was the chance to exploit, as party achievements, both the prosperity and the popularity of the Compromise of 1850.

The Whig convention assembled in Baltimore on June 16, with all 31 states represented. The Northern and Southern wings of the Whig Party were nearly equally represented. The gathering was not likely to be a lovefeast. The bone of contention was the finality of the Compromise of 1850, particularly enforcement of the Fugitive Slave Act. The Northern Whigs generally opposed the compromise while most Southern members of the party supported it and were determined that the convention should nominate no candidate who did not specifically reiterate endorsement. The convention sessions were often lively and sometimes raucous. A minister invited to the hall to deliver a prayer to the convention never had his chance. The delegates, unable to agree when the prayer should be delivered, finally decided to omit it.

President Fillmore aspired to a term of his own. In his view, and in the view of many others, he deserved it. He had finished his first term with the esteem of the country because of his strict enforcement of the Compromise of 1850, including the Fugitive Slave Law. However, after the death of Clay, the prime architect of the compromise in 1852, Fillmore lost the support of many of the Northern abolitionist Whigs. As a result, even though he was their president, he never became an inner-sanctum Whig. He was never permitted to sit in the high councils of his own party; he could make no close connection with any of the great chiefs of Whiggism, and he was unable to develop a potent organization behind him.[74]

Also being pushed for the nomination by Senator William H. Seward was Lieutenant General Winfield Scott, the 66-year-old Mexican War hero. Scott had considerable support in the Northern and Western states but, despite his Virginia birth, was not popular in the South because of his friendship with Seward, a "notorious" antislavery Northerner. Further, Scott had been practicing a masterly silence on any issue connected with slavery, under pledge to his backers determined to keep him the most available candidate. A third candidate in the field was Daniel Webster who coveted the nomination but had ruined his chances with the antislavery element in the party by his support of the Compromise of 1850.

With only three persons under consideration, the Whigs dispensed with formal nominating speeches. Fillmore's service in securing passage of the compromise brought him 133 votes on the first ballot with all Southern delegates except one supporting him. Only 2 votes behind was Scott. On the ensuing ballots the Northern Whigs were able to block the efforts of Southern Whigs to nominate Fillmore and on the fifty-third ballot Scott won the nomination. Secretary of the Navy William A. Graham of North Carolina was given second place on the second ballot without a roll-call vote.

The Whig platform endorsed the Compromise of 1850 only provisionally. The debate over the compromise plank revealed the deep division in the Whig Party. The majority secured the adoption of a so-called "finality plank," which read in part as follows: "That the series of acts of the Thirty-First Congress — the act known as the Fugitive Slave Law included — are received and acquiesced in by the Whig Party of the United States as a settlement in principle and in substance of the dangerous and exciting questions which they embrace" and they promised to maintain them" until time and experience shall demonstrate the necessity of further legislation."[75] Even this lukewarm statement was opposed by 25 percent of the delegates.

The platform was adopted by the vote of 227–66, with most of the dissenting votes being cast by antislavery delegates from the North and West who wanted a stronger statement. Other Northerners seemed to be willing to concede the platform to the South in order to get Southern support for Scott. Scott tried to extricate himself from this dilemma by merely saying "I accept the nomination with resolutions attached."

However, Scott's nomination left Whigs from all sections of the country despondent about the future of the party. The antislavery Whigs of the North swallowed Scott as their standard-bearer but, as Horace Greeley put it, by accepting the nominee they "spit upon the platform." Southern Whigs, who doubted Scott's loyalty to the Compromise of 1850 and especially to the Fugitive Slave Law, accepted the platform but spit upon the candidate.[76]

The Free Democratic Convention, 1852. With the old parties outdoing themselves in getting rid of their Free Soil doctrines to plant themselves on the compromise, the Free Soilers proceeded to attack the compromise, and in the Northwest turned away from the "Free Soil" name to the title "Free Democracy." "Free Democratic" was a broader name which could represent positions on other issues.

When the Free Democratic convention opened in Pittsburgh on August 11, 1852, it was small by the standards of four years earlier. Only about 2,000 attended, compared to the approximately 20,000 at Buffalo. With the Barnburners gone for good the more dedicated antislavery men provided most of the delegates. The unanimous selection of Senator John P. Hale of New Hampshire as the presidential nominee was a foregone conclusion; George W. Julian, a one-term representative in Congress from Indiana, was selected as his running mate.

In their platform the Free Democrats condemned the Compromise of 1850 and the Fugitive Slave Law as inconsistent with all the principles and maxims of democracy, and called for the abolition of slavery. Also included were planks calling for a free homestead policy, river and harbor improvements, and extending a welcome hand to immigrants.

The 1852 Campaign. There was little excitement in the 1852 campaign. The Whigs tried without success to stir up "fife and drum" enthusiasm for their military hero. Forgetting the boomerang they had shaped in 1844, they tried to jeer Pierce back into obscurity with the cry "Who is Frank Pierce?" Pierce was accused of cowardice, intemperance (the hero of many a hard-fought bottle), of being a do-nothing while in Congress, of being anti–Catholic, and in the South of being an abolitionist. Pierce's military record was described in a miniature book, only one inch high and a one-half inch wide, entitled *The Military Services of General Pierce*.

The Democrats responded by forming "Granite clubs" for Pierce and raising "Hickory Poles to the honor of Young Hickory of the Granite Hills." As they rejoiced over their candidate they cried exultantly: "We Polked 'em in '44; we'll Pierce 'em in '52." A flood of anti–Scott pamphlets and broadsides inundated the North and West. William Cullen Bryant's *New York Evening Post* extolled Pierce's talents. Nathaniel Hawthorne, "the most gracious pen in America" and a college friend of Pierce, wrote his campaign biography.[77]

The 1852 Outcome. Pierce was overwhelmingly elected, carrying 27 of the 31 states — receiving 254 electoral votes to 42 for Scott. He also had a large lead in the popular vote as well, receiving 1,601,000 popular votes against 1,386,000 for Scott; which translated into 50.84 percent of the popular vote—the largest plurality any president had received up to that time. Almost all elements of the party had rallied behind Pierce's candidacy, and the Democratic vote rose by 380,000 over that of 1848. The Free Democratic Party made a far poorer showing than it had four years earlier. Hale garnered an estimated 156,000 votes (4.9 percent of the popular vote) but, as in 1848, failed to carry a single state. More than 7,000 Georgia and Massachusetts Whigs—"finality men"—deserted Scott and voted for Webster, although he had died nearly two weeks before the election.[78]

The outcome was a great disappointment to the Whigs. They had lost in every section of the country.[79] "The Whig Party seems almost annihilated by the recent elections," lamented one of its leaders. Another prominent Whig, Thurlow Weed, editor of the *Albany Evening Journal,* confessed, "There may be no political future for us." Weed's pessimism was justified. The Whig Party, which throughout its existence had been little more than an "organized incompatibility," was falling to pieces. In fact, they never again entered a presidential contest with an independent nomination.

The Administration of Franklin Pierce

Franklin Pierce was inaugurated as the fourteenth president of the United States on March 4, 1853.[80] Standing bareheaded in the snow before some 15,000 persons (reduced from 80,000 by the snowstorm), the new president "affirmed"[81] his responsibilities as president. He then delivered his inaugural address without written text or notes—the first American president to do so.[82] The compromise measures of 1850, he said, "were strictly constitutional and to be unhesitatingly carried into effect." The constitutional rights of the South would be respected as resolutely as those of any other section, he pledged. In conclusion, Pierce appealed for maintenance of the status quo. The fearful crisis of 1850 had been surmounted, he said. "Let the period be remembered as an admonition, and not as an encouragement . . . to make experiments."[83]

Although President Pierce sincerely wished to restore national harmony, he was unable to do so. He had almost no capacity for executive direction and none at all for party leadership. He did not appoint a single outstanding man to his cabinet. Its head was William L. Marcy of New York, but the secretary of war, Jefferson Davis of Mississippi, was the most influential member. Friends of the compromise on both sides of the Mason-Dixon Line were surprised that Pierce should have appointed this outspoken opponent of the settlement when several strong Southern supporters of it were available. He was extremely loyal to his cabinet (he was the only president ever to have the same Cabinet through his entire term) and when circumstances forced him to take a stand, he usually allowed his Southern friends in the cabinet to dictate his action.

The administration and its head were held in such low esteem, even among their Southern supporters, that one of the latter wrote: "It has not vitality enough in both houses of Congress to lift it above the sneers and scoffs and ridicule of the veriest dolt that chooses to assail it. . . . Bye and bye . . . the whole country will be ready to write *to let* on the door of the White House."[84]

Uncle Tom's Cabin. For two years the Compromise of 1850 seemed to settle the issue of slavery. Yet, beneath the surface, the tension remained and grew. The person who most likely did more to revive the issue of slavery than any other American was Harriet Beecher Stowe, the author of the novel *Uncle Tom's Cabin.*

Mrs. Stowe's heartrending novel appeared first in June 1851 as a serial in the *National Era,* an antislavery newspaper. It did not create much excitement, however, until it came out in book form in the spring of 1852, and it sold 300,000 copies in its first year. The total soon ran into millions as the tale was translated in several foreign languages. Stowe had brought the issue of slavery home to many who had never before given it much thought. Within a year it had become the most effective piece of antislavery literature ever published. The historian Thomas A. Bailey asserts that no other novel in American history can be compared with it as a political force. Millions of impressionable Northern boys reading it in their teens are said to have imbibed such a deep hatred of slavery that they could only vote the Republican ticket on reaching their maturity.[85]

Although Mrs. Stowe's book was received in the North with great acclaim, the people of the South felt that "that vile wretch in petticoats" had "held up their section in a false light before the world." A Southern minister spoke of it as "that book of genius, true in all its facts, false in all its impressions." Southern protests against the book's unfairness were nullified to a large extent by the indisputable spectacle of the pursuit of black men through free states.[86]

The Kansas-Nebraska Act, 1854

President Pierce had little in the way of a program to offer the new Congress when it met in December 1853. In his message he spoke of a present "bright with promise" because the apprehensions of 1850 had been quieted by distinguished citizens of all parties who had sacrificed their private views and had "restored a sense of repose and security to the public mind." The new president pledged that this repose would "suffer no shock during my official term, if I have power to avert it." It looked as though it would be a quiet year. Then on January 4, 1854, Stephen A. Douglas, the distinguished senior senator from Illinois, brought a bill to the floor of the Senate to organize the Indian country west of Missouri into a huge new territory to be known as Nebraska. Soon, sound and fury filled the halls of Congress and reverberated across the land.

Senator Douglas likely had several motives in having the bill, soon to become famous (or infamous) as the Kansas-Nebraska Bill, enacted into law. For one thing, there was no more anxious prospective tenant for the anticipated White House vacancy than Stephen A. Douglas. Yet Douglas knew that the route to the White House was commanded by Southern Democrats. Before he could become president he had to get the support of the South.

It was also said by many that Douglas's action in the Kansas-Nebraska Act had to do with the building of a transcontinental railroad. For years there had been strong pressure for a government-subsidized railroad link with California. Building the road would involve immense wealth-bringing grants of public land. The South wanted the road to go to the Pacific coast by way of Texas and New Mexico. However, those, such as Douglas, who favored a central route thought that the organization of Nebraska territory would improve their political and personal prospects. Douglas also had a strong personal interest in such a railroad. A heavy speculator in Western lands, including the city site which he expected to be the eastern terminus of the railroad, Douglas knew that if he could make Chicago the eastern terminus he would not only win the political backing of the grateful people of Illinois but he would also benefit his own section and would profit handsomely himself.[87]

Douglas met determined opposition. The bill was opposed by most Southern congressmen because it opened lands north of the Missouri Compromise line which would almost certainly become free states. Missouri, especially, objected to letting Kansas, which would adjoin her on the west, become a free territory. It would be all too easy for Missouri slaves to run away to this free area. For a time Missourians in Washington, backed by Southerners, blocked all efforts to organize the region.

Douglas had hoped to open this territory without raising the slavery issue, assuming that the same phraseology used in the Compromise of 1850 would be acceptable. The trouble was that Nebraska would not fall into the same category as the areas taken from Mexico. As part of the Louisiana Purchase territory, Nebraska was governed by the provisions of the Missouri Compromise of 1820, which prohibited slavery north of the line 36° 30′ except in Missouri. Planters could not take slaves to Nebraska territory unless Congress repealed the ancient compact outright.

Thus, Southerners, led by senators Atchison of Missouri and Dixon of Kentucky, insisted on the outright repeal of the Missouri Compromise. When Douglas balked he was threatened with loss of his chairmanship of the Territories Committee, a post he considered vital to his legislative and political hopes.[88] Douglas finally bowed to their pressure, correctly predicting that his action would raise "a hell of a storm" (although he grossly underestimated its proportions). He brought in a bill to create the territories of Kansas and Nebraska which also contained two special provisions. One embodied the idea of "popular sovereignty" — the concept that the people of each territory would decide for themselves, when time for statehood came, whether to permit or exclude slavery — a concept to which Douglas and his Western constituents had become deeply attached. The other specifically repealed the Missouri Compromise. Despite the public outcry in the North against the Kansas-Nebraska Act, the Free Soilers could not dissuade President Pierce, under the thumb of Southern advisers, from throwing his full weight behind the bill.

But the Missouri Compromise, now 34 years old, could not be brushed aside lightly. A bitter debate raged in Congress for four months over the bill. Despite Douglas's denials, thousands of Northerners were convinced that the sole purpose of the bill was to ensure that slavery would enter Kansas and Nebraska. As Senator Charles Sumner expressed it, "It [the act] annuls all past compromises with slavery, and makes all future compromises impossible. Thus it puts freedom and slavery face to face, and bids them grapple. Who can doubt the result?"[89]

The Appeal of the Independent Democrats. On January 22, 1854, the day after the Kansas-Nebraska Act reached the Senate, the *National Era*, the Washington antislavery newspaper, published an influential "Appeal of the Independent Democrats in Congress to the People of the United States," a document largely drafted by Salmon P. Chase, and signed by all the Free Soil members of Congress. The "Appeal of the Independent Democrats" accused Douglas of being willing to "permanently subjugate the whole country to the yoke of slaveholding despotism," denounced the repeal of the Missouri Compromise with furious indignation, and labeled the Kansas-Nebraska Act as "part and parcel of an atrocious plot" to trample free labor and to make the great West into a "dreary region of despotism inhabited by masters and slaves." The people were urged to "Let all protest, earnestly and emphatically, by correspondence, through the press, by memorials, by resolutions of public meetings and legislative bodies, and in whatever other mode may seem expedient, against this enormous crime."[90]

The North responded to the "Appeal" with a torrent of denunciation for Douglas's disruption of the "finality" of 1850. Northern, Eastern, and Western Democratic papers opposed the measure. Northern clergymen assailed it from hundreds of pulpits. Mass meetings were held in all the chief Northern cities to attack Douglas and his measure. Douglas was labeled a traitor, a Judas, and a Benedict Arnold, who had sold himself to the South in the hope of the presidential nomination. As Horace Greeley's *New York Tribune* noted, "The unanimous sentiment of the North is indignant resistance." Senator Sam Houston of Texas predicted that if the Missouri

Compromise were repealed, "I will have seen the commencement of the agitation, but the youngest child now born, will not live to witness its termination."

After three months of bitter controversy Douglas succeeded in pushing the bill through a sullen Congress. President Pierce signed the bill, although it was in direct violation of the compromises of 1820 and 1850 and despite the fact that he had been elected president on a platform pledging "adherences to those compromises." It almost certainly cost Pierce his party's nomination in 1856 and probable reelection as president. Editor William Cullen Bryant, back in the Democratic Party, begged Pierce to veto the obnoxious bill. "To persist in the foolish scheme of Senator Douglas can only result in whittling away the Democratic Party into shavings," he warned.

The passage of the Kansas-Nebraska Act raised the argument over slavery to a desperate new intensity and brought to a sudden end the "sense of repose and security" which Pierce had promised to protect. The stage was set for the extremists on both sides — the fire-eaters, the men who invited violence with violent words. Many Northerners, previously friendly to the South, now came to feel that the act seemed concrete evidence of a slave power plot to use the federal government to spread slavery against the will of the North, a plot abolitionists had warned about since the 1830s. Worse yet, Kansas was thrown open for settlement under conditions which practically guaranteed bloodshed.

Douglas was hanged in effigy in every free state. He was accused of selling out to the South in return for the Democratic presidential nomination. Horace Greeley kept Douglas under fire with his *New York Tribune* editorials throughout the spring and summer of 1854.[91] When Douglas visited Chicago to speak in his own defense, a crowd of 10,000 hooted and groaned until exhausted. But the senator still enjoyed a high degree of popularity among his own loyal following in the Democratic Party, especially in Illinois, a stronghold of popular sovereignty, whose legislature was one of the few Free Soil states to pass a resolution supporting the measure.[92]

Douglas's fantastic political miscalculation plagued and divided American politics for decades. In the end the Kansas-Nebraska Act fractured both major parties. Northern Democrats split up into pro–Nebraska and anti–Nebraska Democrats. Droves of old-line Democrats deserted the national party in New England, Ohio, Illinois, and Iowa. The Whigs were also hopelessly rent. In one Northern state after another the party split in pieces as a result of the measure. In New England there were Cotton and Conscience Whigs. In New York Whigs became either radical Seward "Woolly Heads" or conservative "Silver Grays," and in other places "Higher Law" and "Lower Law" Whigs. The Southern "Cotton Whigs," alienated by the antislavery attitude of their Northern brethren, began to flock into the Democratic fold, while thousands of other members moved over into the growing Know-Nothing ranks in search of an issue (and a party) that would bring slaveholders and abolitionists together and thus save the Union. The bill's passage brought to a close the six-year history of the Free Soil–Free Democratic Party. Whatever may have been the motives of Douglas or the merits of popular sovereignty, the repeal of the Missouri Compromise opened to contention again the question of slavery and this time it would be closed only with civil war.

The Rise of Nativism

In the first 50 years of independence foreign immigration had been relatively low, first reaching as many as 10,000 in a single year in 1825. Thereafter, the figures mounted rapidly, and between 1846 and 1855 almost 4 million foreigners, mostly poverty-stricken Irish and Germans fleeing famine and revolution, would step ashore. Most of them settled in the slums of Eastern cities where they were dependent on local and state authorities for relief. By the 1850s aliens constituted half of the population of New York City and outnumbered the native-born Americans in Chicago, Milwaukee, and St. Louis. A succession of antiforeign societies and political parties soon began to grow up to curb the increase of this alien population. Such conditions helped to produce the first significant nativist, or antiforeign, movement in American history, a movement that briefly became a major force in both state and national politics.

A part of the concern was religious. The United States was an overwhelmingly Protestant country. But that would change, many "native Americans" feared. The bulk of the arriving Irish were Roman Catholics as were a substantial minority of the Germans. In due course the Catholic newcomers would "establish" the Catholic church at the expense of Protestantism and would introduce "popish idols."

Self-interest also contributed to the antiforeign sentiment, particularly among native laborers, who complained that the aliens, willing to work for low wages, were stealing their jobs. Sometimes they refused to work alongside the sons of Erin. "No Irish Need Apply" (often abbreviated to NINA) was a sign commonly found above factory gates.

Widespread concern also developed among native-born citizens about the increasing political participation and power of foreigners, since immigrants were generally absorbed into the urban political machines of the Democratic party and voted overwhelmingly for Democratic candidates. Old-stock Americans were incensed at seeing recently naturalized foreigners being herded to the polls by the Democratic political bosses in the cities and taking possession of municipal governments. As often as not, the Democratic ward bosses had not bothered with the formality of naturalization papers.

The Native American Democratic Association. In 1827 in New York City a local third party offered an "American Ticket." In 1835 nativists in New York attempted to organize a statewide political party, the Native American Democratic Association, which opposed Catholics, sought to exclude all foreigners from office, and opposed the immigration of paupers and criminals.[93] This type of opposition naturally bound the immigrants more closely than ever to the Democratic organization.

The American Republican Party. In 1841 a state convention in Louisiana founded the American Republican Party, whose chief principles were to put only native-born Americans into office and to extend the naturalization period to 21 years. The party, which also came to be known as the Native American Party, quickly spread to the North where similar problems exasperated the Atlantic seaboard Whigs.

By 1843 an American Republican Party had been organized in New York City with a platform calling for the disenfranchisement of Catholics and the foreign born. It grew so rapidly that it carried the city elections in the spring of 1844. The following year it had six members in Congress. In 1845 delegates from 14 states assembled in Philadelphia to attempt to form a national "American Party," but their effort met no success. Two years later a "national" convention of 100 delegates from 6 Eastern states and Ohio met at Philadelphia and endorsed Zachary Taylor, the Whig presidential nominee. As the Mexican War and the great slavery issue gained public attention, the Native American movement gradually subsided. Its poor showing in 1848 finished its career under that name. However, the uncompromising nativists turned to the formation of a new party. "The Supreme Order of the Star Spangled Banner," or "Sons of the Sires of '76," was organized in New York in 1849 as a superpatriotic society with membership restricted to native-born Protestants. It soon became known as the Native American Party or, more popularly, as the Know-Nothing Party.

The Native American Party:
The Know-Nothing Party

The Native American Party had one simple goal and that was to have "America ruled by Americans."[94] A candidate for membership in the party had to be a native-born Protestant citizen and he had to agree not to vote for any office seeker unless he was a native American Protestant. Those who became eligible to hold either a council or party office to be nominated for a public office took a long oath which included the following: "That if it may be done legally you will, when elected or appointed to any official station conferring on you the power to do so, remove all foreigners, aliens, or Roman Catholics from office or place in your gift."[95] Horace Greeley dubbed the party the "Know-Nothings" because when suspected members were questioned about the party they habitually answered with "I know nothing about it."[96] Greeley also editorialized in the *New York Tribune* that the party had no more substantial unifying principle than an antipotato-rot party would have.[97]

Know-Nothingism mushroomed after the election of 1852. When Franklin Pierce appointed an Irish Catholic as postmaster general in 1853 the worst fears of nativists about the political potency of foreigners within the Democratic party organization were confirmed. Hundreds of thousands of men joined the lodges, including thousands who had never bothered to vote before. After the passage of the Kansas-Nebraska Act the Know-Nothing ranks were swelled by thousands of conservative Whigs from the middle states who sought protection from the storm raised by the Kansas-Nebraska Act. Many of these new members clung desperately to the hope of compromise promised by this nativistic party that placed such emphasis on the glories of union. Many politicians in both the North and South hoped that the issue of immigration and Americanization might supersede the slavery issue and that the Know-Nothings, by focusing on the new problem, might be the instrument by which to unite a divided people.

2. The Republicans
Preservers of American Politics

After the introduction of the Kansas-Nebraska Act into Congress in early 1854, all shades of antislavery men came together to keep slavery out of the territory from which it had been excluded by the Missouri Compromise. The Free Soilers called a series of meetings to convert the anti-Nebraska forces into a new party dedicated to preventing the further spread of slavery. The Republican Party came into being as a result of these meetings, although its place of nativity cannot be clearly identified.

The principal claimant to be the birthplace of the Republican Party was Ripon, Wisconsin, where Alvan E. Bovay of New York—a lawyer, Whig idealist, and a staunch foe of the Kansas-Nebraska Act—had called a protest meeting on February 28, 1854. At this meeting a resolution was approved "to throw old party organizations to the winds and organize a new party on the sole basis of the nonextension of slavery" if the bill passed. At a second meeting held on March 20, as Bovay said, 53 men went into the meeting as Whigs, Free Soilers, and Democrats, but "came out of it Republican."[1]

Jackson, Michigan, also claims to be the city of birth of the new party. That city's claim is based on the fact that a formal meeting was held "under the oaks" there on July 6, 1854—the same day that the Kansas-Nebraska Act passed the House of Representatives—where a resolution was adopted by those assembled that they would suspend all differences on other issues because of the imminent danger that Kansas and Nebraska would be grasped by slavery and 1,000 miles of slave soil be interposed between the free states of the Atlantic and those of the Pacific; that they would act in unison to avert and repeal gigantic wrong and shame; and that, in view of the necessity of battling for the first principles of Republican government and against the schemes of aristocracy, "the most revolting and oppressive with which the earth was ever cursed or man debased," they would cooperate and be known as "Republicans" until the contest was terminated.[2]

Those assembled at Jackson also approved a platform which began by

condemning slavery as "a great moral, social, and political evil." The repeal
of the Missouri Compromise, said the resolution, was a plain departure
from the policy "of the fathers of the Republic in regard to slavery." Its
destruction, therefore, would result in admitting slavery into the territories
and thus sow "the seeds of an evil which like a leprosy had descended upon
their property with accumulated rancor, visiting the sins of the fathers
upon succeeding generations."[3] The official history of the party issued by
the Republican National Committee equivocates by referring to "the movement begun in the Ripon church and 'under the oaks' at Jackson."[4]

No one was more elated with the results at Jackson than Horace
Greeley. "The name under which the opponents of the Nebraska Iniquity
have enlisted for the war," he wrote in the July 11 New York Tribune, "is
simply REPUBLICAN, and this, we think, will be very generally adopted."
Greeley was right. The Republican Association of Washington was established in June 1854, after which the name "Republican" was generally used.

The Congressional Elections of 1854. In the congressional elections of
1854, held six months after the passage of the fateful Kansas-Nebraska Act,
the Democratic Party suffered a disastrous defeat. Although two years
earlier Pierce had carried all but two Northern states, in 1854 his party lost
all but two of these states and gave up its majority in Congress. In the
House of Representatives their number was slashed from 159 to 83. Of the
42 Northern Democrats who voted for the Kansas-Act in the House, only
7 were reelected. The Republicans claimed 108 members, making them the
largest single group, and the Know-Nothings claimed the allegiance of 75
congressmen (some still nominally in the old parties but subscribing to
Know-Nothing principles), primarily from the South. The number of
Democratic congressmen from the free states fell from 93 to 27. An old,
witty black man summed up the history of the Pierce administration: It
"came in with *little* opposition, and it is going out with *none*."[5]

When the Thirty-Fourth Congress met early in December 1855, it was
divided into so many factions that no group was able to secure a majority
vote for its candidate for Speaker of the House. Not until February 2, on
the one hundred thirty-third ballot, did the antislavery forces in the House
succeed in naming Nathaniel Banks of Massachusetts to the Speaker's chair.
Banks had been elected to this Congress on the "Know-Nothing" (American) ticket, but his position on the slavery issue was satisfactory to the Republicans and they supported his election. The Republicans regarded the
election of Banks as a Republican triumph even though 70 of Banks's 103
votes came from Know-Nothings. The presidential election of 1856 was
taking shape as a serious contest for survival for the Republican Party.
However, on the basis of the results of the 1854 elections, the betting odds
favored the Know-Nothings as the coming challengers of the Democratic
Party.[6]

The Issue of Prohibition

As if nativism and the agitation over slavery were not enough to muddy the political waters, a movement to prohibit the sale and consumption of alcohol through the law began to sweep the country. A leader in the prohibition movement was Neal S. Dow of Maine, who, as a mayor of Portland, sponsored the so-called Maine Law of 1851, which prohibited the manufacture and sale of intoxicating liquor. In the next ten years a dozen other states in the North and West followed Maine's example.

The Prohibition movement was a threat to the ballot-box fortunes of the Republican Party, and Republican Party leaders were fearful that it would keep the Germans of the Midwest, who took a jaundiced view of those who wished to prohibit their consumption of huge quantities of beer and schnapps, from joining the new party. The Republican leaders vowed to keep the liquor question out of politics in the future. Oddly enough, into this party with its Know-Nothing and temperance elements came a considerable number of German immigrants, whose opposition to slavery was stronger than their distaste for teetotalers and nativists.

The Struggle for Kansas

After the Kansas-Nebraska Act repealed the Missouri Compromise the slave owners could take their slaves into the territories north and northwest of Missouri. Initially, however, not too many were eager to do so. Kansas lay too far to the north, and planters were generally unwilling to transport valuable slave property into a region that appeared to be unsuited for cotton or tobacco cultivation and that might ultimately resolve for free labor. However, the Northerners were not so reluctant. Thousands of them moved into Kansas, attracted by its fertile lands as well as by the opportunity to strike a blow at black servitude. Around their campfires at night many of the Kansas-bound pioneers sang John Greenleaf Whittier's marching song:

> We cross the prairie as of old
> The pilgrims crossed the sea.
> To make the West, as they the East,
> The homestead of the free!

Southerners, horrified at this attempt to usurp a region allocated to slavery, sent their own parties of settlers. Some carried banners proclaiming:

> Let Yankees tremble, abolitionists fall,
> Our motto is, "Give Southern Rights to All."

These two streams poured into Kansas during 1854 — the Northerners to the interior, where they founded Lawrence and Topeka; the Southerners to Atchison and Leavenworth along the Missouri River, where they could count on help from the proslavery Missourians, who were always ready to swarm over the border to help "clean out the abolition crowd."

By the fall of 1854 the stage was set for a violent struggle. When Andrew C. Reeder, a Douglas Democrat from Pennsylvania chosen by President Pierce to be the first territorial governor of Kansas, arrived there in the fall of 1854, he found several thousand settlers ahead of him. The first elections he called set the pattern for many Kansas elections to follow. The proslavery forces won overwhelmingly, electing a territorial delegate to Congress in the fall of 1854 and a proslavery legislature the following March. In the election for members of the territorial legislature thousands of armed Missourians, living in counties adjacent to the border, poured into Kansas and carried the elections for the proslavery candidates.

When Reeder tried to disqualify 8 of the 31 proslavery members of the territorial legislature on the grounds that they had been elected irregularly, Southern congressmen put pressure on President Pierce to overrule the governor. The president gave in to their demands and appointed a proslavery Ohio politician, Wilson Shannon, to the post. Once in place, the proslavery Kansas legislature adopted a civil and military code designed to drive all antislavery factions out of Kansas. These included a death sentence for anyone who aided a fugitive slave, and a prison term for anyone who merely expressed the opinion that slavery should be outlawed in Kansas.

The antislavery Kansans then denounced the actions of the "bogus" legislature and held a separate convention in Topeka in October 1855, where they drafted a state constitution which provided for the end of slavery by 1857 which they submitted to the voters of the territory. It was approved by an almost unanimous vote in an election in which the proslavery men did not take part. Early in January 1856 the Free State Party, operating under the rules of the Topeka Constitution, elected its own governor and legislature. Now two governments, complete with capitols, governors, and legislatures, confronted each other. On January 24 President Pierce denounced the Topeka Constitution and declared the proslavery legislature to be the legal legislative body of the territory of Kansas.

None of this agitation bore much fruit until May 1856 when the proslavery U.S. marshal and a county sheriff led a posse of 750 men to Lawrence to make some arrests. In the riot which ensued part of the town was burned and a few men were killed. The Eastern newspapers, however, reported that a full-scale battle had taken place. Thereafter, they habitually referred to the incident as the "Sack of Lawrence."

Four days later a crime of still greater enormity was committed at

Pottawatomie Creek by a small group of antislavery men led by John Brown, a gray-eyed and gray-bearded militant abolitionist. According to "Old Brown's" estimate, five antislavery men had lost their lives in the attack on Lawrence at the hands of the proslavery party. To avenge their deaths Brown and six associates (four of whom were his sons) hacked to pieces five unarmed men, allegedly proslaveryites. Brown proclaimed he was acting for "God and the Army of the North." After this fiendish butchery, terror and violence gripped both sides. Pierce removed Shannon and sent yet another governor to replace him. In September 1856 Governor John Geary brought order to the territory with federal troops. Though he persuaded the Missourians to abandon hostilities, nobody believed that the question of slavery in the territories was settled.

On May 19, while the Missourians were putting the torch to Lawrence, Senator Charles Sumner, the tall, dark, and eloquent Republican abolitionist orator from Massachusetts, delivered a blistering speech on the floor of the Senate against the "slave oligarchy," denouncing its "rape of a virgin territory, compelling it to the hateful embrace of slavery." In his speech, "The Crime Against Kansas," Sumner for no apparent reason referred insultingly to South Carolina and its kindly and much-respected Senator Andrew Pickens Butler, who was ill at the time and absent from his seat. Butler, Sumner observed, had chosen "Slavery" as his mistress and "the frenzy of Don Quixote in behalf of his wench Dulcinea del Toboso is all surpassed." The denunciation, a gross exaggeration when applied to the gracious and studious Butler, was symptomatic of the bitterness engendered by the slavery issue.[7]

Representative Preston S. Brooks, a 36-year-old congressman from South Carolina and a nephew of Butler, thereupon took vengeance into his own hands. On May 22 he strode into the Senate and rained 20 or 30 blows on Sumner's head with a thick cane until Stephen Douglas and others restrained him. Sumner was forced to leave his seat for over three years and to seek medical aid in Europe. Meanwhile, the voters of Massachusetts defiantly reelected him, leaving his seat eloquently empty.

A large part of the Northern antislavery press raged over this "ruthless attack" on "liberty of speech" and all decency and held up Sumner as a martyr who had sacrificed himself in a great cause. Cartoons in Northern newspapers showed the noble senator falling before the merciless onslaught of "Bully Brooks," while crude-looking Southern congressmen stood aside and snickered in the background. Mass meetings of protest were addressed by Henry Ward Beecher, William Cullen Bryant, William M. Evarts, Edward Everett, President Charles King of Columbia University, Theodore Parker, Wendell Phillips, and a host of other intellectual and political leaders.[8] Sumner's abusive speech, which otherwise might have been ignored, was printed in pamphlet form and sold by the tens of thousands.

In the main, the Southern press defended Brooks's act as "good in conception, better in execution, and best of all in consequence." The "vulgar abolitionists in the Senate . . . have been suffered to run too long without collars. They must be lashed into submission." So said the *Richmond Enquirer*.

The Republicans were also able to build a highly successful campaign stratagem around the attack on Sumner. Usually, it involved having the Massachusetts senator write a letter to be read at large Republican rallies, reminding the audience that so critical were his injuries that he was not yet able to return to his beloved home. This trick always sparked a sympathetic response and was probably quite effective as such emotional devices go.[9]

Republicans in the House were unable to obtain the two-thirds vote necessary to expel Brooks. A majority of the representatives, however, did vote in favor of expulsion and Brooks resigned his seat, but was triumphantly reelected by a handsome margin. Moreover, since he had broken his cane, many Southern admirers made him presents of new ones usually inscribed "Hit him again." By 1856 America was a nation torn by hatred, bloodshed, and the lust for vengeance. Such was the atmosphere as the nation approached the presidential election.

The Election of 1856

The Republican Pittsburgh Meeting, 1856. In anticipation of the upcoming presidential elections to be held in the fall of 1856, the Republican Party leaders issued a public call on January 17, 1856, inviting Republicans to meet in convention at Pittsburgh on February 22, Washington's birthday, "for the purpose of perfecting the National Organization, and providing for a National Delegate Convention of the Republican Party" to nominate candidates for president and vice president.[10]

On the appointed date party leaders from all the free states and spokesmen from eight Southern states met in Pittsburgh in a festive atmosphere. Horace Greeley, now imbued with Republicanism, telegraphed the *New York Tribune* (correctly, as it turned out): "Its [the convention's] moral and political effect upon the country will be felt for the next quarter of a century." Greeley, Owen Lovejoy, brother of the abolitionist lynched in 1837 by a mob, and Joshua R. Giddings, the Ohio firebrand, delivered radical speeches. A Republican National Committee, with one representative from each state, was created to call the party's first national convention to nominate presidential and vice presidential candidates and to complete the organization of the Republican Party in the states. Edwin D. Morgan, a highly successful merchant banker of New York, became national chairman. The subsequent call was addressed not to Republicans but "to the people of the United States without regard to past political differences or divisions" who were opposed to the Pierce administration and the congressional compromise on slavery.[11]

The Democrats resented this assumption of the name of Jefferson's old party and so, to distinguish it from their parent party, they called the new party the "Black" Republican Party.

The Know-Nothing Convention, 1856. In view of their impressive victories in 1854 and 1855 the Know-Nothings, now using the American Party as its name, seemed certain to be an important factor in the national election to be held in 1856. The *New York Herald* thought that their prospects to elect the president were good. Even a few hostile newspapers, including some Roman Catholic ones, predicted victory (though not very happily) for the American Party candidates.

The National Council of the American Party met on Washington's birthday in 1856 in Philadelphia in what turned out to be a dissension-ridden convention to nominate a presidential slate and to draft a party platform for use in the forthcoming election. Twenty-seven states were represented by a total of 227 delegates. Only Maine, South Carolina, Vermont, and Georgia were unrepresented.

The Council found it easy enough to agree on the purely nativistic portions of the platform, which included demands for the limitation of officeholding to native-born, a requirement of 21 years' residence for naturalization, exclusion of paupers and criminals from entry into the United States, and denial of political station to anyone recognizing allegiance to a "foreign prince, potentate or power." But the members fought for three days over the slavery question. When the "North Americans" tried to commit the party to an antislavery position, violent arguments raged. Kenneth Raynor of North Carolina, who tried to find a middle ground on which the warring factions could meet, proposed that it be declared, in substance, that the party sought to remedy certain evils, with slavery not one of them, and that the party was neither proslavery nor antislavery, but that if the party came to power it would dispose of the question so as to mete out justice to all sections and to all interests. Raynor's proposal was rejected by the North Americans who regarded "the nonintervention doctrine" as a proslavery position. When a resolution was adopted accepting as final the existing legislation on slavery (that is, the Fugitive Slave and Kansas-Nebraska acts), recommending against congressional interference in the territories, and condemning further agitation of the slavery question, about 25 percent of the delegates, including most of the delegates from New England, Pennsylvania, Ohio, Michigan, Illinois, and Iowa, left the hall, organized themselves as a separate party called the "North Americans," and called for a nominating convention in New York in June to select a candidate satisfactory to Northern voters. Thereafter, the Know-Nothings were merely a Southern party.

The remaining delegates then nominated the aging former President Millard Fillmore, who was popular in the South because of his support of compromise measures during his administration. The principal importance of the selection of Fillmore, who had never been a member of the Know-Nothing Party, was to attract conservative Whigs away from the Republican movement. However, Fillmore had never declared himself in favor of nativist principles[12] which ensured that the party would stress national unity and conservatism more than antiforeign and anti–Catholic sentiments.[13] Andrew Jackson Donelson of Tennessee, editor of the *Washington Union*, was chosen as the vice presidential candidate.

The North American Party, 1856. When the seceding "North Americans" (or "Northern Bolters" or "Republican Sympathizers" as many called them) met in convention in New York on June 12, 1856, five days before the scheduled national meeting of the Republican delegates, representatives came from all the Northern states except Ohio. Many of the delegates were Know-Nothings more in name than in fact and, since they were much stronger on antislavery policy than on nativism, it seemed apparent to all that the major object of the convention was to work up some kind of an arrangement or union with the Republicans. They probably would have named John C. Fremont as their candidate for president but for the fears of his friends that it might hurt his chances with the Republicans if his first endorsement came from the nativist Know-Nothings. A way out was found in nominating Nathaniel P. Banks, Speaker of the House of Representatives and a major supporter of Fremont, with at least the tacit understanding that if the Republicans made Fremont their candidate, Banks would retire and direct the North Americans to give Fremont their votes. Former Governor William F. Johnston of Pennsylvania was selected as his running mate. A resolution demanding restoration of the Missouri Compromise was adopted.

The Democratic Convention, 1856. With bullets whining in Kansas, the Democrats opened their convention on June 2, 1856, in Cincinnati, Ohio, the "Porkopolis of the West," with delegates from all 31 states in attendance. The rules of the preceding convention were unanimously adopted, including the two-thirds and unit rules.

The Democratic platform hailed "the liberal principles" of founder Jefferson, but went on to endorse the Kansas-Nebraska Act "as the only sound and safe solution of the 'slavery question'" and announced that the "party will resist all attempts at renewing, in Congress or out of it, the agitation of the slavery question under whatever shape or color the attempt be made." Kansas, it proposed, should be admitted as a free state, and both a railroad to the Pacific and improvements of rivers and harbors should be given the aid of national appropriations. With the Irish and German immigrants (most of them Catholic) already a sizable voting bloc, the platform welcomed more with a condemnation of the Know-Nothings as "a political crusade . . . against Catholic and foreign-born contrary to "the spirit of toleration and enlarged freedom which peculiarly distinguishes the American system of popular government."[14]

As the Democrats convened, Douglas and Pierce were the leading contenders for the nomination. The logic of the situation demanded that the delegates should renominate the president, who was eager for the nomination and who had stood as firmly by popular sovereignty as he was ever able to stand by anything. If Pierce was not to be the candidate, then it should be Douglas, the foremost champion of the doctrine. However, both were so badly tarred with the Kansas-Nebraska brush that the party leadership, which was predominantly Southern, thought it politically unwise to have such obvious targets at the head of the ticket. They were, in consequence, covertly "looking around." Lewis Cass, the perennial candidate, was also making another try for the nomination. However, Cass was now 74 years of age and still living in the shadow of the defeat he had suffered at the hands of Taylor in 1848.

Also being discussed by the delegates was the name of James Buchanan (pronounced by many *Buck*-anan), an amiable but mediocre Pennsylvanian. Buchanan had had considerable political experience. Originally a federalist, he had gone over to the Jackson party in the disputed election of 1824. Elected to Congress in 1828, he staunchly defended Jackson — his acts, policies, and measures; he continued as a Democratic leader in the Senate all during Van Buren's term. When Tyler became president, though neither his foe nor ally, Buchanan was the main defender in the Senate of Tyler's vetoes. As Polk's secretary of state he had settled the long-vexing question of the Oregon boundary line, and during the Mexican War capably handled the foreign affairs of the country. Retiring in 1848 to private life, he was recalled to service by Pierce, who sent him as U.S. minister to England, where he had been away from party squabbles and sectional conflict during the Pierce administration. He had also managed to escape taking definite stands on such party-splitting issues as compromise in the territories. By this means, he was acceptable to the South as well as the North.

Buchanan had further commended himself to the favorable attention of the Southern Democrats by his opposition to the Wilmot Proviso and his coauthorship of the Ostend Manifesto — which had asserted that the United States would be justified in taking Cuba by force if Spain refused to sell — an expansion which would shore up the declining representation of the slave states in Congress. The *Richmond Enquirer*, endorsing Buchanan, summed it up well when it editorialized that the Pennsylvanian had never "uttered a word which could pain the most sensitive heart."

Buchanan's weaknesses before the electorate were his age — at 65 he was considered to be "overripe"; his lack of dramatic and emotional appeal; and his sane, unexciting record. The political historian Franklin Burdette rightfully concludes that in 1856 no candidate could have been found who would better hold together the warring Northern and Southern factions of his party.[15]

Seventeen ballots were taken before Buchanan was finally nominated. On the sixteenth ballot the vote stood Buchanan 168, Douglas 121, and Cass 6, with Buchanan still short of the necessary two-thirds majority. At this point Douglas withdrew his name, and on the next ballot Buchanan received all 296 votes and the nomination. Pierce thus became the first man elected president to be denied a second term by his own party. In accepting the Democratic nomination, the Pennsylvanian publicly stated that he would submerge his private misgivings about the popular sovereignty feature of the Kansas-Nebraska Act and be "the representative of the Cincinnati Platform."

Joined with Buchanan on the Democratic ticket was the 35-year-old John Cabell Breckinridge of Kentucky, a friend of Douglas. So the Democrats were able to offer a "national" program and candidate.

The Republican Convention, 1856. Two weeks later (on June 17, 1856), in a fervency of moral indignation and high enthusiasm, the Republicans gathered in Musical Fund Hall in Philadelphia for their first nominating convention. Sixteen free states, four border slave states (Delaware, Maryland, Virginia, and Kentucky), the District of Columbia, and three territories were represented in some fashion. The territory of Kansas, symbolically important in the slavery struggle, was treated as a state and given full representation. Included among the nearly 2,000 delegates and observers present were Free Soilers, Libertymen, Old Whigs, Know-Nothings, anti–Nebraska Democrats, Barnburners, and men whose political dissidence ran back to Anti-Masonry.[16] The gathering of the party was clearly sectional, only a handful of delegates from border slave states were there, but it represented the populous North and the growing West where electoral votes were already dominant. The delegates cheered wildly when chairman Edwin D. Morgan announced in his welcoming address: "You are here today to give direction to a movement which is to decide whether the people of the United States are to be hereafter and forever chained to the present national policy of the extension of slavery."[17]

The Republicans adopted by voice vote a strong Free Soil platform which strongly condemned the repeal of the Missouri Compromise and asserted: "That the Constitution confers upon Congress sovereign power over the territories of the United States for their government, and that the exercise of this power is both the right and the duty of Congress to prohibit in the territories those twins of barbarism, polygamy and slavery" (a phrase suggested by the Massachusetts radical Ebenezer R. Hoar).[18] The Republicans charged that "bleeding Kansas" was the price of popular sovereignty and accused the Democratic Party of being subservient to slaveholder demands. Kansas, the platform demanded, must be admitted to the Union under the free-state Topeka Constitution. Further, they condemned the Ostend Manifesto (issued by James Buchanan and others which called for the annexation of Cuba – where slavery was legal – to the United States) as an imperialist design of the administration to expand slave territory into the Caribbean. It also called for the building of a government-aided railroad to the Pacific and federal spending for internal improvements.[19]

The Republicans had several impressive possibilities from which to select their first candidate for the presidency. One of these was the perennial hopeful Salmon P. Chase of Ohio, who for years had had his eyes fixed longingly on the White House. Chase was, however, seriously handicapped by his reputation as a "party jumper"; he had already changed parties five times. It was not clear whether his bewildering political zigzags had been due primarily to his hatred of slavery or his political ambition, but nobody disputed the consistency of Chase's record on the slavery question. In the Senate he had led the fight against the Kansas-Nebraska Act. After its passage, Chase had been so active in resisting the enforcement of the Fugitive Slave Law he had been hailed as "the attorney general of the fugitive slaves."[20] There was, however, a repellent self-righteousness about Chase's idealism which led a critic to remark that Chase "thinks there is a fourth person in the Trinity."[21]

Probably the leading contender for the nomination was the slight-statured and weak-voiced former governor and now senator William H. Seward of New York. However, "Higher Law" Seward had come to be regarded as an extremist on slavery. In addition, Seward had many enemies. He had aroused the hatred of the native Americans because as a governor of New York he had championed appropriations for parochial schools and other measures in support of immigrants, and had been kindly disposed toward the foreign-born (particularly the Irish). Furthermore, Seward had split the Whig Party in New York as a result of his open war with Fillmore for control of New York Whigs.

Another contender who had availability of a high order, was the 71-year-old Justice John McLean of the U.S. Supreme Court. McLean was a conservative antislavery man, believing in the power of Congress to prohibit slavery in the territories, but he had upheld the Fugitive Slave Law. He had strong support in the important states of New Jersey, Pennsylvania, and Illinois, and in the South. He would also draw into the fold most of the old National Whigs and the Northern business community which did not like the Democrats but had grown very skittish about antislavery extremists.[22] Most important of all, the Pennsylvania conservatives regarded McLean as the one Republican who might carry that all-important state.

When the Democrats nominated Buchanan, who also hailed from the keystone state, this argument was pushed by McLean's supporters with increased vigor. The chief obstacles to McLean were hostility of radical antislavery men who looked upon him as a "marrowless old lawyer," and the feeling of Greeley and other Easterners that the party needed a fresh young leader with no political past.

Not entirely out of the running was Nathaniel P. Banks, Speaker of the House, who was already the presidential candidate of the North Americans. However, Banks was actively promoting the glamorous 43-year-old soldier-explorer, General John Charles Fremont.

Fremont was attractive for a number of reasons. He had become a hero of sorts as a result of his exploration of Western regions and his military moves against the Mexicans in California (it was said that "He conquered California with sixty-two men") during the Mexican War. Fremont had fired the imagination of the young and not so young as the fabled "Pathmarker of the Rockies" who had explored the craggy peaks of that awesome range of mountains and braved the rigors of a meal with Indians. Also, he had eloped with Jesse Benton, the beautiful daughter of Senator Thomas Hart Benton, the powerful Jacksonian Democratic leader from Missouri, who, in her own right, was an able political strategist.

Fremont's own political experience was minimal. He had been elected as a Democrat in 1850 to a short term as one of California's first senators, but his actual work in Congress had been limited to a few days. However, he was "right" on the slavery issue—he publicly disavowed both the Fugitive Slave Law and the Kansas-Nebraska Act—and that was considerably more important to Fremont's supporters than his lack of national political experience. Also, Fremont, it was thought, would appeal to the German and other immigrant vote. He had never been contaminated with Know-Nothingism, and because German scientists frequently accompanied him on his expeditions, Fremont enjoyed an excellent reputation with German Americans. His association with German scientists had won him the sobriquet "the American Humboldt." To those seeking a winner, Fremont looked like a person peculiarly able to bring about an amalgamation of the political protest groups of his day into a concentrated drive for victory.[23]

On the formal roll call, taken after Chase's friends had withdrawn his name, the Republicans chose the popular young explorer — thereby launching their "young, bold, and determined party [with] . . . a young, bold, and determined candidate." For the vice presidency the convention members cast 110 votes for an Illinois lawyer and one-term congressman, Abraham Lincoln, but finally chose William L. Dayton, a former Whig senator from New Jersey who was acceptable to Know-Nothings and would be an inducement for victory in New Jersey.

The North American Rump Convention, 1856. As soon as Fremont had been nominated by the Republicans, the North American convention reassembled, Banks was withdrawn as planned (with some reluctance on his part), and Fremont and Dayton were accepted. This opened the way for the anti-immigrant, anti–Catholic groups to merge with the Republicans.[24]

The Conservative Whigs, 1856. A conservative remnant of the Whig Party met in Baltimore in September, with delegates from 21 states, to endorse Fillmore as the best hope for peace but also to write their own platform repudiating that of the Know-Nothing American Party which had nominated him.

The Campaign of 1856. The race in 1856 was always clearly between Fremont and Buchanan, although neither became active campaigners. On behalf of Fremont, the Republicans exhausted all the possibilities of "Freedom, Freeman, and Fremont." Shouting "We follow the pathmarker" and "We are buck hunting" and singing, to the revolutionary air of *La Marseillaise:*

> Arise, arise, ye brave!
> And let our war-cry be,
> Free speech, free press, free soil, free men,
> Fre-mont and victory.

"And free love," jeered the Democrats.

The Republican campaign of 1856 was fought in the North, especially Pennsylvania, since the South was solid for Buchanan. The continued outrages in Kansas provided the Republicans with excellent arguing material. The Republican national committee issued a series of campaign documents on such subjects as "The Border Ruffian Code in Kansas," "The Poor Whites of the South," and "The Vacant Chair of Sumner." In response, the Democrats let loose against the Republicans one of the heaviest barrages of mudslinging in American political history. In thousands of tracts, pamphlets, and newspaper stories, members of the new party were branded "Black Republicans," "Nigger Lovers," "Abolitionists," "thugs," "Free booters," and every other vile epithet that could be imagined."[25]

Horace Greeley's *New York Tribune* also did a great deal to keep the Kansas issue alive by printing a stream of reports about innocent Kansas settlers being "proscribed and hunted" like wild beasts, while Greeley organized a Kansas relief fund with great fanfare. The weekly edition of the *Tribune* had wide circulation among a far-flung army of rural subscribers. It was said of them that many read only the Bible and the *Tribune* and that they preferred the latter because it had the added appeal of greater novelty.[26]

Tons of literature were sent out by the Republicans denouncing "Ten

Cent Jimmy" Buchanan. Rallies and torchlight marches were punctuated with floats depicting underfed laborers toiling at various trades beneath the legend: "Buchanan's Work Shop, Ten Cents a Day." Fife and Drum Corps, glee clubs, and Wide Awakes (marching societies whose members paraded the streets) also added to the uproar. The Republicans also reminded the voters that back in 1818 when Buchanan was a federalist he boasted in a Fourth of July speech that "if he had one drop of Democratic blood in his veins he would open them and let it pour out."[27]

Abraham Lincoln, speaking for Fremont in Illinois, declared that the central difference between the two parties was a single question: shall slavery be allowed to extend into the national territories now legally free? "Buchanan says it shall; and Fremont says it shall not."[28] John Greenleaf Whittier wrote Republican campaign songs. James Russell Lowell translated the new party's doctrine into poetry, while Emerson, Bryant, Henry Wadsworth, Longfellow, and Oliver Wendell Holmes were some of the names high in American literature listed on its membership rolls.

Women were active in the 1856 campaign, joining parades and meetings "of the party of freedom," and Protestant clergymen gave political speeches for Fremont from their pulpits. Lyman Beecher, the great revivalist orator, even exhibited a heavy chain with two large padlocks which he claimed had been placed around the legs of free-state men in Kansas. So active in the campaign were the women and preachers that the strongest aids of the Republicans were declared by sneering Democrats to be "Pulpits and Petticoats."[29] Sex was introduced into American politics by having Fremont's beautiful wife, Jessie, campaign with him. The Fremonts were pictured as an ideal couple to grace the White House. Republican floats and emblems attacked Buchanan's bachelor status:

> Who ever heard in all of his life
> Of a candidate without a wife?

The Democrats shouted "Buck and Breck" and urged voters "to take the Buck by the horns." They denounced the Republican Party as a sectional party and predicted that the South would secede were Fremont elected. Prominent Southern "fire eaters" supported this contention with unconcealed threats that the election of a sectional "Black Republican" would be a declaration of war on them, forcing them to secede. The Democrats also charged that Republicans were abolitionists. Some of the sting was taken out of this accusation by the decision of the abolitionists to run Gerrit Smith for president. The Democrats revived (and updated) an old slogan:

> We Po'ked 'em in '44
> We Pierced 'em in '52
> And we'll "Buck 'em" in '56

For his part, Buchanan remained in such complete seclusion at Wheatland, his country estate near Lancaster, Pennsylvania, that his fellow Pennsylvanian, Thaddeus Stevens, suggested that "there is no such person running as James Buchanan. He is dead of lockjaw."[30]

In an effort to break the alliance between Republicans and Know-Nothings, the Democrats attacked Fremont as secretly a Roman Catholic. There were several details to suggest that the charge was, in fact, true. He was French, had been educated at a Catholic school, and had been married on a U.S. Army post by a Catholic chaplain. His adopted daughter had attended a Catholic school. The Catholic press generally were claiming Fremont as one of their communicants. Fremont, under restrictions from his campaign managers, was not allowed to deny these statements.

Eventually, the Republican managers were able to prove that Fremont was Episcopalian and that he had not been educated as a Catholic. They also showed that all of his children had been baptized as Episcopalians. That he was married by a Catholic priest, however, could not be denied, and there can be little doubt that the injection of the religious issue into the campaign was harmful to Fremont in many areas.[31]

The Outcome, 1856. When the presidential elections took place on November 4, 1856, there was a massive outpouring of voters. Out of a national population of about 30 million, more than 4 million cast ballots, or some 900,000 more than in 1852. Buchanan rolled up sizable majorities in such large free states as Illinois and Indiana, and carried his own state of Pennsylvania without difficulty for a total popular vote of 1,833,000 (45 percent). Fremont carried 11 free states, including New York, Ohio, and Michigan, and received a total popular vote of 1,800,000 (30 percent). Buchanan won 174 votes in the electoral college to Fremont's 114 and Fillmore's 8. All of Fremont's electoral votes came from the North, and the Republican Party was revealed as a purely sectional organization.

Although Fillmore, the Know-Nothing candidate, mustered 870,000 votes, nearly 25 percent of all the popular votes, they were so scattered as to win only Maryland's 8 electoral ones. Breckinridge was elected vice president and both houses of Congress were safely Democratic.

The Republican politicians were elated over their "victorious defeat" in this, their first national campaign. They had come very close to winning the presidency, and it was evident that they had a good chance to gain it in 1860 if they could capture Pennsylvania and either Indiana or Illinois. Republicans everywhere echoed Whittier's exultant cry:

> Then sound again the bugles,
> Call the master-roll anew;
> If months have well-nigh won the field,
> What will not four years do?

For rather obvious reasons, Buchanan's election did not reassure many Southerners. Fremont swept large areas of the North previously unshakable in their loyalty to the Democratic Party, and carried states like Maine, New Hampshire, and Michigan which had been Democratic strongholds. Similar defections took place in Illinois. However, the largest number of defections from the Democratic Party came in New York State, where scores of important Barnburner leaders joined the Republicans.[32] Although the Democrats still controlled the key states of the North, the new president was not to confront the irresolute and disunited opposition of the Pierce era but a militant minority already heartened by a taste of victory.

For all practical purposes the "Americans" collapsed after Fillmore's overwhelming defeat in 1856. After the election the Know-Nothing National Council met, authorized each state council to adopt the rules of organization it thought best for its locality, and adjourned, never to meet again. After that date the party only survived at the state level.

The Administration of James Buchanan

On March 4, 1857, James Buchanan took the oath of office as the president of the United States. In his inaugural address he deplored the incessant agitation over the slavery issue and expressed the hope that the long agitation over slavery was now "approaching its end." He also hinted at what the South had long awaited, that the Supreme Court was to hand down its decision in *Dred Scott versus Sanford* — a case pending before the court that would settle the question of slavery in the territories. He urged the public to accept the verdict, whatever it might be, as final.

Two days later, March 6, 1857, the Supreme Court handed down its decision in the so-called Dred Scott Case.[33] When the aged chief justice read the decision to a packed courtroom his words came with the force of a thunderclap. He held that the right to hold slaves was a property right, and since Congress could not interfere with a man's property rights, to exclude slavery would violate the due process of law clause of the Fifth Amendment. Further, Dred Scott's residence in Illinois, which was free soil, had not made him a free man. Also, as a black of slave origins (said Chief Justice Taney) Scott could not be a citizen of the United States in any case. He and all people like him were simply ineligible for citizenship. Finally, Dred Scott could not have gained his freedom by residing in territory covered by the Missouri Compromise, since that act was unconstitutional. It was the first time in over 50 years that the U.S. Supreme Court had declared an act of Congress unconstitutional.

Southerners were exuberant over the decision. "The nation has achieved a triumph," said the *Richmond Enquirer*, "sectionalism has been rebuked and abolitionism has been staggered and stunned. Another supporting pillar has been added to our institution." The North responded with cries of dismay. Shocked Northern newspapers headlined: SLAVERY ALONE NATIONAL — THE MISSOURI COMPROMISE UNCONSTITUTIONAL — NEGROES CANNOT BE CITIZENS — THE TRIUMPH OF SLAVERY COMPLETE! "The Supreme Court," the *New York Tribune* said, "has abdicated its just functions and descended into the political mire. It has sullied the ermine; it has dragged and polluted its garments in the filth of pro-slavery politics. . . . The decision deserves no more respect than the opinion of a majority congregated in any Washington bar room." Abolitionist ministers also concentrated on the Dred Scott decision, claiming that it was fresh proof that "the South was engaged in an aggressive attempt to extend the peculiar institution so far that it could no longer be considered peculiar." Northerners immediately began calling for secession. The state legislature of Wisconsin passed a resolution supporting this principle. In the end this decision, which was to settle the slavery controversy once and for all, in fact settled nothing. In reality it greatly intensified the conflict between the sections.

One thing it did was to split the Democratic Party by precipitating a clash in the party between the champions of Southern rights and those of popular sovereignty. Triumphant Southerners were soon demanding that the party go beyond the older principles — to the more radical position that Congress could not force slavery *out* of the territories — to the even more extreme position that it was obliged to defend slavery *in* them. This was the ultimatum of the South to the Northern wing of the Democratic Party which had put its faith in the doctrine of popular sovereignty. As Alexander Johnston has said, the Dred Scott Case marks the point at which "the Northern (or Douglas) Democrats, who had supported the South heretofore, refused . . . to follow the Southern lead further, and chose rather to divide the party."[34]

Nor did "Buchanan's decision" silence the Republicans. The president never explained why he imagined that the Republicans and others who had insisted on the right of Congress to regulate slavery in the territories since 1840 would capitulate as soon as a court with a Democratic majority rendered an opinion.

The Kansas cauldron had cooled somewhat as Buchanan took office as president. President Pierce, by sending in federal troops, had quieted the civil war in the territory, and when Buchanan assumed the presidency in 1857 he appointed Robert J. Walker, former secretary of the treasury, as the fourth territorial governor of Kansas. Walker, a native Pennsylvanian who had moved to the slave state of Mississippi, quickly recognized that most Kansans wanted to bar slavery from their state (only 200 slaves were there). Accordingly, Walker worked to help them turn their preference into law.

The proslavery leaders in Kansas soon came to detest Walker. In September 1857 a proslavery constitution was drawn up at Lecompton. Under the provisions of this constitution, Kansas citizens were not allowed to pass on the constitution as a whole but were given only the privilege of deciding whether, in the future, slaves were to be admitted or kept out. Even if they voted to keep slavery out, slave property already in Kansas was to be protected. The Free Soilers refused to go to the polls on December 21, 1857, and the Lecompton Constitution was overwhelmingly ratified with the slavery clause. It was clear, however, that the great majority of the people of Kansas did not want slavery. When a newly elected territorial legislature called for another election to permit a vote on the Lecompton Constitution as a whole, the Kansas voters rejected it by a huge majority on January 4, 1858. This time the proslavery voters refused to participate.

Walker, disgusted with these proceedings, went to Washington to urge the president to use his influence against the Lecompton Constitution and to convene a new, more representative, convention in Kansas. Buchanan, however, alarmed at Southern criticism of Walker and influenced by Southern cabinet members, refused Walker's request and on February 2, 1858, submitted the proslavery constitution to Congress and called for the admission of Kansas as a slave state, in spite of the overwhelming rejection of the Lecompton Constitution by the voters of the territory. Kansas, he asserted, was "as much a slave state as Georgia or South Carolina," and warned that refusal to admit Kansas as a slave state would be "keenly felt" by the South. As the leader of the Democrats, he ordered the Democratic House to accept this and take Kansas out of politics. Walker resigned in disgust.

Buchanan's support of the proslavery constitution angered Stephen Douglas and his followers and widened the rift in his already divided party. In a dramatic confrontation at the White House the president tried to force Douglas into line. "Mr. Douglas," he said, "I desire you to remember that no Democrat ever yet differed from an administration of his own choice without being crushed." "Mr. President," Douglas replied contemptuously, "I wish *you* to remember that General Jackson is dead!"[35]

The administration struck back through the power of patronage and every other pressure available to it. Douglas postmasters, revenue collectors, marshals, and other federal officers were purged. Anti-Lecompton congressmen found the White House doors closed to them. The test now was, Were you for or against Lecompton? Despite a heroic fight by Douglas, the president had his way in the Senate, where only three Democrats (all from the North) joined Douglas and the Republicans in opposition; but in the House of Representatives the anti–Lecompton Democrats were stronger, and the statehood bill failed. Despite administration coercion, Northern Democrats knew that a vote for the proslavery Kansas constitution would be political suicide.[36]

In the end Douglas won. A compromise measure known as the English Bill was adopted under which the Lecompton Constitution would be submitted to the voters in an honest election with the provision that if it was accepted, Kansas would receive about 4 million acres of public lands, as well as 5 percent of the proceeds of the sale of another 2 million acres. Rejection by the voters would mean a delay in statehood and in the land grant of perhaps two years, or until Kansas had sufficient population for a representative to Congress (about 90,000 people). The bait was not taken in Kansas and the Free Soil men thronged to the polls and snowed it under by the overwhelming margin of nearly 10–1. Here the matter rested until January 21, 1861, when Kansas entered the Union as a free state after much of the South had seceded.

The Panic of 1857. By late summer in 1857 the nation, particularly the North, was gripped by a financial panic brought on by extended credit at home and abroad, inadequate banking facilities, high prices, and inflation. Misery among the unemployed of the cities of the industrial Northwest was greater than at any previous time in America's history. Huge "hunger meetings" were held and thousands of jobless people paraded demanding "work or bread." Demonstrations of the poor occurred frequently. The panic of 1857 helped to widen the cleavage between North and South. As it happened, the South, enjoying favorable cotton prices abroad, passed through the crisis relatively unscathed, which was proof of the virtues of slavery to its ardent defenders. "The wealth of the South is permanent and real," exulted *De Bow's Review*, a New Orleans journal, while "that of the North [is] fugitive and fictitious."

The panic also brought the tariff issue back into the political spotlight. Many aggrieved Northern manufacturers blamed their troubles on the tariff reductions enacted in the closing days of the Pierce administration, which had been pushed through the Congress by the South. They felt that the "slave power" had once more sacrificed the nation's well-being to its own sectional interests. Northerners clamored for tariff protection against the inroads of cheaper industrial products from abroad, and Westerners called for low-cost homestead legislation and internal improvements as a cure for the nation's economic ills. The South opposed these programs as only sectional benefits.

Although the panic was relatively brief it had a far-reaching political impact. With Northerners and Westerners clamoring for financial relief, the Republicans embraced that issue as well as tariff protection and attracted many laborers and farmers who were little moved by the question of slavery. At the same time some who regarded the revenue-only Tariff of 1857 as the result of a conspiracy joined the Republican Party.

The Emergence of Abraham Lincoln

The Congressional Elections of 1858. As depression gripped the country a Republican convention met in Springfield, Illinois, on June 16, 1858, and nominated Abraham Lincoln as its senatorial candidate to run against the redoubtable Douglas. It was not a nomination which all Republicans were happy about. Lincoln was little known except as a local politician in Illinois. Also many Eastern Republicans, including Horace Greeley, thought that Douglas's reelection should be unopposed in Illinois because of his stand against Buchanan and hinted at an alliance of Republicans and Douglas men in 1860. In fact, the forming of a new party composed of Republicans, Douglas Democrats, Know-Nothings, Whigs, and whoever was seriously suggested, and arrangements were proposed such as allowing the Republicans to name the presidential, the others the vice presidential candidate. In the end, however, the Illinois Republicans, who knew Douglas for himself as well as for the enemies he had made, would not go back on their principles by supporting the author of the Kansas-Nebraska Act.

Abraham Lincoln was born in Kentucky in 1809 in a log cabin to impoverished parents. In 1815, when Abraham was 7, the family moved to Indiana and in 1830 pushed west again into southern Illinois. Abraham received almost no formal schooling although he did a pretty good job of educating himself by reading widely. He read a little law and was admitted to the bar in 1836 at the age of 27. As a trial lawyer he was immediately successful. From the onset of his legal career he was familiarly known as "Honest Abe," partly because he would refuse to accept cases that he could not conscientiously defend.

From the practice of law it was an easy step into local politics where he soon got a reputation as a shrewd politician. He was plain and unassuming, a man whom folks liked. Like most visiting lawyers arguing before the county court, Lincoln usually spent the long evenings after the adjournment of court swapping jokes, drinking, and talking in the local inn or debating current issues before the assembled farmers. He soon gained a great reputation as a "country style" (the long, earthy, and funny story) storyteller—"he could make a cat laugh," was a common assessment.[37]

In 1834 Lincoln was elected to the Illinois legislature as a Whig where he served several terms. Also as a Whig, he was elected in 1846 to a single term in Congress, where he opposed the Mexican War and introduced his famous "Spot Resolution" to embarrass the Polk administration and show the war to be unnecessary and unconstitutional. However, by accepting the strategy of the Whig caucus in criticism of Polk's Mexican War policy he lost favor with his ardently prowar constituency back home. Wilfred Binkley, the political historian, has suggested that Lincoln's only misinterpretation of sentiment at home was his attitude toward the Mexican War while in Congress.[38]

However, the passage of the Kansas-Nebraska Act in 1854 stirred Lincoln again to take an active part in the politics of his state. His first prominent speech was in October 1854 at Peoria, Illinois, at a great rally against Douglas and the Kansas-Nebraska Act. During the speech he said that Congress had no more moral right to repeal the Missouri Compromise, a great sectional compact, than to repeal the law against importing slaves from Africa. He asserted that all national legislation should be framed on the principle adopted by the fathers of the republic, that slavery was an institution to be restricted and ultimately abolished. And the popular-sovereignty principle, he contended, was false, for slavery in the West was the concern not merely of the inhabitants there but of the whole United States. "What better moral right have thirty-one citizens of Nebraska to say that the thirty-second shall not hold slaves than the people of thirty-one states have to say that slavery shall not go into the thirty-second state at all?"[39]

Lincoln stated the issue simply. "But if the Negro is a man, is it not to that extent, a fatal destruction of self-government, to say that he too shall not govern himself?" "No man is good enough to govern another man, without that other's consent. I say this is the leading principle — the sheet anchor of American republicanism."[40] Lincoln's "Peoria Statement" was soon being praised as the best statement of Free Soil principles thus far presented.

Lincoln had barely missed election to the U.S. Senate by an anti-Nebraska legislature in 1855 and, as we have seen, he had received strong support for the vice presidential nomination on the Fremont ticket in 1856. After retirement from Congress, Lincoln devoted himself primarily to the practice of law in central Illinois. Ostensibly, he had "taken the veil" as far as politics were concerned.

In 1858 the Illinois senatorial election claimed the national spotlight. Senator Douglas's term was about to expire, and the Republicans had selected Abraham Lincoln, a rustic Springfield lawyer, to run against him. Because Douglas was considered unbeatable in Illinois, despite his role in the Kansas-Nebraska Act, the Republican nomination was generally considered a worthless nomination.

However, Lincoln accepted the 1858 senatorial nomination with a ringing and memorably prophetic speech at the Illinois state Republican convention at Springfield in June, which echoed the apprehensions of the Free Soil states. "A house divided against itself cannot stand! One side or the other would have to prevail. Either the opponents of slavery will arrest the further spread of it, and place it where the public mind shall rest in the belief that it is the course of ultimate extinction; or its advocates will push it forward till it shall become alike lawful in all the States, old as well as new, North as well as South. I believe the government cannot endure permantly half-slave and half-free." This address subsequently became known as the "House Divided" speech.

The Lincoln-Douglas Debates

In July, to further his senatorial campaign, Lincoln boldly challenged the "Little Giant" to a series of joint debates in the various election districts up and down the state. To the amazement of the nation, Douglas, who was sublimely self-confident, accepted the challenge. They appeared on the same platform seven times, once in each congressional district except the two where they had already appeared.[41]

Douglas presented an impressive figure in contrast to Lincoln. Well dressed and immaculately groomed, Douglas became all fire and frenzy in his speech — his voice a powerful bark that had brought many an opponent to heel. Douglas traveled about in a private car with a flatcar coupled to his train mounting a brass cannon that was fired in a crashing salute when the train approached the prairie towns, sounding, as one of the newspapers lyrically reported, "like some great deliverer, some mighty champion who had saved a nation from ruin."[42]

Lincoln, an awkward, lanky giant of 6 feet 4 inches in baggy clothes and unshined shoes, whose grotesquely long arms, legs, and neck and whose homely countenance was crowned by a shock of coarse, black, and unruly hair, presented an extraordinary contrast to Douglas. Moreover, the "Tail Sucker" had a piercing, high-pitched voice and was often ill at ease until he began to speak. He traveled through the state on a day coach frequently on the same train with Douglas. On at least one occasion Lincoln arrived for the debate riding in the caboose of a freight train.

These debates captured the interest and imagination of the nation. Thousands of listeners thronged to each meeting place where they stood in the heat, humidity, and rain showers of late summer and early fall to hear the arguments of the debaters. Throughout the nation an unseen audience of millions was kept informed by excellent newspaper coverage.

Douglas's strategy was to make Lincoln look like an abolitionist because he had declared that slavery would either expand or die. He charged that Lincoln's "House Divided" philosophy could only end in "a war of extermination." Why, Douglas asked, did the Republicans say that slavery and freedom could not peaceably coexist? He accused Lincoln of refusing to abide by the decision of the Supreme Court in the Dred Scott case.

Lincoln replied that his party did not propose to interfere with slavery where it already existed but, in keeping with the Republican program, he flatly opposed the further extension of slavery. With regard to Douglas's charge that he did not accept Taney's opinion as final, he said that he would respect the Dred Scott decision and the jurisdiction of the court that decided it. However, since the Supreme Court had reversed itself on previous occasions, he urged the Republicans to look ahead with this in mind. All efforts must be directed "to have it reversed if we can, and have a new judicial rule established upon this subject."

The climax was reached at the second debate in August 1858 at Freeport, a town northwest of Chicago near the Wisconsin line. Here Lincoln put the question to Douglas: Was there any lawful way in which the people of a territory could exclude slavery? If, as Douglas maintained, the Dred Scott decision must be respected as the law of the land, how, asked Lincoln, could there be any place for popular sovereignty to prevail? The Supreme Court had said that slavery was legal everywhere under the American flag and that no legislative enactment could render it illegal. How, then, could there be any popular sovereignty in the face of that? Could popular sovereignty restrict what the Constitution, as interpreted by the Supreme Court, said could not be restricted? How would Senator Douglas get around that?

The Freeport Doctrine. Douglas replied that the answer was obvious. Slavery could not live a day unless it were supported by protective local legislation. It mattered not what the Supreme Court decided as to whether or not slavery might go into a territory under the Constitution, he said, slavery would stay down if the people voted it down. Laws to protect slavery would have to be passed by the territorial legislature and these would not be forthcoming in the absence of popular approval. He then stated what has become famous as the Freeport doctrine (or, in the South, as the Freeport heresy). "If the people are opposed to slavery they will elect representatives who will by unfriendly legislation effectually prevent the introduction of it into their midst," and vice versa.[43] Lincoln had no difficulty pointing out the rather obvious inconsistency in Douglas's argument. Although the Freeport doctrine saved Douglas his seat in the Senate, it almost certainly cost him the presidency.[44]

The Freeport doctrine also split the Democratic Party in two. It displeased many in the North because it glossed over the moral question of slavery, and it horrified the South because it suggested a loophole whereby a territory could exclude the "peculiar institution." Many Southerners urged President Buchanan to exclude Douglas from the Democratic Party. The Little Giant, who had been the Democrats' favored candidate for the presidency in 1860, thus found himself on the eve of the election deserted by one whole wing of the party.

The actual choice of the next senator lay, of course, in the hands of the Illinois legislature, so in reality, Douglas and Lincoln were campaigning for candidates for the legislature who were pledged to support them for the Senate seat. The legislature of Illinois, in a joint ballot of its two houses, reelected Douglas by 54–46, even though Lincoln supporters running for the legislative seats had gained a plurality of 4,000 votes. Inequalities in legislative apportionment permitted Douglas's legislative supporters to dominate. A few minutes after the Illinois legislature had selected Douglas, Lincoln was asked by a friend how he felt. Lincoln reportedly replied: "I feel like the boy who stubbed his toe; I am too big to cry, and too badly hurt to laugh."[45] Other defeated candidates, in other times, would describe their feelings pretty much the same way.

For Douglas the price of victory was high. He was snubbed by his colleagues and displaced from his important post as chairman of the Senate Committee on Territories. His enemies continued to harass him throughout 1859 and 1860 by demanding a federal code to protect slavery in the territories, irrespective of the wishes of local inhabitants. The Freeport doctrine and its author was almost as obnoxious to the proslavery Democrats as a Black Republican.[46]

Somewhat ironically, defeat did Lincoln no harm politically. He had more than held his own against one of the most formidable debaters in politics and he had, in addition, beaten his opponent in the popular vote by enough to prove that there was a man who could beat Douglas in Illinois and if he could do it there, why not all over the country? Indeed, Lincoln's political career was revitalized. After this year he was a national figure and one of the foremost spokesmen of the Republican Party.

The Return of John Brown. Before long, sectional strife again became acute. During the night of October 16, 1859, John Brown, who had dropped out of sight after the Pottawatomie Massacre, suddenly descended, with a band of 18 men, on the town of Harper's Ferry, Virginia, seized the federal arsenal there killing 7 innocent people (one being a free black), and called upon the slaves to rise and claim their freedom. Not a single slave responded, and the wounded Brown and the remnants of his tiny band were soon captured, found guilty of murder and treason against the state of Virginia, and hanged early in December 1859. Several of his followers later encountered the same fate.

Abolitionists and other Free Soilers were outraged that the Virginians had hanged so earnest a reformer who had sacrificed himself in a righteous cause. The day of Brown's execution became one of public mourning in New England. Free Soil centers in the North tolled bells, fired guns, half-masted flags, and held mass meetings. Some spoke of "Saint John" Brown and Ralph Waldo Emerson declared that Brown would "make the gallows glorious like the cross." Henry Thoreau called him an "angel of light" and John Bigelow, the New York journalist, suggested that it was easier to put John Brown upon a scaffold than to get him down again.

To many Southerners, Brown's raid appeared as the invasion of a state by a murderous gang of abolitionists bent on inciting slaves to murder helpless women and children. They became more indignant when they learned that several Republican newspapers hailed Brown as a hero — which only confirmed the Southerners' belief that Republicans were indistinguishable from abolitionists, and that if the Republicans came into power they would send other John Browns into slave territory to rouse the blacks to arson, rapine, and murder. In the November elections the Democrats charged that the Republicans were implicated in Brown's diabolical scheme, and that the Kansas martyr had drawn his misguided inspiration from the doctrines of the Republican Party. The political system was being strained to and beyond its limit by the issue of slavery. The chance that the bitter sectional argument could be harmonized faded close to the vanishing point.

Within two years blue-clad soldiers were marching south to the tune of:

> John Brown's body lies a-mouldering in the grave,
> But his soul goes marching on.

The Election of 1860

From early 1859 until the Democratic National Convention in April 1860, the rift between Stephen Douglas and the Southerners widened. In early February 1860, Jefferson Davis issued the Southern ultimatum to Douglas in the form of a series of resolutions introduced into the U.S. Senate demanding a national code for the protection of slave property in the territories and a congressional declaration that personal liberty laws and attacks on slavery were unconstitutional. Davis's purpose was to test the Northern Democrats' support of the South and to set forth the program Southern Democrats would insist on in return for party loyalty. The ensuing debate between Douglas and Davis over the resolutions was immediately recognized as presaging the formation of an independent Democratic party in the North unless the upcoming Democratic National Convention could heal the breach. The resolutions remained unpassed when the Democrats met for their convention in 1860.[47]

The Democratic Convention, 1860. On April 23, 1860, the Democratic National Convention assembled in Charleston, South Carolina, the headquarters of secession sentiment, to name candidates for the presidency and vice presidency. On the surface Charleston wore a gay and festive air. But the atmosphere there was not conducive to the spirit of unity the convention so much needed if it were to weather the approaching storm.

As the delegates assembled, the favored candidate of most of the Northern Democrats was the 47-year-old Stephen A. Douglas — the Little Giant. However, the Southern leaders were determined to block Douglas's nomination or, failing that, to make his nomination worthless. Knowing that Douglas cared not whether slavery was voted up or down, they had no confidence that he had any real concern over Southern rights or that he would really exert himself to protect them.[48] Also, they had supported Douglas's popular sovereignty in 1854, expecting to get Kansas; but Kansas had slipped the other way. Its territorial legislature was now in the hands of antislavery men, encouraged by Douglas's Freeport doctrine to flout the Dred Scott decision.

The Southern Democrats had no candidate of their own. Their leader was the eloquent William Lowndes Yancey of Alabama, the "Prince of Fire Eaters," who made no attempt to conceal his desire for an end to the party which allegedly "binds and divides and distracts the South."

On the first day the Douglas supporters pushed through a resolution permitting delegates to vote without the "unit rule," which meant that state delegations were not bound to vote as a unit. The result of this was that more than 40 pro–Douglas delegates were released from the control of delegations where the majority was anti–Douglas. Thus the prospects for the nomination of Douglas looked hopeful. However, at this point the Little Giant's floor leaders made a major blunder. Instead of insisting on an immediate vote for the candidate, they yielded to a proposal for completing the platform before the nominations began.[49] That evening the delegates representing the cotton states caucused and agreed to withdraw from the convention if their demand for a plank in the party platform declaring that neither Congress nor a territorial legislature could abolish slavery or impair the right to own slaves — essentially a commitment to the Dred Scott decision — was refused.

On April 27, platform day at the convention, the Buchanan-dominated Committee on Resolutions brought in two reports: a majority anti–Douglas report and a minority pro–Douglas report. The majority report began by suggesting the readoption of the platform from the Cincinnati convention of 1856 which simply stated that slavery was permitted by the Constitution and the Democratic Party supported the Constitution. In addition, it declared that no government — local, state, or federal — could outlaw slavery in the territories.

The pro–Douglas minority report also endorsed the Cincinnati platform, but took a more moderate position by saying that the party would "abide by and faithfully carry out" future decisions on slavery handed down by the Supreme Court.

For hours the convention boiled with bitter debate. Pleas for party harmony were useless. "We are for principles," a Mississippian shouted: "Damn the party!" H. B. Payne of Ohio warned the delegates that if the anti–Douglas report was adopted, "you cannot expect one Northern electoral vote, or one sympathizing member of Congress from the free states."

Without those the Democrats could not win the presidency. Yancey, speaking for the South, chided the Douglas men for lack of courage. Democratic Party defeats in the North, he said, were the result of pandering to antislavery sentiment. Not one state voting against the majority report, Yancey said, could be relied on with certainty to cast Democratic electoral votes, while every one, with the possible exception of Maryland, supporting it was surely Democratic.

Finally, Yancey laid it on the line. "Ours is the property invaded," he said, "ours are the institutions which are at stake; ours is the peace that is to be destroyed; ours is the property that is to be destroyed; ours is the honor at stake — the honor of children, the honor of families, the lives, perhaps of all — all of which rests upon what your course may ultimately make a great heaving volcano of passion and crime, if you are unable to consummate your designs. Bear with us, then, if we stand sternly here upon what is yet that dormant volcano, and say we yield no position here until we are convinced we are wrong." The Douglas men, he said, must take the position that "slavery was right and therefore ought to be."[50]

Immediately, Senator George A. Pugh of Ohio, regarded as the Douglas spokesman, rose to reply. The party's troubles in the North, Pugh said, began with the fact that Northern Democrats had worn themselves out defending Southern interests. They were being asked to eat dirt once again and that they absolutely refused to do. "Must the Party be harnessed to the chariot of 300,000 slave masters?" Pugh asked. "Gentlemen of the South, you mistake us — you mistake us — we will not do it!" Pugh called on Southern moderates to remember Jefferson, Madison, Jackson, and other Southern founders of the democracy who had denounced slavery and sought to find some peaceful way to rid the nation of it. He named men present in the convention, former senators and representatives, who had suffered defeat in their states and districts because of their support of Southern doctrines. He begged the Southern delegates not to ask Northern Democrats to commit political suicide.[51]

The convention decided along sectional lines to recommit the various platform resolutions to the committee. All the following day, Sunday, the platform committee worked on the language of the platform. Finally, on Monday, April 30, the eighth day of the convention, the platform committee acknowledged that a difference of opinion existed within the party with respect to slavery, and submitted a revision of what had been the pro-Douglas minority report which carried 165–138. The Douglas minivictory was short-lived when the thoroughly angered cotton delegations walked out of the convention. Yancey and the Alabama delegation led the way, followed by Mississippi, Florida, and Texas, and a majority of delegates from Virginia, South Carolina, Georgia, and Arkansas.

The remainder of the original states met as scheduled the following day, voted to reaffirm the 1856 platform, and prepared to nominate Douglas. In a surprise move, the permanent chairman, Caleb Cushing of Massachusetts, a dedicated Buchanan man, announced that the old party rule—that a winner must have two-thirds of the delegates—was still in effect. The two-thirds rule made agreement on candidates difficult even under normal circumstances, but Cushing blandly explained that he meant two-thirds of the original 303 delegates, not those 252 delegates still in the convention! This meant that some candidate must receive 202 votes. The ruling of the chairman was sustained after Virginia and other states threatened to withdraw unless it was done.[52] Buchanan's men had also persuaded the New York delegation to vote for the measure, and the nominations began with Douglas facing a totally impossible task.

By the end of the first day of balloting, after 12 ballots had been taken, it was obvious Douglas was blocked. Favorite sons Robert M. R. Hunter of Virginia, James Guthrie of Kentucky, and Andrew Johnson of Tennessee clung to their delegates under orders from the president. Although the Douglas delegates sent frantic telegrams to Buchanan, warning him that he could not "afford to be the last President of the United States," nothing changed—the embittered president refused to yield. On the tenth day of the convention, after 57 fruitless ballots, the weary delegates agreed to adjourn and reconvene in Baltimore on June 18 after recommending that the party in different states fill any vacancies in their delegations.

The Constitutional Democratic Convention, 1860. The adjournment of the main convention suddenly left the seceders with nothing to do. Most of their strategy had been geared to the expectation that Douglas would eventually withdraw, either in recognition of defeat or for the sake of the party, and that a candidate acceptable to the seceders would be chosen. But when this had not happened the Southern faction was sure they had the nomination and a little more than 100 of them moved to Military Hall in Charleston, denominated themselves "Constitutional Democrats," and agreed to meet again in Richmond, Virginia, on June 11. When only a handful appeared on that date, an adjournment was taken to Baltimore on June 21 to await the outcome of the Baltimore adjourned session.

The Constitutional Union Convention, 1860. On May 9 a group of old border-state Whigs, Know-Nothings, and moderate men of both North and South from 24 states gathered in Baltimore to form the Constitutional Union Party and nominate former Whig Speaker and Senator John Bell of Tennessee, one of the best known of the old Whigs. For vice president the convention selected the great Massachusetts scholar, orator, preacher, and former Senator Edward Everett, also an old Whig. This was a "Kangaroo ticket," so-called because its hind legs were presumed to be stronger than the front. It was, however, a slate which was believed to have much strength in the South, where the considerable number of Union-loving

conservatives might well vote it in preference to Douglas or a radical secessionist.[53]

The new party wrote no platform and took no stand on the crucial
question of the expansion of slavery into the territories. They were content
to declare simply for "the Constitution of the country, the union of the
states, and the enforcement of the laws." To this negative standard they
sought to rally all those who wished to preserve the Union by compromise
and conciliation — the way it had always been preserved before. With no
platform and no program except to preserve the Union and uphold the
Constitution, the Constitutional Union Party soon became known derisively as the "Do-Nothing Party." A New York newspaper scornfully
dismissed the Bell platform as "no North, no South, no East, no West, no
anything."[54]

The Republican Convention, 1860. The 1860 Republican convention
opened in Chicago on May 16 with 465 delegates from all the Northern
states and the territories of Kansas and Nebraska, the District of Columbia,
and the slave states of Maryland, Delaware, Virginia, Kentucky, Missouri,
and Texas present. Only Alabama, Arkansas, Florida, Georgia, Louisiana,
Mississippi, North Carolina, South Carolina, and Tennessee were not
represented. In contrast to the demoralized Democrats, the Republicans
were optimistic and confident of victory. The most influential newspapers
in the country were on their side and the trend of the elections had been
uniformly in their favor. The presidential prize now seemed within their
grasp.

The convention was held in the newly finished Wigwam, a huge box-
like 10,000 seat wooden structure built especially to house the convention.
The hall was gaily decorated with red, white, and blue streamers and
brilliantly lit by flaring gas jets.[55] A new feature was a special press gallery
to accommodate the more than 900 reporters who applied for space.[56] The
Republican convention attracted more spectators and generated more excitement than any previous party gathering in American history. A car-
nival atmosphere enveloped Chicago. Marching groups, known as the
"Wide Awakes," convoyed each arriving delegation to its headquarters
through streets choked with welcoming crowds.

As the delegates to the convention assembled, Senator William H.
Seward, the 56-year-old New York leader, appeared to be the most likely
nominee. The talkative, good-natured, and good-hearted Seward had constructed an impressive career in the politics both of his state and the nation
as an able governor and an outstanding senator. The Republican Party
itself was in large part his creation. The most astute correspondents
reported that Seward's candidacy was irresistible, and he was clearly preferred by a majority of the delegates. Horace Greeley, once Seward's dear
friend, now his bitter enemy (primarily because Seward, Weed, and company

had not satisfied Greeley's longing for office), practically conceded a
Seward victory. Even the Southern press conceded Seward to be "the
greatest man in the government."

However, Seward's past dogged him. Everyone knew that he was a
"war to the knife" abolitionist who had predicted during the campaign of
1858 "an irrepressible conflict" between the North and South, and that in
his speech against the Compromise of 1850 he had appealed to "a higher law
than the Constitution." As the governor who had once procured financial
aid for Catholic and parochial schools he was handicapped in New
England, Pennsylvania, New Jersey, and Indiana, where the Republican
Party was saturated with Know-Nothingism. Seward had also been
associated with the "money power" centralized in the East and hence was
no favorite in the Democratic strongholds of the West. Horace Greeley
frankly, openly, and vigorously opposed him, and the New York Tribune
would carry weight with the voters. In addition, Seward's long and close
association with Thurlow Weed (and Weed's malodorous political
machine) in New York's turbulent politics led many potential voters to
believe (incorrectly) he was engaged in corrupt politics. Even so, Seward
seemed to be the man to beat.

In addition to Seward there was Salmon Portland Chase, the deeply
religious and capable Republican governor of Ohio.[57] Unfortunately for
Chase his home-state politicians were not prepared to support him and his
low-tariff views hurt him in Pennsylvania and elsewhere. Also, he was well
recognized as a "party-jumper" who had used and discarded Whigs,
Democrats, and Know-Nothings in his rise to power. Chase's ambition to
be president had reached inordinate proportions by 1860. His transparent
ambition coupled with ostentatious self-righteousness was a repellent combination at best and, as historian George H. Mayer put it, Chase made it
seem more offensive with a "bland and patronizing smile."[58]

Somewhat behind Seward and Chase was white-haired Judge Edward
Bates of St. Louis, Missouri, an ex–Whig and former slaveholder. Bates
would attract the support of Republicans and old Whigs who sought compromise on the slavery issue or settlement without conflict. If the convention tried to placate the South, Bates would be a good compromise. His age,
however, was against him — he was 67 years of age; his flirtation with the
Know-Nothings had alienated the German vote and he would most likely
be a loser in any state where the foreign-born vote was essential; and the
antislavery radicals made it clear that they would bolt the party if Bates
were chosen. They did not insist that the party accept their first choice —
Seward — but they did demand that "a Republican candidate" be chosen,
one who had supported Fremont in 1856.[59] The judge had the support of
Horace Greeley and the famous Blair family and was from a border state,
all of which were in his favor.

Abraham Lincoln of Illinois was also a possibility. In 1859, after his dramatic senatorial contest with Douglas, "The Rail Splitter of Sangamon County" had taken a 4,000-mile tour with extended stops at Indianapolis, Columbus, Pittsburgh, Cleveland, Buffalo, Harrisburg, and Philadelphia, ending at the Cooper Union in New York City on February 27, 1860. At the Cooper Union before a sophisticated audience that included Horace Greeley and William Cullen Bryant, Lincoln had outlined with powerful simplicity the historical basis for Congress's right to exclude slavery from the territories. Moreover, he had made clear that his ultimate goal was not merely the nonextension of slavery — although he was inflexible in his adherence to this objective — but its "ultimate extinction."[60] The Cooper Union speech with its moderation on the slavery issue, its emphasis on constitutional procedure, and its strong appeal for national peace and harmony, was widely reported and favorably received. Soon, Lincoln was being widely discussed as a leading candidate for the Republican nomination.[61]

National Chairman Edwin D. Morgan called the convention to order at noon on Wednesday, May 16. The moderate (even conservative) platform, drafted by a group including Horace Greeley and Carl Schurz was designed to have a much wider appeal than the antislavery manifesto of four years earlier. On the slavery question it clearly denied "the authority of Congress, of a territorial legislature, or of any individuals, to give legal existence to slavery in any territory of the United States." The infamous Lecompton Constitution was denounced, and the immediate admission of Kansas to the Union as a free state was called for. It rejected the Dred Scott decision as "a dangerous political heresy" and denounced lawless invasion of any state (without mentioning John Brown) as "among the gravest of crimes." Passed over were such explosive questions as enforcement of the Fugitive Slave Law, the admission of additional slave states, and the abolition of slavery in the District of Columbia.

The platform also promised federal aid to a Pacific railroad and the improvement of rivers and harbors; endorsed a tariff "that would encourage industrial development" which was gratifiying to the industrialists of Pennsylvania (a doubtful state); and pledged to enact a law granting free homesteads to actual settlers — a pledge that was certain to gain votes for them in the old Northwest and on the Pacific coast. When the party platform was passed by unanimous vote, there followed 15 minutes of deafening applause.[62]

When the nominations began, William M. Evarts the chairman of the New York delegation placed the name of Seward before the convention in 26 words. Norman B. Judd, a member of the Republican National Committee from Illinois (who had persuaded the RNC to have the convention in Chicago), then used only 27 words to nominate Lincoln. "I desire on behalf of the delegation from Illinois to put in nomination as a candidate for the President of the United States, Abraham Lincoln of Illinois." The galleries, packed with Lincoln supporters, cheered mightily when Lincoln's name was called. As Bruce Catton described it: "Imagine all the hogs ever slaughtered in Cincinnati giving their death squeals together, a core of big steam whistles going . . . and you can conceive something of the same nature."63 After the nomination of Seward and Lincoln, there were several others: William L. Dayton of New Jersey, Cameron, Chase, and Judge McLean.

Seward's supporters were convinced the nomination was theirs for the taking. Even before the nominations were completed, they set up a clamor for "a roll call of the States!" However, to their astonishment, something that "couldn't possibly happen" did. The clerks could not find the tally sheets. In the confusion, somebody made a motion to adjourn. Before Seward's forces realized what was happening, the convention was adjourned for the day.

Even so, the Seward supporters were not overly upset. That night the champagne flowed freely in the headquarters of the New York delegation, and the delegates boastfully informed visitors that the nomination of Seward was assured. They were convinced that they were celebrating victory but one day early. But even as they partied, Judge David W. Davis, who was organizing the support of Lincoln, and the Lincoln managers began rounding up delegate support for the lanky rail splitter from Illinois "by paying their price."64 They made a deal with the Pennsylvania delegation under which that state agreed to vote for Lincoln, provided that Simon Cameron would be appointed secretary of the treasury if the Republican Party won the election. Another cabinet post was "half-promised" to Caleb Smith in exchange for the votes of Indiana. In entering into these agreements, Davis and the other Lincoln managers had plainly ignored Lincoln's telegraphed instructions to "Make no bargains for me."65

The balloting started late on May 18, 1860, and was all over by noon. The first ballot gave Seward 173.5, Lincoln 102, Cameron 50.5, Chase 49, and Bates 48; 42 votes were scattered elsewhere. On the second ballot Seward gained only 11 while Lincoln picked up 79 as Pennsylvania swung away from Cameron to Lincoln as prearranged. Seward had been stopped. The remaining anti-Seward delegates made a dash for the Lincoln bandwagon.

On the third ballot Lincoln had 231.5, only 1.5 votes away from victory. New Jersey gave the signal midway through the third ballot by switching 8 votes to Lincoln. States further down the alphabet followed suit. At the end of the third ballot Ohio shifted 4 votes from Chase to Lincoln after a whispered promise from a Lincoln manager that Salmon P. Chase "could have anything he wanted," thus giving Lincoln the nomination. As the result was announced, Thurlow Weed, Seward's manager and friend of over 30 years, sat and wept. His 20-year purpose — to elevate his friend to the presidency—had been defeated "by a combination of the disappointed."[66]

After some haggling with New York, Senator Hannibal Hamlin, whom Lincoln had never met, was quickly nominated for the vice presidency. Hamlin had served several terms in the House of Representatives and finally in the U.S. Senate, always as a Democrat until he left the party over the Kansas-Nebraska Act. He had been one of the chief organizers of the Republican Party in Maine and in 1856 was elected as a Republican governor of Maine. The choice of Hamlin for the vice presidency was a recognition of the desire to balance the ticket in geographic and political backgrounds. His selection was a recognition of the Democratic element in the Republican Party. Also, Hamlin could speak for the antislavery element in New England, having strong sympathies with abolition. The convention closed on the motion of one delegate "to meet at the White House on the 4th of March next."[67]

When the word of Lincoln's nomination was flashed to the nation, joy in the old Northwest was unbounded. Companies of uniformed "Wide Awakes" and mobs of assorted well-wishers marched in torchlight parades through the streets of the larger cities, singing and yelling throughout the night, repeating over and over the party song:

> Ain't you glad you jined the Republicans?
> Jined the Republicans—Jined the Republicans!

In the South the news of Lincoln's nomination was received with dismay. Southern secessionists promptly served notice that the election of the "baboon" Lincoln—the "abolitionist" rail splitter—would split the nation.

The Baltimore Convention, 1860. The Northern faction of the Democratic Party reconvened in Baltimore on June 18 to try again to find a suitable candidate for the presidency. Bitter wrangles marked the opening sessions when it was discovered that many of the Southern states had sent new delegations to the convention and these were vying for the seats of the original delegates. Should the Southern bolters be reseated or should they be replaced by the contesting delegates who were favorable to Douglas? Caleb Cushing, serving again as chairman, ruled that the old delegations should be admitted as official representatives, but the affair was passed on to the pro-Douglas credentials committee which returned with two conflicting reports. The majority report suggested that the new delegations should be seated from Alabama, Louisiana, and Arkansas, with a compromise made between the old and the new in the case of Georgia. The minority report, on the other hand, demanded the seating of the original Charleston delegations.

In the end the convention adopted the majority (pro–Douglas) report. The Virginia delegates then left the hall, followed by those from South Carolina and Tennessee. Kentucky retired to caucus and some Maryland delegates withdrew, followed by scattered groups from a few Northern states and a substantial block from the Pacific coast where the party was dominated by pro–Southerners. As each delegation left, the Douglas men hissed their hatred after them. By the time the shambles ended, only 13 states were left with full delegations.

When the uproar had subsided, the convention, consisting of less than two-thirds of the original delegates, finally moved on to the nomination itself. On the first ballot Douglas received 173 out of 190.5 votes cast and, on the second, gained 181.5 out of 194.5; (over John C. Breckinridge of Kentucky who received 7.5 votes). It was clear that it would be impossible for Douglas to gain two-thirds (202) of the votes allocated. A delegate then moved that since Douglas had received two-thirds of all the votes, he should be declared the nominee. The motion passed on a voice vote. In an unsuccessful unity move, Senator Benjamin Fitzpatrick of Alabama, who had been selected by a caucus of the remaining Southern delegates, was named as the vice presidential candidate, but he declined and Herschel V. Johnson, a former governor of Georgia, was chosen by the national committee to take his place.

While the Northern wing was nominating Douglas, some 200 members of the anti–Douglas faction convened in the Maryland Institute Hall in Baltimore where Breckinridge was nominated on the first ballot. Senator Joseph Lane of Oregon, who was markedly sympathetic to the South, was named for the vice presidency. President Buchanan, as expected, publicly endorsed Breckinridge. The nation was now faced with two Democratic parties, two Democratic candidates, and two Democratic platforms—one Northern and one Southern.

The Campaign of 1860. The Republicans drove into the battle to help Lincoln maul Democrats. Lincoln enthusiasts staged roaring rallies, barbecues, and torchlight parades attacking the Buchanan administration as wasteful and corrupt and extolling "High 'Old Abe' the Great Railsplitter of the West"[68] and the "Little Giant Killer," while groaning dismally for "Poor Little Doug." Republican "Wide-Awakes" carried lighted torches on fence rails in parades, marching in zigzag formations in imitation of rail fences. Campaign buttons with a picture of the beardless Lincoln,[69] campaign biographies which fully exploited the qualities of a folk hero (which were so conspicuous in Lincoln), and medals with inscriptions which dramatized Lincoln's youthful struggles against poverty were sold or given away.

Lincoln made no speeches, asserting that he had already made his position clear on every issue. He did receive a stream of visitors—friends, politicians, office seekers, reporters, photographers, and painters — during the campaign, and selections from the Lincoln-Douglas debates and his Cooper Union address were printed and widely circulated. Lincoln's chief rivals at the convention responded loyally, and Seward and Chase entered the campaign wholeheartedly, making a number of very strong speeches for Lincoln all around the country. As they campaigned, they repeatedly flogged the issue that was bothering the free laborer of the North: "How can the free laboring man ever get two dollars a day when a black slave costs his master only ten cents a day?"[70]

The Republicans were successful, too, in enlisting such strong support from business groups that they were far better provided with money than four years earlier. The panic of 1857 had stimulated a widespread demand in industrial communities for a protective tariff and, in commercial and financial circles, for a better banking system. The Republican Party promised to satisfy these yearnings. For the Democrats, August Belmont and William B. Astor reminded rich businessmen that a Republican victory would jeopardize nearly $200 million owed to Northerners by Southern customers.

Republicans were well aware of the Democratic hope that even if they could not elect they might still prevent any candidate from obtaining a majority in the electoral college and thereby throw the election into the House of Representatives. The Democrats hoped that, in case no compromise candidate could be agreed upon, the Senate might then elect Breckinridge's running mate, Joseph Lane, as vice president, who would then step into the presidential vacancy.[71] During the campaign the Republicans consequently hammered away with the slogan: "It's Lincoln or Lane."[72]

Douglas, ignoring public opinion, took his case to the people in a vigorous nationwide tour, asserting the merits of popular sovereignty and taking a stand for the Union. He "demeans himself," the *North Iowan* editorialized, "as no other candidate ever yet has, who goes about begging, imploring, and beseeching the people to grant him his wish. . . . He should be attended by some Italian, with his hand organ to grind out an accompaniment."[73]

In August, after wild stories began to circulate around the South about slave revolts and uprisings and massacres if the Republicans won, the bone-weary and physically sick Douglas turned his attention to the South, not to gain votes, for his cause was hopeless there, but calling upon the people to accept the outcome of the election peacefully. He declared that no grievance could justify secession. The night before the election Douglas was saying these things in Mobile, Alabama, the home state of William L. Yancey.

The Constitutional Unionists, calling themselves "Bell Ringers," went into battle ringing bells of all sizes, shapes, and sounds for Bell, and voicing the slogan, "The Union, the Constitution, and the Enforcement of the Laws." Like the Democrats, their strategy was that of preventing a majority in the electoral college, thus throwing the election into the House of Representatives. In that contingency they believed they occupied the strategic middle ground, both ideologically and geographically, with which to break the impasse that might occur in the electoral college and the House of Representatives. A people distracted with factional strife might then welcome the happy solution of an election of Bell and Everett. For his part, Bell respected the no-campaign tradition. He left Nashville only once during the canvass, and his trip had nothing to do with politics.

The Northern Democrats, in a desperate effort to win some Southern support for Douglas, emphasized their candidate's stand on slavery: "I do not care whether it is voted up or down." If the Democrats did not win the election, they warned, the South would surely secede from the Union.

Breckinridge also declined to campaign personally, but, after the Democrats lost the Kentucky state election in August, he consented to speak once at a great barbecue in his home county.

The 1860 Outcome. The balloting for president took place on November 6. Thirty-three states with a population of 31,443,790 cast 4,676,853 votes in the election. Lincoln received 1,867,000 popular votes (less than 40 percent of the popular vote), and 180 (a clear majority) in the electoral college. His total Southern vote amounted to 26,000. He secured no votes in the ten states of the future Confederacy; his name was not even permitted on the ballot. Vice President Breckenridge carried the Deep South, Delaware and Maryland with 854,000 popular and 72 electoral votes. Bell finished third with 592,000 popular and 39 electoral votes from two upper South states — Virginia and Tennessee — and one border state — Kentucky. Douglas received 1,380,000 popular and 12 electoral votes — carrying only Missouri and winning half the electoral votes of New Jersey.

Farmers and intellectuals joined by businessmen were at the core of Lincoln's victory; once again most of business had feared the unsettling effects of change. Republicans were strongest in the rural areas of New York, Massachusetts, Vermont, and northern Ohio. In the Midwest their margins of victory were slimmer, and in California and Oregon they won only through the division of opposition. In the states of the Northeast and Midwest, however, the Republicans had replaced Democrats as the dominant party.[74]

The victory of the Democrats in the presidential election of 1856 was their last as a national organization, for in 1860 the party split. The national party system now lay shattered. The major outcome of this event was a new political alignment.

In mid–December Vice President Breckinridge cheerlessly performed his ceremonial duty of counting the ballots cast by the members of the electoral college and declaring Lincoln elected.[75]

In the elections for the House of Representatives and the Senate the Republicans failed to secure a majority in either branch of Congress. Only when the senators and representatives of the seceding states withdrew from Congress were the Republicans able to gain a majority in the national legislature and take complete control of the federal government.

The Secession of the Southern States

The secession of the lower South began while James Buchanan was still serving out the closing months of an unhappy administration. South Carolina acted first. The South Carolina legislature had remained in session over election day and when it became apparent that Lincoln had been elected, it called for a convention to provide for the state's secession from the Union.[76]

When the convention met on December 20, 1860, it unanimously declared that the ratification of the Constitution by the South Carolina Convention of 1788 was rescinded, and that the "Union now subsisting between South Carolina and the other states, under the name of the 'United States of America' is hereby dissolved." On this occasion, unlike the nullification crisis of Jackson's time, South Carolina gained the support of her sister states. The secession movement had begun.

The supreme and sole impulse of Buchanan's last three months in office was to prevent the spread of the secession movement by avoiding any coercive measures that might annoy the upper South. On December 4 he sent to the "lame duck" Congress a labored and inconclusive "straddle" message, deploring Northern agitation of the slavery question but also asserting that secession was not a constitutional right, as practically all of the Southerners said it was, but revolution. On the other hand, he believed that no power to coerce a state was lodged with the federal government, and that the exercise of such power under these circumstances would be of doubtful wisdom anyway. "Oh for one hour of Jackson!" cried the advocates of strong-arm tactics.

Nor did President-elect Lincoln, in the four months between election and inauguration, do anything to head off catastrophe. To Lincoln, to whom the Union was most dear, slavery was a moral wrong; but it should be contained only constitutionally, and only in the territories could it be denied by federal power without constitutional change. He saw fit, perhaps mistakenly, to issue no statement to quiet Southern fears. Meanwhile, others tried to restore the Union.

The Crittenden Compromise. The most seriously considered proposal to save the Union came from Senator John J. Crittenden of Kentucky, the successor to Clay's seat in the Senate, on December 18, 1860, two days before South Carolina's formal departure from the Union. In addition to four resolutions, it proposed six unamendable amendments, the most important of which provided for the extension of the Missouri Compromise line of 36° 30' to the Pacific and the establishment of slavery with federal protection south of that line. The proposal also promised that no future amendment would tamper with the institution in the slave states, and offered other guarantees to the South.

The Southern leaders refused to accept Crittenden's proposal unless it was acceptable to Lincoln and the Republican Party. The Republican leaders in Congress were inclined to favor the compromise but they waited to hear what the president-elect would say about it. When Lincoln's answer came, it was "No." Lincoln was sure that the slave power, if not contained, would press for new slave areas in the Union and would seek annexation in the Caribbean or perhaps even in Mexico. He had concluded that on this issue the time had come to take a stand and run a risk. The Republicans, following the leadership of Lincoln, opposed the measure and the bill died in a Senate committee. The congressional plans to achieve compromise had failed.

By February 1, 1861, five other states of the Deep South (Mississippi, Florida, Alabama, Georgia, and Louisiana) had seceded, and on that day Texas followed. In the next two months the Confederacy seized federal forts, post offices, and customs houses throughout the South, leaving under federal control only Fort Sumter in the Charleston, South Carolina, harbor and three other forts off the coast of Florida. When South Carolina demanded that federal troops be withdrawn from the fortifications in the Charleston harbor, Buchanan replied in Jacksonian accents that Fort Sumter would be defended "against hostile attacks from whatever quarter they may come." The Unionists hailed the president's policy but it came too late.

Many people in the North, including some abolitionists, were willing to let the "erring sisters go in peace." Many Northerners rejoiced that the secession of the cotton states had relieved the nation of just that much responsibility for the "curse of slavery." Horace Greeley, in an editorial in his *New York Tribune*, declared: "If the cotton states shall decide that they can do better out of the Union than in it, we insist on letting them go in peace."[77]

The lame-duck Congress of 1861, after the withdrawal of members from seceding states, admitted Kansas as a free state. Ironically, when Kansas finally became a state, it entered the Union with a constitution that forbade slavery but which gave the vote only to white males.

Formation of the Confederate Government. Even before the process of secession had gone far enough to include the states of the upper South, a convention of six of the seven rebel commonwealths met at Montgomery, Alabama, on February 4, 1861, to form a new government. The delegates settled on Jefferson Davis of Mississippi as provisional president and the diminutive (he weighed in at 80 pounds) Alexander H. Stephens of Georgia as vice president.[78]

A month later James Buchanan stumbled out of the office which (as he said) "was not fit for a gentleman" with a sigh of relief. To his successor he said frankly, "If you are as happy to be entering the White House as I shall feel on returning home, you are a happy man indeed." The decision whether the seceding states should be allowed to depart in peace or whether the Union would be preserved at the cost of war was Lincoln's to make. The entire country anxiously awaited the new president's decision.

Abraham Lincoln as President

Angry, black clouds filled the skies as Abraham Lincoln solemnly took the oath of office on March 4, 1861. The weather of the day suited the gravity of the occasion. Stephen Douglas appeared on the inaugural platform and, according to legend, held Lincoln's stovepipe hat on his knee as a gesture of support.

In his inaugural address Lincoln was conciliatory but firm and he left no room for doubt as to the policy he was determined to follow. He would agree to enforcing the return of fugitive slaves and to the inviolable rights of the states to their own institutions. He said he had no objections to a proposed constitutional amendment guaranteeing that "the Federal Government shall never interfere with the domestic institutions of the states" — including slavery. The secession ordinances, he said, were "legally void" and pledged to use his office "to hold, occupy, and possess property and places belonging to the Federal Government." But he promised not to begin hostilities.

Lincoln then made a direct appeal to the people of the South. "In your hands, my dissatisfied fellow countrymen, and not in mine, is the momentous issue of civil war. The government will not assail you. You can have no conflict without yourselves the aggressors." Lincoln then added his famous, eloquent paragraph:

> I am loath to close. We are not enemies, but friends. We must not be enemies. Though passion may have strained, it must not break our bonds of affection. The mystic chords of memory, stretching from every battlefield and patriot grave to every living heart and hearthstone all over this broad land, will yet swell the chorus of the Union when again touched, as surely they will be, by the better angels of our nature.

In the North and in the border slave states reaction to the inaugural was pretty much along party lines. The deep South regarded it as a declaration of war.

To the dismay of his advisers and against their advice, the new president chose to construct a "balanced" cabinet representing a wide range of opinion instead of putting together a group of harmonious advisers who could help him face the crisis. Many thoughtful observers found his selections alarming.

William H. Seward, who accepted the post of secretary of state, was the ablest and best known of the appointees. The New Yorker, nursing his disappointment over twice missing the Republican presidential nomination in 1856 and 1860, had agreed to accept the post only after much urging and only after being persuaded that Lincoln would be unable to govern, necessitating Seward's taking over the actual administration of the country. Seward would be prime minister to Lincoln's powerless monarch. Also, Seward represented the power of New York and the Free Soil Whigs. But throughout the entire war, whatever may have been his personal idiosyncrasies, Seward's loyalty to the party, to the national cause, and to the administration were never in doubt.

Gideon Welles, a Connecticut "War Democrat" who looked like an Old Testament prophet, was named to be the secretary of the navy to represent New England. Montgomery Blair of Maryland, a conservative on slavery and emancipation, became postmaster general. Blair soon became anathema to the radicals in the cabinet and Congress and was forced to resign. The attorney general was Edward Bates of Missouri, an archconservative former Whig, chosen to represent the border states. Representing the radical Western group was Senator Salmon P. Chase of Ohio, who Lincoln named secretary of the treasury. Soon Chase had destroyed much of Lincoln's confidence in him by meddling in every department as though he actually were president and intriguing for the office in the next election. Chase detested Seward, agreeing with him only in thinking Lincoln a weakling. Seward and Chase were to sit at the cabinet table as bitter rivals.

The president honored two commitments made at the convention and appointed Simon Cameron of Pennsylvania as secretary of war and Caleb B. Smith of Indiana as secretary of the interior. Cameron, who had a justly deserved reputation as a spoilsman and corruptionist,[79] proved to be inept if not corrupt and was replaced by Lincoln in January 1862, with the eccentric but brilliant Edwin M. Stanton, of Steubenville, Ohio, a Breckinridge Democrat and attorney general in Buchanan's cabinet. Stanton, who had dubbed Lincoln the "original gorilla," immediately sided with the radicals in the cabinet. Before he had been in office six months the wily Stanton was weaving intricate political webs.

Picking a cabinet, however, was simple in comparison with handling the greedy hordes of office seekers of the new party who crammed the White House rooms, stairways, hallways, and even closets, or bombarded Lincoln with petitions and endorsements. As the first president of his party, it was up to Lincoln to clean house—replace all the Democrats with Republicans—as soon as possible, and he did his best to comply. Eventually, Lincoln removed 1,195 of the 1,520 presidential officeholders and distributed jobs to build up support for his policies.[80] As usual, there were more applicants than jobs. At a time when he needed a clear mind for pressing affairs of state, the new president complained that he was forced to worry about the "postmastership at Pepperton."

After hostilities started, Lincoln dispensed patronage to War Democrats as well as to Republicans. He gave commissions to a number of influential Democratic politicians whose support he deemed essential. He appointed six major generals, five of whom were Democrats. Of the 110 brigadier generals appointed that first year, 70 were Democrats—including Benjamin F. Butler of Massachusetts, John A. Logan and John McClernand of Illinois, and Daniel Sickles of New York. Although from a purely military point of view most of these appointments were indefensible, they contributed greatly to national unity.[81]

On Inauguration Day Lincoln received word from Major Robert Anderson, in command at Fort Sumter, that his supplies were running low and that the garrison must either get food by April 15 or be withdrawn. The president, after a period of hesitation, decided not to surrender the fort. A month after his inauguration Lincoln notified the governor of South Carolina that he would attempt to send a supply of provisions to Fort Sumter. The Confederate government regarded this announcement of Lincoln's policy as equivalent to a declaration of war, and President Davis ordered General Beauregard to demand the immediate surrender of the fort. Anderson promised to evacuate by April 15, unless he was relieved or ordered to remain. But the Confederates would not wait. Anderson was given until 4 A.M. on April 12 to capitulate. At 4:30 A.M. the batteries from the Charleston shore opened fire on the Fort. In the afternoon of April 13 Anderson surrendered. "The first gun at Fort Sumter," wrote James Russell Lowell, "brought all the free states to their feet as one man."

Beauregard's cannon temporarily ended Northern division. Pierce and Buchanan announced they would support Lincoln. Stephen Douglas met confidentially with the president to offer his hand in "preserving the Union and maintaining the government." In May 1861, in a ringing Chicago speech (his last as it turned out) delivered to 10,000 people, Douglas declared: "Every man must be for the United States or against it. There can be no neutrals in the war; only patriots or traitors." Editors like Horace Greeley, preachers like Henry Ward Beecher, and politicians like Edward Everett, who only recently had opposed the use of force, now joined in the call to arms. Pacifist groups like the American Peace Society quietly evaporated. Men from all walks of life and from all parties rallied to the support of the government.

Partisan politics were altered by the war but not suspended. The president never succeeded in obtaining bipartisan support. The death of Stephen Douglas on June 3, 1861, six weeks after the fall of Sumter, left the Democrats leaderless and on the point of following the Whig Party into limbo. Douglas's loss was indeed, as Greeley said, "a national calamity." After the death of their leader most of the Douglas Democrats rushed to the support of the Lincoln administration and the Union cause. However, many Northern Democrats remained loyal to their party, and offered a vigorous if not always loyal opposition.

The Peace Democrats, former Breckinridge and Bell supporters, professed loyalty but opposed Lincoln's war policies. Most of them demanded that the war should be ended by some kind of negotiated settlement. Breckinridge himself entered the Confederate cabinet as secretary of war.

Lincoln's own party was badly divided over the slavery question. The regular Republicans were first and foremost Unionists. Such men as Senator Orville H. Browning of Lincoln's state of Illinois, James R. Doolittle of Wisconsin, John Sherman of Ohio (the general's brother), and Jacob Colamer of Vermont, rejected every suggestion that the war was a fight to free slaves.

In opposition were the radicals, who made emancipation the primary objective. They demanded swift and decisive movement, both against slavery and the Confederacy. The radicals in the Senate were led by three experienced politicians: Charles Sumner, who had resumed his seat in 1860 after a four-year absence and was more or less recovered from his caning and brimful of hatred for slaveholders; Benjamin "Bluff Ben" Wade of Ohio, an educated but profane frontier firebrand who took a dim view of caution in politics; and the vengeful Zachariah Chandler, a prosperous and hard-fighting merchant from Michigan. "The rebel," Chandler announced, "has sacrificed all his rights. He has no right to life, liberty, or the pursuit of happiness. Everything you give him, even life itself, is a boon which he has forfeited."

In the House of Representatives the 73-year-old Thaddeus Stevens of Pennsylvania, the chairman of the powerful Ways and Means Committee, was the most influential and vindictive of the radicals. One of the ablest champions of blacks' rights, Stevens nourished a dislike for the Southern planter aristocracy which did not vanish with the Confederacy. The South, he insisted, must be beaten into submission no matter what the cost. Outstanding among Stevens's lieutenants in the House were the Indiana congressmen George W. Julian and Schuyler Colfax. This group, backed by Horace Greeley and the *New York Tribune*, kept up an incessant criticism of the administration.

The radicals took a distinctive view of the war between the states and the nature of the peace to be concluded. Whereas Lincoln assumed that the

Southern states never left the Union, the radicals insisted that the separation of the sections had been complete and that readmission was to be permitted only under the most stringent conditions. In general the radicals
favored total and immediate emancipation, accompanied by the immediate
grant of full civil and political rights to the former slaves (including the
right to vote). By their criticism of Lincoln's conduct of the war, they early
earned the epithet "Vindictives," which was not unacceptable to them.

   The Emancipation Proclamation. From the start of his administration,
Lincoln had resisted the radical demand that all slaves in and out of the
Union should be declared free. He had been too keenly aware of the likely
response of the border slaveholding states — Delaware, Maryland, Kentucky, and Missouri — to risk such a step. They had been kept in the Union
with the understanding that slavery was not the issue between North and
South. When the cries of the Northern radicals became too insistent, Lincoln in 1862 again stated his position in positive terms: "My paramount object in this struggle is to save the Union, and is not either to save or to
destroy slavery."

   Later in the year, however, Lincoln had come to recognize that "it was
a military necessity, absolutely essential for the salvation of the nation, that
we must free the slaves or be ourselves subdued." In April 1862 Congress
had declared itself willing to cooperate with the border states in a policy
of gradual compensated emancipation, by which the federal government
would purchase the slaves from their owners. This announcement did not
meet with a cordial reception. Congress abolished slavery in the District of
Columbia in April 1862. About two months later, on June 19, 1862, it prohibited slavery in all the existing territories of the United States and any
that might be acquired at any time in the future.

   For some time Lincoln had been considering the advisability of
liberating the slaves in the Confederacy as a war measure, through his
authority as commander in chief of the U.S. Army. The battle of Antietam
on September 17 offered the desired opportunity, and on September 22, on
the eve of the 1862 Congressional elections, Lincoln made the announcement that on January 1, 1863, the slaves would be declared free in all parts
of the Confederacy that were still engaged in rebellion. However, rebels
who surrendered in 90 days could keep their slaves. "It is my last card," he
said, "and I will play it and may win the trick."[82]

   The reception of the proclamation was mixed. The regular Republicans, who were not abolitionists but were opposed to slavery, accepted the
proclamation as a necessary expedient for defeating the Confederacy and
a proper objective of the war. The radicals, however, viewed it as a too-
timid effort at abolition for its own sake and were, consequently, impatient
to get along much faster with the business. The regular Democrats denounced it as further evidence that the Republican Party was waging war

not to preserve the Union but to free the slaves. Abroad, the British public hailed the proclamation. Mass meetings all over England congratulated Lincoln on his stand and adopted resolutions of support for the Union. Thereafter the expectations of the South for English intervention began to fade.

The president's foes seized upon the Emancipation Proclamation as proof of Lincoln's hypocrisy:

> Honest old Abe, when the war first began,
> Denied abolition was part of his plan;
> Honest old Abe has since made a decree,
> The war must go on till the slaves are all free.
> As both can't be honest, will someone tell how,
> If honest Abe then, he is honest Abe now?[83]

The Emergence of the Union Party

The first real test of the impact of emancipation on Northern voters came in the state and congressional elections of 1862 and the results were deeply distressing to the administration. Although their supporters retained majorities in Congress, in the House of Representatives the margin was narrow. In that body the Democratic forces increased from 42 to 75 with 6 important states (New York, Pennsylvania, Ohio, Indiana, Illinois, and Wisconsin), which had voted for Lincoln in 1860, shifting to the Democrats. Somewhat ironically, the Democratic gains strengthened the radicals, since many Republican moderates lost their seats in the swing. Also, the Democrats won the governorship in a number of important states, including New York, where Horatio Seymour was elected.[84]

It was evident to Lincoln that to reduce the influence of the radicals in the Republican Party — and to broaden the base of political support for the war and the policies of the administration — it would be necessary to create a new coalition of moderate Republicans and pro-administration Democrats. The name Union Party came into use for this coalition. Republican policies were to be dropped, and a simple program of supporting the war adopted. Slavery was not to be an issue. All differences were to be submerged in the common cause.[85] Henceforth, the president deliberately avoided reference to the Republican Party. Lincoln was, in fact, creating a new party, distinguished in its purpose and personnel from the Republican or any other previous party.

Into the Union Party came many Democrats like Daniel S. Dickinson of New York, Edwin M. Stanton of Pennsylvania, David Todd of Ohio, Andrew Johnson of Tennessee, Ben Butler of Massachusetts, and John A. Logan of Illinois. Those Democrats who still clung to their own party became the political opposition to the administration and the emerging Union Party. Insisting that they were the true unionists, the Democrats refused to accord that term exclusively to Lincoln's supporters, but sought to deter further defections of Democrats in that direction by fastening upon the Lincoln men the opprobrious epithet of "Black Republicans." Radical Republicans for the most part complained bitterly about the new coalition, but they remained reluctantly but necessarily with the coalition.

Meanwhile, in local politics the term "Union" began to replace "Republican." In Ohio a war Democrat was nominated and elected as governor. In other states, such as Pennsylvania, New Jersey, and Delaware, Union tickets were also formed; and even in New England Republicans adopted the Union name.

On December 13, 1862, came the disaster of Fredericksburg. Three days later, the Radical Republican senators met in a secret caucus on Capitol Hill. Their immediate objective was to force the president to dismiss Seward, whom the radicals regarded as a conservative influence. Ultimately, however, they had a far more sweeping goal — to force Lincoln to replace his coalition cabinet with a group of radicals who would then govern the country with Lincoln as a figurehead.

In this the radicals were encouraged by Salmon P. Chase, who always thought of himself as the key man in the administration and who had hopes of succeeding Lincoln in the presidency. In December 1862, when Seward learned of the caucus action, he submitted his resignation but Lincoln would not accept it. He had come to value Seward, and he was aware of Chase's ambitions; also, he did not want to bow to the radicals. Knowing that Chase was conniving with the radicals, the president arranged a showdown meeting between his cabinet and the congressional leaders. Caught in the open between both sides, Chase put on so poor a show that he also wrote out his resignation, which he presented reluctantly to Lincoln. The president now had what he wanted, resignations from both Seward and Chase. He then asked both Seward and Chase to stay and kept his cabinet intact. Once again, Lincoln had beaten the radicals. "Now I can ride," he said. "I have got a pumpkin in each end of my bag."[86]

The Draft Riots. In the spring of 1863 Congress passed a draft law (the first in American history) to aid in the manning of the military forces. Opposition to the law was widespread. The provisions for relief by paying $300 or hiring a substitute were especially offensive to laborers and immigrants who usually could not afford to do either. To working men in the North, the administration in Washington appeared to be uninterested in their problems while it showed profound concern about those of blacks in the South. Lincoln's Emancipation Proclamation of January 1, 1863, seemed to many white laborers in the North less a humanitarian act than an invitation for more and more freed slaves to pour into the cities and compete for jobs.

In several Northern cities this animosity erupted into violence. The worst of these riots broke out in New York City in mid–July 1863 (after the Union victories at Gettysburg and Vicksburg), and for a week the city was at the mercy of a burning, drunken, pillaging mob. Blacks, alleged to be the cause of it all, proved to be the rioters' special target. Many blacks were beaten; some of them were hanged to lamp posts; and even more brutally murdered. At least 72 people died during the violence, which raged out of control for four days.

The Democratic governor of New York, Horatio Seymour, issued proclamations and authorized the arming of the police. At length, federal troops returning from Gettysburg were brought in to quell the riot. Seymour, who had opposed the law anyway, wanted the draft to be suspended until the results of the recruiting of volunteers in New York were known. Since Seymour was well known as a peace Democrat, the Republican press charged that his attitude in the dispute was due to political motives and blamed him and the Democrats for the riots and their bloody consequences.[87]

The Peace Democratic Movement

The peace Democratic movement gained strength rapidly after the Emancipation Proclamation, particularly in the states just north of the Ohio River. The peace Democrats began to gather around the handsome and articulate Clement L. Vallandigham of Ohio, a member of the House of Representatives representing a southwestern Ohio district, who was a vitriolic critic of the war. Vallandigham, an active manager of the Douglas presidential campaign, saw himself as the successor to the mantle of the deceased "Little Giant."

Because of his antiwar activities, Vallandigham was defeated for reelection to Congress in 1862. Then in May 1863 he was arrested because of a "disloyal" speech which he delivered at Mt. Vernon, Ohio. Convicted of treason by a military court, he was sentenced to close confinement for the duration of the war. The Democratic leaders protested the conviction, declaring that Vallandigham stood for free speech and had been arbitrarily condemned. President Lincoln, who was anxious to avoid creating a martyr, instructed the military authorities to send Vallandigham into exile in the Confederate states, subject to the original sentence of imprisonment should he return. Vallandigham soon ran the Union blockade and escaped to Canada. While he was there, the Democrats of Ohio defiantly nominated the exile as their candidate for governor in the Ohio state elections to be held in the fall of 1863. When he came back to Ohio he was unmolested. Even so, the long-lasting effect of Vallandigham's candidacy was to fix suspicion in Northern minds that the peace Democrats toyed with disloyalty.

The activities of the peace Democrats reached a climax in June 1863, when a huge mass meeting in Lincoln's hometown of Springfield, Illinois, adopted resolutions demanding the immediate end of the war that "tends to subvert the Constitution of the Government" and "the restoration of the Union as it was." The meeting was a signal for hundreds of smaller peace gatherings throughout the nation. Soon rumors of traitorous plots by clandestine political societies like the Knights of the Golden Circle, the Order of American Knights, and the Sons of Liberty were rife. Their activities at a time when thousands of men were risking their lives in battle infuriated many Northerners.

These critics of the government and the war were soon being called "Copperheads" by the Republicans. Though they must have known that the Republicans had in mind the poisonous reptile of that name, these Democrats chose to ignore the opprobrious implications of the title "Copperhead" and turned it into a compliment to themselves and a reproof to their enemies by wearing badges made of the copper cent bearing the head of the goddess of liberty.[88]

The Union League of America. In 1862 the Union League of America was organized in Ohio as a counterforce against the antiwar organizations by uniting the influence of all who wished the war pushed to a successful conclusion. In less than a year Union League clubs, long to be important adjuncts of the Republican Party, were in existence in 18 Northern states and had also made extensive inroads into the loyalist areas of the South. The results were eminently satisfactory. In the October 1863 elections war supporters won handily in Pennsylvania and Ohio. In the latter state Vallandigham, the peace Democrat, was swamped, losing to Union candidate John Brough by more than 50,000 votes. Yet more than 185,000 civilians and soldiers voted for Vallandigham. Union victories at Gettysburg and Vicksburg in July 1863 had made his defeat a certainty. In November Union Leaguers triumphed in all Northern states with the exception of New Jersey.

The Thirteenth Amendment. The Emancipation Proclamation did not offer a complete and final solution to the slavery problem. At best, it reached only a small number of the slaves. It did not apply to the border states but only to the states in rebellion. Permanent and complete emancipation could be secured only by the voluntary action of the slaveholding states or by an amendment to the federal Constitution. Meanwhile, public opinion was mobilizing in favor of universal emancipation by constitutional amendment. In January 1864 a resolution for an amendment to the Constitution abolishing slavery throughout the United States was introduced in Congress, sponsored by the radicals. About a year later, in January 1865, it received the requisite two-thirds vote in both houses. It was then sent to the states for their consideration.

Lincoln's 10 Percent Plan. Important steps were taken during the war for reestablishing loyal governments in the South. President Lincoln assumed the initiative in these proceedings. He recognized a loyal government in Virginia which had been contrived in the summer of 1861 to sanction the separation of West Virginia. When Tennessee, Louisiana, and Arkansas passed under Union control in 1862 and 1863, he appointed military governors to take charge until suitable civil governments could be formed. On December 8, 1863, the president issued a proclamation of amnesty which set forth a general policy.

Lincoln's plan excluded from participation in politics all high military and civil officers of the Confederacy or its states. To all other Confederates who would take an oath of loyalty to the Constitution and "solemnly swear . . . [to] abide by . . . all acts of Congress passed during the existing rebellion with reference to slaves . . . and faithfully support all proclamations of the President . . . having reference to slaves," a general amnesty would be granted and any confiscated property other than slaves would be restored. As soon as a number equal to 10 percent of those voting in the 1860 election had taken this oath they could establish a state government and send representatives and senators to the U.S. Congress. Such governments had to be republican in form, must recognize the permanent freedom of blacks, and provide for the education of blacks.

These were the most generous terms toward a helpless opponent ever offered by a victor. This 10 percent plan reflected Lincoln's moderation and lack of vindictiveness, and also his political wisdom. The rebellion must be forgotten, he believed, and every Southern state should be readmitted to full privilege in the Union as quickly as possible. Operating under this plan, three states, Tennessee, Louisiana, and Arkansas, succeeded, during the year 1864, in re-creating state governments and were accorded presidential recognition.

The radicals in Congress disliked the 10 percent plan, partly because of its moderation and partly because many leading Republicans were fearful that the return of the Southern states to the fold would pave the way for the rise of the Democratic Party to power, and they were particularly aggrieved that the president should have taken into his own hands a matter so important. In opposition to Lincoln's conciliatory policy, Thaddeus Stevens, Charles Sumner, and the militant minority of radical Republicans drew up the Wade-Davis Bill, which they rammed through Congress in July 1864, an hour before the session ended (and in the midst of the presidential campaign).

The Wade-Davis Bill would have made readmission extremely difficult. It required a majority of citizens, not just 10 percent, to swear loyalty to the Union before an acceptable state government could be established in a seceding state. The bill also required that new state constitutions in the South must abolish slavery, repudiate state debts, and disenfranchise ex–Confederate leaders. The radical strategists intended by this bill to commit the Republican Party to the radical reconstruction program in the impending presidential and congressional elections.

Lincoln was unable to block the passage of the Wade-Davis Bill, but he did slow down its progress so much that it did not reach him until July 4, 1864, the day of the adjournment of Congress, which enabled him to kill the bill by a pocket veto. He then issued a proclamation declaring that he would neither set aside his own work nor acknowledge the power of Congress over slavery in the states, which infuriated the radicals. To Thaddeus Stevens the proclamation was "infamous." Henry Winter Davis (a coauthor) received word of the fate of the Wade-Davis Bill while he was still at his desk, although the House had adjourned. Shaking with fury, he rose to his feet and delivered an extemporaneous denunciation of Lincoln to the empty chamber.[89]

The Election of 1864

A struggle for power appeared within Republican ranks as Lincoln's first term drew to a close in 1864. A group of New York pessimists, headed by James Gordon Bennett, publisher of the *New York Herald*, who were sure that Lincoln was not reelectable, were boosting General Ulysses S. Grant as a surefire winner. However, when emissaries were sent to Grant to find out if he could be induced to try for the nomination, he was not interested. Some of them backed Salmon Chase, Lincoln's secretary of the treasury, and others favored General Benjamin F. Butler, a Democrat turned Unionist. Chase seemed to have the best chance of success.

For several reasons, Chase was a highly available rallying point for the opponents of Lincoln. To begin with, as secretary of the treasury he had patronage of nearly 15,000 places which he used effectively to build a personal organization. The treasury post also gave him considerable power in financial circles. He had the personal and financial backing of Jay Cooke, a Philadelphia banker and fiscal agent of the treasury in selling government bonds. Also, by arranging for his portrait to appear on the new $1 national bank notes, Chase had placed a "campaign picture in every man's pocket."

In early February 1864 Chase persuaded Senator John Sherman of Ohio to send out under his congressional frank a pamphlet titled "The Next Presidential Election" which savagely denounced Lincoln. In February Chase induced Senator Samuel C. Pomeroy of Kansas to father a new assault on Lincoln known as the "Pomeroy Circular," a confidential letter designed to prevent Lincoln's renomination. It was essential, said the circular, that "friends of the Union of freedom must act." Since Lincoln's reelection was impossible — even undesirable because of his tendency to temporize and compromise—it was obvious that the man cut out for the job was Salmon Chase.[90]

Lincoln, who always thought Chase was "a little insane" on the subject of the presidency, overlooked these breaches of loyalty with his customary magnanimity. When the Ohioan again offered to resign as secretary of the treasury, Lincoln again, to the dismay of both friends and critics, declined to accept Chase's resignation.

The Chase boom rapidly waned after the Unionist members of the Ohio legislature caucused in February 1864 and declared for Lincoln. Ohio's example was followed by other states and in March the secretary of the treasury announced that he was not a candidate.

The Radical Democrats, 1864. Several second-rank radicals (including John C. Fremont, Wendell Phillips, and Benjamin Gratz Brown) were determined to organize against Lincoln, despite Chase's defection. To this end, about 400 assembled in a special convention in Cleveland, Ohio, on May 31, 1864, and there organized a new party which they named the Radical Democracy. This party adopted an extreme antislavery platform which demanded, among other things, that slavery be universally prohibited by a constitutional amendment, that the reconstruction of conquered territory be left entirely to Congress, and rebel lands be confiscated and divided among the Union soldiers. It denounced Lincoln in the most vituperative language and accused him of bringing his country to ruin in order to grab for himself four more years of power.

John C. Fremont was nominated by acclamation for president, and former Tammany Congressman John Cochrane of New York for vice president. Fremont promptly qualified his endorsement of the platform and announced that a spirit of vengeance ought not to prevail in dealing with the South. This statement ruined Fremont's last chance of securing support from the radical leaders in Congress, who had seen a certain nuisance value in the Fremont candidacy.

The Regular Republican (National Union) Convention, 1864. The Regular Republican Convention, called by the national committee chosen by the Republican convention of 1860—but now without mention of the Republican name—met in the border state city of Baltimore on June 7, 1864.[91] Thirty-one states were represented, including the slave states of Arkansas, Florida, Louisiana, Tennessee, South Carolina, and Virginia. No less hospitable site could have been chosen for a Unionist gathering outside the rebel states themselves.

That the convention was convened as a Union convention was made clear by the temporary chairperson in his keynote speech. "I see before me," said he , "not only primitive Republicans and primitive abolitionists, but I see also primitive Democrats, primitive Americans, and primitive Whigs. . . . As a Union Party I will follow you to the ends of the earth and to the gates of death; but as an abolitionist party, as a Republican party, as a Whig party, as a Democratic party, as an American party, I will not follow you one foot."[92]

On June 8 Lincoln was easily renominated on the first ballot: only the radical delegates from Missouri voted against him. They cast 22 votes for General Grant, who had given no one encouragement. Much as they would like to have come out in favor of some other candidate, the radicals were realists who had no intention of ending up on the losing side.

Lincoln did not publicly declare his preference for a vice presidential running mate, leaving the selection to the convention. Andrew Johnson of Tennessee, a well-known war Democrat who had supported Breckinridge in 1860, was nominated on the first ballot, even though Hannibal Hamlin, the incumbent vice president and the choice of the radicals, wanted the nomination. Johnson was a rarity — a Southerner who opposed slavery and supported the North in the Civil War. When Lincoln accepted Johnson as his running mate, Thaddeus Stevens of Pennsylvania, the most powerful Republican in Congress, expressed the view of a good many Northerners: "Can't you get a candidate for Vice President without going down into a damned rebel province for one?"

The platform was approved without debate. The Union Party, "laying aside all differences of political opinion," resolved to support the war and to offer to the Southern states no terms of peace except upon "unconditional surrender of their hostility and a return to their just allegiance." The platform also called for the eradication of slavery by constitutional amendment, endorsed the encouragement of immigration for a new supply of labor, and supported the speedy construction of a transcontinental railroad. After Lincoln had been renominated, Chase, miffed over a trivial patronage difficulty, again offered his resignation, and this time, to the treasury secretary's surprise and chagrin, Lincoln accepted it.[93]

The Democratic Convention, 1864. The Democratic convention convened in Chicago on August 29 with 23 states participating. Although the border states were represented, the territories and seceded Southern states were not. August Belmont, the chair of the Democratic National Committee, had postponed the convention from the beginning of August until the end of the month in the hope that a decisive battle might occur during the interval and give the delegates a fresh clue about public opinion. None was forthcoming, and the convention opened amidst manifestations of bitter discord.

By 1864 most of the Democratic presidential possibilities had run into trouble. As we have seen, Vallandigham had been defeated for reelection to Congress and for election as governor of Ohio. In New York Governor Horatio Seymour had ruined his chances by his participation in the draft riots of July 1863. The Democrats finally turned to the personally popular

Major General George B. McClellan, a war Democrat (the party's only war hero if indeed he was one), who was nominated on the fourth ballot. McClellan had no political experience or record. After graduation from West Point, he had served with distinction in the Mexican War. He was president of the St. Louis and Cincinnati Railroad Company when the Civil War began. He immediately reentered the army, where his work in organizing the Army of the Potomac was recognized as of tremendous value. After the retirement of General Winfield Scott, "Little Mac, the Young Napoleon," as McClellan's supporters dubbed him (and as he liked to be called), was placed in charge of the Union armies. As commander in chief, he won the Battle of Antietam. However, the president had then removed McClellan (he was accused of having the "slows") from his command because of the failure of the operations of 1862 in the eastern theater. Unwittingly, Lincoln himself had given the Democrats their candidate.[94]

George Hunt Pendleton, an Ohio peace Democrat, was selected as the vice presidential candidate as a concession to the peace party. The combination of war hero and a peace platform seemed to be contrived to attract united Democratic support for the ticket in the face of a quarreling, disunited Union Party.

Although the candidate was a war Democrat, the peace faction led by Vallandigham wrote most of the platform, which declared the war a failure and called for an immediate end to hostilities and a negotiated peace which would restore the Union with "the rights of the states unimpaired." They also denounced the Lincoln administration for wholesale disregard of the Constitution, and the abridgment of state and civil rights. The Democratic platform provided Unionist orators with ample ammunition for their thesis that the Democratic Party harbored treasonable elements.[95]

McClellan, in his letter accepting the Democratic nomination, decisively repudiated the peace planks of his own party platform and rejected the statement that the war had been a failure by declaring, "I could not look into the face of my gallant comrades of the army and navy who have survived so many bloody battles and tell them that their labors and the sacrifice of so many of our slain and wounded brethren had been in vain; that we have abandoned the Union for which we have so often periled our lives."[96]

The Radical Democrats, 1864. McClellan's repudiation greatly confused the party position. A group of Western peace Democrats attempted to put another candidate into the field, and at a meeting at Columbus, Ohio, chose Alexander Long, a Cincinnati member of Congress, but he refused to run.[97]

So great was the split in the Republican Party (along with the adverse war news) that Lincoln, in the summer of 1864, was ready to admit defeat in the upcoming November elections. Some of his advisers, including

Thurlow Weed and Henry Raymond, chairman of the Republican National Committee, were urging him to withdraw from the presidential campaign for the good of the party. Even Lincoln seemed to agree. "This morning as for some days past," he confided to his personal diary on August 23, "it seems probable that this Administration will not be reelected." Needless to say, there were many anxious days for the Unionists as the campaign got under way.

The 1864 Campaign. During the 1864 campaign the Democrats damned Lincoln and the Republican Party not only for failure to win the war but for every unpopular thing that had been done during the war — the draft, the income tax, the suspension of the writ of habeas corpus, the high prices, and everything else that stirred the political bile. Democratic papers called the Union candidates "a rail-splitting buffoon and a boorish tailor, both from the backwoods, both growing up in uncouth ignorance."[98] The Democrats cried, "Old Abe removed McClellan, We'll now remove Old Abe." They also sang, "Mac Will Win the Union Back." To the tune of "Dixie" McClellanites sang:

> For rebel traitors we've a halter
> They falsely swore at freedom's altar
> Cheer away, cheer away,
> Cheer away, cheer away,
>
> We've tried all means to keep 'em quiet,
> Shot and shell their only diet,
> Cheer away, cheer away,
> Cheer away, cheer away.

Or to the air of "The Battle Cry of Freedom," they would sing:

> We'll extend the hand of peace,
> That this wicked war may cease,
> Shouting McClellan, boys, and freedom.

Democratic campaign posters, bandannas, banners, and badges featuring General McClellan surrounded by the sheathed sword, and the gun and cannon that were not able to be fired, showed the party emphasis on what the country longed for — peace and unity. Lanterns with McClellan's picture on one side and the slogan "Union and the Constitution" on the other side were carried in torchlight parades — which by 1864 had become a favorite kind of campaign rally.

The Union Party men shouted for "Uncle Abe and Andy," and against "Mac the Unready" and urged, "Vote as you shot." An effective anti-McClellan cartoon showed McClellan restoring slave owners to power in the South, while Lincoln is shown requiring unconditional submission to the government. Lincoln's official campaign button presented his platform "War for the Union." Their most notable slogan was "Don't swap horses in the middle of the river."[99]

In the midst of the presidential campaign Wade and Davis responded to the president's veto of the Wade-Davis Bill with a bitter "manifesto" severely attacking the president, in which they accused him of the "most studied outrage of the legislative authority of the people" ever perpetrated. They also charged him with holding the electoral votes of the rebel states at the "dictation of his personal ambition," and called upon the country to put an end to this executive usurpation (presumably by electing Fremont). Greeley published this Wade-Davis Manifesto in the *New York Tribune* on August 5. Two weeks later he and the radicals began to circulate a call for a new Republican convention to reconsider Lincoln's candidacy. Lincoln, instead of condemning the insurgent Republicans, shrewdly offered conciliation by acknowledging the Wade-Davis plan and agreeing to recognize any state that wished to come in under its provisions.

However, military victories quickly reversed the political situation. On August 23 a federal fleet under Admiral David Farragut captured Mobile Bay, the last open Confederate port, and on September 3 General William Tecumseh Sherman wired Halleck: "So Atlanta is ours, and fairly won." Six weeks later a Union army under Major General Philip H. Sheridan routed the troops of General Jubal Early from the Shenandoah Valley of Virginia. Almost every day in October news of another Union victory appeared in the press. These victories utterly discredited the Democratic Party that had staked its future on the "war is a failure" platform.

The news of Sherman's gift to the Union Party also ruined the radical's plot. They had no interest in causing a Democratic victory — they hated Democrats more than they feared Lincoln. Senator Zachariah Chandler quickly negotiated Fremont's withdrawal. Fremont came out for Lincoln and most of his followers immediately joined the National Unionists and worked hard for the president's reelection. Lincoln helped a little by rewarding the radicals with the amicable removal from the cabinet of the moderate postmaster general, Montgomery Blair of Maryland. Even Wade and Davis went on the stump; but it was reported that Davis did not mention Lincoln's name.[100]

The 1864 Outcome. Election day, November 8, 1864, was cold and wet in the national capital. After the nation's polls closed, President Lincoln went to the telegraph office in the War Department across the street from the White House to await the wires. When they came, they carried news of a decisive victory for the president.

When the final returns were in, Lincoln and Johnson had won 55 percent of the popular vote and an electoral vote of 212 against McClellan's

21. The Democrats carried only three states: Kentucky, Delaware, and New Jersey. Still, Lincoln's popular majority was only 400,000 in approximately 4 million votes. After the election *Harper's Weekly* ran a cartoon showing an extraordinarily tall Lincoln with the caption: "Long Abraham Lincoln a Little Longer."[101]

Lincoln's reelection caused widespread demoralization in the Democratic Party. McClellan's departure for a stay of several years abroad left the party without a titular leader. The only Democrat holding a major national office was Vice President Johnson. But who could be sure how much of a Democrat the Union vice president would continue to be?

Despite the nation's preoccupation with the Civil War, the Republican administration, with the help of Congress, built an impressive record of progressive national legislation.

The Homestead Act, 1862. In 1862 Congress enacted the long-wanted homestead law providing inexpensive land for Western settlers that it had promised.[102] President Lincoln endorsed the Homestead Act "so that every poor man may have a home." In the presidential election of 1860 the Republican Party had rallied support with the cry "vote yourself a farm," and promptly after it took over the government in 1861 it resurrected the Homestead Law that Buchanan had vetoed the previous summer under pressure from the Southern members of Congress, who had opposed such an act because it was not compatible with slavery. The secession of the South now made it possible to pass the law.

Under the Homestead Act of 1862 any person, man or woman, head of a family or 21 years old, and either a citizen or an alien who had declared his intention of becoming a citizen, could enter a claim to 160 acres on the public domain by occupying it for five years and making certain improvements on it. Excluded from this right to free land were all persons who had borne arms against the United States or given aid and comfort to the enemy. The free land was to go to loyal Unionists, including soldiers in the Union army. A soldier in the Confederate army, since he had borne arms against his country, was denied the right of acquiring land under the act.

Because the plains had long been called the Great American Desert, anyone taking up land under the act took a risk. "The Government is willing," said one writer, "to bet the homesteader 160 acres of land that he'll starve to death on it in less than five years." The reality was that unless the "steader" bent the law, he could lose the bet. Even so, thousands thronged to the great plains. Although most found that the best sites had to be purchased from railroads or speculators, "Free Land for the Homeless" was a compelling magnet. Eventually, the Homestead Act earned the Republican Party the gratitude of millions of farmers (and voters).

The Pacific Railway Act, 1862. In 1862 Congress also authorized aid for a Pacific railway in that year's Pacific Railway Act, which chartered the Union Pacific Railroad to build west from the Missouri River and the Central Pacific to build east from Sacramento until the two lines met. Each was given a land grant of five sections to a mile, increased to ten in 1864, and a subsidy in federal bonds of $16,000 a mile in level country, $32,000 in the hilly regions and $48,000 in the Rocky Mountain area. Thus was launched one of the most dramatic races in American history: for each was determined to outbuild the other to win the loans and land grants. On May 10, 1869, when the golden spike was hammered home at Promontory Point, Utah, the whole country celebrated. Within 15 years four twin bands of steel spanned the continent and opened the vast province of the great plains for the march of the frontiersmen.

After 1862 the Western settler could buy a one-quarter section outright from the national government under the terms of the Preemption Act of 1841, or he could purchase his farm from one of the land-grant railroads or from one of the states whose holdings of public domain were enormously increased by the passage of the Morrill Act (1862) which had given every state establishing a public agricultural college 30,000 acres for each senator and representative then in Congress. Lastly, the Western settler could secure his one-quarter section free from charge under the Homestead Act of 1862.

The National Banking Act, 1863. From 1836 to the outbreak of the war, state banks had dominated banking and inundated the country with their paper notes, some sound, some unsound, with others fluctuating wildly in value. To cope with financial disorders and help the sale of bonds, Congress in 1863 enacted the National Banking Act which created the National Banking System. Providing for a policy of nationally chartered banks, it gave the country a more stable bank-note currency based on the national banks' holdings of U.S. bonds. The new national banks chartered under the act were required to invest one-third of their capital in government bonds and to deposit those bonds with the Treasury Department. The bank could then issue bank notes, which would serve as legal tender, up to 90 percent of the face value of the deposited bonds. The scheme was useful to the government, profitable to the banks, and convenient to the public. The next year, in 1864, Congress made provision for forcing all banks chartered by the states entirely out of the currency business by laying a prohibitive annual tax of 10 percent on state bank notes. The system thus created lasted without serious modification until 1913 when the Federal Reserve System was created by Congress.

The Morrill Tariff, 1861. When the Congress came together in December 1861 for its first regular war session, it was faced with a financial crisis. At the outset of the Civil War the federal budget amounted annually to about $70 million, or roughly $150,000 a day. Within a year, however, the war was costing $1.5 million to $3.5 million a day. The Morrill Tariff, which had been passed in March 1861 by the Republicans before hostilities had broken out and signed by President Buchanan two days before he left office, was not producing enough income to prosecute the war. After Lincoln's inauguration Secretary of the Treasury Chase suggested an increase of tariff duties as a war measure to bring in more revenue, and tariff measures enacted in 1862, 1864, and 1865 were frankly protective. By the end of the war the duties averaged 47 percent, the highest thus far in the nation's history, and more than double the prewar rate. The 1865 bill, passed under heavy pressure from the industrial interests, left President Lincoln with many misgivings and he observed that he signed it only on condition that it was to be repealed after the war.

The Greenback Controversy. During the Civil War the Republicans also (probably unintentionally) laid the groundwork for what became one of the most perplexing and complex of the issues which confronted the parties in the post–Civil War era — the "money question." Initially, it centered in a controversy over the issuance of "Greenbacks."

Secretary of the Treasury Chase, who feared the political effects of taxation, initially tried to pay all government obligations in specie, relying for funds on the tariff, short term loans, and treasury notes. This policy, together with hoarding and the repudiation of Southern notes, made money tight, and in December 1861 the government and the banks were forced to suspend specie payment.

As gold and silver became scarce, Congress, in desperation, on February 25, 1862, passed the first Legal Tender Act, which provided for the issue of $450 million in paper money on "the credit of the United States." The new notes were to be legal tender, or lawful money, for the payment of all debts, public and private, except customs duties. The official name of the new notes was United States Notes, but since they were printed on green paper they soon came to be known as "Greenbacks." This paper money had no specie backing and could not be converted directly into either gold or silver. The notes were simply promises of the government to pay at some future date, and their value depended upon the credit of the government (and its ability to win the war).

Since the greenbacks had no gold or silver backing, they fluctuated widely in value. In 1864 a greenback dollar, relative to a gold dollar, was worth only 39 cents, and even at the close of the war its value had advanced to but 67 cents. The existence of the greenbacks also contributed heavily to a severe wartime inflation. In the five years between 1860 and 1865 the general cost of living nearly doubled.

At the same time, borrowing by the government continued to be authorized and a variety of bonds and notes were issued. Eventually, 75 percent of the money needed during the four war years was to be borrowed.

To service the debt and to retire the greenbacks, a tax on incomes was levied for the first time in 1861, when a 3 percent tax was imposed on incomes over $800.[103]

Several extremely complex political problems resulted from the issuance of the greenbacks. Since the unbacked notes fluctuated widely in value as compared with gold, they never reached par, and their fluctuations encouraged speculation. The law permitted the public to buy government bonds with greenbacks which the treasury was required to redeem at maturity in gold dollars, and many speculators bought bonds with greenbacks worth 40 cents to the dollar in gold. They then received interest in gold (thus converting the presumed 6 percent into an actual 15 percent).

The greenbacks were also popular with long-term debtors like farmers, who held few bonds but used them to pay their fixed mortgage obligations. If the greenbacks were retired and the currency restored to a gold value, they would have to pay both the interest and principal of their loans in gold dollars. With the purchasing power of the dollar thus increased commodity prices would fall; the farmer would receive fewer dollars for his products but the number of dollars which he owed the Eastern mortgage holder would not decrease. In consequence, the farmers of the West opposed even gradual retirement. They did not want any deflation; on the contrary, they became convinced that the country needed more rather than fewer greenbacks, and they advocated the retention of the notes as a permanent financial policy.

The greenbacks had been issued as emergency currency and as soon as the Civil War ended the new secretary of the treasury, Hugh McCulloch, who regarded greenbacks with abhorrence, took steps to enable the country to resume specie payments. In April 1866 Congress passed the Contraction Act, which authorized the treasury to withdraw a maximum of $10 million of the greenbacks in the first six months following passage and up to $4 million a month thereafter. Throughout the remaining months of 1866 McCulloch "cremated" greenbacks and substantially reduced the country's currency supply.

On June 30, 1864, when the issuance of greenbacks was terminated by the U.S. Treasury, $432 million was outstanding. By February 1868 the amount in circulation had been reduced to $356 million. The gold value of a greenback dollar was 73 cents. Prices of commodities fell, and evidence of economic dislocations began to appear.

The "Ohio Idea." In the summer of 1867 George H. Pendleton, a prominent Democrat from Ohio, came up with his "Ohio Idea" to pay the Civil War debt in greenbacks rather than in gold. Pendleton's proposal was peculiarly appealing to the debtor farmers of the West (and also to many hard-pressed businessmen of the East) who wanted to avoid paying in gold a debt incurred in greenback values. The "Ohio Idea" was epitomized in the slogan: "The same currency for the bondholder and the ploughholder."

On the other hand, most of the national banks, creditors in general, exporters and importers whose business transactions depended on a stable currency, academic economists, and a large part of the Eastern Republican press were arrayed against the "Ohio Idea" (which they vilified as the "greenback heresy") and the idea of cheap money generally. Charles Dana is, of the *New York Sun*, said: "If we mean to be honest at all, there is no escaping payment in specie. Anything else is repudiation, disguise it as we may." Horace Greeley was even more outspoken when he rejected the "Ohio Idea" in the *New York Tribune* in October 1867: "Should I ever consent to argue the propriety and policy of wholesale swindling, I shall take your proposal into consideration." Thus by the end of the war a strong sentiment had developed in financial circles for the retirement of the greenbacks and for a restoration of the gold standard. However, the protests of the farmers were strong enough to cause Congress to stop further withdrawals of the greenbacks in 1868.[104]

3. The Radical Republicans
Despoilers of American Politics

On March 4, 1865, Abraham Lincoln took the presidential oath and delivered his second inaugural address. With victory certain, Lincoln spoke for tolerance, mercy, and reconstruction. As for the future, he summed up its immediate task in his noble and concluding words: "With malice toward none; with charity for all; with firmness in the right, as God gives us to see the right, let us strive on to finish the work we are in; to bind up the nation's wounds; to care for him who shall have borne the battle, and for his widow, and his orphan — to do all which may achieve a just and lasting peace, among ourselves and with all nations."

On Good Friday, April 14, 1865, just five days after General Robert E. Lee's surrender at Appomattox Courthouse, President Lincoln held a cabinet meeting where he announced that he had decided to lift the blockade of the Confederate ports, the first step in his plan for reconstruction of the South. That night the South's greatest and most powerful Northern friend was shot and mortally wounded as he sat in his box at Ford's Theatre. Herman Melville sensed the future when he wrote:

> They have killed him, the forgiver —
> The Avenger takes his place.

Lincoln's death heartened many radicals. Vice President Johnson had already made it clear that he was not only a firm adherent to the Union but was also a stubborn enemy of the Southern planter aristocracy. "Treason is a crime and must be punished," he had said; "treason must be made infamous, and traitors must be impoverished." When he offered rewards for the arrest of Jefferson Davis and certain other Southern leaders as accomplices in the terrible deed, radical chieftains confidently expected the new president to pursue a vindictive course toward the South. Ben Wade, one of the authors of the Wade-Davis Bill, exulted: "By the gods, there will be no trouble now in running the Government." In their intimate circles

113

Wade, Sumner, Julian, and other radical leaders referred to Lincoln's assassination as a "Godsend to the country." Even the pastor of Saint George's Church in New York City told his congregation, "I do not know but God intended that Lincoln should be removed in order that the proper punishment should be imposed upon the authors of the Rebellion."[1]

Andrew Johnson as President

Three hours and 33 minutes after the death of Lincoln swarthy, strong-visaged, combative Andrew Johnson quietly took the oath of office as the seventeenth president of the United States. Although he had some experience in politics, few men who have reached the presidency have been less prepared for that high office than was Andrew Johnson.

He had entered politics when elected as an alderman of the mountain town of Greenville, in his native state of Tennessee. His east Tennessee neighbors then sent him to the state legislature and then to the national House of Representatives. Later Johnson was elected governor of Tennessee for two successive terms, and in 1857 became a member of the U.S. Senate.

In June 1861, when Tennessee voted to join the Confederacy, Johnson had to flee from the state. He had stubbornly opposed the secession of Tennessee and, alone of the 22 Southern senators, remained in his seat in the Senate when his state left the Union. But after Union forces seized western and central Tennessee in 1862, while still a senator, he was appointed by President Lincoln to be military governor of that state. He became a loyal supporter of the Lincoln administration and, as we have seen, it was largely because of Lincoln's insistence that he became the Union Party candidate for the vice presidency in 1864.[2]

Johnson foolishly kept Lincoln's cabinet intact. He infuriated the radicals by retaining Seward as secretary of state. The radicals had hated Seward from Lincoln's day as a moderate conservative who could destroy their dominance of the Union Party. Stanton stayed on as secretary of war, even though Johnson had been warned repeatedly about his disloyalty. Stanton was soon using his vast influence in the Freedman's Bureau and the army to undermine his chief. Unfortunately for Johnson, he inherited little of Lincoln's personal political following and no party machine responsive to his own directions.

Congress was in recess when the new president took office in mid-April and, to the distress of the radicals, could not convene without the president's call until the following December. By that time, Johnson hoped to have state governments restored throughout the South. On May 29, 1865, he granted a broad amnesty to former Confederates who would take an oath of loyalty to the Constitution and the federal laws. Their property was to be restored to them, except for slaves and any lands and goods that were already being confiscated by federal authorities. Fourteen classes of persons were excepted from the general amnesty, including the highest ranking civil and military officers of the Confederacy, all those who had deserted judicial or seats in Congress to serve the Confederacy, and persons whose taxable property was worth more than $20,000. Those men were to make individual applications for amnesty, which the president promised to judge fairly.

Johnson recognized the governments already established in Virginia, Arkansas, Louisiana, and Tennessee and appointed provisional governors in the other seven states. He authorized the loyal white citizens to draft and ratify new constitutions and to elect state legislatures, which were to repeal ordinances of secession, repudiate the Confederate debt, and ratify the Thirteenth Amendment to the Constitution freeing the slaves.

The radicals were soon fighting mad at Johnson. They thought that he was in agreement with their view that Southern states were conquered territory subject to military rule, to be controlled and reconstructed under policies enacted by Congress and supervised by its committees. However, he had taken action without even consulting with them — an independence which would soon open old wounds. The more radical leaders had suffered much frustration under Lincoln and they were not going to yield to Johnson the influence they had been forced to accord to Lincoln. In particular, the radicals resented Johnson's failure to require enfranchisement of the blacks. Republican agitation for black suffrage was prompted by both idealistic and political motives. Idealists like Senator Charles Sumner regarded the ballot as an inherent human right. However, the least idealistic radical Republicans, like Thaddeus Stevens, saw in the enfranchisement of the blacks a means of preventing the return of the Southern bloc to the control of Congress which it had held before the war. They were determined that the Democratic Party must not regain its sway. Consequently, a Republican Party must be built up in the South to control these states.[3] The radical leaders calculated that the grant of suffrage would enable blacks in combination with white Union men to control the Southern states. Ultimately, they hoped to create a coalition of Northern Republicans and Southern blacks which could control the nation.

As Congress prepared to meet in December 1865, it was confronted by the fact that Reconstruction (on the president's terms) had been virtually completed without Congress having any voice in the matter. The provisional governors had called constitutional conventions, and in every state but Texas the conventions had met, organized governments, accepted the new Thirteenth Amendment abolishing slavery, and elected senators and representatives to Congress.

The first elections that were held showed that, for the most part, the leaders of the Confederacy were still regarded by the voters as the leaders of the South. The newly organized states between them elected to Congress 4 Confederate generals, 5 Confederate colonels, 6 Confederate cabinet officers, and 58 Confederate congressmen. Also, there was Alexander Stephens, former vice president of the Confederacy, still under indictment for treason. The choice of these former Confederates sat poorly with Northern public opinion.

Further, the radicals were well aware that a restored South would be stronger than ever in Congress. Before the war, a slave had counted as 60 percent of a man in apportioning congressional representation. Now, 100 percent of the blacks would count in apportioning representatives. Ironically, the South, although it lost the war, was now entitled to 12 more votes in Congress than it had had before the war. Unless heroic measures were promptly adopted, the radicals perceived that they could easily become an impotent minority.

On December 4, 1865, when Congress assembled, the radicals rushed through a ruling that no congressman-elect from a former state would be allowed to take his seat until there had been a full investigation. A joint (House-Senate) committee of 15 was appointed to investigate—with the vengeful Thaddeus Stevens as its chairman. Eight of these members of this joint committee turned out to be radicals. Two weeks later Stevens, in a speech before the House of Representatives, served notice that Southerners would not be readmitted to Congress until the supremacy of the Republican Party had been assured. Predictably, none of the Southerners were allowed into Congress. Schuyler Colfax, the Speaker of the House, thereupon defined the duty of Congress: "the door of Congress having been shut in the rebel faces, it is still to be kept bolted."

In reality, by turning down the South's new senators and representatives, Congress had rejected both Lincoln's and Johnson's plan for reconstruction. Many Southerners expressed their defiance of Congress, the president, and the Union with the song:

> I'm glad I fought against her,
> I only wish we'd won;
> And I ain't asked any pardon
> For anything I've done;
> And I don't want no pardon for what
> I was or am;
> I won't be reconstructed and
> I don't give a damn.

The Black Codes. The radicals soon had another reason for discontent. In the fall and winter of 1865 the Southern legislatures began to enact "Black Codes" which denied to the Southern blacks many of the rights of citizenship

—including the right to vote and to serve on juries—and also excluded them from certain types of property ownership and certain occupations. Such laws, apparently designed to get around the Thirteenth Amendment, excited great opposition in the North and were attacked there as attempts to restore slavery under another name. Northern newspapers, such as the *Chicago Tribune*, denounced the black codes and proposed that "we tell the white men of Mississippi that the men of the North will convert the state of Mississippi into a frog pond before they will allow any such laws to disgrace one foot of soil in which the bones of our soldiers sleep and over which the flag of freedom waves."[4]

The Freedman's Bureau. On March 3, 1865, Congress with Lincoln's approval created the Freedman's Bureau under the War Department to perform humanitarian work among the blacks. However, the Freedman's Bureau quickly became engaged in numerous political activities. The most significant of these came to be the organization of an extension of the Union League. These Southern branches, known as Loyal Leagues, engaged in extensive efforts to enlist black membership to work toward black suffrage. So the Freedman's Bureau commissioners early became political organizers devoted to the creation of a Republican Party in the South.[5]

In February 1866 Congress passed a bill expanding and extending the Freedman's Bureau indefinitely. A part of the purpose of the 1866 act was to give the bureau authority to bring before military courts Southerners violating the civil rights of the blacks.

President Johnson vetoed the Freedman's Bureau extension bill on the grounds that to continue the agency in peacetime would be to invade the right of Southern states to supervise their own internal affairs. In a rambling speech defending the veto on Washington's birthday, 1866, Johnson denounced Stevens and other radicals as traitors, accused them of seeking to enslave the white South, and suggested that they wanted to kill him. This performance opened a wide breach between him and the radicals and increased their influence in Congress. In the House the president's veto was quickly and overwhelmingly overridden.

In the Senate, despite the fact that it had originally passed the bureau extension bill by more than a two-thirds margin, five Unionist senators reversed themselves and three who had been absent for the first roll call also supported the president, with the result that the veto was sustained 30–17, thus barely defeating the measure. This was Johnson's last victory over Congress. From this point on, Johnson's messages to the House were laid aside unread, and members jeered whenever his name was mentioned.[6]

The Civil Rights Act of 1866. On April 9, 1866, Congress again struck at the Black Codes by passing a civil rights act which empowered the federal government to intervene in state affairs when necessary to protect the rights of citizens. It was enacted without a single Democratic vote.

Undoubtedly, part of the motivation for the measure was a humanitarian concern for the rights of blacks after the termination of the military occupation. However, another part of the motivation was concern for the protection of the white man in the North.

When the bill was presented to President Johnson he vetoed it, even though he had expressed no objections to the measure during its course through Congress. Now even the Republican moderates in Congress, who had formerly opposed many radical measures, realized that they had to present a united congressional front in order to protect their prerogatives against the president. With moderates and radicals acting together, the Senate promptly overrode the veto by an overwhelming majority. The House did not even bother to debate the veto but overrode it the same day. It was evident that Johnson's inflexible stubbornness had alienated congressional leaders and had driven most of the moderates into the ranks of the radicals.

The Fourteenth Amendment. As the quarrel with Johnson intensified, the radical Republican leaders grew more insistent in their demands for the political proscription of the ex-Confederates. In April 1866 the Joint Committee on Reconstruction proposed the Fourteenth Amendment to the U.S. Constitution. In section one of the proposed amendment citizenship was conferred on every person born or naturalized in the United States (to override the Dred Scott decision). Section two left the matter of suffrage with the states, because its framers feared that a direct enactment by the federal government extending the vote to blacks would lead to an adverse reaction in the North. However, under the amendment, states which deprived blacks of the right to vote were to suffer a reduction of representation in Congress.

Also, under the amendment anyone was barred from holding national and state offices who had previously taken an oath to support the Constitution of the United States and then had "engaged in insurrection or rebellion against the same, or given aid or comfort to the enemies thereof." Since nearly every Southern official of pre-Civil War days had taken oaths to support the Constitution, this clause effectively eliminated all those prewar leaders from an active role in political life. Even so, the provisions were not as harsh as many Republican radicals had wished.

In June 1866, when the Fourteenth Amendment was sent to the states for ratification, Johnson advised the Southern states to reject the amendment.[7] However, on July 19 Tennessee, under radical control, ratified the amendment, and the radicals in Congress rushed an admission resolution through the House admitting Tennessee back into the Union. The impression was deliberately left that other Southern states would receive identical treatment when they ratified. In July 1866 the radicals passed the Freedman's Bureau Bill over a second presidential veto and admitted the congressmen and senators from Tennessee only. Congress had served notice that it intended to control Reconstruction. Victory in the struggle between the president and Congress appeared to turn on the election of a new Congress in the fall of 1866.

The National Union Convention, 1866. To strengthen congressional support for the president's lenient Reconstruction program and to elect a Congress that would quickly admit their Southern brethren, the Democratic friends of Johnson organized an unprecedented midterm national convention at Philadelphia in August 1866 on the eve of the congressional election campaigns in the North. The delegates included a large number of the war Democrats who, like Johnson, had joined the Union Party. Although great pains were taken to exclude conspicuous Copperhead Democrats (particularly Clement Vallandigham and Fernando Wood), they were there anyway. Several former Confederates responded to the call and participated fully. Only a few leading Republicans attended and the Johnson leaders had difficulty keeping the convention from becoming a purely Democratic rally. The "arm in arm" convention (so-called because Governor Orr of South Carolina walked down the aisle with Governor Couch of Massachusetts) acclaimed the statesmanship of Johnson, demanded the restoration of Southern representation in Congress, and appealed to the country to elect congressmen who would support the president. The radicals denounced the convention with the charges of rebellion and Copperheadism.

The Congressional Elections of 1866. The congressional elections of 1866 caught the voters in the widening rift between president and Congress. Election of Johnson's supporters, the radicals said, meant rejection of the Fourteenth Amendment, the repudiation of the national debt, and the assumption of the Confederate debt. Roscoe Conkling put the issue succinctly: "Do you want to give up your interest once more to this alliance with the two-fifths added to the old slave power?" The campaign of 1866 was vicious and bitter, with riots in many Southern cities.

Between August 28 and September 15 President Johnson, accompanied by secretaries Seward and Welles, General Grant (reluctantly), and Admiral Farragut, made an unprecedented "swing around the circle" — a grassroots campaign tour of the country — in support of numerous Democrats that would support his program. In his speeches the president denounced the Republicans in intemperate, often irrational language, frequently taunting the Republicans for demanding that blacks be permitted to vote in the South while denying them suffrage in Northern states. Unfortunately, when hecklers planted in the crowds by the radicals made him angry, he shouted back angry retorts, making a fool of himself personally and demeaning his high office.

The radicals were quick to turn the president's indiscretions to their advantage. They spread reports that Johnson was habitually drunk and had "sunk the Presidential office to the level of the grog house," an appeal which had a powerful influence with temperance forces. Thomas Nast, the cartoonist, and David Ross Locke, writing dime tracts under the pseudonym of Petroleum V. Nasby, did their best to make the president appear ridiculous.

The Grand Army of the Republic. To help the radical cause, the Union army veterans formed the Grand Army of the Republic (GAR), an organization which was to play a peculiar role in American politics. For decades, the GAR worked closely with the Republican Party and the devotion of 1 million discharged Union soldiers to the party under whose banner they marched to victory was reinforced by generous pensions and land grants. In November 1866 the GAR held its first national encampment in Indianapolis. The radicals made a big play for the soldier vote by reviling the Democratic Party as the standard-bearer of rebellion, repression of the blacks, and financial repudiation.

The 1866 Outcome. The election of 1866 was a triumph for the president's enemies. In most congressional districts in the North voters had to choose between a radical Republican and a Copperhead Democrat. Faced with this prospect, many moderate Republicans went over to the radical camp. When it was over, Johnson could count on the support of less than one-third of both House and Senate. The radicals and their allies now had the necessary two-thirds majority in both houses to allow them to pass any legislation they proposed over a presidential veto. Radical legislatures were also elected in most Northern states, which in turn forced the retirement of several moderates from the Senate.

The First Reconstruction Act, 1867. The radicals, acclaiming the results of the fall elections as a vindication of their "thorough" policy toward the South, launched their own program. On March 2, 1867, the Thirty-Ninth Congress passed the First Reconstruction Act "to provide for the more efficient Government of the Rebel States." This act stripped the white Southerners of the power Johnson had given them. The rebel states (except Tennessee, which had been readmitted to the Union) were grouped into five military districts, each to be commanded by a Union general and policed by blue-coated soldiers. It further provided that senators and representatives would be admitted to Congress when the states had framed constitutions acceptable to Congress and had ratified the Fourteenth Amendment; but blacks must be allowed to vote not only in electing delegates to the constitutional conventions and in ratifying the work of those conventions but permanently under the terms of the new constitutions. Former Confederate leaders were disqualified from voting. Johnson's veto, expected, condemned the bill as "utterly destructive" to the "principles of liberty," but his veto was promptly overridden. The insolence of the radicals aroused all Johnson's qualities of combativeness and dogmatism. He became increasingly bitter, stubborn, and relentless.

Then in June 1867 Congress authorized the readmission of seven of the reconstructed states to the Union on the "fundamental condition" that they ratify the Fourteenth Amendment and that they never change their constitutions to exclude blacks from the ballot. Arkansas was admitted first on June 22 and North Carolina, South Carolina, Louisiana, Georgia, Alabama, and Florida were brought in by the Omnibus Bill of June 25. An important reason for hurrying action in the case of the seven had been the radical desire to secure their electoral support in the impending presidential election.

During the last half of 1867 most of the remaining Southern states wrote acceptable constitutions under military supervision, called their new legislatures into session, and ratified the Fourteenth Amendment. All except three were readmitted to the Union in 1868 — Virginia and Texas, which had not yet finished adopting constitutions; and Mississippi, which had rejected the Fourteenth Amendment, and thus continued under military rule. It was 1870 before those three states won congressional approval of their constitutions and were permitted to reenter Congress. Georgia, admitted in 1868, then cast out again when its new legislature dismissed duly elected black delegates, was readmitted in 1870. Under the rules laid down by Congress, the army carried out a new registration of the voters in the recalcitrant states. When the radicals got through rearranging the voting lists, only about 627,000 whites in the South had the right to vote. In five states they were outnumbered by the votes of their former slaves.[8]

The Impeachment of President Johnson

The Congressional leaders next moved to secure the presidency by removing President Johnson from office by impeachment and replacing him with Ben Wade of Ohio, the vulgar and vituperative president pro tempore of the Senate. The plan was almost foolproof since the Republicans possessed the two-thirds majority necessary to convict in an impeachment proceeding.

To lay the basis for impeachment, the radicals secured the passage of the Tenure of Office Act early in 1867, requiring the consent of the Senate for presidential removals as well as appointments. The act was specifically designed to guard against the removal of Secretary of War Stanton, who was in league with the radicals, and like-minded independents. Convinced that the Tenure Act was an unconstitutional invasion of executive powers,[9] Johnson ordered Stanton to resign and appointed General Grant as temporary secretary of war while Congress was in the 1867 summer recess.

When Congress reconvened, the Senate refused to consent to Stanton's removal, whereupon Grant relinquished the office back to Stanton, protesting that he had never agreed to join the president in breaking the law. Grant's critics suggested that it was more likely that the "old hero" had done so after a hint from the radicals that he might himself become a presidential candidate — a conclusion which was probably correct. From that moment, General Grant, who had almost sullenly stayed out of politics, became the conspicuous favorite of Republican leaders for the presidential nomination in 1868.[10]

On February 28, 1868, the House voted to impeach the president for "high crimes and misdemeanors" by a vote of 126–47, with all "yeas" cast by Republicans. Eleven articles of impeachment were drawn, ten centering upon Stanton's removal. The tenth article charged that Johnson had attempted to bring "ridicule and contempt" upon the Congress. The remaining article, drawn up by Thaddeus Stevens, charged, among other things, that Johnson used unseemly language and spoke in a loud voice.[11] Johnson exploded when he heard the charges against him.

Seven of the most restive radicals were chosen by the House to present the case for conviction to the Senate: Thaddeus Stevens, Ben Butler, John Logan, John A. Bingham of Ohio, George S, Boutwell of Massachusetts, Thomas Williams of Pennsylvania, and James F. Wilson of Iowa. Since Stevens was in ill health, Butler assumed the actual though not official leadership.[12] Chief Justice Chase presided.

The two-month-long trial of Johnson aroused intense public interest throughout the North. Popular sentiment was against Johnson. Even the Annual General Conference of the Methodist church, then in session at Chicago, set aside an hour of prayer that the senators might be directed to do their "high duty."[13] Johnson, fortunately, kept his dignity and sobriety, and maintained a discreet silence.

Despite the use of political pressure by the radicals, when the critical test vote was taken on May 16, the Senate stood at 35–19 for conviction. The radicals had failed by one vote to secure the two-thirds majority of the Senate required for conviction. Seven Republicans voted for acquittal. The proceedings, they had concluded, properly dealt with a criminal case, and they decided that Johnson had committed no crime. The radicals were infuriated. "The country is going to the Devil" cried Stevens as he was carried from the hall. Undaunted, Stevens drafted new impeachment articles from his deathbed.[14]

Saved from impeachment by a single vote, Johnson had no further influence over Reconstruction policy. He retired to private life in 1869. Six years later he made a political comeback: he was elected a senator from Tennessee as an independent, but died before the end of his first year in office.

The Election of 1868

The Republican Convention. The Republican (or Republican National Union) Party convened its first postwar convention in Chicago on May 20, 1868, in the midst of the impeachment proceedings against President Johnson. All the states — North and South — were present except Texas. A dozen or more blacks were present among the delegations of the old Confederacy. The delegates had no difficulty in finding their candidate — squat, firm-mouthed, and stubbily bearded General Ulysses Simpson Grant, the "Hero Who Saved the Union."

From the day of Lee's surrender at Appomattox, Grant had been the most popular person in the North. After a lifetime of failure, he had suddenly become a roaring success. Admiring Unionists showered him with swords, horses, libraries, and testimonial dinners. The citizens of Philadelphia, Washington, and his hometown of Galena, Illinois, each presented him with a house. New Yorkers tendered him a check for $105,000, universities awarded him honorary degrees, and the press reported his activities with worshipful enthusiasm. Congress accorded him the greatest honor, when they made him a full general — the first since George Washington.[15]

Before the Civil War Grant had exhibited little interest in politics. In 1865 he had voted for Buchanan because, as he explained, "he knew Fremont." He is believed not to have voted in 1860 (although, ironically, he apparently favored Douglas) and to have voted the Union ticket of Lincoln and Johnson in 1864. Under the circumstances, there was nothing inconsistent in the Democrats considering Grant their logical candidate for 1868. Early in 1866 New York Democratic leaders quietly launched a Grant for president movement. However, as we have seen, Grant had joined hands with the radicals in their misunderstanding with President Johnson over Stanton's removal from office, and the radicals in turn, although they preferred Wade, were ready to "let him into the church" because he appeared to be more electable. However, when the radicals tried to pin the general down on where he stood on public issues, they had no success. After an interview with Grant, Ben Wade reported in disgust: "As soon as I'd talk politics, he'd talk horses."[16]

The most troublesome responsibility of the convention was the drafting of a platform for what it referred to as the "National Union Republican Party," as if the new party was the result of an analgamation rather than a contraction since the days of the war. The radical congressional reconstruction policy was commended and President Johnson, "who had acted treacherously to the people who elected him and the cause he was pledged to support," was denounced as deserving of impeachment. The platform tiptoed around the issue of equal suffrage (black suffrage was generally unpopular in the North) by guaranteeing equal suffrage in the South but making it optional in the "loyal states" of the North.[17] The monetary plank was even more ambiguous. It denounced repudiation and declared for the payment of the national debt in "the spirit of the laws" under which it had been contracted, which meant in gold instead of greenbacks. Unable to reconcile differences between high-tariff Northerners and low-tariff Westerners, the delegates allowed the platform to remain silent on the subject, although the Republican Party had tacitly given their promise to "do something about the tariff." The Republicans apparently meant to make Reconstruction the big issue, while subordinating economic questions that might divide the party.

With the platform out of the way, Grant received the unanimous vote of the 650 delegates present on the first presidential nominating ballot. As white doves were released in the convention hall, the bunting at the back of the stage was dramatically parted, unveiling a huge Thomas Nast drawing of General Grant as a boastful scoff at the Democrats: "Match Him!"[18]

Grant declined to express a preference for the vice presidential slot. Ben Wade, "robbed" of the presidency by one Senate vote and defeated for reelection to the Senate in 1867 by the new Democratic legislature in Ohio, wanted the place. Senators Reuben E. Fenton of New York, Henry Wilson of Massachusetts, and the amiable but undistinguished Radical Republican Speaker of the House, Schuyler Colfax of Indiana (always known to his friends as "Smiley"), were also in hot pursuit. In all, 11 candidates received votes on the first roll call. Wade led for four ballots, but on the fifth Pennsylvania threw a sizable block of voters to Colfax and other delegations moved quickly on to the Colfax bandwagon. The choice of Colfax was made unanimous after the result of the sixth ballot was announced.

On May 29 Grant wrote his letter of acceptance. In it he endorsed the platform and announced as his aims economy in administration and the restoration of nationwide tranquility and prosperity. His concluding words, "Let us have peace," struck a popular chord and did much to enhance his chances for election.

The Democratic Convention. In 1868 the Democrats were thoroughly demoralized. They had yet to rid their party of the taint of disloyalty and they had no leaders capable of replacing their prewar spokesmen. In an effort to revive their reputation for patriotism, they called their convention to order on July 4 in New York City, in the newly constructed Tammany Hall, six weeks after the Republican convention which nominated Grant. This convention was the first national convention since 1860 in which all states were represented.

The platform, which was adopted before nominations were allowed, was carried on a voice vote without debate. It began by declaring that the questions of slavery and secession had been settled "for all time" by the Civil

War. It pledged "the immediate restoration of all the states to their rights in the Union" and called for "amnesty for all past political offenses." The platform did not mention black suffrage, being content to dispose of the subject by stating that suffrage was purely a state question; it called for a tariff that would primarily raise revenue but also protect American industry; and called for an increase in the volume of notes in circulation and for the payment of both principal and interest of the bond issues with these "greenbacks," the first time the question of the coinage and printing of money was discussed in a party platform. Other sections of the platform denounced the radicals for their "unparalleled oppression and tyranny," declared the Reconstruction acts "unconstitutional, revolutionary, and void," expressed support for President Johnson who was "entitled to the gratitude of the whole American people," and decried the attempts to impeach him. The Democratic platform opened the party to the charge that it was soft on the South.

In spite of the fact that prospects for success were slim in the coming campaign, the struggle for the Democratic Party nomination was bitter and long. Among those who desired the nomination for president was President Johnson himself. He had a few delegates, mostly Southerners. However, the leaders of the party regarded him as a potential liability. In addition, most of them sensed that the president cared less about the office than about receiving a vindication. In any case, the progress of other candidates during the impeachment trial had so committed the party leaders that the president had little chance.[19]

"Gentleman George" H. Pendleton of Ohio, McClellan's running mate in 1864, was the leading aspirant. The 43-year-old Pendleton was gaining a following in the economically depressed Midwest because of his "Ohio Idea." However, because of his soft-money views, he had little appeal in the Eastern states. Another serious obstacle to Pendleton's nomination was the fact that his greatest strength lay for the most part in states which the Democrats could not hope to carry with any candidate, and his candidacy would weaken the party in those states where success was possible. Also, Clement Vallandigham, who was also from Ohio, was hostile to Pendleton's nomination.

Chief Justice Salmon Chase, the old Democrat who had served in Lincoln's cabinet, also wanted the nomination and he had powerful support from opponents of radical reconstruction and military rule. Chase's impartiality in presiding at the impeachment trial of President Johnson had enhanced Democratic opinion of him. However, his support of black suffrage was a serious barrier.

After 22 ballots it was clear that the convention had stalemated, and a compromise was sought. A Pendleton-Vallandigham truce in the Ohio delegation gave all that state's vote, in a surprising maneuver, to Horatio

Seymour, a "sound-money" man, whose name was not even mentioned in the first 21 ballots. Seymour declined to be a candidate and so informed the convention, but Ohio refused to change its vote. New York then changed its votes to Seymour and the bandwagon began to roll. When the vote switches were completed Seymour, despite his sincere protests, was the unanimous nominee.[20]

The Democratic candidate had played a prominent role in New York politics since 1841, when he was elected as a Democrat to the state assembly. In 1862 he was elected governor. As war governor, he had been a bitter and outspoken critic of President Lincoln. He had openly denounced the Emancipation Proclamation, and his handling of the draft riots during the war had made him popular with Southern whites but also made him a standing target for the radicals. Unlike Grant, Seymour had won no military laurels.

The convention then nominated General Francis P. Blair, Jr., from Missouri, a staunch Unionist (who gladly accepted the honor), as the vice presidential candidate. Blair added little allure to the ticket. In his letter accepting the nomination, Seymour repudiated the soft-money plank in the platform. The Democrats were thus faced with the problem of electing a hard-money candidate on a soft-money platform.

The Campaign of 1868. The ensuing campaign was spirited. Republicans whipped up enthusiasm for Grant, "The Man Who Saved the Nation." (When they thought Grant was a Democrat they called him "Grant the Butcher.") However, during the greater part of the campaign Grant refused to speak or release statements on the issues, remaining in semi-seclusion at his home in Galena. A Democratic pamphlet entitled "The Lively Life of U.S. Grant, the Dummy Candidate," suggested that Grant "has nothing to say and keeps on saying it day in and day out." The *New York World* concluded that the Republicans had a "deaf and dumb candidate when the country couldn't afford a deaf and dumb President."[21]

Grant did make a few trips to scenes of his prewar life in Ohio, Illinois, Missouri, and Kentucky, and in company with generals Sherman and Sheridan to Denver. The union of these three heroes of the war was made the subject of much ecstatic oratory by the party workers. Grant's supporters formed clubs called "Tanners" (Grant had once been a tanner) to make sure that the Democrats were "tanned" in the best Appomattox fashion. Rallies of Union veterans, known as Boys in Blue, were organized, at which Republican orators "waved the bloody shirt,"[22] picturing themselves as the party that had saved the Union and the Democrats as the party of rebellion. The Democratic Party had forfeited all rights to govern the nation by its dubious war record, they said. "Scratch a Democrat," cried the *New York Tribune*, "and you'll find a rebel under his skin."[23] Indiana Senator Oliver Morton, in the apogee of "bloody shirt" rhetoric, described the Democratic Party as "a common sewer and loathsome receptable into which is emptied every element of reason North and South, and every element of inhumanity and barbarism which had dishonored the age." Congressman Bingham of Ohio put it more simply: "I do not wish to sit side by side with men whose garments smell of the blood of my kindred." As we shall see, the bloody shirt proved to be the most effective political issue until nearly the turn of the century.

To attract the Eastern business vote Republican orators denounced the "Ohio Idea," pleading that redemption of war bonds in anything but gold smacked of repudiation of a sacred debt that had been contracted to preserve the Union. At the same time they promised business that when the time came all bondholders would be paid in gold. The official campaign button pictured Grant and Colfax on a shield of flags and eagles with the inscriptions "The Will of the People Is the Law of the Land" and "Loyalty Shall Govern What Loyalty Has Preserved."

The Republicans enjoyed the support of the Union veterans (the GAR by now was being referred to as "Generally All Republicans"), the multitude of officeholders, and of the carpetbag governments in the South. Also, many influential journals backed Grant. *Leslie's Weekly* referred to Seymour alliteratively as a "poor, paltering, politician," while *Harper's Weekly* considered him "the obsequious servant of the only aristocratic class in the country," apparently referring to his friendships among the New York bankers.[24]

Seymour did not take an active public part in the campaign until near the end. He felt that the dignity of a presidential candidate precluded him from actively campaigning on his own behalf. However, in letters to friends he identified himself as a hard-money man, although he did not repudiate the greenback plank. President Johnson, although not favorably disposed toward Seymour, eventually endorsed his candidacy but made no speeches on behalf of the ticket. Pendleton endorsed the ticket and pronounced Seymour the foremost statesman of the day. Vallandigham played a minor role in the campaign.[25]

The choice of Blair as Seymour's running mate proved to be unfortunate. His political speeches were frequently misconstrued to mean that he favored the overthrow of the new Southern state governments. The Republicans were also able to make a major issue of a letter Blair had written shortly before the convention in which he said that the president should refuse to enforce the unconstitutional Reconstruction acts and should "compel the army to undo its usurpations at the South."[26] It argued that the next president elect should disperse the carpetbag state governments and allow the white Southerners to organize their own governments. The Blair letter enabled the Republicans to hammer on the idea that Blair was a revolutionary, while Grant favored peace.[27]

The 1868 Outcome. Grant was elected but not by a convincing margin—only slightly more than 300,000 out of a total of 5,715,000. The electoral college divided 214 for Grant and Colfax and 80 for Seymour and Blair. The margin of victory was provided by the Union League clubs which helped deliver the vote of about 700,000 blacks who had been given the ballot in the seven reconstructed Southern states. The Republicans carried every New England state and all states in the Northwest central region, which now included Nebraska. The Midwestern farmers had stayed in the Republican Party. Democratic appeals for "the same currency for the bond-holder and the ploughholder" had gone over their heads. With blacks voting for the first time, the party was able to carry West Virginia and the Carolinas. In the border states of Missouri, West Virginia, and Tennessee the disenfranchisement of many Democrats gave Grant a narrow victory.[28] In Texas, Mississippi, and Virginia, which were still "unreconstructed," no elections were held.

The Democrats carried several states. In Maryland and Delaware the blacks did not vote and both states went into the Democratic column. New York, home of the Democratic candidate, also went to the Democrats; the first time since 1852 that the empire state had yielded a Democratic major-ity. In the solid South, the Democrats managed to carry Georgia and Loui-siana. Charges, "probably true," immediately flew that the victory in Georgia was mainly due to intimidation of the black Republican vote by the Ku Klux Klan.[29]

The Issue of Black Suffrage. The election of 1868 marked the beginning of the extremely complex and highly explosive issue of black suffrage, a problem faced in both the North and the South. In 1865 blacks had been permitted to vote in all the New England states except Connecticut and under a special tax qualification ($250 freehold) in New York. In the next three years blacks were granted the vote in Nebraska, Iowa, Minnesota, and Wisconsin: Minnesota and Iowa had only a handful of blacks; Nebraska entered the Union with black suffrage as a congressional require-ment; and Wisconsin obtained black suffrage by decision of her Supreme Court. During this period efforts in some Northern states to give blacks the ballot were defeated: in 1865 Connecticut, Minnesota, Wisconsin, and Col-orado Territory had voted the proposal down; in 1867 Ohio and Kansas— and Minnesota by a reduced majority—rejected black suffrage; in New Jersey it was thrust aside as an issue in a legislative campaign; but in 1868 the advocates of black suffrage carried Iowa, Minnesota, and Wisconsin, but lost in Missouri and Michigan. So by the end of 1868 ten Northern states had admitted blacks to the franchise.

The Fifteenth Amendment. The implications of the election returns were abundantly clear. The part the blacks played in winning the election—or rather the fact that blacks in certain states like Louisiana and

Georgia had been prevented from casting their votes—prompted the radicals to strengthen the Fourteenth Amendment's provisions protecting the right of the blacks to vote. When Congress convened early in 1869, it promptly proceeded to erect the last constitutional pillar of Reconstruction, the Fifteenth Amendment. This amendment was sent to the states in February 1869 and was declared ratified in March 1870, while Union troops were still stationed in most Southern states. Most of the reformers convinced themselves that their long campaign on behalf of the blacks at last was over, that with the vote they should be able to take care of themselves.

However, the Fifteenth Amendment was not as effective in ensuring the right to vote to blacks as many radicals had hoped. It did not *give* the votes to blacks, but merely prohibited states from denying it on the basis of color. This loophole allowed Southern states later to exclude blacks without appearing to do so because of race. After the adoption of the Fifteenth Amendment in 1870 they simply turned it into a dead letter by establishing poll taxes, rigging educational tests, and using other underhanded devices, unfairly administered by whites for the benefit of whites.

The Politics of Terrorism

The election of 1868 also marked the emergence of widespread terrorism as a political force in the South. To discourage black voting, thousands of Southern whites banded together in terrorist organizations like the Ku Klux Klan, the Knights of the White Camelia, the White Brotherhood, the Pale Faces, and the '76 Association.

The Ku Klux Klan. The most effective and notorious of these terrorist organizations was the Ku Klux Klan. The Klan started in 1866 at the little town of Pulaski in southern Tennessee as a social club for returned Confederate veterans who, just for fun, rode about the countryside after dark dressed in white robes and hoods on white-sheeted horses visiting cabins of "uppity" blacks and white members of Loyal Leagues. The "Pulaski Idea" spread like wildfire and in April 1867 a secret gathering at Nashville combined the units or "dens" under the name of the "Invisible Empire of the South."

In 1868 the Klan opened a campaign of intimidation on a broad front. Fright was usually enough to persuade the blacks to desist from political activities. However, when fright and threats failed, the Klansmen resorted to violence: beating and murdering blacks who refused to be intimidated. A congressional investigating committee reported that in Louisiana alone just before the election of 1868 close to 2,000 people had been killed or wounded. The blacks soon learned to stay home on election day. In state after state "white supremacy" was reestablished as the Democrats took over Southern state governments.

Angry Northern radicals struck at the Klan by passing two so-called Force Acts, the Enforcement Act of May 30, 1870, and the Second Enforcement Act and the Ku Klux Klan Act of 1871. Together, the acts provided that the use of force or intimidation to prevent citizens from voting was to be punished by fine or imprisonment. The Enforcement Acts authorized the president to suspend the writ of habeas corpus in order to deal with the violence that regularly erupted at elections. The federal courts, rather than the Southern state courts, were given exclusive jurisdiction in all suffrage cases. The Force Acts were not popular in either the North or the South — the practice of using soldiers to supervise elections was too abhorrent to many people on both sides of the Mason-Dixon line. Moreover, since most of the federal judges in the South were white, few of the 7,300 persons indicted under the Force Acts were convicted. The Ku Klux Klan Act empowered the president to end the societies with armed force if necessary.

In the summer of 1871 President Grant sent federal troops into the South to areas where the Klan was strong. After scores of arrests, fines, and imprisonments, the Klan's power was finally broken, and "Ku Kluxing" had almost disappeared by early 1872. By then, however, the resourceful whites had learned they could frighten blacks away from the polls by the mere threat of maltreatment.[30]

President Grant in Office

The 47-year-old General Ulysses S. Grant took the oath of office on a chilly March 4, 1869. His brief inaugural address was disappointing. "The responsibilities of the position I feel," he said, "but accept them without fear." About the only near controversial thing he said was that he would pay all government obligations in gold.[31]

For the most part, Grant's cabinet was a hodgepodge of mediocrities. To head the Treasury Department, Grant asked Alexander T. Stewart, a New York merchant prince who ranked third among America's richest men. Soon, however, an old statute came to light forbidding the choice of a businessman for this responsible post, and Grant was forced to withdraw the nomination. Stewart was replaced with George S. Boutwell, a Massachusetts politician with no special fitness for the office. Adolph E. Bories, a wealthy Philadelphia financier who had contributed generously to the Republican campaign chest, was designated secretary of the navy.

There were, however, some excellent appointments. The State Department was given to Hamilton Fish, a talented and conscientious New Yorker who had been a one-term congressman, governor, and senator. Fish served through eight stormy years and brought real distinction to the State Department. Two other excellent appointments were Jacob D. Cox in the Department of Interior and Ebenezer Rockwood Hoar as attorney general, both of whom resigned in a little over a year and were replaced by more pliant souls. Zachariah Chandler, a heavy-drinking, big-bellied man with an imposing fringe of whiskers and a weakness for flashy clothes, diamond rings, and stickpins, replaced Cox.[32]

Grant was singularly unprepared for the presidency and soon fell under the sway of the surviving radicals—who were now generally known as Stalwarts. In the Senate Oliver P. Morton of Indiana became the administration's floor leader. Also there to help out when needed were senators Simon Cameron and Roscoe Conkling, and in the House were General John A. Logan of Illinois, head of the Grand Army of the Republic, General James A. Garfield of Ohio, and James G. Blaine of Maine, who was elected Speaker of the House in 1869. Congressman Benjamin F. Butler of Massachusetts became Grant's House leader. These men had ample partisan reason—chief among them the wish to protect wartime tariff, railroad, and banking legislation from attack by returning Southerners—for keeping ex–Confederates disenfranchised and the black voters safe in the Republican camp.

Scandals in the Grant Administration. After the Civil War corruption was widespread throughout the United States, in the North as well as the South. Neither by temperament nor by training was President Grant qualified to set a high standard of political ethics in such a political and social climate. His frank admiration for people of wealth involved him unwittingly in several scandals.

A notorious event occurred on "Black Friday," September 24, 1869. For months before that date the undersized and cunning Jay Gould and the corpulent and unprincipled "Jubilee Jim" Fish had been plotting to gain control of the gold supply of the country that was not held in government vaults. They hoped, eventually, to dispose of their holdings in the precious metal with vast profit to themselves. They realized, however, that they could not control the market if the federal government chose to sell its gold. At the time the country held a supply of gold available for use by businessmen in settling foreign trade balances. When the price of gold rose too high, the government would sell enough to stabilize the market. The group went to President Grant and convinced him of the desirability of limiting the sale of gold by the U.S. treasury. To make doubly sure that Grant would not interfere, Gould arranged to have him take a vacation in the secluded village of Little Washington, Pennsylvania, 40 miles from a telegraph office.

Assured of Grant's cooperation, Fish and Gould went to work buying gold. The price of gold shot up until it reached $162 an ounce, $30 above normal, on September 24. When he was finally informed of the severity of the situation, President Grant ordered the secretary of the treasury to sell $4 million of government gold to New York banks. Immediately, the price dropped to $135 an ounce. Although the corner was broken, hundreds of investors were ruined.

The sordid event shook the business world severely and added to the growing demands of agrarians for reform of banking and currency practices. The investigation of the whole matter by Congress exonerated the president from any intentional wrongdoing, but his bad judgment was hard to explain away.

One affair hit close to the president himself — the uncovering of the "Whiskey Ring," a conspiracy of hundreds of distillers who had bribed treasury officials in order to evade federal taxes. An investigation by Secretary of the Treasury Benjamin H. Bristow, a new reformer in Grant's cabinet, revealed that Orville Babcock, President Grant's private secretary, had shared in the profits from the forgery of revenue stamps. Although Grant declared "Let no guilty man escape," he ignored the evidence and ensured Babcock's acquittal by serving as a character witness for him during the trial. He then named Babcock inspector of lighthouses. When Secretary Bristow expressed an interest in investigating other officials, Grant decided that it was time for the reformer to go and forced him to resign — which led many citizens to the false conclusion that the president was as corrupt as Babcock.

The Tweed Ring. Corruption also seeped down into state and local politics. When Grant became president of the United States, the "Grand Sachem" of Tammany Hall was the "honorable" William Marcy "Boss" Tweed. Of Tweed it was said that he was "a chairmaker by trade, a vulgar good fellow by nature, a politician by circumstances, a boss by evolution, and a grafter by choice."[33]

In 1863 Tweed and his henchmen had captured the Tammany organization and through it, control of the Democratic Party and the New York City government. Tweed and his associates then proceeded to plunder the city year after year, until at the height of their power they were splitting among themselves 85 to 90 percent of the total expenditures made by the city and county. The Tweed Ring had been estimated to have cost New York City at least $75 million and possibly $200 million. Lavish gifts to charity silenced much criticism and to those demanding reform, Tweed retorted, "Well, what are you going to do about it."[34]

The answer came with a crusading political cartoonist, Thomas Nast, whose drawings in *Harper's Weekly* aroused public opinion. Nast's cartoons really hurt Tweed. As the "Boss" put it, newspaper revelations of his grafting did him no damage among his constituents because so few of them could read, but he declared wrathfully, "they can't help seeing them damn pictures." Tweed offered the owner of the *New York Times* $0.5 million to call the whole thing off and Nast $0.5 million to "study art," but they refused. A citizen's committee headed by Samuel J. Tilden and Charles O'Conor launched an investigation that was able by the end of 1872 to drive every member of the Tweed Ring out of office. Tweed himself died in prison in 1876, friendless and penniless. Yet Tweed lost little of the esteem and admiration in which he had been held by the thousands of impoverished New Yorkers who had responded with regular votes for the jovial boss. "Well if Tweed stole," people in the slums would say, he was "good to the poor."[35]

The Liberal Republican Movement

Although the worst of the scandals, such as the Whiskey Ring affair and the defalcations of Secretary of War Belknap in the management of Indian affairs, did not become public knowledge during Grant's first term, they were well known among several members of the administration and Congress, including senators Charles Sumner, Carl Schurz, and Lyman Trumbull, and former Ambassador Charles Francis Adams. Secretary of Interior Cox and Attorney General Hoar, when ousted from the cabinet, also joined the opposition to Grant.

In the Senate the revolt against Grantism was led by Trumbull and Schurz. In 1870 Schurz, in league with former Senator and former Democrat B. Gratz Brown, secured the nomination of Brown as the anti-administration candidate for governor of Missouri. The president threw the administration's support against the liberals but to no avail. Brown was elected to the governorship and the coalition ticket captured both the state legislature and the Missouri congressional delegation. Encouraged by the triumph of the liberals in Missouri, and the growing dissatisfaction with Grantism in other areas, Schurz stumped the country during 1871 promoting a fusion of civil service reformers, low-tariff advocates, and critics of the administration's harsh reconstruction policy. The earnest, articulate, and bespectacled Schurz soon became the national symbol of reform. Schurz's success encouraged the anti–Grant Republicans to think they could prevent the president's renomination in 1872 and thus renovate the party from within. Calling themselves liberals, this group hoped to capture the regular Republican organization and to nominate one of the reformers for the presidency. When the radicals, despite this growing volume of criticism, made known their determination to bring about the president's renomination, a split in the Republican Party became inevitable.[36]

Grant and the radicals belatedly attempted to head off the liberal Republican movement by stealing its program. In March 1871 the president established competitive examinations for federal jobs on a trial basis in the federal offices at Washington and New York City from January 1, 1872. But Grant was not really very interested in reform, and even if he had been he could not have persuaded his followers to accept a new system that would undermine the very basis of party loyalty — the patronage. The experiment came to nothing when Congress neglected to renew the commission's appropriation. For the Grant administration the issue of civil service reform was closed.

In 1872, fearful that criticism of the high-tariff wall might hurt the Republicans, Grant ordered an across-the-board slash of 10 percent from all duties. In the same year Congress passed the Amnesty Act, which restored voting and office holding privileges to all but about 500 former Confederates. These gestures undercut the liberal Republican program and dampened their enthusiasm, but not the enmity of the dissidents.

The Election of 1872

The Liberal Republicans, 1872. When the anti-Grant reformers met in a convention in Cincinnati May 1, 1872, the Republican critics called it "a conclave of cranks." "There were," wrote "Marse Henry" Watterson of the Louisville, Kentucky, *Courier-Journal* — who was there as a delegate — "anti-Grant soreheads, tariff reformers, currency experimenters, the opponents of centralization, woman suffrage advocates,[37] and opponents of Radical Reconstruction." They all agreed on only one thing — that while Grant remained president their special desires would not be realized.

A number of prominent political figures sought the party's nomination for president, including Chief Justice Chase, who was suffering his quadrennial attack of "Potomac Fever"; Justice David Davis (already a candidate of the National Labor Reform Party); Senator Lyman Trumbull of Illinois; Jacob Cox of Ohio, who had been secretary of the interior under Grant until he was fired; Gratz Brown, governor of Missouri; Charles Francis Adams of Massachusetts, the son of one president and grandson of another; and Horace Greeley, who had the support of the professional politicians and (not surprisingly) the *New York Tribune*.

Adams was probably the first choice of the earnest reformers and of the leading Eastern Democrats, who were anxious for a liberal whom they could support. Unfortunately for the patrician reformer, Adams — like his father and grandfather before him — suffered from an acute oversupply of New England frigidity. In addition, he refused to do anything that would promote his own candidacy.

Greeley was the favorite of the anti-Grant Tammany politicians. He was also imagined to have strength in the South where he was viewed as a friendly candidate. He had signed the bail bond upon which Jefferson Davis, ex-president of the Confederacy, was released from imprisonment, and he was an early advocate of universal amnesty and reenfranchisement of former Confederates. He was also presumed to be popular in the West where he had counseled so many young men to go. Greeley was regarded as an intellectual and an eccentric — both of which were perilous reputations to have in politics. He sported strange chin whiskers and had taken up every fad of the last few decades, ranging from spiritualism to a crusade against the evils of drinking tea.

When the first ballot was taken, Adams had 203 delegate votes to 147 for Greeley. On the second ballot Greeley jumped to a 2-vote lead. But then on the third and fourth ballots a vociferous demonstration supporting Greeley took place which proved to be the turning point of the convention. Greeley took a decisive lead on the fifth ballot and was nominated on the sixth. Gratz Brown, a Greeley supporter, was nominated for the vice presidency on the second ballot after many reform-minded delegates, disgusted with the selection of the eccentric New York editor, left the convention.[38]

The platform attacked Grantism and called for an end to radical Reconstruction with its carpetbag governments; for a grant of universal amnesty to Southern citizens; for civil service reforms that would smash partisan tyranny; and a return to local self-government. On the matter of the tariff, which many liberals wanted to see lowered, the convention collided head-on with Greeley, a high-tariff protectionist, who threatened to desert the cause if a low-tariff plank were adopted. A compromise plank was eventually agreed upon, which stated that the party's position on the issue should be left to the decision of Congress without executive interference.[39]

The nomination of Greeley came as a shock to many people. It was said of the New York editor, rightly as it turned out, that he understood politics well but not well enough to know that he was a poor candidate. It was generally agreed that the New York editor had more "first class weaknesses" than any candidate ever nominated by a major party. He had taken strong stands on several controversial issues — temperance (he was for prohibition, which offended many Germans), women's rights (for), abolition of slavery (for), organization of labor (for), civil service reform (lukewarm), and having a protective tariff (for).

What is perhaps more important, he did not even look like a president. With a cherubic face and innocent blue eyes peering through steel-rimmed spectacles, he would amble along in a white coat and hat clutching a green umbrella — like a character stepping from the pages of Charles Dickens. It was a simple matter for cartoonist Thomas Nast to ridicule Greeley, and he did so unmercifully. At a small dinner the night after the nomination, Schurz expressed his discouragement by playing Chopin's Funeral March on the piano.[40]

The Democratic Convention, 1872. At the beginning of 1872 the Democratic Party was so nearly dead that many Democrats were asking themselves, "Shall we enter a candidate in the Presidential election and be beaten or shall we help elect some Republican?" When they met in convention in early July, inspired by a determination to take "anything to beat Grant," they also nominated Greeley and Brown and gave their approval to the liberal Republican platform. The choice of Greeley by the Democrats was an amazing choice. There was not a man in the United States who had been a more venomous critic of the Democratic Party and all its works than Horace Greeley. As editor of the *New York Tribune* he pilloried the Democrats as traitors, slave whippers, saloonkeepers, horse thieves, and idiots. Commenting on the general reception given to Greeley's nomination by the Democrats, the *New York Times* candidly remarked: "There was no joy in the fact or if there was it was concealed with most consummate art."[41] As if it mattered, Thurlow Weed, the Republican boss of New York, said he could not believe that any gathering "outside a lunatic asylum" could have nominated such a man.

The "Straight-Out" Democratic Party, 1872. A handful of the bitter end anticoalition Democrats, calling themselves the "Straight-Out Democrats," held a convention at Louisville on September 3 and nominated Charles O'Conor, one of the prosecutors of the Tweed Ring. Charles Francis Adams was chosen as his running mate. O'Conor was the first Roman Catholic to be nominated for the presidency. When informed by telegram of his nomination, O'Conor peremptorily refused to accept it. James Lyon of Virginia was then named in O'Conor's stead, but Lyon also declined the honor. The convention finally decided to let the original ticket stand, no matter if O'Conor and Adams did not like it.[42]

The straight-out Democrats succeeded in putting themselves on the ballot in 23 states. No Democrats of standing supported the movement; but Republican leaders looked upon it as a means of weakening Greeley and so they helped to distribute the group's literature.

The Republican Convention, 1872. A few weeks after the liberal Republican convention the regular Republicans met in Philadelphia and unanimously renominated Grant. The tone of the convention was summed up by the remarks of one delegate. Told that another delegate was not for Grant, he asked, astonished: "What's he doing here, then?"[43] Vice President Colfax was dropped from the ticket because he had presidential aspirations which displeased Grant, and Senator Henry Wilson of Massachusetts ("The Natick Shoemaker") who was popular with labor, was substituted.

In the platform the Republicans stood pat on their record and gave Grant a beautiful coat of whitewash in the following paean of praise: "We believe that the modest patriotism, the earnest purpose, the sound judgment, the incorruptible integrity, and the illustrious services of Ulysses S. Grant have commended him to the heart of the American people, and with him at our head we start upon a new march to victory."[44]

The National Prohibition Party Convention, 1872. The Prohibition

Party entered the presidential contest for the first time in 1872. The new party was formed in September 1869, at a convention in Chicago attended by almost 500 delegates from 20 states. Women had equal status as men as delegates for the first time in American politics. The assembled delegates voted to form an independent party and issued a call for a nominating convention to be held in Columbus, Ohio, in February 1872. When they assembled, the Prohibitionists issued a declaration of principles in which they denounced the old parties for competing for the "liquor vote" and asserted that a party not openly committed to the righteous cause "will barter away the public morals, the purity of the ballot, and every object of good government for party success."[45] They then nominated James Black of Pennsylvania and the Reverend John A. Russell of Michigan, two of the party's founders.

The Prohibitionists adopted a platform which demanded legal suppression of the liquor traffic; denounced the spoils system and called for a return to honesty, accountability, and economy in government; proclaimed in favor of a direct election of senators, the president, and the vice president; and called, for the first time, for the admission of women to the rights of suffrage. A few newspapers printed excerpts from the Prohibitionist platform but most ignored it entirely.

The Equal Rights Party, 1872. The Equal Rights Party nominated Victoria C. Woodhull, the first woman presidential candidate.[46]

The Campaign of 1872. The campaign of 1872 was a curious one. General Sherman pointed out the obvious paradox in the two major candidates of 1872 in a letter to his brother John: "Grant who never was a Republican is your candidate and Greeley who never was a Democrat, but quite the reverse, is the Democratic candidate."[47]

The president remained aloof from politics, but Republican spellbinders once again vigorously waved the bloody shirt and told the voters that Grant's defeat would mean pensions for the ex–Confederate veterans, if not the secession of the South. Roscoe Conkling belabored the obvious on behalf of the president: "If the name and the character of the administration of Ulysses S. Grant have been of value to the nation, no one knows it so well as the men who represent the property, the credits, the public securities and the enterprise of the country."

To most people's surprise, Greeley turned out to be a vigorous and hard-hitting campaigner, speaking with dignity, breadth of vision, and restraint to large and enthusiastic gatherings. However, his lifelong flirtation with fads, cults, and causes made him an easy mark for ridicule. Greeley was called an athiest, a communist, a vegetarian, and a congenital idiot (with elaborate phrenological charts to "prove" the charge). Besides all this, countless Republican pamphlets charted Greeley's bewildering zigzags on the major issues of the Civil War era. His violent attacks on the

Democrats were exhumed and reprinted.[48] The vast barrage of abuse heaped on Greeley from all quarters, led him to say, when it was all over, that he did not know at times whether he was running for the presidency or the penitentiary.[49] Grant in turn was denounced as a dictator, a loafer, a swindler, an ignoramus, a drunkard, and an "utterly depraved horse jockey."

The liberal Republicans and the Democrats were handicapped by the fact that conditions were good and the American people were in no mood for a change. Indicative of the new trend of politics, the great business and financial interests of the country, pleased with Grant and his party, contributed generously to the Republican campaign, Jay Cooke's subscription alone totaling over $50,000.[50]

The 1872 Outcome. The result was never in doubt. Grant, the man of no ideas defeated Greeley, the man of too many ideas, by a majority of 763,000 and carried all but six states — Texas and Georgia, where the troops had been withdrawn, and the border states of Missouri, Kentucky, Maryland, and Tennessee. The reformers garnered only 66 out of 352 electoral votes. The Democratic effort at coalition had been a failure. Although many Grant supporters pointed to the president's landslide majority (the largest popular majority of the century) as a clear verdict against anti-Grantism in any form, many observers merely concluded that the voters had decided that there was no object in putting out a knave merely to put in a fool.[51]

The Republicans retained their two-thirds majority in both houses of Congress. All liberal Republicans in the House were defeated in the election. In the Senate Schurz, Sumner, Fenton, and Trumbull lost their committee assignments and were excluded from the party caucus. Sumner died before his political future was settled; Trumbull rejoined the Democratic Party, which he had left in 1854; and Schurz became a genuine Independent. The bulk of the liberal Republicans in the House imitated Trumbull, closing their careers as Democrats.[52]

For Greeley, the end was tragic. He emerged from the campaign exhausted by his efforts and by long vigils at the bedside of his dying wife. When he found that he had also lost control of the New York Tribune, he sank into a final and fatal illness and died on November 27, 1872. It was said by many that he had died of a broken ego. The liberal Republican movement died with him.

President Grant's Second Administration. President Grant was either unwilling or unable to put his political house in order, and his second administration was marked by a distressing series of governmental scandals.

On September 4, 1872, while the campaign of 1872 was in progress, the New York Sun rocked the country with its charge that prominent public officials, including Vice President Schuyler Colfax and Congressman James

A. Garfield, had exchanged political influence for shares of stock in the Credit Mobilier Company of America, a railroad construction company, formed by the insiders of the transcontinental Union Pacific Railway. The accusations were so damaging that Congress could not avoid an investigation. When it was completed, the results were vividly described by the *Nation* as a "total loss, one Senator; badly damaged and not serviceable to future political use, two Vice Presidents and eight Congressmen."

Among the more notorious revelations was Postmaster General Creswell's admission that he had authorized the payment of nearly $500,000 for services which the claimant himself later estimated to be worth $176,000. Another cabinet officer, William A. Richardson, was found to have grossly abused his authority as secretary of the treasury in order to divert department funds, through unearned commissions, into the pockets of a political henchman of Ben Butler. Richardson hurriedly resigned to avoid a vote of censure by the House. President Grant then immediately appointed him to a high-salaried, life-tenured position on the Court of Claims.

However, the ultimate outrage to both the reformers and the public was the "Salary Grab Act" of 1873 by which congressmen raised their own salaries from $5,000 to $7,500 and made the raise retroactive for two years, thereby voting themselves a virtual gift of $5,000. This act also raised the salary of the president from $25,000 to $50,000 (the first increase since George Washington's time). Both the press and public protested so vehemently that in 1873 Congress repealed the measure. Many of those who accepted the back pay were speedily retired from public life by the voters.

The Panic of 1873. During Grant's second administration the nation was also subjected to a disastrous economic recession. Since 1850, except for short intervals, the economy in the North and West had enjoyed unparalleled prosperity. However, signs of trouble in the American economy had begun to appear by 1871, when the number of business failures reached 3,000. By 1872 more than 4,000 additional firms had collapsed. A serious financial crisis came in September 1873 as a result of the failure of Jay Cooke and Company, one of the most respected banking firms in the nation. The shock to the business world could hardly have been greater if the U.S. government itself had become bankrupt. Since Cooke's huge fortune had been freely at the disposal of the Republican Party, the reformers were quick to say that Republican chicanery and graft had brought the disaster upon the country. Before the close of 1873 there were more than 5,000 commercial failures, involving $228 million.

The panic spread rapidly. In 1874 three million men were thrown into the ranks of the unemployed. By 1875 6 to 8 percent of the laboring force was unemployed, and the proportion increased to 13 percent at the bottom of the depression in 1876. The nation was in the throes of its first economic depression, and the economic and political effects would be felt for several decades.[53]

The Issue of Cheap Money

The Panic of 1873 and the ensuing depression inevitably turned public attention to the nation's currency system. The Western farmers sought relief from the depression through currency inflation. A depreciated currency, they believed, would result in higher prices. Thus the farmers would receive more dollars for their crops with which to pay off the interest and the principal of their debts. As we have already seen, the expenses of the Civil War were met by the government to a large extent by the issuance of greenbacks. These were simply promises of the government to pay at some future date and their value depended upon the credit of the government. As these greenbacks increased in number, they naturally declined in value. Before the conflict had closed the government had issued $450,000 in greenbacks.[54]

After the war a policy of gradual retirement of the greenbacks was instituted by the government. This action, however, quickly encountered determined opposition. The farmers, particularly those in the West, had borrowed paper dollars (greenbacks) when they were worth only about 50 cents in gold or silver. If the greenbacks were retired and the currency restored to a gold basis, they would have to pay both the interest and principal of their loans in gold dollars. With this increase in purchasing power of the dollar, commodity prices would fall; and though the farmer would receive fewer dollars for his products, the number of dollars which he owed the Eastern mortgage holder would not decrease. The protests of the farmers were strong enough to cause Congress to stop withdrawals of the greenbacks in 1863. By 1870 the value of the greenback dollar reached 88 cents, where it remained for several years.

The Inflation Bill, 1874. In April 1874, since an election was imminent, the Republican-dominated Congress passed the Inflation Bill, sponsored by Representative Benjamin Butler, which increased the amount of greenbacks in circulation from $382 million to a maximum of $400 million. But even this halfway measure was too much for the hard-money advocates who clamored for President Grant to wield his veto. After much pondering of the political and economic alternatives, the president vetoed the inflationary measure, thereby winning the plaudits of the business interests but incurring the condemnation of the farmers. It was an election year and Congress did not dare to override the veto. However, Grant's "bottling up of Butler" aroused inflationist indignation against the president in and out of Congress. The Republicans were now adopting the twin principles of political economy that would become the party's articles of faith in the decades to come—high tariffs and hard money.

The issue of the value of money remained a divisive and central question in American politics, in one form or another, for the remainder of the century. It was, however, an issue which Congress refused to face.

The Congressional Elections of 1874. The new exposures of the scandals of "Grantism" and the pocketbook issues of unemployment and the scarcity of cash helped the Democrats to gain 80 seats and a majority in the House of Representatives in 1874 for the first time in 18 years. It was the first political defeat for the Republicans in a national election since the Civil War. The Senate still remained Republican by a margin of 45–29, but several members of the majority were unreliable.[55] When the new Congress met in 1875 the Republicans would no longer be in control as they had been since the beginning of the Civil War. The congressional results, along with victories in key gubernatorial elections, gave the Democrats reason to believe that after 20 years of wandering in the wilderness they had real prospects of capturing the White House.

During the congressional election campaign of 1874, Thomas Nast invented the Republican elephant. The first appearance of the animal showed him (labeled "Republican Vote") with a collection of other animals (representing various papers, states, and issues) being frightened by a donkey (the *New York Herald*) in a lion's skin ("Caesarism"). A fox resembling Samuel Tilden, the Democrat's candidate for governor of New York, was surveying the chaos from under a bush. The Republicans quickly adopted the elephant symbol; they said it showed their size and strength.[56]

The Specie Resumption Act of 1875. Early in 1875 the Republican-controlled, "lame-duck" Congress made haste to settle the money question before the newly elected Democratic congressmen took office. At Grant's insistence they passed a Resumption Act, which called for the issuance of new bank notes but required that $80 in greenbacks be retired for every $100 of the new notes. It also specified that the entire greenback issue would be redeemed through the accumulation of a gold reserve by January 1, 1879. The statute sought to appease both the greenback notions of the West and the gold-standard sentiments of the East.

The Civil Rights Act of 1875. A Civil Rights Act sponsored by Senator Charles Sumner was approved by Congress on March 1, 1875. It guaranteed equal accommodations in such public places as inns and theatres. It also forbade exclusion of blacks from jury duty. School integration, which Sumner had proposed, was quietly dropped from the final bill. However, the Grant administration made little effort to enforce the law.[57]

On March 4, 1875, the new Congress was sworn in. The Senate was still Republican, but most of the radical Republicans of the 1860s were gone and so also were many stalwart Republicans. In their places were Democrats from the South, eager to undo the effects of Reconstruction, and Democrats from the North, just as eager to expose the evils of Grantism.

When Congress opened its session the Democrats chose their first speaker since the beginning of the Civil War. Although Samuel J. Randall of Pennsylvania was, for all practical purposes, the leader of House Democrats, the party chose Michael C. Kerr of Indiana, a congressman with fewer political scars. The Democrats now set about the task of investigating Republican corruption. Their findings would furnish excellent campaign material for the next election.

They did not have long to wait. In February 1876 Grant's ambassador to Great Britain was forced to resign and leave England; he had been selling worthless mining stock to British investors. A month later it was discovered that Grant's third secretary of war, William W. Belknap, had grown wealthy by taking bribes from traders at Indian trading posts under his jurisdiction. When his impeachment appeared imminent, Belknap took the precaution of offering his resignation to the president. The House proceeded with Belknap's impeachment, despite his resignation. However, when the case came before the Senate for trial, a majority voted for conviction but not the necessary two-thirds majority, on the ground that by leaving office and becoming a private citizen, Belknap had removed himself from the jurisdiction of the Senate. He might be prosecuted in the courts (he never was), but could not be impeached.

Although none of the scandals involved Grant personally, the revelations of early 1876 showed that the easygoing president had been shockingly unaware of what had been going on in his administration.

The Emergence of the Greenback Party

While the financial effects of the Specie Resumption Act of 1875 would not be felt for several years, its political consequences were quickly apparent. On May 17, 1876, some 200 delegates, representing almost half of the states in the Union, gathered in Indianapolis to launch the National Independent or Greenback-Labor Party. Included among the delegates were agrarian radicals, labor reformers, and a handful of true believers in greenbackism. The platform adopted by the delegates focused entirely on the currency issue. Opening with a statement that the party had been called into existence to oppose the ruinous policies of the old parties which had done nothing to relieve the new three-year-old depression, the platform militantly demanded immediate and unconditional repeal of the 1875 Specie Resumption Act, and the issuance of U.S. legal tender notes or greenbacks.

The delegates named the 85-year-old ironmaster-philanthropist Peter Cooper of New York for president. Cooper was rich enough to supply his own campaign fund and most delegates assumed that he would. General Samuel Fenton Cary of Ohio, a former congressman with a good labor record and an early advocate of the Ohio Idea for payment of the national debt in greenbacks, was chosen to be their vice presidential candidate. Once again, the complex question of government monetary policy was injected into American politics.

The Disputed Election of 1876

With the approach of the national nominating conventions dissension again began to divide the Grand Old Party (GOP) as the Republicans had taken to calling themselves. The "Stalwarts," the hard-core political professionals closest to Grant, wanted the general to run for an unprecedented third term to ensure the wherewithal for party machines and party workers. Within the Republican Party those who opposed a third term for the president were branded by the Stalwarts with the epithet, "Half-Breeds."[58]

Grant himself was thinking about running again. However, his third-term plan quickly received its death blow when the House of Representatives in December 1875 passed a resolution supported by nearly half the Republicans, declaring a third term "Unwise," unpatriotic, and "fraught with peril to our free institutions." The president took the hint and agreed that he would retire from office when his term ended on March 4, 1877.

With Grant eliminated, several would-be candidates came to the fore. The best known of these was James G. Blaine of Maine — whom Thaddeus Stevens had nicknamed "The Magnetic Man" — from 1869 to 1874 the energetic, gregarious and much idolized Speaker of the House of Representatives. After the Republican defeat of that year Blaine had lost that post, but he was still the leader of the half-breed Republicans in Congress. The man from Maine had many of the qualities that make a great leader: personal dynamism, imagination, political intuition, oratorical ability, and a broad view of the national interest. He enjoyed widespread support throughout the North. However, he was only 46 years old, too young for the presidency in the view of many.

Blaine had never waved the bloody shirt before, but now he set out to do it with a vengeance. In January 1876 he taunted the House Democrats by offering an amendment to exempt Jefferson Davis, the "late President of the so-called Confederate States," from the provision of their general amnesty bill, charging Davis with being personally responsible for deaths of captured Union soldiers at Andersonville and Libby prisons. Although Blaine's attack on Davis won him the applause of South haters in many states, it also antagonized many more sober-minded citizens. In addition, many voters doubted Blaine's honesty and integrity. Blaine had been connected with some chicanery involving railroad securities. As Speaker of the House he had acted as bond salesman for the Little Rock and Fort Smith Railroad. Later he permitted the Union Pacific and certain other corporations to relieve him of a large block of their securities at a sum far in excess of their market value. Blaine categorically denied any improper connection. He went before Congress in April 1876 to defend himself, claiming that his dealings with the railroad had been a simple business transaction. The following month the Democratic-controlled House Judiciary Committee began to investigate Blaine's relationship with the Little Rock and Fort Smith. The Democrats knew as well as Blaine that the Republican convention was only a few days off and Blaine needed a clean slate to enter it.

Unfortunately for Blaine, about that time James Mulligan appeared in Washington with letters in his possession written by Blaine to Mulligan's former employer, Warren Fisher, a Boston businessman who had close relations with the management of the Little Rock and Fort Smith Railroad. The letters, Mulligan said, would reveal the nature of Blaine's connection with the railroad. By a trick Blaine got possession of the letters, and when the time was ripe, rose in the House and with virtuous indignation held aloft the packet of letters, announcing that he would read them aloud. He then read the letters out of order, adding his own comment and interpretation to confuse their implications. However, even his edited comments revealed a suspiciously close association with railroads seeking financial favors from the government.

Another handicap to Blaine was the opposition of Senator Roscoe Conkling, the vain and pompous Stalwart boss of New York. Conkling had hated Blaine since 1866, when the two men had clashed in a debate in the House of Representatives. Conkling had made some slighting remark about Blaine. Blaine had then withered Conkling into silence by referring in sharp, contemptuous tones to his "majestic, supereminent, overpowering, turkey-gobbler strut." Cartoonists thereafter portrayed Conkling as a turkey gobbler with one "Hyperion curl" dangling carefully over a broad forehead. Conkling never forgave Blaine for the jibe.

Also, Blaine had further antagonized Conkling when he denounced the Stalwarts as "all desperate bad men, bent on loot and booty." The Stalwarts never forgot or forgave. "Anyone but Blaine" was a creed with them. Perhaps most damaging to Blaine's chances was the fact that the liberal Republicans threatened to bolt the party again if Blaine should be nominated.[59]

A third contender was Senator Oliver P. Morton of Indiana. Morton, the last of the radical Republicans, could count on the votes of the carpetbaggers and scalawags in the South, and his cheap money ideas won backing for him in the farming states of the Midwest. But Morton had no followers in the all-important Northeast, where he was feared as a narrow-minded, vengeful person whose monetary policies were unsatisfactory to the bankers and whose racial views were so extreme that many felt they could lead to a new civil war if he were elected. Morton, too, was a member of Grant's faction of the party, which opened him to charges of corruption. Worst of all, his health was poor; though he was only 52, he suffered from a paralysis that forced him to use crutches at all times, and it was doubtful that he could survive the strain of the presidency.[60]

Another strong possibility was Benjamin H. Bristow of Kentucky, whose ruthless warfare as secretary of the treasury against the "whiskey gangs" had endeared him to the reformers. In major Eastern cities "reform clubs" containing such prominent conservatives as John Jacob Astor, Joseph Choate, Theodore Roosevelt, Sr., William E. Dodge, and John Hay heartily endorsed Bristow.[61] His management of the treasury had won him considerable support among financial interests. Carl Schurz tried to rally the remnants of the liberal Republican movement behind Bristow, but Bristow was too much of a threat to the Stalwarts to get the nomination. Also, unfortunately for Bristow's chances, he lacked personal magnetism.

Far back in the race was Rutherford B. Hayes, the governor of Ohio, a doubtful and strategically important state. Although Hayes was little known to the rank and file of the party, he had many strong recommendations. He had an outstanding military record. Although he had a wife and family to support, when the Civil War came he volunteered for service within weeks after the first shell fell on Fort Sumter. He had participated in several Civil War engagements, was wounded twice, was praised by Grant for "conspicuous gallantry," and rose to the rank of major general. He was elected to Congress in 1864 and 1866 and then to the governorship of Ohio in 1867 and 1869. In 1872 Hayes demonstrated his regularity by campaigning for President Grant, who was then under heavy attack by the liberal Republican reform faction of his own party. Running for a seat in Congress in 1872, Hayes was defeated, the only political loss of his career. In 1875 he ran again for governor of Ohio and won, thus recapturing an important state from the Democrats. In his third term as governor, Hayes had established a reputation for honest administration and constructive reforms.[62]

On the whole, Hayes was the most available candidate. He was obscure enough to be dubbed "the great Unknown"; he had shown some vote-getting ability in state elections; he was moderately well liked by the Independents; and the regular Republicans regarded him as a safe man who would be careful of the party's interests, mindful of its policies, and amenable to its discipline. He gained the endorsement of Carl Schurz and the reformers when he came out solidly for reform of the civil service, sound money, and "permanent pacification of the South." His fine Civil War record would attract soldier votes. Hayes appeared to many to be the ideal nominee for a party bedeviled by besmirched reputations and beset by scandal.

The Republican Convention, 1876. The Republicans met for their sixth national convention in Cincinnati on June 14, 1876, the centennial year of the birth of the nation. The call to the convention extended the olive branch to the dissident liberal Republicans, who were encouraged to "come home" to the party of their first love. Ironically, the convention was held in Exposition Hall where the ill-fated reform movement had nominated Greeley four years earlier.

The platform adopted by the delegates pointed with pride to the past, reminding the country who had won the Civil War, but also promised reform in the future when it said: "We rejoice in the quickened conscience of the people concerning political affairs and will hold all public officers to a rigid responsibility, and engage that the prosecution and punishment of all who betray official trust shall be swift, thorough, and unsparing." It also pledged "honesty, fidelity, and capacity" in all appointments to public office, and called for the extension of civil rights, civil service reform, increased rights for women, the abolition of polygamy, and the distribution of public land to homesteaders. The touchy matter of cheap money was mentioned only in the vaguest terms. The Democratic Party was charged with being the same in character and spirit as when it sympathized with treason. A Democratic victory, the platform declared, "would reopen strife and imperil national honor and human rights."[63]

On June 16 Oliver Morton was placed in nomination with a speech that foolishly called attention to his disabilities. Bristow was nominated next with a speech calculated to enrage the Stalwarts. "His mode had been to execute the law; and if the Republican Party contained offenders who betrayed their trust, or who were thieves, he let them be punished, as well as anybody else."[64] In nominating Blaine Colonel Robert G. Ingersoll, with an illusion to Blaine's great self-defense in the House of Representatives, extravagantly described Blaine as "the plumed knight who threw his shivering lance full and fair against the brazen foreheads of the defamers of his country and the maligners of her honor." This flowery rhetoric brought roars of enthusiasm from the delegates and won for Blaine the appellation "the plumed knight," which he carried with considerable pleasure for the rest of his political career. Conkling and Hayes were also nominated.[65]

On the first ballot Blaine forged into a comfortable lead, though short of the majority needed for nomination.[66] When it looked as though Blaine would be nominated by acclamation, the lights in the convention hall went dead, which forced an early adjournment. When voting resumed the next day, Blaine held his own until the fifth ballot, while Hayes gained and the others lost. On the fifth ballot the Blaine vote went to 308, only 70 less than the required majority. At that point the anti–Blaine forces concluded that the convention would have to take Hayes if it were to stop Blaine and they quickly concentrated on the Ohioan. On the next ballot Hayes received the bulk of the New York and Pennsylvania delegation and this gave him the nomination. Ironically, Blaine had been defeated through a union of the worst and best factions of the party, the extreme spoilers and the extreme reformers.

The ticket was then balanced by the nomination of William Almon Wheeler, a New York congressman. The Republicans had acted, as they were to act again and again, to choose their presidential candidate from one of the crucial doubtful states of the Midwest, and to balance the ticket with a name from the doubtful state of New York. Joseph Pulitzer, whose reform-minded *New York World* had been for Bristow, found little to praise in the candidate; "Hayes has never stolen. Good God, has it come to this?"[67] Zachariah Chandler, against the candidate's wishes, became chairman of the national committee and ran the campaign virtually without consulting Hayes.

The Democratic Convention, 1876. The Democrats met in St. Louis on June 27, 1876, two weeks after the nomination of Hayes and Wheeler by the Republicans. For the first time a national convention was being held west of the Mississippi River. The Democrats naturally hoped to capitalize on the growing public disenchantment with the Republican Party, and their chances for capturing control of the government appeared to be good. The principal contenders for the nomination were two governors: Samuel Jones Tilden of New York and Thomas Andrew Hendricks of Indiana.

Tilden had been an old Van Buren barnburner, but he had remained loyal to the Democratic Party when the antislavery faction passed through the Free Soilers to the Republican Party. In 1845 he won election to the legislature of New York State. In 1871, although a staunch Democrat, Tilden had not hesitated to turn against Tammany's corrupt Tweed Ring and aid in its overthrow. Despite the opposition of Tammany, he was triumphantly elected as the party's candidate for governor of New York in 1874. In the governorship Tilden enhanced his reputation for honest administration by uprooting another powerful organization of grafters known as the Canal Ring, who had defrauded New York State of more than $10 million. Soon cries of "Tilden for President" were being heard in a nation weary of corruption in high places. However, Tilden's conservative economic views and hard-money doctrines were more pleasing to the business community of the East than they were to the South and West. Popular enthusiasm for Tilden's candidacy was further limited by his railroad associations and his poor health—he had suffered a stroke in February 1875.[68]

Hendricks had served Indiana as a member of the U.S. Senate from 1863 to 1869. In that body he symbolized the Northern discontent with the war effort which earned him the label "Copperhead." In 1872 he was elected governor of the hoosier state, and in December, after Horace Greeley's sudden death, received 42 of Greeley's 62 electoral votes as a compliment. An engaging personality, political craft, and love of spoils made him an effective campaigner. Hendricks, a "sound-money" Midwesterner, was proposed because questions of currency and credit had come into prominence along with postwar inflation and agricultural depression.

As the convention opened, Tilden had a large lead in delegates and he was enthusiastically nominated on the second ballot. The strongly inflationist Western wing of the Democratic Party forced the nomination of Hendricks as the candidate for vice president.

The Democratic platform of 1876 was a call to arms for reform in government. It declared that the primary issue of the campaign was the elimination of rascals from government and the installation in their place of "honest men." Tilden, who had been responsible for most of the planks in the platform, believed in a strong currency backed with gold, and the platform advocated that position. The Western faction of Greenbackers rose to amend that platform to call for an immediate issue of paper money. When the issue came to a vote, the hard-money forces won, 550–219. The platform also called for a tariff for revenue purposes only, restrictions on Chinese immigration, and a new policy on the distribution of public land that would benefit the homesteaders and not the railroads.[69]

The Campaign of 1876. The campaign of 1876 was one of the most brutal contests of a brutal era. Once again the bloody shirt was waved as the Republicans assailed the Democrats as the party of treason and rebellion. "Avoid Rebel Rule" and "Vote as You Shot" they shouted. Colonel Robert G. Ingersoll in a flight of hyperbole (seldom equaled in American politics) told an assembly of Union veterans: "Soldiers, every scar you have on your heroic bodies was given you by a Democrat."

The Democrats bore down hard on Republican corruption in high places and alleged misrule in the South. When Republican orators pointed with pride to Hayes's spotless record, and proclaimed, "Hurrah! For Hayes and Honest Ways!" the Democrats countered with "Turn the Rascals Out" and "Tilden and Reform." Nothing, of course, effectively obscured the real issue of the day.[70] Unfortunately, the main thrust of the campaign zeal turned toward personalities and many irrelevant issues. The Democrats produced a 750-page book vividly describing in detail the Republican scandals. In turn, the Republicans republished a book detailing Tilden's railroad reorganization manipulations and sang about "Sly Sam, the Railroad Thief." Cartoons pictured "Tweedle-dee and Tilden-dum," linking Tweed and Tilden as cronies in graft. A book called *Samuel J. Tilden Unmasked* called him a criminal, "A disgrace to the State of New York," and "a menace to the United States."[71]

A good money raiser for the Democrats was *The Tilden Illustrated Campaign Song and Joke Book,* which contained 50 pages of songs and jokes and sold for a dime. Popular Republican campaign songs were: "Hurrah for the Hayes Ticket, All," "Brave Rutherford Hayes," and "We Will Not Vote for Tilden." Zachariah Chandler, the Republican national chairman, drained money out of every Republican holding public office. Any who declined to contribute 2 percent of his salary to the Hayes campaign could expect (and received) swift vengeance.[72]

The Outcome in 1876. When election day, November 7, 1876, finally arrived, it looked like a decisive Tilden victory. The popular vote gave him a clear majority over Hayes (4,300,590 against 4,036,298 for Hayes) of over 250,000 votes.

The press proclaimed Tilden the winner. Even the Stalwart Republican organ, the *New York Tribune,* conceded the defeat of Hayes, and indeed Hayes admitted his defeat in his personal diary. However, they were a little premature. The electoral votes of four states—South Carolina, Florida, Louisiana, and Oregon—were apparently in doubt. Without the votes of these states, Tilden had only 184 electoral votes with 185 necessary for election. Tilden needed only one of them to win; Hayes needed them all.

Quickly realizing that the 19 electoral votes of these states were exactly enough to elect their candidates, the Republican and Democratic leaders went into action. "Visiting statesmen" (Republican and Democratic politicians) descended upon the three Southern state capitals to look after the interests of their party. Soon two sets of returns, one Republican and one Democratic, were sent to Washington from the three states in question.

In Oregon, where Hayes had received a majority of 1,000 votes, it was discovered that one of the Republican electors had been constitutionally ineligible because he held a federal office as postmaster. The state law stipulated that the remaining electors should fill the vacancy, but the Democratic governor insisted that the highest Democratic candidate for elector should have the place. The Democratic governor then replaced him with a Democrat.

In the three Southern states the disputes were even more complex and involved. In Louisiana, although the Democratic electors had a majority of some 9,000 votes, the Republicans claimed that this success was because of the intimidation of the free blacks, the majority of whom clearly would have voted for Hayes. Flatly rejecting all evidence submitted by the Democrats, the Republican-dominated hearing board transformed the Democratic majority of 9,000 into a Republican majority of 4,000. The result in Louisiana, therefore, was that both Republican and Democratic electors presented their votes in Washington. In South Carolina a state canvassing board, also controlled by Republicans, certified to the election of the seven Republican presidential electors. In Florida, as in South Carolina, a Republican returning board certified the Republican electors. In Florida both Republican and Democratic electors cast their ballots and forwarded them to be counted in Washington. Congress was soon in an uproar over finding a solution to the dilemma of which set of election returns from South Carolina, Louisiana, Florida, and Oregon should be counted.

When Congress convened shortly after January 1, 1877, the situation became urgently threatening. The Republicans and Democrats were taking sides with such earnestness that people feared that civil war might break out if some way was not found to settle the dispute. Finally, to the great relief of many people, the Congress resolved the difficulty by passing a special act creating an electoral commission to consist of 15 members drawn in equal numbers from the Senate, the House, and the Supreme Court. Seven were to be Republicans, seven Democrats, and one, as expected, to be Justice David Davis, an Independent. The decision of the commission was to stand, unless rejected by both houses of Congress voting separately.[73]

But then, once again, the situation grew momentarily darker. Justice Davis became ineligible when the Democrats of the Illinois legislature elected him to the U.S. Senate. With Davis gone, the last hope of the Democrats faded. Only Republicans were left on the Supreme Court, and Associate Justice Joseph P. Bradley of New Jersey became the fifth judge on the commission.

In the Florida dispute the commission voted, 8 Republicans to 7 Democrats, not to go after the original returns. This, of course, meant accepting the electoral votes for Hayes. On the eve of the commission's decision in the Florida controversy, Justice Bradley was apparently ready to vote in favor of Tilden. But the Republicans subjected him to such tremendous political pressure that when he read his opinion of February 8, it was for Hayes. The Democrats assailed Bradley until, as the *New York Times* put it, he seemed like "a middle-aged St. Sebastian, stuck full of Democratic darts." South Carolina and Louisiana were disposed of in the same manner.

Enraged by what they denounced as a "conspiracy" to defraud them of their victory, many Democrats refused to abide by the vote of the commission. Some spoke ominously of a filibuster that would prevent the recording of the electoral vote and leave the country on March 4 with no president. "Tilden-Hendricks Minute Men" clubs readied themselves to march on Washington to force the inauguration of the man who had been "cheated out of the presidency." The slogan "Tilden or Blood!" was heard in many places. During the election crisis Hayes received many threatening letters, and one evening someone even fired a bullet into his house while he was at dinner. Sensational pro-Tilden newspapers virtually invited someone to shoot Hayes.[74]

The Compromise of 1877

The highly explosive issue was finally resolved when a group of conservative Southern Democrats in the House of Representatives, after negotiating with spokesmen for Hayes, reached an informal understanding that these Southerners would vote to accept the commission's report if Hayes would agree to the inclusion of at least one Southerner in his cabinet, control by the Southern conservatives of federal patronage in their sections, support of generous appropriations for internal improvements, and withdrawal of the troops. Hayes would then become the winner if Congress accepted the commission's findings. Congressional acceptance, however, was not certain. Democrats controlled the House and had the power to filibuster to block action on the vote.

In the end, however, most Democrats agreed to abide by the decision.[75] On March 2, 1877, Hayes was declared the president of the United States by the margin of 185 to 184 electoral votes. Soon he was being pilloried in the press as "Rutherfraud," "Old Eight to Seven," and "His Fraudulency," and was cartooned with "Fraud" on his honest brow.

It was the conclusion of P.L. Haworth that in a free election, Hayes would have won. Many thousands of Southern blacks who had wished to vote for Hayes were denied their then incontrovertible legal right to vote. "All things considered," concluded Haworth, "it appears, both legally and ethically, the decision was a proper one."[76] However, Malcolm E. Moos disagrees: "The consensus of historical research favors his [Hayes's] claims to the electoral votes of South Carolina and Louisiana, but supports the Tilden ticket in Florida, and thus, the election of Tilden."[77] Probably the evaluation closest to the realities of the events of 1876 was that the Democrats stole the election in the first place and then the Republicans stole it back.

President Hayes in Office

Three days later Hayes was inaugurated. Some 30,000 spectators, including a considerable number of security officers, cheered as the bearded man from Ohio took possession of the White House. In an unpretentious inaugural address, which the Democrats boycotted, Hayes acknowledged that the circumstances under which he came into office were unusual and promised to be as nonpartisan as possible as president. The most pressing need of the South, he said, was the restoration of "wise, honest, and peaceful local government" — which, Wayne Morgan suggests, most hearers took to mean that he was going to withdraw the troops and let the whites take over control of the state governments.[78]

Rutherford B. Hayes entered the White House without enthusiastic support even within his own party.[79] In choosing his cabinet, he ignored the advice of the Stalwarts and defied their power. The Republican managers wanted to have Roscoe Conkling as secretary of state, but Hayes appointed William M. Evarts of New York. He had been Andrew Johnson's attorney general and had brilliantly defended the president in the impeachment trial. John Sherman, brother of the Civil War general, was appointed secretary of the treasury. The leaders urged the appointment of the notorious spoilsman Thomas Collier Platt for postmaster general, but instead Hayes named David M. Key, an out-and-out Tilden Democrat from Tennessee and former Confederate general. Key would be in charge of dispensing patronage below the Mason and Dixon line. To the horror of Conkling and the Stalwarts who had surrounded Grant, Hayes also appointed to his official advisers Carl Schurz, an outspoken critic of Grant's policies, as interior secretary. The *Washington Post* suggested editorially that Hayes had put together a cabinet of "rare and quaint mosaics" (no compliment intended).[80] Senator Zachariah Chandler summed up the disgust of the Republican leadership when he complained "Hayes had passed the Republican party to its worst enemies."[81] Conkling, Blaine, and Morton tried to block senatorial confirmation of Hayes's choices. Only with Southern support did Hayes get his cabinet approved.

Civil Service Reform. The increase of corruption in Grant's second term demonstrated vividly the need for civil service reform and President Hayes made a determined effort to implement this policy. In his inaugural address he had emphasized the need for a permanent federal civil service beyond the reach of thieves and grafters and hungry party hacks. The reforms, he declared, should be "thorough, radical and complete." The appointment of the reformers Evarts as secretary of state and Schurz as secretary of the interior foreshadowed a new patronage policy. With the approval of the president, a new code was drafted governing the selection and removal of subordinate officeholders. On June 22, 1877, the president issued an executive order forbidding political assessments on federal officeholders for party purposes and banning all appointive officials from the management of party affairs. Although his orders were widely ignored, a reasonable start had been made.

The principal center of the spoils system was the New York Customs House, the center of Senator Conkling's machine. Two-thirds of the nation's revenue came through that port, and a bevy of corrupt officials drew profits from it. In the view of Hayes the responsibility for the evils in the Customs House at New York rested with the collector Chester A. Arthur, the high-living Republican boss of New York City, and his associate, Alonzo B. Cornell, chairman of the Republican state committee. When an investigation of Arthur's office in the summer of 1877 confirmed charges of bribery, political assessments, and underappraisals of imports, Hayes dismissed him and appointed a new collector. Conkling saw to it that the

Senate refused to approve the new appointments. But the president stubbornly persisted, and after Congress adjourned in the late summer of 1878 he removed Arthur anyway and filled his position with a man of his own choice.

The fuming Conkling coined new expressions of contempt for the president; he became, for instance, "Granny Hayes with his snivel service." At a special state Republican convention at Rochester in September 1877 Conkling bitterly denounced the president and climaxed his remarks by declaring that "when Dr. Johnson defined patriotism as the last refuge of a scoundrel, he was unconscious of the then undeveloped capabilities and uses of the word refawr-rm!"[82]

Hayes's relations with Congress were far from happy, however, for the Democrats controlled the House of Representatives during his entire administration and also the Senate during his last two years. The Democrats repealed the Force Acts that had been passed in 1870–71 during the Ku Klux Klan troubles. By holding up the appropriations bill, the House in June 1878 forced the Senate and president to accept a bill barring the use of troops at the polls.

Labor Unrest. The new president had been in office only a few months when the first nationwide strike produced the first labor rioting that reached into numerous states. The trouble started when the principal railroads decreed a 10 percent cut in wages. The workers hit back. Violence by the strikers provoked the use of troops by the government and the use of troops provoked more violence. Before it ended, President Hayes had to send federal troops to Maryland, West Virginia, Pennsylvania, Illinois, and Missouri to restore order. He had thus set the fateful precedent of using federal troops to intervene in a strike in order to restore order.

The president incurred additional ill will from labor, especially on the West coast, when he vetoed a bill passed in 1879 to exclude the Chinese "coolie" labor which he felt would violate the Burlingame Treaty of 1868, providing for mutual freedom of migration between the two countries. Hayes then called for a new treaty — a pact eventually signed in 1880 — which acknowledged the right of the United States to "regulate, limit, or suspend" but not absolutely prohibit Chinese laborers. In 1882 Congress passed a bill putting an end to Chinese immigration for the following decade.

Though Hayes's bitterest foes were in his own party, the Democrats worked tirelessly to discredit him and his administration. Although Tilden had gone into semiretirement, his associates kept alive his image as a victim of fraud. By keeping the issue alive, they hoped to sweep the country in 1880 in a dramatic campaign of vindication.

The logical issue to reopen, it was decided, was the presidential "steal" of 1876. A committee, headed by Representative Clarkson Potter of New

York, went to work with zeal. But what was not known to this committee was that a farsighted Republican Senate clerk had failed to return to Western Union some file copies of Democratic telegrams subpoenaed by earlier investigating committees. Several hundred of the most interesting-looking specimens were sent to Whitelaw Reid of the *New York Tribune* which that paper published in the original cipher. The readers were invited to try their hands at decoding them. At exactly the right moment, the *Tribune* broke the code. These telegrams, when decoded, revealed the efforts of the Democrats to bribe the Florida and South Carolina returning boards. Thanks to someone's foresight, Republican telegrams sent at the same time could not be found. Most of the Democrats implicated by the "cipher dispatches" did not deny the essential charges. Rather they attempted to justify their actions on the plea that they were merely trying to "ransom stolen property from thieves."[83]

Henceforth, the Democrats were declared (though not by the committee) equally culpable for the election irregularities of 1876, and the "martyred" Tilden was removed as an election issue. When Tilden, at his own request, appeared before the committee, he answered clearly every question that helped his case, but to others he gave such evasive replies as "I presume I did," "I do not remember," "I guess not," "I may have done so," "I do not think I did, so far as I remember," "I think not," and "I may have seen it." This sensational episode shook the confidence even of many of Tilden's followers. The development destroyed "Whispering Sammy" Tilden's political future, despite his personal innocence. Overnight, 40 years of Tilden's devotion to reform were obliterated by the brush of scandal.[84]

The Establishment of One-Party Government in the South

In the South the system of radical reconstruction was gradually overthrown, and in its place there developed political organizations and state governments founded upon the principle of white supremacy. After the Amnesty Act of May 1872 restored voting and officeholding privileges to all Southern whites except for a few hundred of the highest surviving Confederate dignitaries, Democrats came to power in the Southern states. Republican control ended in Virginia, North Carolina, and Georgia in 1870, in Texas in 1873, in Alabama and Arkansas in 1874, and in Mississippi in 1875. By 1876 only Louisiana, South Carolina, and Florida remained "unredeemed" in the view of Southern Democrats. Once installed in office, Hayes lost no time in recalling the federal troops from the South. With their removal, the last of the radical regimes collapsed and white Democratic governments were quickly installed in their places.

When President Hayes ordered the last federal troops out of the South on April 10, 1877, Republican governments survived in only two Southern states: South Carolina and Louisiana. The Republican government in Florida had already collapsed. In the fall of 1877, when President Hayes made a goodwill tour of the South, conservative Democratic leaders greeted him cordially and assured him that peace and racial harmony now reigned in the South. Hayes tried hard to believe it, because he hoped so much that it was true.

President Hayes's withdrawal of the last Southern garrisons in 1877 marked the end of active federal intervention on behalf of the exslaves. Southern whites were left in undisputed control. In effect, the North, having become increasingly absorbed in the problems of its emerging industrial order, turned the race question over to the South to solve in its own way. After 1877 general concern for the blacks quickly abated and the freedman was left to work out his own redemption.

The most obvious political result of the restoration of white supremacy in the South was the adherence of almost all Southern whites to the Democratic Party as a result of the radial Reconstruction policies. Since the radicals in the South were, or became, Republicans, the conservatives inevitably associated themselves with the Democrats. Since the blacks stuck to the Republican Party with undeviating loyalty, Republicanism came to symbolize black and carpetbagger rule.

Thus was born the "Solid South." The Democratic Party was in power in all Southern states. The Republican Party in the South functioned only for the power it could wield in national conventions. It survived on whatever federal patronage was thrown its way, delivering no votes for the national ticket nor any support in Congress. Thus, the end of Reconstruction brought a new problem for Republican national conventions – the "demoralizing influence" that went with the shameful scramble for the votes of Southern delegates.[85] For more than 40 years after 1876 the Republicans were unable to win a single Southern state. A reasonable conclusion was that the Republican Party in the South was as "dead as a doornail."[86]

The Congressional Elections of 1878. The first opportunity to test the policy of conciliation in the South occurred in the congressional elections of 1878. The president took a beating as the Democrats carried both houses of Congress for the first time since 1856. The Democrats achieved an almost solid South vote. Hayes told the press: "I am reluctantly forced to admit that the experiment was a failure." The only consolation for the Republicans was a solid North, whose electoral college votes could still elect a Republican president in 1880.

Perhaps more significant to the development of American politics in the post–Civil War era was the fact that in the congressional elections of 1878 over 1 million votes were cast for greenback candidates as against 80,000 two years before, and 15 of them were sent to Congress. In the Senate the greenbackers came close to holding the balance of power.

The Money Question

President Hayes viewed the growing agitation for easy money with increasing concern. He was, by conviction, a hard-money advocate and had strongly backed the Specie Resumption Act of 1875. In 1877 his secretary of the treasury, John Sherman, began to build up a gold supply to pay for the retirement of the greenbacks provided for in the act. When the reserve reached $142 million, Sherman initiated the project. By September 1878 the greenbacks were worth their face value in gold, and when resumption took place in 1879 there was no difficulty; people deposited more gold in banks for safekeeping than they demanded in exchange for greenbacks. With $200 million worth of gold in the treasury representing a solid bullion backing for the paper currency, no one bothered to redeem greenbacks. After 1879 greenback agitation died out, partly because of a revival of trade which temporarily boosted farm prices, but mainly because interest in expansion of the currency turned to the silver question.

The Silver Controversy

From the 1870s to the close of the century a debate raged, at time with great ferocity, between the conservatives (or deflationists) and the radicals (or inflationists) over the country's monetary policies. Conservative financial theorists were bullionists — that is, they held that paper money without gold or silver backing could never be made the basis of a reliable money supply. Paper money, they argued, was only a token of metallic currency held at any time by the government or by banks. The value of such paper money would be determined by the value of the metallic currency backing it and the government should not try to interfere with this economic law by issuing other forms of money.

Up to 1873 the American monetary system in theory was bimetallic. Both gold and silver were coined with the number of grains of each in the dollar being periodically adjusted to reflect the commercial value of the two metals. An act of 1792 established a 15 to 1 ratio (coins of 15 units of silver equaling in value coins of 1 unit of gold). In fact, on the market gold was worth nearly 16 times as much as silver, so it paid to take silver to the mint to be coined, while gold was of greater value if used as a metal. In 1834 the ratio was changed to 16 to 1. Gold became slightly overvalued at the mint, and silver almost disappeared from circulation. But when the Gold Rush of 1849 lowered the price of gold in relation to silver, Americans sold their silver on the open market rather than have it coined at a loss. Since few people brought in silver to be minted, silver dollars nearly disappeared from circulation. In 1873, after debating the question for four years, Congress abolished their coinage. The coinage of silver for domestic use thus stopped at almost precisely the time when the silver mines of Nevada and Colorado began to expand their output.

Within a short time after 1873 the price of silver relative to gold began to fall. When the price of enough silver to make a silver dollar went below a dollar it would have been profitable again for the silver miners to have their metal bought by the government for coinage into dollars, but the coinage act of 1873 deprived them of this market. When the discovery was made that only a few men, including Treasury Secretary Sherman – who had the bill introduced into Congress – and John Jay Knox, comptroller of the treasury, had known that the bill demonitized silver, a storm of protest arose from the Western bloc in Congress. After 1876 the free silver men began talking of the crime that Congress had committed in secretly repealing free coinage of silver as the "Crime of 1873." About the same time farmers and debtors adopted the cause of "free and unlimited coinage of silver at sixteen to one."

The interest of the debtor farmers of the Midwest was slightly different from that of the silver miners. They were not really interested in a higher price for silver. They simply wanted to raise prices by whatever means possible. In their view money was hard to come by because it was scarce, and the proper remedy was to increase the supply of money in one way or another. If silver would to it, very well and good. Farmers and others had favored the greenbacks, but silver seemed to provide a better leverage for inflation than the greenbacks. It met the demands of the bullionists that hard currency must stand behind paper; and it brought the farmers into an alliance with the mine owners who had money to spend on free silver propaganda. For these reasons, free silver replaced greenbackism among the demands of the inflationists during the 1870s and 1880s. The silver issue continued as a constant factor in American politics for the rest of the nineteenth century.

The Bland-Allison Act. The first important test for the silver inflationists in Congress came in November 1877 when Representative Richard P. ("Silver Dick") Bland of Missouri introduced a bill in the House of Representatives calling for unlimited coinage of silver at the old rate of 16 to 1. The law authorized the secretary of the treasury to purchase not less than $2 million and not more than $4 million of silver each month. The secretary then had the option of coining the silver or issuing silver certificates based upon it. This meant limited coinage instead of unlimited and the act did not satisfy the advocates of silver inflation. Although he had no objection to coinage of both gold and silver dollars, President Hayes was against reducing the real buying power of money and he vetoed the measure, but Congress passed the bill over his veto.[87] Treasury Secretary Sherman adopted a policy of balancing silver coinage with gold coinage, thus preventing an inflationary currency. The monetary issue continued to cause the political pot to boil for many years to come.

4. The Mugwumps, Populists, and Other Assorted "Cuckoos," "Crackpots," and Reformers:

Shakers and Rattlers of American Politics

Following the Civil War, the concerns of the Americans and inevitably of their political parties shifted from the complex issues surrounding slavery and the preservation of the Union to the meanings and consequences involved in economic reorganization and action stimulated by the war itself. The immense stimulus given to business and industry by the war brought forth a new generation of captains of industry and masters of capital, whose frenzied moneymaking, vulgarity, selfishness, and lawlessness led the writer Mark Twain to call this period "The Gilded Age" (dazzling on the surface, base metal below) but which Vernon L. Parrington, the social historian, dubbed the "Great Barbecue," a time when everyone rushed to get his share of the national inheritance like hungry picnickers crowding around the savory roast at one of the big political outings common in those years.[1]

The Growth of Trusts. The most conspicuous feature of American industrial development in the period after 1870 was the rise of the great trusts. The first of these examples of business consolidation on a grand scale was the Standard Oil Company created by John D. Rockefeller in 1870. Within a decade Rockefeller had cornered about 95 percent of the refining capacity of the country and had captured almost the entire world market for his products. In 1881 Chicago journalist and reformer Henry Demerest Lloyd summed up Rockefeller's success: "The Standard had done everything with the Pennsylvania legislature except refine it."[2] So successful did the trust device prove that, between 1884 and 1887, it prompted the formation of trusts in other fields, notably the American Cottonseed Oil Trust, the National Lead Trust, the Distillers and Cattle Feeders' Trust (the Whiskey Trust), the Sugar Trust, and the National Cordage Assocation.

159

When the Civil Service Reform Act of 1883 began to limit patronage as a political resource for the national parties, politicians turned increasingly to businessmen for money and support. A new type of political boss soon appeared—a business type who resembled and worked closely with the corporation executives, made few speeches, and conducted his activities in legislative corridors, caucuses, and committees. Zachariah Chandler of Michigan, a wealthy lumber merchant; Pennsylvania's Simon Cameron, a banker and railroad director; New Yorker Tom Platt, a banker and president of a lumber company; and Leland Stanford, a railroad builder of California, were bosses of this new breed. Some had entered the Senate to protect their interests. Inevitably, the growth in number and influence of these special interests in the nation produced a change in the whole pattern of the American political party system. The party system which had begun as an instrument of democracy would become, by the end of the century, the servant of those special interests.

The Politicization of Labor. Under the impact of war and of soaring prices, some labor organizations shattered by the panic of 1857 were pieced together again. In August 1866 the National Labor Union (NLU) was founded by William H. Sylvis, an iron molder and veteran leader of the union movement. Although the NLU was politically oriented from the outset seeking various political and social reforms—such as the eight-hour day, currency reforms, woman's suffrage, and government lands for genuine settlers only—its convention in 1867 made no move to launch a party. However, in a meeting at Baltimore in 1868 the leaders of the union urged political action as the most effective means of promoting the workers' interests. However, the advocates of economic rather than political action were able to defeat a motion for the immediate formation of a straight-out political labor party. The conference, nevertheless, agreed that one should be established "as soon as possible."[3]

The Labor Reform Convention, 1872. At its annual convention at Columbus, Ohio, in 1872 the NLU formed a National Labor Reform Party to participate in that year's presidential election. The some 200 delegates from 17 states adopted a platform calling for the government to issue more legal tender, pay the national debt in greenbacks, reserve the public lands to actual homesteaders, and establish an eight-hour day.[4] Other planks called for the exclusion of Chinese laborers, abolition of contract labor in prisons, government regulation of railway and telegraph corporations, and civil service reform.

Going outside the ranks of labor for its candidate, the convention nominated David Davis of Illinois, a wealthy Supreme Court judge. On being notified of his nomination, the judge wired his thanks without committing himself to an acceptance. In June, after he had missed both the liberal Republican and the Democratic nominations, he declined to stand as the

Labor Reformers' candidate. Hastily, the Labor Reformers named Charles O'Conor of New York, whom the straight-line Democrats had already chosen as their presidential nominee. In November O'Conor received only 29,489 votes and the Labor Reform Party ended its days. The party held no other national conventions.

After the collapse of the National Labor Union following the crash of 1873, the forces of labor were represented by the Noble and Holy Order of the Knights of Labor. The Knights sought to unite all labor and welcomed all "toilers" of whatever race, nationality, or craft, whether skilled or unskilled. The Knights did not view favorably the idea of a labor party and sought to remain primarily an industrial rather than a political organization. They supported the eight-hour day, preferred boycotts and arbitration of strikes, advocated a national income tax, and organized producers' and consumers' cooperatives.

For a time the Knights of Labor flourished. By 1866, the year of the Haymarket Riot, nearly 6,000 local assemblies had a total membership of more than 700,000. However, the increasing dissatisfaction of skilled craftsmen with the aims and methods of the Knights resulted in the formation in 1866 of the American Federation of Labor (AFL). The founder of the American Federation, and its head until his death in 1924, was squat, square-jawed, Samuel Gompers, an immigrant cigar maker in New York City. Gompers was convinced that labor must avoid all efforts to establish a separate labor party. The road to well-being for labor, he insisted, did not lie through independent political action but through "pure and simple" trade unionism. Though stoutly opposed to the formation of a separate labor party, the AFL did, nonetheless, put forward at its annual conventions specific demands for new laws to be won by political action. At elections members of the federation resorted to the political tactic of "rewarding our friends and punishing our enemies," regardless of party.

The Politicization of Agriculture. The decade of the 1860s had been a prosperous one for farmers with the demand for foodstuffs stimulated by the Civil War, the various European conflicts of the period, and poor harvests in Europe. By 1873 migrants to the opening prairies were streaming westward over the newly completed rail facilities and by prairie schooner. By 1880 almost 20 million acres had been entered by homesteaders. Inevitably, the scores of farmers who got land under the provisions of the Homestead Act came to look upon the Republican Party as their benefactor.

The swift expansion of agriculture in the post–Civil War period did not prove to be a complete blessing. Many farmers borrowed heavily during the wartime boom to finance expansion and when farm prices declined precipitously after the war in wheat, corn, and cotton—the three great American staples—thousands of farms had to be abandoned. The wagons that had rolled westward with such great expectations began to move eastward again, this time displaying legends such as "Going home to the wife's folks" and "In God we trusted, in Kansas we busted."

For the most part the farmers blamed hard times upon the new economic forces with which they had to reckon. They resented the fact that their products yielded small returns, while the protective tariff kept up the price of manufactured goods and the farm machinery which they bought. The economic dilemma of the farmers rapidly became a major political problem. In the 1870s and 1880s exotic new agrarian parties and movements appeared on the American political scene to protest the subjection of the agrarians to industry and finance.

The Granger Movement. The Granger movement was launched in 1866 when the commissioner of agriculture sent a clerk from his bureau, Oliver Hudson Kelley, on a trip through the Southern states to gather information on the conditions of agriculture.[5] From his observations of the farmers, Kelley became convinced that something should be done to help the farmers solve their problems. The first local chapter, or Grange, was founded in Washington, D.C., in 1867. The group was called the National Grange of the Patrons of Husbandry. During the hard times of the early 1870s the Granger movement spread like wildfire, especially in the Midwest and cotton South. By 1875 there were Granges in almost every state, and membership had reached about 800,000.

Although the Grange began as a secret fraternal society, created to promote social and intellectual intercourse among the nation's farmers, that soon changed. Before long the meetings of the local Granges became centers for the discussion of agrarian problems. Soon the Grangers were involved in politics, despite the prohibition against political discussion or activities in their constitution. This was called politics "outside the gate," even if it was within the walls.[6]

When Granger political action came, it appeared first on the state level as the various independent, reform, antimonopoly, and farmers' parties of the Midwest carried on what resembled a battle royal against the railroads, stockyards, banks, and corporations. Their most eloquent voice was that of Ignatius Donnelly of Minnesota, a self-educated Irish intellectual who afterward became one of the foremost orators of populism.[7] In several states the Grangers were successful in electing their members to the legislature where they pushed through so-called "Granger Laws," regulating railroads and warehouses.

The Growth of Cities. Another significant characteristic of the post–Civil War industrial order was the growth of cities both in size and influence as the offices and factories of business enterprises drew thousands of immigrants from Europe and native-born Americans from the farms and villages. At the beginning of the Civil War no single city had as many as

1 million inhabitants. Thirty years later New York had 1.5 million, and Chicago and Philadelphia each had more than 1 million. As time passed, the great cities became more and more dominated by recent arrivals. The foreign-born population of Chicago in 1890, for example, almost equaled the total population of Chicago in 1880; four out of every five residents of New York City in 1890 were either foreign born or the children of immigrants.

The post–Civil War city was an ideal area for the development of the urban political machine — a political party organization providing services and sympathy in return for the votes of the new immigrants, who were often bewildered and overwhelmed by the difficulties of life in the slums in which they found themselves. With the immigrant votes the machines placed their party operatives in the offices of city, state, and federal government, and managed — however inefficiently and corruptly — to run them. As we have already seen, one of the most efficient of these machines was the Tweed Ring which controlled New York City int the 1860s and 1870s.

Machine politics led to widespread corruption in government. The historian Henry Adams wrote in 1905, "The period was poor in purpose and barren in results. . . . One might . . . search the whole list of Congress, judiciary, and executive during the twenty-five years 1870–1895, and find little but damaged reputations."

The National Greenback-Labor Party. When the panic of 1873 intensified the agricultural depression and the Granger movement failed to relieve the situation, farmers took over the Greenback movement. In August 1874 the Indiana Independents, a group of farm leaders and reformers who had abandoned the major parties, issued a call for all greenback men to meet in Indianapolis during the coming November to form a new national party. The convention, in the hands of the Greenbackers, declared the money problem was the key question affecting the welfare of the people. In March 1875 a national convention met at Cleveland to launch the National Independent Party. This was followed by a nominating convention at St. Louis in May 1876, which chose Peter Cooper of New York for president and General Samuel F. Cary of Ohio for vice president. Its platform called for repeal of the National Specie Resumption Act of 1875 and issuance of U.S. Notes. As we have already seen, the election of 1876 gave the Greenbackers 1 percent of the popular vote — 80,000 — mainly from agrarian voters.[8]

After 1876 the Greenback-Labor Party received accretions from labor, in part because President Hayes had used the army to suppress the rioting which accompanied the railroad strike of 1877. Since many of the labor parties were friendly toward greenbackism, their leaders and the leaders of the Greenback Party readily saw the advantages of fusion on a national scale. A call, therefore, was issued for a meeting of labor reformers and Greenbackers at Toledo, Ohio, in February 1878.

The platform adopted by the 1,100 delegates from 28 states who gathered at Toledo opened with the traditional broadsides against the major parties and the pronouncements in favor of currency inflation. It then enumerated the demands of the labor reform groups. It called for a reduction in hours of daily toil; the national and state governments were urged to establish bureaus of labor and industrial statistics to gather and publish information on wages and working conditions; and an end was demanded to child labor, the use of prison contract labor, and to the importation of Chinese laborers. But labor was a junior partner in the combination, and although the party polled over 1 million votes in the midterm elections of 1878 and elected 14 congressmen, they were mostly from the Midwest, and the workers gradually drifted away.

The Election of 1880

Fortunately for the Republicans, prosperity had returned by the time of the presidential election of 1880. Even so, the Grand Old Party was sadly torn by internal strife. In the eyes of his contemporaries Hayes's administration was a failure — it was being said that the president was "almost without a friend." The Republican leaders had several excellent reasons for looking for a new candidate. In 1876 they had won the presidency by the smallest majority, that of a single electoral vote. In 1880 they were certain to lose the 19 votes of Florida, Louisiana, and South Carolina, which had been voted for them in 1876. Enough votes had to be found to compensate for this loss and the prospects were not bright. On the other hand, the Republicans could count upon that most valuable of all political allies — prosperity. A feeling of optimism had replaced the feeling of gloom that had characterized the depression years.

Hayes's pledge against a second term cleared the way for the Stalwarts to engineer a comeback for former President Grant, who had recently returned from a triumphal tour of the world and was willing to try a third term. Supporting Grant's renomination were the powerful Stalwart bosses of three states — Roscoe Conkling of New York, Don Cameron of Pennsylvania, and James A. Logan of Illinois. In doing so, they were ignoring the resolution of the House of Representatives, adopted in 1875 for the express purpose of blocking such a move. The "Old Hero" was anxious to run and they were anxious to have him run.

Grant's most conspicuous rival was James Gillespie Blaine. "The Man from Maine" was now 50 and at the peak of his career. He had moved from his familiar place in the lower house to the Senate after six years of wielding the powerful Speaker's gavel. John Sherman, the grey-bearded, cool-eyed secretary of the treasury also waited on the sidelines. Sherman had the backing of big business, although he apparently did not have the support of President Hayes. Sherman's availability was impaired by a reputation as an icicle, due to his lack of an attractive personality. Also he was considered by many persons to be pro–Catholic. Sherman would probably have withdrawn in favor of Blaine but he had been offended by Blaine's insistence on seeking convention delegates in Ohio, Sherman's home state.

The Republican Convention, 1880. When the Republican convention opened in Chicago in the great amphitheater in the Interstate Exposition Building on an usually hot Wednesday, June 2, 1880, every state was represented – the first Republican convention where this happened. Grant had more delegates than any other candidate, but he lacked the necessary majority. Although the anti–Grant delegates were numerous enough to control the convention if they could unite, they had not agreed upon any one nominee. Under these circumstances, it was good strategy for the opposition to aim at the defeat of Grant; eventually, they might find an acceptable candidate.

For the Grant men, on the other hand, the proper strategy was to attach to their side an appreciable number of delegates from the opposition. This they attempted to do, under Roscoe Conkling's leadership, by forcing the convention to adopt the unit rule by which every delegation would have to cast its entire vote as a majority of the delegation directed. The anti–Grant minorities in the various delegations, in spite of themselves, would thus be enrolled on the Grant side.

Unfortunately, for the Grant supporters, the plan leaked out. When James A. Garfield, John Sherman's floor manager, learned of the plan he assumed command of the anti–Grant forces. In a masterful speech which appealed to the sense of fair play and individualism of his audience, he turned aside Conkling's design, while a storm of applause broke over the hall. Even before the Ohioan concluded his speech, Conkling passed a short (sarcastic) note to Garfield's seat: "New York requests that Ohio's real candidate and dark horse come forward. We want him in our seats, while we prepare our ballots."[9] Conkling then withdrew the motion; there would be no unit rule.

When the nominating speeches were in order, Blaine's name was placed in nomination by an obscure delegate from Michigan (possibly a fatal mistake). Nevertheless, a pandemonium of approval for Blaine broke out. General Logan, the commander of the GAR from Grant's own state of Illinois, followed with the nomination of Grant in a single sentence that provoked more pandemonium. "In the name of our loyal citizens, soldiers and sailors – in the name of loyalty, of liberty, of humanity and justice, I nominate Ulysses S. Grant for President."[10]

Conkling then seconded the nomination of Grant, with a speech rivaling Ingersoll's presentation of Blaine in 1876. "Never defeated in peace or war, his name is the most illustrious borne by living man. His fame was earned not alone by things written and said but by the arduous greatness of things done. He never betrayed a cause or a friend. Select no man without a record. Pull no skulkers from under the ammunition wagon; take the tried and true old hero — with the Old Guard behind him who have never kept step to any music but the music of the Union. Show me a better man, and I am answered. Nobody now is really disquieted about a third term except those who are longing for a first time. This convention is master of a great opportunity. It can speed our nation to certain and lasting victory with its great Marshal at its head."[11]

As Conkling concluded, Exposition Hall erupted into a bedlam of hurrahs, aisle marching, and general confusion. Herbert Clancy, the historian of the election of 1880, concludes that if the balloting had begun at that moment, Grant would probably have won on the first ballot as he had in 1868 and 1872.[12]

Garfield followed with a 15-minute nominating speech for Sherman in which he subtly but effectively emphasized his own virtues. When he finally mentioned Sherman's name in the last sentence of the last paragraph, it was to commend the Ohioan "not as a better Republican or a better man than thousands of others, . . . but . . . for deliberate and favorable consideration." The consensus of the delegates was: "He has nominated himself."

For 35 ballots Grant ran ahead of Blaine and Sherman but could not get a majority. Most of the Sherman and Blaine delegates at last united and shifted their votes to Garfield on the thirty-sixth ballot, and he was nominated over the opposition of the most powerful group of party bosses that ever sought to manage a convention and nominate a candidate. The Grant loyalists, the "Immortal 306," voted for the general on every one of the 36 ballots.[13]

James A. "Boatman Jim" Garfield, who was born in an Ohio log cabin in 1831, had grown up in poverty.[14] His education was almost Lincolnesque. He had succeeded in earning enough — as a canal boat driver and carpenter — to put himself through college. He began his public career as a schoolteacher and as a Christian evangelist, which led to his being called to be president of Hiram College in Ohio at the age of 26. In northern Ohio he became known as a powerful antislavery speaker. Although he was only 29 when the Civil War broke out, Garfield had volunteered and was mustered out as a major general in 1863 after he won a seat in Congress. There he served for 18 years, emerging in 1880 as Republican floor leader. He was a Senator-elect when nominated for the presidency at the age of 48.[15]

The delegates, to conciliate the Stalwarts, then offered the second place on the ticket to the tall, handsome, and well-dressed Chester A.

Arthur, the Conkling henchman just dismissed from office by Hayes. Arthur had never held an elective public office. Garfield, who would have much preferred the New York banker Levi P. Morton, an able organizer and fundraiser with connections in Eastern business and high society, as his running mate, acquiesced in Arthur's selection in an effort to heal the split in the party. Arthur accepted the nomination, despite Senator Conkling's advice to reject it.

The candidates having been chosen, the delegates proceeded to frame a platform which opened with the usual Republican claim of having "transformed 4,000,000 human beings from the likeness of things to the rank of citizens," and of having made a "sovereign nation" out of "Confederate states." It then declared for veterans' pensions, Chinese exclusion, and the protective tariff, and against the use of public funds for sectarian schools. It adopted a special resolution approving civil service reform which was vague enough to satisfy both spoilers and reformers.[16]

The Democratic Convention, 1880. When the Democrats assembled in Cincinnati on a hot and humid June 22, they were as badly divided as the Republicans. Lacking in leadership and in strong candidates and tainted with treason and with pacifism, the prospects appeared gloomy. Samuel J. Tilden was too old and too ill to be a candidate and the delegates had no enthusiasm for him. Even so, the Sage of Greystone ardently wanted the nomination. The crime of 1876 should not go unpunished, and Tilden was anxious that the American people should have an opportunity to vindicate his name. Also placed in nomination were Governor Thomas A. Hendricks of Indiana, Supreme Court Justice Stephen J. Field of California, Senator Thomas F. Bayard of Delaware, and General Winfield Scott Hancock, a 56-year-old professional soldier with no experience in politics. Hancock's military record would be a plus because it matched that of Garfield, the Republican candidate.

General Hancock, one of the Union heroes at Gettysburg, had later pleased the South by the way he conducted himself as military commander of Louisiana and Texas during Reconstruction. "Nominate Hancock and the bloody shirt will be folded away," his supporters urged. "He will . . . be alike acceptable to the North and to the South." The general's nomination would be an effective answer to the customary Republican charges of Democratic disloyalty during the Civil War.[17] Justice Field had support from the far West and from conservative businessmen. But he also had enemies who were circulating rumors that his nomination effort was being financed by Jay Gould. Also the judge had incurred the hostility of the Democrats of California by his decisions suporting the constitutional rights of the Chinese. Bayard had strong support among the Southern delegates.

On the third ballot the convention chose Hancock. William H. English, a wealthy banker with a hard-money record as a congressman, was nominated for vice president. In nominating Hancock and English, the Democrats took into account sectional prejudices. Hancock was from Pennsylvania, while English made his home in Indiana, a state both doubtful and pivotal, so the party helped to attract voters from all parts of the country. The short platform was accepted without debate or opposition. It called for decentralization of the federal government with increased "home rule," "honest money, consisting of gold and silver, and paper convertible into coin on demand," a tariff for revenue only, civil service reform, "a free ballot" (without mentioning blacks), and it opposed Chinese immigration "except for travel, education, and foreign commerce, and that even carefully guarded," and the subordination of the military to the civil power. In its harshest language the platform proclaimed the "great fraud of 1876–77" as the issue that "precedes and dwarfs every other."[18]

The Greenback-Labor Convention, 1880. Greenback hopes were high in 1880 as they met in convention in Exposition Hall in Chicago on June 9, where only the day before Garfield had been chosen as the standard-bearer of the Republican Party. Present were representatives of all the rival Greenback factions, as well as 41 delegates from the newly formed Socialist-Labor Party. James Baird Weaver of Iowa, a Civil War Union general, was nominated for president with B.J. Chambers of Texas as his running mate. The selection of Weaver, a Western agrarian, who had gone from Democratic to Free Soil doctrine to Republicanism and finally to greenbackism, dissatisfied the Eastern labor leaders. (Before Weaver was finished with his party jumping he would move on to populism.)

The platform adopted by the Greenbackers went beyond the currency issue and attempted to appeal to the discontented and reformist elements. It repeated the demand of the farmers for a graduated income tax, called for increased public land for settlers, denounced large monopolies, and proposed that Congress control passenger and freight rates. To broaden their appeal to labor, the platform was expanded to include such matters as the support of the eight-hour labor law; the abolition of child labor; the inspection of mines, factories, and workshops; the curtailment of Chinese immigration; and improvement of the sanitary conditions in industrial establishments. The Greenback platform also called for women's suffrage.

The Prohibition Party Convention, 1880. The Prohibition Party met in convention in Cleveland on June 17, 1880. Twelve states were represented by 142 delegates. A platform was adopted which graphically enumerated the disastrous effects of alcohol upon the individual and upon society. With the platform out of the way, the delegates nominated General Neal Dow of Maine, with A.M. Thompson of Ohio as the vice presidential candidate.

The Campaign of 1880. The campaign of 1880 was hard fought but not as fiery as some previous ones. In the absence of real issues the campaign degenerated into one of personal abuse and vilification.

The Republicans dismissed Hancock as "a good man weighing two hundred and fifty pounds" (the ultimate dismissal). Hancock, whose exploits on the battlefield had won him the sobriquet, "Hancock the Superb," they said, was in reality "General Went Off Half-Cock." A large, elegantly bound book titled *Record of the Statesmanship and Achievements of General Winfield Scott Hancock,* consisting of blank pages, was a particularly effective piece of anti–Hancock literature. To emphasize Hancock's unfamiliarity with the issues, Thomas Nast highlighted the general's response to an interviewer's question about the tariff with a cartoon in which Hancock whispers to a companion: "Who is Tariff, and why is he for revenue only?" One of Garfield's correspondents rightly concluded that Hancock had given "one interview too many."[19]

The Republicans gave the bloody shirt a new shake by stressing the danger of the solid South, which, by a combination with a few Northern states would control the government, undo the result of the war, and pay rebel claims and pension Confederate soldiers. Hancock silenced the latter charges in a letter stating that not one dollar would be spent for any such purpose.

In parades and rallies for Hancock a wooden mechanical rooster, symbolic of the Democratic Party, was seen feeding the ballot box with votes for the Democratic candidate. The rooster was also used in parades in support of Hancock.[20]

The Republicans also made the most of their candidate's rise from a barefoot canal boy in Ohio. However, "the Canal Boy'" encountered troubled waters. The Democrats pointed to the Credit Mobilier scandal of the early years of the decade, when Garfield had been "touched a little with the mud stick," as one old reporter noted. Although he had been cleared of receiving $329 from the gift of the stock, energetic Democrats now chalked these telltale figures on sidewalks, streets, doors, fences, walls, posts, on the steps of Garfield's home in Washington, on hats, napkins, and even, according to one amused Republican, "on underclothing and the inside of shoes."[21]

Contrary to precedent, Garfield personally campaigned intensively, stressing the tariff issue. In August Grant took to the stump and made several short speeches for Garfield in the East and West. Conkling also took to the field to battle for the ticket. The Republican spellbinder Robert Ingersoll, campaigning for Garfield, plumbed the depths of partisan nonsense: "I believe in a party that believes in good crops; that is glad when a fellow finds a gold mine; that rejoices when there are forty bushels of wheat to the acre. . . . The Democratic Party is a party of famine; it is a good friend of the early frost; it believes in the Colorado beetle and the weevil."[22]

In securing the funds for the campaign the Republicans assessed officeholders, usually 2 percent of their salaries.[23] Indiana and other doubtful states were "plastered with $2.00 bills." Vice President Arthur at a postelection banquet jestingly referred to these bills as "political documents."

The 1880 Outcome. Garfield barely squeaked into office. His popular plurality—less than 3,000 votes out of a major-party popular vote of almost 9 million votes—was the smallest in American history. Seventy-eight percent of the voters had balloted, indicating the campaign's importance. Weaver, after a vigorous cross-country campaign, polled 308,500 votes (about 3 percent of the total), a disappointing drop from the 1 million cast for Greenback candidates two years earlier. Soon that party would cease to matter. However, Weaver's success was a warning that agrarian discontent still survived, particularly in the Midwest, and that a third party might make a serious bid for power if farmers were struck by another economic depression. Some 10,000 people voted for Dow, the Prohibitionist.

In the electoral college Garfield had 214 votes to 155 for Hancock. The South placed her entire 138 electoral votes in Hancock's column. It was the first solid South since Reconstruction. With Garfield's victory in 1880 begins an era of the closest balance of party strength in American history until about 1900. Republicans carried all of the North except New Jersey, but their majorities in House and Senate were both razor-thin and unstable.

President Garfield in Office

In the White House Garfield showed signs of being a strong executive, as unconcerned with party as Hayes had been. His independence of party quickly precipitated a fratricidal struggle between party factions over patronage. Garfield, encouraged by Blaine, particularly resisted the demands of Senator Conkling for appointments for the Stalwarts. When Blaine was picked for the State Department, Conkling considered the appointment a personal affront, as it was probably intended to be. For the treasury, Garfield appointed not the New York financier the Stalwarts wanted but a Westerner, William Windom of Minnesota. Appointment as secretary of war went to Robert T. Lincoln of Illinois, one of the diehard "306" who stayed with Grant through the last of the ballots at Chicago. Lincoln's appointment was a concession to the Stalwarts; almost the only one Garfield made. The post of postmaster general (the cabinet official having the most to do with patronage) went to Thomas L. James, a civil service champion, and a Southerner, William H. Hunt, nominally of Louisiana, was chosen for the Navy Department. The West got a representative in Samuel J. Kirkwood of Iowa, as secretary of the interior.

In making federal appointments, Garfield further infuriated Conkling by nominating J.S. Robertson, the leading opponent of the Conkling faction in New York, to be collector of the Port of New York. Not only was the office the most lucrative in the whole public service, but its possessor would control 1,300 appointments. It was a position absolutely necessary to political control of New York State.[24] The circumstances suggest that the nomination of Robertson was a purely political move for the purpose of handing the New York Republican machine over to Blaine's Half-Breeds.

When it became clear that he could not prevent Robertson's confirmation by the Senate, Conkling staged a melodramatic resignation from the Senate, dragging along with him his Stalwart subordinate, New York's junior senator Thomas Collier Platt, who ever after would be tagged with the derisive nickname "Me Too" Platt. Two days after the dramatic resignation of Conkling and Platt, Robertson was confirmed without a roll call. Garfield and Blaine had won a great victory. Cartoonists drew Conkling as an exploding gasbag, with a lesser balloon labeled "Me Too" trailing behind. Sometimes, they simply pictured Conkling carrying his head under one arm.

On July 2, 1881, less than four months after taking office, Garfield was shot in the back as he waited for a train in the Washington railroad station by the Stalwart Charles Guiteau, who had failed to get the minor office he wanted, shouting: "I am a Stalwart and Arthur is President now!" After a gallant ten-week fight, the president died on September 19.[25]

The assassination of Garfield at the hands of a disappointed office seeker, coming so soon after Lincoln's death, produced both a nationwide expression of sympathy for Garfield and a revulsion against the system of patronage and spoils associated with the tragedy. Whether or not he would have done much for civil service reform had he lived, the dead president effectively symbolized the crucial need for some kind of reform. "The assassination of Mr. Garfield," declared the *New York Evening Telegraph*, was a natural "outcome of the debased and debasing machine politics that his nation has suffered from ever since the War closed."[26] Demands for civil service reform swept the Congress. On August 11, 1881, the National Civil Service League was founded.

In July, after the shooting of Garfield, a combination of Half-Breeds and Democrats in the New York State Senate blocked Conkling's reelection to the U.S. Senate as vindication and Conkling and Platt were replaced by unknowns. Conkling retired permanently to private life. Soon he was just "a gorgeous reminiscence." Platt, who had earlier withdrawn from the Senate race "in order not to hurt the chances of Conkling,"[27] went into temporary oblivion and then on to fame as one of the most odious of the political bosses, doing what he could to run the Republican Party in New York from the barroom of the Fifth Avenue Hotel (called the "Amen Corner").

Chester A. Arthur as President

Although the nomination and election of the dark-horse Garfield surprised many Americans, the nomination of Chester Arthur as vice president was a real shock, and many citizens feared the worst when Garfield died in September 1881 with 3.5 years of his term remaining. There were reasons for the public to be worried. Arthur, a "foppish" man whose tastes ran to rich food and drink, expensive carriages, and sable-lined overcoats with broad mink cuffs, had been associated with and apparently enriched by the corrupt New York Republican machine for almost 20 years. When Arthur became president there was every expectation that the freewheeling spoils system that had reigned in New York would be firmly established in Washington. Even some Republicans shared the dismay of the man who groaned, "Chet Arthur President of the United States! Good God."[28]

The nation's fears about the new administration were further heightened when Arthur dismantled Garfield's cabinet, replacing the martyred president's appointees with friends of Grant and Conkling, most of whom were mediocre men. Only one member of the Garfield cabinet was retained – Robert T. Lincoln – who had been appointed as a concession to the Stalwarts in the first place. Blaine left the State Department. He could not countenance working under a Stalwart who had been reviling him for years.

However, fortunately for the nation, Chester Arthur fooled everyone – friends and enemies alike. Somehow the responsibilities of the high office of president turned this petty politician into a man sincerely dedicated to the good of the country.

Tariff Revision. There had been some discussion of tariff revision in the campaign of 1880, and after Arthur became president the low-tariff Democrats set up a clamor for reduction of the import duties, which were still at the record levels imposed in 1864 while the Civil War was still on – 1,450 dutiable commodities had been burdened with an average tariff of 47 percent of their value. Perhaps more important, several moderate tariff Republicans pointed out to the president that the prosperity-bred surplus of $100 million which had accumulated in the treasury during 1881 and 1882 threatened to upset the prosperity by keeping investment money in government vaults.

To deal with this unusual problem, the Republicans had authorized the president to appoint a tariff commission. When he did, Nelson Aldrich – a staunch Republican elected to the Senate from Rhode Island in 1882 – pointed out "there was a representative of the wool growers on the commission; there was a representative of the iron interest on the commission; and those interests were very carefully looked out for."[29] When the last back had been scratched and the last log had been rolled, the Tariff Act of 1883, the "Mongrel Tariff" as it was contemptuously called, reduced rates by an average of 5 percent. Real tariff revision had been prevented by wholesale lobbying and by the clever maneuvers of strong protectionist congressmen. Even so, it was signed by the president.

The Civil Service Reform Act of 1883. In his first message to Congress, President Arthur firmly told the members that action on civil service reform "should no longer be postponed" and he promised his full cooperation. Mugwumps (a group of independent Republicans, from the Indian word for big chief) were fulsome with praise. E.L. Godkin, the Mugwump editor of the *Nation*, that stern critic of politics and politicians, reported: "He takes the reform bull by the horns in the most manfull [*sic*] fashion."

But the solidly Republican Congress was not to be hurried into a reform which would deprive the members of accustomed perquisites. However, in the fall elections of 1882 the Democratic candidates were so successful that papers headlined it "A Democratic Cyclone." In the Forty-Eighth Congress 200 Democrats would face 119 Republicans in the House of Representatives, though the GOP still controlled the Senate by the slim margin of 4 votes. The setback of 1882 endangered Republican control of federal spoils.

The "lame-duck" Republican Congress, fully aware of the Republican defeat and fearing a more drastic law at the hands of the Democrats, now hastened to enact legislation to protect Republican partisans already in office. The Pendleton Act, sponsored by Democratic Senator George H. Pendleton of Ohio, was passed by large majorities in both houses of Congress.[30] President Arthur, who had risen to power through the sort of patronage excesses the Pendleton Act was designed to wipe out (and who could have killed the bill with a veto), unhesitatingly signed it into law on January 16, 1883.[31]

The act established a three-man bipartisan Civil Service Commission, appointed by the president with Senate approval, who were to administer "open" competitive examinations for new applicants for federal positions (but not to incumbents) and select appointees on the basis of merit. A key provision was the statement that congressmen's recommendations of applicants for the offices covered by the system should receive no consideration whatever in the appointment process. To insulate officers from political persuasion, the law forbade, at least on paper, assessment of officeholders for political purposes. Arthur demonstrated his good faith by naming as head of the commission Dorman B. Eaton, an outstanding reformer who drafted the act, and appointing two prominent friends of reform as the other commissioners. When the commission promptly applied merit rules, he did not inhibit their effectiveness in any way.[32]

The Pendleton Act was as weak as Congress had dared to make it. Aside from offices in Washington, the new Civil Service Commission got jurisdiction only over custom houses plus post offices in large cities. Initially, the great majority (about 85 percent) of the 100,000 federal jobs remained outside the merit regulations. Arthur also extended the merit system to some 14,000 additional positions in order to protect his partisans against replacement by his successors. He had, however, established a precedent, and in the years that followed each outgoing president extended the merit system to more jobs.

The Rivers and Harbors Veto. Arthur also antagonized the Stalwarts by vetoing two key measures (which presidents just never veto). The first came in 1882, when the Republican Congress voted $18.7 million for river and harbor improvements in 500 different localities. The press called the rivers and harbors bill "the great divide," and compared it to "a jack pot, with everyone in." Godkin pulled out the stops: "No appropriation bill was ever more wanton in its lavishness." When Arthur, with an eye on the upcoming congressional election, vetoed the bill as a pure and simple graft-ridden raid on the "pork barrel," he got some good press coverage for a change. However, the president's veto was quickly overridden by an angry Congress.

The Chinese Exclusion Bill. The second veto came later in the same year when Arthur disapproved the Chinese Exclusion Bill in the face of the unanimous and excited demands of the far Western states for its enactment into law. Congress irritably sustained the veto, then passed an act restrictng immigration for ten years, which Arthur signed.[33]

After four years, although he was not an inspiring leader of men, he had earned the nation's gratitude. Said Mark Twain, the political humorist: "I am but one in 55,000,000; still in the opinion of this one-fifty-five millionth of the country's population, it would be hard to better President Arthur's Administration."[34] Even the *Nation* concluded that Arthur had been a far better president than the country deserved for having elected a vice president of his spoils-system antecedents.

The Election of 1884

As the time for the 1884 Republican convention came closer, the field was cluttered with aspirants for the presidential nomination. President Arthur hoped to be nominated for a term of his own. However, although he had given the country a surprisingly conscientious and able administration, Arthur had almost no support outside the South. His independence had pleased neither the Stalwarts nor the Half-Breeds. Nor was he acceptable to the reformers who had no doubt about whom they did *not* want to be president, but were not sure who they did want in the office. Most of the reformers eventually settled in on the honest and upright (and equally undistinguished) senator George F. Edmunds of Vermont.[35]

Another hopeful was General John A. ("Black Jack") Logan of Illinois, a popular figure among the nation's boys in blue. Logan gained fame in the Civil War and capitalized on it afterward as a founder (and later commander) of the Grand Army of the Republic and instigator of Memorial Day. In 1880 he was one of the bitter-end Stalwarts. He faced open opposition from Chicago Republicans, as well as downstate supporters of James G. Blaine. General William Tecumseh Sherman, John Sherman's red-haired and red-bearded brother, also had a few supporters. The general soon removed himself emphatically from the contest, however. When asked if he would accept the Republican nomination, he wired back what came to be regarded as the ultimate turndown in American politics: "If nominated, I will not run. If elected, I will not serve."

However, the leading candidate for the Republican presidential nomination was James Gillespie Blaine, one of the most widely respected Republican leaders in the country at the time and the unquestioned leader of the Half-Breeds. His name had been placed before two previous Republican conventions, in 1876 and 1880, but he had lost out both times, and he was determined to do or die in a crucial third try. Blaine's chances to realize his great ambition for the presidency appeared to be excellent. Conkling, his bitter enemy, was out of politics and Platt, the Republican leader of New York, had announced his support.

The Republican Convention, 1884. When the Republicans assembled in Chicago on June 3, 1884, Blaine's supporters were the most numerous.[36] When his name was placed in nomination by the famous "Blind Orator," Judge William H. West of Ohio, one of the wildest demonstrations in convention history took place. A forest of white plumes waved on the floor and in the galleries. The delegates chanted "Blaine! Blaine! The Man from Maine!" The hullabaloo was climaxed by the appearance of a helmet festooned with a large white plume which was rushed up to the speaker's platform. In the stampede which followed, Blaine became the standard bearer of the Grand Old Party.[37]

Since Blaine was an Easterner and a Half-Breed without a war record,[38] his candidacy was balanced by the nomination of General John A. Logan. Blaine was not pleased with the selection of Logan as his running mate and said so. For one thing, the general represented the Stalwart wing of the party and could be counted on to give his support to Conkling and his friends. He was, in addition, a coarse-grained, illiterate sort of person, the exact antithesis of Blaine. Before the campaign had hardly begun, a very marked coolness developed between the two men.[39]

The chairman of the Resolutions Committee, Representative William McKinley of Ohio, presented a short and somewhat ambiguous platform which halfheartedly called for revision of the tariff without endangering domestic industries, an eight-hour day, sound money, civil service reform, the exclusion of Chinese labor, regulation of corporations, and increased availability of public lands for settlers. It also promised "quick and faithful response to the demands of the people for the freedom and equality of all men; for a united nation assuring the rights of all citizens; for the elevation of labor; for purity in legislation." Many of the reformers were disappointed with the platform. It spoke, they said, "for a party which had lost almost all reason for being except to win elections."[40] It was, however, the sort of platform on which four campaigns had been fought and won since the Civil War.

The Mugwump Revolt. Many reform-minded Republicans, especially in the New York and Massachusetts areas, were profoundly displeased with the nomination of Blaine, who as Speaker of the House, senator, and secretary of state had been too influential too long in the old system—the system they had been fighting for years—to satisfy the Independents. Since Blaine had never been a committed advocate of reform, the Independents refused to believe that he would change his spots: they were determined to prevent their nascent reform program from falling into his hands. Blaine, for his part, dismissed the reformers: "Oh, they have re-enacted the moral law and the Ten Commandments for a platform . . . and have demanded an angel of light for President."

To this end, a group of them, including Henry Ward Beecher, William Everett, George William Curtis (the reformist editor of *Harper's Weekly*), Carl Schurz, and E.L. Godkin—all of whom had been identified with the Republican Party from its earliest years—indicated to Democratic leaders that they would bolt their own party and support a Democrat, provided he was a decent and honorable man. Although they insisted that they were still Republicans and formally retained the Independent Republican title, their attachment was not to the party's present corrupt leaders but to the old party's ideals.

Inevitably, the deserters earned a number of more widely used nicknames. The loyal followers of Blaine scornfully derided them as Mugwumps (Indian chiefs whose egos were so big that they would not be bound by decisions of a tribal council). The bolters themselves eventually developed a sentimental attachment to the term Mugwump, defining it as a man of principle willing to stand for his convictions.[41] The appellation soon became the regular method of distinguishing the dissenters from the regular Republican Party.[42]

Many Republicans who had opposed Blaine before the Chicago convention decided against joining the Mugwumps and extended their support to Blaine. One of these was the young New Yorker Theodore Roosevelt, who thoroughly understood the virtues of party regularity. However, Blaine's old enemy, Roscoe Conkling, was unreconcilable. "I do not engage in criminal practice" was his reply to requests for support.

In 1884 the Democrats appeared to have a reasonable chance of winning the presidency for the first time since the Civil War. The division in the Republican Party, and an economic depression in the farm areas and cities accompanied by widespread unemployment, raised Democratic hopes for a return to power. It would be a hard fight. By 1884 the United States had become normally Republican in politics and, in order to win, the Democrats would have to draw heavily from the liberal and independent elements ordinarily Republican.

Even though he was not 70 years old — older than any man ever elected to the presidency at that time — and in failing health, Samuel Tilden still had friends who wished to see him in the White House. But Tilden was not interested in running. He declined publicly, saying, "I but submit to the will of God in deeming my public career forever closed." Anyhow, most of the younger Democratic politicians did not want Tilden. They more often called for reform than for Tilden, and looked to Grover Cleveland, the outspoken and profanely hot-tempered reform governor of New York to lead them to victory.

Grover Cleveland entered public life in 1863 through an unsought appointment as assistant district attorney for Erie County, New York. His performance in that office prompted his party to nominate him in 1869 for the office of sheriff of Erie County. The expectation was that he would lose, yet he won the election. The Democratic Party then nominated him for the office of mayor of Buffalo to which he was elected in 1881, even though the Republican state ticket carried Buffalo by a 1,000-vote majority. As mayor of Buffalo, Cleveland turned down so many crooked appropriations measures proposed by the city council that he came to be known as the "veto mayor" and as "His Obstinacy, Grover of Buffalo."[43]

Based on his reputation as a reform mayor, the Democrats nominated Cleveland for the governorship of New York in 1882 in order to overthrow the established Republican control. Cleveland won in the election in a supposedly Republican state by the remarkable plurality of 192,000 votes out of almost 900,000 cast, defeating Secretary of the Treasury Charles J. Folger, the handsome, handpicked candidate of President Arthur. Overnight the "Burly Buffalonian" became a national figure.

As governor, Cleveland gained popularity and showed his courage by refusing to court favor with the politicians, particularly those of Tammany Hall (then near the peak of malodorousness). In return, he was heartily disliked by the ruling spirits of Tammany Hall. Cleveland's conservatism was shown by his veto of a bill requiring Jay Gould's street railways to reduce their fares to a nickel because he thought it a violation of a contract between the street railway company and the city. He also risked the wrath of labor by vetoing a bill limiting the working day of New York streetcar conductors to 12 hours. Cleveland's defense of his vetoes made him into a champion of strict construction of the Constitution, a fact that impressed businessmen. To the Democrats looking for a winner, Grover Cleveland looked like a mighty good prospect.

The Democratic Convention, 1884. The Fourteenth Democratic National Convention opened in Chicago's Exposition Hall on July 8, 1884, five weeks after the Republicans had nominated Blaine. It was a generally harmonious convention. The only sour note was sounded by the Tammany delegation, a minority of the New York delegation, which came to the convention determined to defeat Cleveland. When Cleveland's name was put into nomination, Wisconsin's fiery "old Warhorse," General Edward S. Bragg—mindful of Tammany's earnest desire to prevent Cleveland's nomination—stated, in seconding the nomination, "We love him most for the enemies he has made." A member of Tammany sprang up and roared back, "on behalf of his enemies I reciprocate the sentiment." The anti-Cleveland delegates attempted to block his nomination by disposing of the unit rule to permit individual voting by delegates when a state's vote was challenged, but the move failed and on the second ballot Cleveland was nominated as the presidential candidate.

The Democratic platform of 1884 called for honest civil service reform and the diffusion of free education by common schools "so that every child in the land may be taught the rights and duties of citizenship." It straddled the tariff issue by pledging the party "to revise the tariff in a spirit of fairness to all interests." The tariff plank was, in the view of many delegates, a "mongrel resolution . . . which meant anything or nothing as one chose to construe it"—which was exactly the way the majority wanted it.

The Greenback-Labor Party, 1884. The dying Greenback-Labor Party held its convention in Indianapolis two weeks later, and after some dissension nominated the ever-available General Benjamin F. Butler, the Democratic governor of Massachusetts (who had earlier been nominated by the antimonopoly national convention). The stout and bald Butler, derisively called "Old Cock-Eye" because his eyes were not quite in line, was a bundle of contradictions. A Democrat until the Civil War, like many Democrats he had switched parties and been elected to the House of Representatives as a radical Republican and subsequently managed the impeachment of Andrew Johnson and popularized the term "bloody shirt" by waving one to emphasize black rights. In 1878 Butler had gone back to the House as a Greenbacker. Then in 1882 he became Democratic governor of Massachusetts; and now in 1884 Butler sought the Greenback Party's nomination. Alonson M. West of Mississippi was chosen to be his running mate. Butler delayed accepting the nomination, however, hoping something more promising would develop at the upcoming Democratic convention. When the Democrats totally ignored Butler, he had no choice but to accept the Greenback nomination.

The Prohibition Party, 1884. On July 23 the National Prohibition Party met in Pittsburgh to name John P. St. John, a former Republican governor of Kansas, for president and William Daniel of Maryland for vice president, on a platform declaring that both the other parties, either in their platforms or candidates, were competing for the liquor vote and were partners in the liquor crime. It unequivocally demanded the admission of women to full and equal suffrage rights with men. Even this was implicitly linked with the sacred cause of Prohibition. St. John spent most of his time on the campaign trail speaking about the virtues of a dry mouth and a pure heart.

The Equal Rights Party, 1884. The election of 1884 saw still another third party enter the lists when the Woman Rights Convention met at San Francisco and nominated Mrs. Belva A. Lockwood, the first woman lawyer to practice before the Supreme Court, for president. The platform, written largely by Mrs. Lockwood, recommended suffrage for women, equal rights as property holders for women, a moderately protective tariff, discouragement of liquor traffic, civil service reforms, and urged that public land be granted only to actual settlers.[44]

The Campaign of 1884. The campaign of 1884 was one of the most frenzied, if meaningless, campaigns in American history. As Henry Adams put it: "Everyone takes part. We are all doing our best, and swearing like demons. But the amusing thing is that no one talks about real issues." But then how could they? There was no significant difference between the party platforms and so, from the beginning, the campaign could be little more than a mudslinging contest centering on the personal fitness, or more accurately unfitness, of the candidates. Blaine made some 400 speeches stressing the protective tariff as support for high wages, and on appropriate occasions employing his magnificent oratorical powers in waving the bloody shirt, raising the spectre of the solid South and of "the South once more in the saddle." Cleveland was sneered at because he had not enlisted in the army but had sent a substitute. To this it was answered that he was then the sole support of a widowed mother, and that Blaine had neither enlisted nor sent a substitute.

Cleveland said little at all during the campaign. The Democrats revived their claim that Blaine had sold his influence in Congress to business interests by resurrecting the "Mulligan Letters" which had been so embarrassing to Blaine in the 1876 campaign. Blaine had added the damning postscript "burn this letter" to one of these incriminating letters addressed to Warren Fisher, in which Blaine asked the railroad executive to state that he had no knowledge of any dishonest dealing involving Blaine. The Democrats and bolting Republicans adopted this postscript and set it to music. As they marched in procession for Cleveland they threw lighted bits of paper into the air and joyously chanted:

Burn, burn, burn this letter
Regards, regards to Mrs. Fisher!
Burn this letter![45]

When Mulligan released additional Blaine-Fisher letters which made it obvious that Blaine had systematically lied and equivocated when he testified before the House of Representatives in 1876, the plumed knight was nakedly exposed. After the new Mulligan disclosures, when the Republicans rent the air with their chief campaign cry,

Blaine! Blaine! James G. Blaine!
The White Plumed Knight
from the State of Maine

the Democrats hooted back:

Blaine! Blaine! Jay Gould Blaine!
The Continental Liar
from the State of Maine!

Resolute Republicans, eager to retaliate, dug deeply into the past of bachelor Cleveland. What they found appeared to them pure dross. On July 21, 1884, the *Buffalo Evening News* made the sensational charge that the Democratic candidate as a young man had fathered an illegitimate child by a Mrs. Maria Halpin. The scandal quickly filled the nation's press. Church groups passed resolutions and religious organs printed long editorials with quotations from the Book of Revelation. Numerous sermons were preached on "Absalom the Fast Young Man." Cleveland did not deny this misadventure and, whether guilty or not, he had agreed to support the infant (perhaps to shield others involved) and made financial arrangements for the child.[46]

When distraught party leaders asked Cleveland how to reply to the scandal he astonished them by replying: "Tell the Truth." Though shocked by the Halpin story, the Mugwumps decided to stick with Cleveland. As one of them put it: "We are told that Mr. Blaine had been delinquent in office but blameless in private life, while Mr. Cleveland had been a model of official integrity but culpable in his personal relations. We should therefore elect Mr. Cleveland to the public office which he is so well qualified to fill, and remand Mr. Blaine to the private station which he is admirably fitted to adorn."[47] This directness and honesty was publicized and won Cleveland applause.

Reminders of his illegitimate son were chanted through the streets in Great Republican parades.

Ma! Ma! Where's my pa?
Ma! Ma! Where's my pa?
Ma! Ma! Where's my pa?

To which question the Democrats gleefully provided the answer:

Going to the White House
Ha! Ha! Ha!

The political cartoonists played a great part in the campaign. *Harper's Weekly,* which had shifted its support to Cleveland, featured Nast's vicious anti–Blaine cartoons throughout the campaign. One widely circulated cartoon showed Blaine with plumes emerging from his top hat and quotations from the Mulligan letters. Another depicted Blaine as a traveling salesman, wearing a beaver hat decorated with a bedraggled white feather and carrying a carpetbag upon which a variety of uncomplimentary legends appeared, as if to illustrate the unsavory bill of goods Blaine was trying to sell the voters. A picture in *Puck* of Blaine as a tattooed man was so personally offensive to Blaine that his friends had difficulty restraining him from instituting a criminal prosecution.[48]

Clergymen, in particular, pointed to Cleveland as a monster of evil because of his well-known tobacco chewing, beer drinking, and card playing habits. Many ministers assured their congregations that Cleveland was excluded from all decent houses. However, it may have been a Republican clergyman who made Cleveland's election a certainty. On October 29, just six days before the election, a conclave of Protestant clergymen was meeting at the Fifth Avenue Hotel in New York where Blaine was spending the night. The clergymen, wishing to show their support for the plumed knight, arranged to give him a short address when he descended to the lobby. It seemed to Blaine to be a good and harmless idea for him to meet with a large delegation of friendly Protestant ministers to stress his moral acceptability.

The Reverend Samuel Dickinson Burchard, a staunch Presbyterian and an equally staunch Republican, spoke first. As Blaine arrived, Burchard welcomed him in ringing tones, promising "We are Republicans and don't propose to leave our party and identify ourselves with the party whose antecedents have been Rum, Romanism, and Rebellion." These last words, so blatantly indiscreet when publicly addressed to a candidate who was the son of a Catholic mother, brother of a Catholic nun, and who hoped to carry the pivotal state of New York by the aid of Catholic voters, were heard by Blaine, but their significance was not instantly appreciated.

Although the anti–Catholic slur apparently made no immediate impression on Blaine (he later contended that he did not hear the offending words), it did on a Democratic reporter who was present. The reporter headed straight back for Democratic headquarters. The leaders there took one look at Burchard's unhappy phrase and went into action. In less than 24 hours every Democratic paper in the country had spread before its readers the Burchard alliteration. The following Sunday as Irish Catholics filed out of their churches, they were handed bills containing the phrase, attributed to Blaine himself. Blaine's supporters hastily scattered handbills at the doors of Catholic churches in New York and other parts of the country, but the explanation and denial came too late to undo the damage.

On the same day Cyrus Field, Jay Gould, and other "money kings" tendered a lavish testimonial dinner to the Republican candidate, attended by several of the wealthiest men in the nation. The affair would ordinarily have caused little stir, but in the midst of a mild business recession the opposition press quickly made a liability out of it. Joseph Pulitzer headlined the event the next day in the New York World: "The Royal Feast of Belshazzar Blaine and the Money Kings." In case any of the paper's 200,000 readers did not understand the biblical allusion, an accompanying cartoon made the meaning abundantly clear. It showed Blaine and the other diners glutting themselves on a sumptuous meal, while a starving family held out their hands for a crumb. The Mugwumps roundly criticized Blaine's close association with moneyed rogues, noting that the banquet had come too late in the campaign for any of its proceeds to be used for honest purposes.[49] Ironically, the money kings did not care for Blaine, having no fear of Cleveland, and he collected very little from them, while receiving a lot of bad publicity.

The 1884 Outcome. When the ballots were counted it was found that Cleveland was elected by a narrow margin of less than 63,000 popular votes out of the approximately 10 million cast.[50] He had, however, a substantial majority in the electoral college—219 electoral votes to 182 for his Republican opponent. New York, which Cleveland carried by the hair-thin margin of 1,149 votes out of a total of 1,127,000, turned out to be once again, the decisive state in the election. After the results were known, the president-elect received a wire from Jay Gould expressing confidence "that the vast business interests of the country will be entirely safe in your hands."[51] His confidence, Gould was to learn, had not been misplaced.

The Prohibition Party ticket received slightly more than 150,000 votes—25,000 of them in the pivotal state of New York—a sharp increase over the 10,364 the party's candidates had received in 1880. Only about 134,000 votes were cast for Butler, the Greenback candidate. Cleveland faced a divided Congress with Republicans still in control of the Senate.[52]

The victory of the Democrats in 1884 has been variously explained. Some experts believe that a rainstorm in upstate New York may have swung the final votes to the Democrats, as the rain prevented many rural

Republicans from getting to the polls: the cities were all predominantly Democratic and for Cleveland. Others suggested that the votes won by the Prohibition and Greenback candidates in New York were responsible for Blaine's defeat. Others credited Cleveland's victory to Mugwump support or to the "Soft Soap Dinner." Most Republicans, however, singled out the Burchard incident as the primary cause for their defeat and Blaine himself supposedly told friends: "I should have carried New York by 10,000 if the weather had been clear on election day, and Dr. Burchard had been doing missionary work in Asia Minor, or Cochin China."[53]

For whatever reason, the victorious Democrats had the last word, which they sang on high in serenading their successful candidate:

> Hurrah for Maria
> Hurrah for the kid;
> We voted for Grover,
> And we're damned glad we did!

The jubilant Democrats had come back to the White House after an absence of more than two decades. Somewhat ironically, Cleveland had never been to Washington before he went there to be inaugurated as president. For the Republican Party, it was its first defeat for the presidency since its entry into national politics with Fremont. After 24 continuous years in the White House, the Grand Old Party would have to learn to be an opposition party.

President Cleveland in Office

Grover Cleveland was inaugurated as the twenty-second president of the United States on a clear and sunny March 4, 1885. "No President has ever had a finer day for his coming in than Cleveland has; no President has ever had so many onlookers and so cold a reception. . . . The Democrats have come there to look over the man they have elected, rather than to honor him. They are not yet proud of him, and they are afraid of how he may conduct himself, for the charge that they have elected a Republican is current among their leaders."[54] So wrote a correspondent reporting the event.

In his brief inaugural address President Cleveland promised sectional accord, peace in foreign affairs, and less government at home. Civil service reform, he said should be "in good faith enforced," which helped pacify the Mugwumps who had deserted their own party to vote for him. He also promised to adhere to "business principles," and his cabinet included mostly undistinguished business-minded Democrats of the East and South. Thomas F. Bayard of Delaware was made secretary of state, not because he had any diplomatic experience but simply because he had been the other leading Democratic contender for the presidency. Cleveland rewarded Daniel Manning, the manager who had done so much for him, by making him secretary of the Treasury, while William C. Whitney, the leading financier of his campaign, had obviously earned his spot as head of the Navy Department. Toward healing the wounds of the Civil War, he appointed L.Q.C. Lamar of Mississippi to the post of secretary of the interior and A.H. Garland of Arkansas as attorney general. Lamar and Garland were the first Southern Democrats in the cabinet since Rutherford B. Hayes had chosen David M. Key as his postmaster general in 1877. No one represented agriculture, labor, or blacks. Even though Theodore Roosevelt dubbed Cleveland's cabinet "the Apotheosis of the Unknown," they were respectable men, and Cleveland's administration was unmarred by scandal in high places — which was a welcome change after 20 years of "grab and run" politics.

Civil Service Reform. Cleveland ran head-on into the same demand for jobs that had frustrated so many presidents before him. The job-hungry Democrats had been out of office for a quarter of a century and they wanted the "loaves and fishes." The true path to reform, they said, "meant turning out of office of Republicans and putting honest Democrats in their places" — all their places. Some of the more ravenous of the Democrats even talked about repealing the Pendleton Act.[55]

Cleveland permitted the reformed civil service system to continue as it had been under Arthur. The Mugwumps hoped he would concern himself with broadening the reach of the merit system. It would require no additional legislation for him to do so, for the Pendleton Act had granted the president sole authority to extend the reform. By way of compromise, Cleveland added approximately 12,000 offices to the classified list, after which he turned over the task of decapitating Republicans to the first assistant postmaster general, Adlai E. Stevenson. Within a short time, "Adlai's Axe" had chopped off the heads of about 40,000 Republican postmasters, who were replaced with deserving Democrats. The compromise did not completely satisfy either Cleveland's own party or the Mugwumps, who insisted that only merited removals be made. In reality, Cleveland had not opposed the broadening of the civil service system because he was learning the hard way that federal patronage had become a burden instead of a partisan asset. Every appointment seemed to produce at least two disappointed Democratic applicants and several offended civil service reformers.

In office Cleveland proved to be a thoroughgoing conservative. His concept of government was almost entirely negative. He hated paternalism in whatever form: the tariff, land grants to railroads, pensions, and social welfare legislation. He rejected out of hand the idea that the government should relieve individual suffering through the use of public funds. He demonstrated this in 1887 when he vetoed the Texas Seed Bill, which would have supplied free seed to farmers in that drought-stricken state with a stern declaration that "though the people support the Government the Government should not support the people." Cleveland's message accompanying the veto was frequently quoted in later years by opponents of the welfare state.

The Federal Treasury Surplus Issue

Cleveland, like his predecessors, was confronted with a treasury surplus which by inauguration day in 1885 had climbed to over $500 million. The surplus had been accumulating steadily throughout the 1880s when the treasury had taken in, on the average, $100 million more than it spent each year – which was in the neighborhood of $265 million.

The extra money was a surprising political headache. The leaders of the business community did not like the surplus. The country was growing robustly and needed a large volume of money in circulation to carry on its business – a shortage of circulating medium meant tight credit, low prices and wages, and a threat to the pace of growth. To them it made no economic sense for the federal government to collect millions of dollars in excess of its needs and then lock them in the vaults of what some called the treasury octopus. Moreover, the surplus was a standing temptation to extravagance of the pork barrel and pension grab variety.

Since the principal source of federal revenues, and thus, of the surplus, was a stiff protective tariff which alone accounted for some 50–60 percent of the total federal revenue, President Cleveland resolved to reduce the tariff. He dramatized the problem by devoting his entire State of the Union message in December 1887 to a plea for tariff reduction. It raised the cost of living unconscionably; it increased the cost of imports, which in a rapidly expanding nation were still needed in great volume. Moreover, tariffs gave domestic producers a sheltered market in which they could jack up the costs of basic necessities like clothing and canned goods for working families. The burdened masses, he warned in closing, might "insist upon a radical and sweeping rectification of their wrongs."

The Mills Bill, 1888. Immediately, the Southern and Western Democrats rallied to the support of the president. On April 2, 1888, Democratic Representative Roger Q. Mills of Texas introduced a South-favoring low-tariff bill incorporating Cleveland's recommendations. Far from radical, it did place such raw materials as lumber, wool, and flax on the free list and made moderate reductions of about 7 percent in rates for finished goods.

Led by William McKinley and Thomas B. Reed, the Republicans in the House of Representatives made a spirited attack on the Mills Bill, calling it "a direct attempt to fasten upon this country the British policy of free foreign trade." The president cracked the patronage whip over Democratic Representatives and the bill passed the House in July by virtually a straight party vote. Doubtless, some Eastern Democrats went along in the knowledge that the Republican-controlled Senate would kill the measure. In the Senate the Republicans, under the leadership of Nelson W. Aldrich of Rhode Island, defeated the Mills Bill, but also enacted a highly protective substitute measure. In reality, the supporters of free trade were in the minority. American laborers were largely convinced that without the tariff the country would drown in inexpensive goods produced by foreign "cheap labor," to whose abysmal wage levels they would be reduced to stay competitive. Farmers in large numbers also believed that the tariff protected American living standards.

The Democratic House would not accept the Senate bill and the Republican Senate would not accept the house bill. Both parties had been committed to positions that they could not possibly abandon in the coming presidential campaign. The deadlock ensured that the tariff issue would have top priority in the upcoming presidential race.

Warned of the political risk, Cleveland had growled endearingly, "What is the use of being elected or reelected unless you stand for something."

The only other significant federal taxes were on whiskey and tobacco. To cut either of these levies on "sin" would offend important blocs of religious voters. The only viable alternative, therefore, was to spend the surplus away. But on what? One possibility was to speed the payoff of the remaining Civil War debt of more than $1 billion. But to buy back wartime bonds from the banks and major investors who held them would mean paying premium prices. In effect, it would transfer the surplus to the pockets of the rich, yet another impossible choice.

Cleveland early incurred the enmity of the Union veterans when he foiled a series of pension grabs inspired by the Grand Army of the Republic. Petitions to the Pensions Bureau were made on behalf of soldiers who had injured themselves while drunk or to avoid hazardous duty, or who had suffered accidents while "intending to enlist," or had contracted postwar illnesses that they blamed on wartime stress. If the Pension Bureau rejected a veteran's definition of a service-connected disability, he could ask his congressman for a "private bill" for relief, and in the opening months of Cleveland's administration hundreds of private pension bills were pushed through by individual members of Congress for the benefit of constituents who, despite the extremely liberal general pension law, were not entitled to pensions.[56] When the president vetoed several hundred of these bills, his critics in both parties accused the "veto president" of having fallen victim to the "tyranny of the trivial." Soon, even school children were singing:

> A fat man once sat in a President's chair,
> 　　Singing Ve-to, Ve-to,
> With never a thought of trouble or care,
> 　　Singing Ve-to, Ve-to.[57]

The Dependent Pension Act, 1887. In January 1887 Congress, responding to pressure from the powerful GAR, passed the Dependent Pension Act, sometimes referred to as the "Pauper Pension Bill," which gave a pension to every veteran who had served at least 90 days and who was unable to work no matter when or how the disability had been incurred.

Although the bill had passed both houses of Congress virtually unanimously, Cleveland defied the wrath of the GAR and its half a million members and vetoed the bill, arguing that it would encourage further "dishonesty and mendacity." The vote on the motion to override the veto fell short of the necessary two-thirds. But this action was only a temporary check and pension payments continued to grow. Republican and GAR orators quickly pointed to the vetoes as one of the perils of placing a Southern-dominated Democrat in the White House.

In April 1887 the veterans had an excellent chance to show their dislike for the president. When the adjutant general suggested that the captured Confederate battle flags then gathering dust in the attic of the War Department building might be returned to their former owners, Cleveland approved the proposal. The long accumulating wrath of the GAR broke loose. "May God palsy the hand that wrote the order!" roared General Lucius Fairchild, the national commander in chief of the GAR. During the next few days he expanded the theme in an Eastern speaking tour, while Cleveland drew fire from all quarters of the country. The order was rescinded.[58] In the same year, 1887, the annual GAR encampment was scheduled to meet at St. Louis, and President Cleveland had tentatively accepted an invitation to be present. But so great was the bitterness over his pension vetoes and over the battle flag incident that the acceptance was canceled.

The Politics of Utopianism

In the latter decades of the nineteenth century two philosophers of protest emerged who were to drastically affect the development of American political thought and ultimately American political party practice: Henry George and Edward Bellamy.

Henry George (1839–1897). Henry George rejected social Darwinism, the prevailing economic and social philosophy of the day, and its emphasis on the "survival of the fittest" as specious. Poverty was made to appear the inevitable result of the operation of natural forces that destroyed any possibility of alleviating poverty's effects in any sustained way. George was not satisfied with that: the best way to further progress, he believed, was to end poverty. Thus he broke with the traditional view which held that poverty was always an inevitable consequence of progress.[59]

In 1879 George published *Progress and Poverty: An Inquiry into the Cause of Industrial Depression and of Increase of Want with Increase of Wealth* in which he argued that in the United States progress was accompanied by poverty because of the iniquitous system of private land ownership. Since land took on value because of the people who lived on it, George argued, this unearned rent should return to the public in the form of a "single tax" on land values.

George, therefore, proposed a tax on land, so adjusted as to take away the increased value arising from advantages of location and the growth of the community. This single tax – his proposed solution – would yield so much revenue that the government could dispense with all other taxes. The government, possessing abundant funds, could then take over the railroads and telegraphs and embark on a vast variety of social services, such as playgrounds, new schools, museums, libraries, and other badly needed social and cultural services.

When *Progress and Poverty* was published in 1879, it broke into the best-seller lists and ultimately sold some 3 million copies and its author became a national figure. Single tax clubs sprang up throughout the nation. Innumerable Americans, like the millionaire tractor manufacturer Tom L. Johnson of Cleveland who became a model mayor, dated their conversion to social democracy from their first reading of Henry George.

George edited a newspaper and spoke widely. In 1866 he ran for mayor of New York City supported by laborers, Irish nationalists, single taxers, Greenbackers, antimonopolists, and socialists calling themselves the United Labor Party. Alarmed by this threat, Tammany Hall nominated Abram Hewitt, an unusually able and respected businessman; but even so the election was exciting and close. George received the thumping vote of 68,110 citizens, nosing out Theodore Roosevelt, the poor third, while the Democratic winner, Hewitt, polled 90,552.[60] George continued to agitate tirelessly, gaining his greatest influence during the depression of the 1890s. He ran again in 1897, but died five days before the election.

Edward Bellamy (1850–1898). Edward Bellamy, George's contemporary, also rejected the conservative fatalism of the social Darwinists, but unlike George, Bellamy concentrated his attack on the competitive system itself in his utopian novel *Looking Backward, 2000 – 1887*, begun at the end of 1886 – the year of the George campaign, bloody strikes, and the violence at Haymarket Square in Chicago – and set in the year 2000.[61]

The society of the year 2000 was pictured by Bellamy as a sane and plentiful life under a system of state socialism (although the book never used the words socialism or communism). The people were incredibly happy. Poverty, vice, and politics were unknown; hospitals served in the place of prisons; and the creative energies of mankind were released for unparalleled cultural and technological achievement. All this came about through a peaceful and evolutionary process: trusts had gone on combining with one another until they formed one big trust, and the government had taken this over. A peculiar twist was his idea that labor should be organized as an "industrial army" in the service of all the people. He argued that inasmuch as the organization of the people into armies for destructive purposes was generally accepted, there was no reason why people should not be organized in an army for peaceful and productive purposes.

To a nation already alarmed by the trust evil, the book had a magnetic appeal. Within two years after its publication, *Looking Backward* was selling at the rate of 10,000 copies a week and 150 "nationalist clubs" were gathering in a wide variety of middle-class reformers and socialists. Although Bellamy and many of his supporters hoped that "a party aiming at the national control of industry with its resulting social changes" would evolve from the nationalist clubs, that never happened. However, by the mid-1890s the nationalists, although they did not call themselves socialists, had presented socialist ideas and programs to a large American audience.

The Election of 1888

The Democratic Convention, 1888. Breaking a longstanding custom, the Democrats held their convention first, meeting in St. Louis on June 5, 1888. The meeting was gaveled to order by the chairman with a solid silver gavel, a gift of the grateful Colorado miners "to that party which restored silver to the monetary plane from which it was degraded by the Republicans." President Cleveland was renominated by acclamation, the first such endorsement since Van Buren was renominated in 1840. Although the party bosses disliked Cleveland, they felt they were stuck with him since he was the only candidate in 30 years who had carried them through to the spoils.

Since Vice President Hendricks had died on November 25, 1885, former Senator Allen G. Thurman of Ohio, a popular "old-fashioned Democrat," was named to replace him for the second place on the first ballot. "The noble old Roman," as the 75-year-old Thurman was frequently called, habitually wiped his nose with a large, red bandanna handkerchief after taking a pinch of snuff. Predictably, the red bandanna became the Democratic campaign emblem. The selection of the aged and infirm Thurman was an unfortunate choice. Since the president had made it clear that he intended to stay in the White House, that meant that no national figure would campaign.

The platform lauded the policies of President Cleveland and the Democratic Party, opposed the existing protective tariff, supported legislation to modify it, and proposed a reformation of the tax laws. "All unnecessary taxation is unjust taxation," the platform declared. The "demoralizing surplus in the national treasury" had been "drawn from the people and [out of] the channels of trade" by Republican-sponsored "extravagant taxation." The Democratic remedy was to enforce frugality in public expense and abolish needless taxation.

The Republican Convention, 1888. As the Republican convention opened in Chicago on June 19 (two weeks after the Democrats selected Cleveland), Blaine – vacationing in Scotland with Andrew Carnegie – could have had the Republican nomination by acclamation. The Republican delegates were already chanting: "Blaine, Blaine, the man from Maine. We had him once, we'll have him again." However, they were greeted with a decision by Blaine not to run again. He gave no reason except "considerations personal to myself." Even so, many delegates were sure the Mainite would welcome a draft.

After Blaine, John Sherman of Ohio was the leading contender. He had been a leading member of the Republican Party from its inception. As a member of Congress, he served as chairman of the powerful House Ways and Means and Senate Finance committees, became secretary of the treasury under Hayes, and returned to the Senate in 1881. In 1880 he came close to the GOP nomination for the presidency. Sherman had a deserved reputation for expertise in financial matters. However, he was colorless and stiff – he was called the "Ohio Icicle." Also he had inherited many old Stalwart connections – and some of the attendant hostilities. Despite his advanced age and infirmities, Sherman clung tenaciously to the hope of victory; but he had too many enemies and too few backers for a nomination.

Other possible candidates were Benjamin Harrison, from the doubtful state of Indiana; Walter Q. Gresham, Arthur's postmaster general and an advocate of reduced tariffs; Senator William Allison of Iowa; Chauncey Depew, president of the New York Central and Hudson River railways; and former governor Russell A. Alger of Michigan.

When the balloting began, Sherman led on the first six ballots. On the fourth ballot Harrison, who was the second choice of many of Blaine's friends, began to creep up on Sherman and on the eighth ballot received the nomination when Pennsylvania swung its support to him after receiving a coded telegram from Carnegie in Scotland, reading, "Too late. Victor immovable. [Blaine will not run.] Take Trump [Harrison] and Star [Phelps]."[62] The nomination of Harrison, if it was not greeted with much enthusiasm, met with an almost unanimous feeling of relief.[63] For vice president the convention chose Levi P. Morton, a wealthy New York banker and diplomat. Morton never forgot that he had declined a vice presidential nomination with Garfield.

Benjamin Harrison had several Republican assets for the presidency. He had interrupted a prospering law career to serve in the Civil War, where he fought courageously in several major battles rising from the rank of lieutenant to that of brigadier general. He was a graceful orator, a faithful Presbyterian elder, and a distinguished corporation lawyer from the doubtful and electorally potent state of Indiana. Also, as the grandson of President William Henry Harrison—"Old Tippecanoe" of log cabin and hard cider fame (and great-grandson of a signer of the Declaration of Independence)—he carried a distinguished American name.

On the other hand, Harrison had at best only a moderately distinguished record in politics. Shortly after returning to Indiana after the war, he entered politics but was defeated when running for governor. After one term in the U.S. Senate, he failed to be reelected in 1887. As a senator his voting record was inoffensive. He supported high tariffs and sound money, favored railroad regulation, generous land laws, and internal improvements. Also, although the 5-feet, 6-inches tall Harrison loved politics, he disliked politicking and politicians and his glacial but dignified manner gave rise to the saying: "Harrison sweats ice-water." It was said that he was such a cold man that when he entered any room the temperature immediately went down ten degrees. Probably more important, Harrison's handshake, it was said, was "like a wilted petunia."[64]

The platform adopted called for a protective tariff, supported the use of both gold and silver as money, called for veteran's pensions, and strongly opposed the Mormon practice of polygamy.

The Labor Parties, 1888. Two parties, voicing the agricultural and industrial unrest of the period, entered the 1888 campaign. In 1886, as we have seen, a United Labor Party had nominated Henry George, the single-tax advocate, as candidate for mayor of New York City and although he was probably cheated out of thousands of votes he placed second in a three-cornered race. Because the result of the contest was regarded both by the workers and by the general public as being a victory for George, the United Labor Party felt inspired to seek larger fields to conquer. At the 1887 United Labor Party convention, after an acrimonious debate between socialists and single taxers, George managed to expel the socialists and the platform adopted explicitly repudiated socialism.

In the same year a Union Labor Party, composed mostly of Midwestern farmers, held a national organizing convention in Cincinnati where the delegates organized the National Union Labor Party and adopted a platform which endorsed farmer and labor demands.[65]

In May 1888 both labor parties held simultaneous conventions in Cincinnati, but they were unable to reconcile their differences. Each party nominated its own candidates: the Union Labor Party chose Anson J. Streeter of Illinois, a former president of the Northwestern Farmers' Alliance, and Charles E. Cunningham of Arkansas; the Georgites named Robert H. Cowdrey of Illinois with W.H.T. Wakefield of Kansas as his running mate.

The Union Labor Party adopted the chief principles put forth by the Cincinnati meeting, including opposition to land monopoly and immigrant

Chinese labor, and favoring people's ownership of transportation and communication, a graduated income tax, and direct election of senators. The United Labor Party displayed more radical propensities. Among other things, they approved an increased taxation of land values and government ownership and control of railway and telegraph lines.

The Prohibition Party, 1888. The Prohibition Party met in their fifth national convention at Indianapolis on May 20. In a spirit of enthusiasm and earnestness Clinton B. Fisk of New Jersey, a Civil War major general and founder of Fisk University, and John A. Brooks of Missouri were nominated by acclamation.

The platform adopted by the Prohibitionists reflected some expansion of outlook. In addition to the usual proposal that the manufacture, importation, exportation, transportation, and sale of alcoholic beverages should be made public crimes and prohibited, it also covered other issues including the support of import duties that would both protect American industry and raise revenue, called for the extension of voting rights, favored immigration restrictions, and proposed the abolition of polygamy.

The Campaign of 1888. The Republicans entered the 1888 campaign with fewer factional differences than they had had since the best days of Grant. The Republican campaign manager Senator Matthew S. Quay, boss of a ruthless machine in Pennsylvania, carried on an astute and vigorous campaign built around voter pilgrimages to Harrison's Indianapolis home. Between July 7 and October 25 Harrison delivered 80 impromptu addresses to 300,000 people who followed in the wake of these appearances. Many of Harrison's remarks were reported in the press and provided effective texts for his followers.

The campaign was waged almost wholly on the tariff issue—the first campaign since the Civil War that involved a question of economic differences between the parties. The Republicans charged that Cleveland's "British free trade" policy (as they insisted on labeling the mild reforms of the Mills Bill) would ruin American manufacturing and betray American workers to the "pauper labor" of Europe. The Republican campaign hymn was

> Protection, oh protection, the joyful sound
>   proclaim
> Till each remotest nation has heard the Tariff's
> name.

The Republican campaign fund was more than $30 million; the largest sum hitherto collected (and spent) by a political party in a presidential contest. The big beneficiaries of the tariff were put over the fire by the GOP fundraisers and the fat fried out of them. John Wanamaker, treasurer of the

Republican National Committee, put it on the line: "How much would you pay for insurance upon your business? If you were confronted by from one to three years of general depression by a change in our revenue and protective measures affecting manufactures, wages, and good time, what would you pay to be insured for a better year?" The funds collected were used to carry on an extensive campaign of education, and to get out the vote (and in key states to buy votes on election day).

"Little Ben" was joyously hailed as "Young Tippecanoe" and the voters were urged (in an update of the highly successful campaign slogan of 1840) to cast their ballots for "Tippecanoe and Morton Too." Harrison was also pictured as wearing his grandfather's military hat. A popular Republican jingle of the campaign went thus:

> Yes, grandfather's hat fits Ben — fits Ben;
> He wears if with dignified grace, Oh, yes!
> So rally again and we'll put Uncle Ben
> Right back in his grandfather's place.

The Democrats responded with: "Grandpa's pants won't fit Benny," and cartooned him as rattling around in the oversized martial headgear and as a very small figure sitting in a gigantic chair which represented the presidency. Still another pictured Harrison as a midget sitting behind an oversized desk with a bust of his grandfather, President William Henry Harrison, behind the desk and a large raven with the head of Blaine perched on the bust.[66]

Harrison attacked Cleveland's veto of the Dependent Pension Bill by saying that "it was no time to be weighing the claims of old soldiers with apothecary's scales" to the delight of the GAR. Harrison's official campaign button was a stickpin in the form of a five-petaled flower with a word on each petal proclaiming, "Protection, Reciprocity, Nation's Pride, Harrison."

Cleveland refused to campaign on the ground that it would be undignified for the president to go about soliciting votes. Much was made by the Clevelandites of the fact that the bachelor president had married Francis Folsom on June 2, 1886, during his first term as president. Advertising cards featuring Cleveland's young and beautiful new wife and plumping various commercial products appealing to women, such as Merrick Thread, were widely distributed during the campaign.

The Republicans also made effective use of the somewhat stupid British minister in Washington, Sir Lionel Sackville-West. In September this diplomat received a letter requesting advice on how to vote from Pomona, California, signed by C.F. Murchison. Which candidate, Cleveland or Harrison, the American asked, would better serve the interests of

England? The minister, forgetting that diplomats ought never to interfere in domestic politics, replied that Cleveland, the low-tariff candidate, would best serve the interests of Britain's free-trade policy and was to the preferred. When the Republican *New York Tribune* gleefully published Sackville-West's correspondence with a telling comment: "The British Lion's paw thrust into American politics to help Cleveland," a wave of anger swept over the country. The crucial Irish vote in New York, normally Democratic, began to slip away. Thoroughly frightened, Cleveland first complained to Lord Salisbury, and when the prime minister hesitated about withdrawing Sackville-West, the president dismissed the "damned Englishman." A Midwestern newspaper reported that "Queen Victoria keeps a pet dog named Cleveland." The *New York Tribune* gloatingly published a jingle, accompanied by a cartoon, in which Cleveland addressed John Bull:

> Believe me that I made him go
> For nothing that he wrote,
> But just because, as well you know,
> I feared the Irish vote!

Meanwhile, crowds of gleeful Republicans marched through the streets of New York chanting:

> Sack, Sack, Sackville-West
> He didn't want to go home,
> But Cleveland thought it best.

And carrying signs which read:

> No frigid North,
> No torrid South,
> No temperate east,
> *No Sackville-West!*

The 1888 Outcome. Cleveland's popular vote of 5,540,000 topped Harrison's by more than 100,000, but Harrison's popular votes were better distributed for gaining electoral votes and he won the electoral college 233 to 168.[67] The Grand Old Party also captured both houses of Congress. Republican strength would also be increased by the admission in 1889 and 1890 of six new Republican states: Wyoming, Idaho, North and South Dakota, Montana, and Washington. The new senators, although Republicans, added to the already strident clamor for free silver.

As usual, the outcome had hung on a few evenly divided states — Indiana, New York, and Ohio — each of which Harrison had carried by a few thousand votes.[68] As Harold Faulker points out, the most surprising thing about the election was that the outcome was gracefully accepted by both Cleveland and the Democrats. Nobody proposed overthrowing by force a system which could produce such a bizarre and unjust triumph of geography over numbers.[69]

Close or not, the Republicans had won and they exulted:

> Down in the cornfield
> Hear that mournful sound;
> All the Democrats are weeping —
> Grover's in the cold, cold ground!

After the election, national chairman Matt Quay, who never had any doubt that he made Harrison president, went to Indiana to congratulate President-elect Harrison and to make arrangements to collect his "just deserts" (that is, a cabinet post). He expected fervent and grateful thanks; instead, he found that Harrison preferred to attribute his success to the intervention of providence. "Think of the man!" Quay said, in reporting the episode to a journalist friend. "Benny says that God did it." "He ought to know that providence hadn't a damned thing to do with it." Harrison, he said, "would never know how close a number of men were compelled to approach the gates of the penitentiary to make him President."[70]

Benjamin Harrison in Office

Benjamin Harrison was inaugurated president in the midst of a violent rainstorm on March 4, 1889, the outgoing president obligingly holding an umbrella over him. The torrential splashing of the rain made the words of the new president's extremely long inaugural address inaudible to the 60,000 rain-drenched persons shivering in the raw East wind. The new president urged good foreign relations, expanded trade, and opposition to trusts. He had a few crumbs for the civil service reformers. "Honorable party service will certainly not be esteemed by me a disqualification for public service, but it will not, in no case, be allowed to serve as a shield of official negligence, incompetence, or delinquency."

The new chief executive quickly found that he could not even name his own cabinet. Without his knowledge, his party managers had sold out every place to pay the election expenses.[71] He made Blaine secretary of state, but only after he had sent the flamboyant Mainite a long detailed letter informing him of the rules for acceptable conduct in the administration.[72]

The other cabinet posts were filled by a "pretty scrubby lot" (as Blaine's friends put it) of politically obscure, businesslike representatives from the East and West, including the Philadelphia merchant, John Wanamaker, who had contributed heavily to Harrison's campaign, as postmaster general. Although the president promised to carry out the Pendleton Act in distributing patronage, within a year Wanamaker had cleared out over 32,000 of the 55,000 fourth-class postmasters, most for "notorious partisanship." Before he left office, Harrison extended the civil service list to an additional 14,000 jobs; it covered some 43,000 employees.[73]

Harrison's chief contribution to civil service reform, as it turned out, was his appointment to the Civil Service Commission of young Theodore Roosevelt, who had earned the appointment as a reward for Republican regularity during the campaigns of 1884 and 1888. Once aboard, the energetic and colorful New Yorker proceeded to make himself obnoxious to the Republican professionals by trying to make the commission "a living force." Roosevelt could accomplish little and soon became frustrated with Harrison's administration.

Harrison made no effort at legislative leadership, and the leadership passed largely to the conservative Republican leaders in Congress. In the Senate, Nelson Aldrich and Matthew Quay, supported by a small group of elder statesmen, controlled the deliberations of that body. These men formed the nucleus of what soon became known as the "Old Guard" or the "Stand Patters."

In the House, when Congress convened in December 1889, Thomas B. Reed defeated William McKinley, Harrison's choice for the post, to become Speaker of the House. Reed, a masterful debater, wielded a verbal harpoon of sarcasm which caused strong men to cringe at "the sound of his quip." He had enraged the Democrats when he remarked, in debate, that the Democratic Party was the organized incompetence of the country and that Democrats never opened their mouths without subtracting from the sum of human knowledge. Reed further antagonized the Democrats by insisting on counting as present Democrats sitting silent at quorum calls and by his precedent-breaking ruling that the House could continue its business without frequent quorum calls to round up every Republican member. Speaker Reed was also physically intimidating, filling the Speaker's chair with 6 feet 3 inches and nearly 300 pounds.[74]

The new Speaker quickly won the nickname "Czar" because of the autocratic way in which he expedited House business. A new set of rules adopted by Reed permitted him to dominate that body as no Speaker had done before him. Soon Reed had created a system of centralized control of committees and congressional procedure by which conservative domination of the speakership could prevent the introduction of reform bills or facilitate their emasculation in committees or on the floor.

The Billion Dollar Congress. Under Harrison the Fifty-First Congress, by distributing subsidies to steamship lines, passing extravagant rivers and harbors bills, offering large premiums to government bondholders, and returning federal taxes paid by Northern states during the Civil War, distinguished itself by expending, for the first time in a period of peace, more than $1 billion in a single session. When the Democrats cried out against this "Billion Dollar Congress," Speaker Reed cheerfully replied that we were now a "billion-dollar country."[75]

Congress was also extremely freehanded in the matter of veteran's pensions. To please the Union veterans of the Civil War, the president appointed as commissioner of pensions James "Corporal" Tanner of Indiana, a notorious pension lobbyist for the GAR, who was, he said, for "the old flag and an appropriation for every old comrade who needs it." In a thunderous demand for a $4 a month minimum, he contributed the slogan of the hour: "No man ought to be down on the pension roll . . . for less than the miserable pittance of one dollar per week, though I may wring from the hearts of some (who may oppose the spending) the prayer, 'God help the surplus!'" Tanner practiced what he preached so thoroughly that the embarrassed president had to remove him from office within six months.

The Dependent Pension Act, 1890. In office Tanner worked diligently at increasing pension expenditures, and Congress supported the good work with a new law when, in 1890, it revived the "everybody line up" pension bill to aid indigent exservicemen, which Cleveland had vetoed.[76] As a result, almost 1 million pensioners were on the rolls by 1893. Meanwhile, federal outlays for veterans' benefits leaped to $165 million in 1893. As expected, the aging veterans were grateful to the GOP for the measure the GAR hailed as "the most liberal pension measure ever passed by any legislative body in the world."

The McKinley Tariff. President Harrison showed even less comprehension of the economic aspects of the tariff than Cleveland. He proceeded on the assumption that American prosperity was solely the result of the high tariff. His argument was simple enough for anybody to follow: the tariff makes for business expansion; to increase business, raise the tariff rates. Harrison stated firmly, if somewhat illogically, that he was against "cheaper coats" because cheaper coats seemed "necessarily to involve a cheaper man and woman under the coat."[77] Harrison applied his reasoning to the troubles of the farmers. He would bring prosperity to them by imposing duties on agricultural products. And, in general, they believed him.

The Republican leaders were determined not to reduce the tariff unless they could do so without reducing protection. To this end the Republican Congress on October 1, 1890, passed the McKinley Tariff (entitled "An Act to Reduce the Surplus"), which established the highest protective rates thus far in American history. The bill was sponsored by the chairman of the Ways and Means Committee, William McKinley of Ohio, who, it was said, could make a tariff schedule sound like poetry. A son and grandson of iron manufacturers, McKinley had long held high protection in almost religious veneration. His bill, McKinley boasted, was "protective in every paragraph and American in every line."

In effect, as it was finally passed, the McKinley Tariff was a prohibitive tariff that virtually excluded manufactured goods from importation. It was said that whereas earlier tariffs may have "nourished" the so-called "infant industries," the McKinley Tariff had the distinction of protecting industries not yet born. Raw sugar, which had contributed over $50 million annually to the budget, was placed on the free list. The act then compensated the hitherto protected American sugar growers by giving them a bounty of 2 cents a pound. Coffee and hides stayed on the free list, which also included such essentials as acorns, beeswax, and dandelion roots.

As a gesture to farmers, duties were raised on certain agricultural products, such as eggs, butter, potatoes, wheat, and barley, though few of them needed proteciton. It was not long, however, before the farmers began to see that the Republicans were more interested in their votes than in their well-being. Explaining the bill's faults, McKinley freely admitted that they were necessitated by politics rather than economics.

The Sherman Silver Purchase Act, 1890. The Republicans, to win Western votes for the McKinley Tariff in 1890, were forced to agree to support a silver bill to replace the Bland-Allison Act of 1878 which had not satisfied the advocates of silver inflation. The result was the passage in July 1890, over the heavy opposition of the silver interests, of the Sherman Silver Purchase Act, which provided for government purchase of 4.5 million ounces of silver bullion every month (approximately the total output of the Western silver mines) at the current market price, rather than the artificially high legal ratio of 16 to 1, and to pay for the purchased bullion with treasury notes that would be redeemable in gold or silver coin. It thus provided for a substantial addition to the amount of money in circulation.

In practice, the Sherman Silver Purchase Act failed entirely of its object. It did not go far enough to please the silver men while it alarmed conservative financiers. The price of silver continued to drop because of increasing supplies of silver and a worldwide trend among governments to adopt a single gold standard. The lower the price of silver fell the less the treasury had to pay out each month for the 4.5 million ounces it was obligated to buy. Soon the "silverites" began to feel they had been tricked into allowing the government purchases to be stated in terms of a set amount of silver bullion instead of in terms of dollars, as under the Bland-Allison Act. A wave of despair swept over the West and South. In the end the Sherman Silver Purchase Act failed to abate the outcry for free silver.[78]

The Sherman Antitrust Act, 1890. Three years after the passage of the Interstate Commerce Act of 1887, a congressional investigation brought to light facts about the Standard Oil Trust, the Beef Trust, and the Sugar Trust which influenced President Harrison to recommend legislation to restrict their operations. In December 1889 Senator John Sherman of Ohio, who was back in Congress as a Senator, introduced in Congress a bill declaring illegal "every contract, combination in the form of trust or otherwise, or conspiracy in restraint of trade or commerce among the several states, or with foreign nations." The bill glided through Congress, becoming law in July 1890. Most of the congressmen who voted for it understood that it would not be effective. The passage of the Sherman Act signaled not so much effective opposition to the monopolization of industry as a token to the small businessman and farmer. It put the Republican Party on record as theoretically favorable to competition.

The immediate results of the Sherman Antitrust Act were disappointing. Early prosecutions of the trusts by the Justice Department under the act were neither vigorous nor successful. By the end of the Harrison administration only one case had been concluded, the Tennessee coal case, which ended in victory for the government. In 1895 the Supreme Court, in the E.C. Knight case, by defining "commerce" so narrowly as practically to exclude all forms of interstate commerce except transportation, almost consigned the law to oblivion. Confronted by this rebuff, the government made little further effort to enforce the Sherman Act.

By 1893 the unloved surplus had shrunk to less than $2.5 billion. Then came a crushing depression and six straight years of red ink. The century ended with a war-swollen 1899 deficit of nearly $90 million. What was good for the trusts had not proved to be good for the nation. The cautious man who was afraid of the new electric lights in the White House had failed to convince the country that he could lead them on to better times.

Thunder on the Political Left

Following the economic depression of 1884 there was another epidemic of strikes, over 500 in the first few months, with twice as many strikes occurring in 1886 as in any previous year. The situation became so disturbing that President Cleveland in 1886 delivered to Congress the first presidential message devoted to labor problems.

The Haymarket Riot, 1886. A national strike in behalf of the eight-hour work day took place in 1886. On May 3 pickets at the McCormick Harvester works in Chicago became the targets of police guns, which, according to newspaper reports, killed six men and wounded several others. The following day a protest meeting was held at Haymarket Square. When a large force of police officers ordered the crowd to disperse, a bomb was thrown, 7 persons were killed, and over 60 injured. Eight strike leaders were promptly brought to trial, and all were found guilty. One committed suicide, 4 were hanged, and 2 were given terms of life imprisonment. The latter men were pardoned in 1893 by Governor John Peter Altgeld.

The Haymarket episode smeared parts of the labor movement, especially the Knights of Labor, with the charge of anarchism and subjected labor to public suspicion and hostility. Although the Knights had nothing to do with the Haymarket riot, the skilled workers—who had furnished most of the leadershihp—began to desert the Knights in large numbers. By 1890 the membership had fallen to 100,000.

For a time the leaders of the Knights of Labor sought to combat this trend by turning toward political as opposed to industrial activity, and by 1889 Terence Powderly, the grand master workman, was urging the Knights "to throw strikes, boycotts, lockouts, and such nuisances to the winds and unite in one strike through the legislative weapon in such a way as to humble the power of the corporations who rule the United States today."[79]

In the final stages of decline, the agrarian element within the Knights of Labor began to overshadow the influence of industrial workers. Powderly was ousted in 1893 and his post of master workman taken over by James R. Sovereign of Iowa, who was exclusively interested in reform politics. By 1894 the Knights of Labor had ceased to be important in the affairs of organized labor.

The Homestead Strike, 1892. Six years after Haymarket (that is, in 1892), after Harrison became president, a conflict broke out between the Amalgamated Association of Iron and Steel Workers and the Carnegie Steel operators at Homestead, Pennsylvania, when strikers attacked 300 private guards brought in to protect strikebreakers, killing 7 of them and forcing the rest to "surrender." Eight thousand state militiamen made it possible for the plant to resume operations with nonunion workers, an action which broke the strike and the Homestead Union.

The Homestead affair left much scar tissue. Most of it refused to heal before election day, and much of it persisted in the memories of the working men who lived through it or heard of it from afar. The sharp reduction of wages in the highly protected steel industry that touched off the Homestead strike eloquently refuted the Republican argument that high protection means high wages.

When employers sought to blame all trade unions for the Haymarket bomb in order to discredit their economic demands, labor turned to politics in self-defense.

The thunder on the left coming from the factories and mines was soon matched by that coming from the farms of America. Despite everything that had been tried, farm prices continued to decline. As prices dropped debts increased. In the Midwest and South foreclosures came thick and fast.

The Grange dwindled in importance following a temporary revival of farm prosperity in the late 1870s. However, the seed planted by the Grange in the form of farmers' groups, variously called clubs, associations, unions, wheels, and alliances, began in the late 1870s to consider common grievances and propose remedies as conditions on the farm worsened.

By 1878 the farmers of the Northwest had formed an alliance, the object of which was to "unite the farmers of the United States for their protection against class legislation, and the encroachment of concentrated capital and the tyranny of monopoly." In a short time two great organizations developed in the cotton belt: the National Farmers' Alliance, started in 1879, and the Agricultural Wheel, started three years later. After 1885 the alliance movement spread rapidly. By 1889 the five largest farm alliances in the South were the Texas Farmers' Alliance, the Louisiana Farmers' Union, the Arkansas Agricultural Wheel, the Brothers of Freedom, and the North Carolina Farmers' Alliance and Industrial Union. The NFA and IU, or simply the Southern Alliance as it came to be called, spread into every Southern state and several Northern ones, ultimately registering a membership of nearly 3 million white members.[80] There were also the Colored Farmers' Alliance, which claimed a membership of 700,000 adult members in 1891 and was strong in several states of the South; the National (Northern) Farmers' Alliance, which by 1887 was estimated to have about 400,000 members, chiefly in the Northwest; and the Farmers' Mutual Benefit Association, which by 1889 appears to have had a membership of about 150,000 in ten states, chiefly in the Northwest.

At first the organized farmers pinned their faith on nonpolitical measures. Taking a lead from the experience of the Grangers, local groups launched cooperatives, setting up stores, cotton yards, grain elevators, creameries, insurance companies, and the like. But when these undertakings failed, as most of them did because of poor business direction or the cutthroat competition of regular merchants, the farmers began to seek political solutions for their problems.

In December 1889 all the major farm organizations met at St. Louis to talk merger. The fusion attempt failed, although their platforms were substantially the same. The Northwest Alliance wanted to take independent political action. However, the Southern Alliance preferred to work for control of the Democratic Party because the white farmers of the South were afraid that the founding of a new party would endanger white supremacy. The Northern Alliance did not relish being absorbed in the larger Southern body. Although the proposal for Union failed, the meetings were not a total loss. Both alliances drew up platforms, a move which itself pointed toward political action. The only questions remaining were where and how that political action would manifest itself. It was the Harrison administration's lack of interest in their proposals (problems) which finally triggered a coalescing of alliance members into a political movement.

The People's Party. As it turned out, political action began in less than a year. A convention met in Topeka, Kansas, in June 1890, made up of delegates from the alliance, the Knights of Labor, the Farmers' Mutual Benefit Association, and the Patrons of Husbandry. Before the convention adjourned, the delegates had established a new party called the People's Party based on the principles proclaimed at the St. Louis meeting the year before. Adherents of the new party were soon being referred to as "Populists"; sometimes as "Populites" or "Pops."

The Congressional Elections of 1890. The congressional elections of 1890 took place at the very moment when public sentiment was most deeply stirred against the record which the Republicans had established. In less than two years the treasury had been emptied, the cost of living had been enormously increased, and no one had received any benefit save the multimillionaires of the protected industries and the Sugar Trust.

The ensuing elections thus became a great social and political revolution. The Kansas journalist, William Allen White, wrote that it was a "religious revival, a crusade, a Pentecost of politics," in which "a tongue of flame sat upon every man, and each spoke as the spirit gave him utterance."[81] All through the West and South, after a hard day in the fields, farmers hitched up their buggies and with their wives and children jogged off to the local church, Grange hall, or the schoolhouse and applauded the impassioned oratory of the grass-roots leaders as they blasted Wall Street, the gold standard, the railroads, the trusts, the tariff, and "standpat" politicians of both parties.

Several colorful eccentrics presented the agrarian argument. There was William A. "Whiskers" Peffer, the editor of the *Kansas Farmer*, whose whiskers were so luxuriant that none could tell whether he wore a shirt (they reached to his beltline), and his shaggy figure and clipped oratory enlivened national debates[82]; and his fellow Kansan, Jerry Simpson, the "Socrates of the Prairies." Simpson, a one-time Greenbacker, single taxer, and Union Laborite, received the nickname "Sockless Jerry" during the 1890 congressional campaign when his accusation that his opponent wore silk stockings was answered with the observation that Simpson wore no socks at all. Also, there was Ignatius Donnelly, "The Sage of Nininger (Minnesota)," a plump, genial, self-taught Irish intellectual with a reputation for quips and politicking, whose widely read novel *Caesar's Column* depicted a revolution against the capitalists. Donnelly, who had been an original Republican, then a liberal Republican, a Granger, a Greenbacker, and a Union Labor nominee for governor, was conceded to be the most brilliant speaker among the Populists.[83]

From Georgia came the fiery Thomas E. Watson, a picturesque lawyer-politician with an oratorical style straight out of the hills of Georgia, who waged a campaign for Congress that has been described as "hot as Nebuchadnezzar's furnace."[84] South Carolina's Ben Tillman, the "One-Eyed

Plowboy," preached Populist doctrine without leaving the Democratic Party.[85] In Texas there was the massive orator James H. "Cyclone" Davis, whose volcanic harangues, interlarded with Jeffersonian quotations, could hold farm audiences spellbound for hours.

On the sunbaked prairie of Kansas, the bony-handed and sad-faced Mary Elizabeth Lease, who was called, not lovingly, the "Kansas Python-ess," speaking with unladylike ferocity about unladylike topics "left a trail of fire throughout the state."[86] "Mary Yellin," as she came to be called, traveled widely throughout the farming sections denouncing the East, before whose manufacturers, she said, the West and South were bound and prostrate and little more than slaves. "Wall Street owns the country," she declaimed, "it is no longer a government of the people, by the people, but a government of Wall Street, by Wall Street, and for Wall Street. Our laws are the output of a system that clothes rascals in robes and honesty in rags." She cried that the people of Kansas should "raise less corn and more HELL."[87] They were happy to oblige. To the tune of "Good-bye My Lover, Good-bye," the rebellious Jayhawk farmers sang "Good-bye, My Party, Good-bye," and "The Girl I Left Behind Me" became "The Party I Left Behind Me."

> I was a party man one time,
> The party would not mind me,
> So now I'm working for myself,
> The party's left behind me.

The shock felt by respectable Easterners was reflected by the *New York Evening Post*, which caustically commented: "We don't want any more states until we can civilize Kansas."

The tariff was the dominant issue. Democratic campaigners never let their audiences forget for a moment that "Bill McKinley and the McKinley Bill" were responsible for increasing and holding up commodity prices to the consumer. The Republicans, with tea, coffee, and sugar on the free list, tried to offset the consumer discontent by pointing to "the free breakfast table" they had provided.

When the votes were counted, the Republicans discovered that they had received the sharpest reversal in the history of their party. In the Senate the Republican majority was reduced from 14 to 6 and would have been wiped out altogether but for the holdover senators from the newly admitted states of the Northwest. Even the East, where the reaction to the new tariff was highly unfavorable, had gone Democratic. In the House the Democrats took 235 seats — an enormous majority — the Republicans being reduced to 88, the smallest number in 30 years. In all the agrarians elected 44 Alliance candidates to Congress. The appearance of this group of congressmen representing farm interests and not associated with either of the major parties, indicated that a third-party revolt was shaping up in the far West, Midwest, and South and that a new phase in American politics was under way.

William McKinley, the architect of the Tariff Act of 1890, lost his seat. Among the things said to account for McKinley's defeat was the device of the Democratic local chieftains who hired an itinerant vendor to peddle tin dippers in McKinley's congressional district. His instructions—so it is said—were to greet housewives by asking if they would care to purchase a drinking water dipper for $1. The anticipated reaction to such a statement, of course, was that the housewife would immediately protest that such a price was outrageous, with the comment that any fool would know a tin dipper could easily be purchased for 10 cents. "I know, madam," was the stock reply of the peddler. "But since the passage of the McKinley Tariff Law we are now forced to charge a dollar instead of ten cents."[88]

The Populist Party

Encouraged by the local successes of the new People's Party in the election of 1890, a meeting was held in December in Ocala, Florida, attended by delegates representing the Southern Farmers' Alliance, the Farmers' Mutual Benefit Association, and the Colored Farmers' Alliance to plan political action. Also present were agents of the Northern Alliance, who urged the formation of a national political party. A few Southern leaders were agreeable, but most Southerners still hoped to bend to their will the Democratic Party in the South. By way of compromise, it was agreed to defer decision on the question of a national party until February 1892, the presidential election year, when a convention of delegates from "all organizations of producers" should be held.[89]

Although the Northern Alliancemen had agreed to delay the decision on a national party until February, many Westerners were unwilling to wait that long and they convened a convention in Cincinnati, Ohio, in May 1891 for the purpose of launching the People's Party as a national organization. Once assembled, the delegates adopted a platform which demanded the free and unlimited coinage of silver; the issue of paper money which should be loaned to the people at no more than 2 percent per annum on the security of nonperishable agricultural products; the national ownership of railroads, telegraphs, telephones, and steamship lines; a graduated income tax; and the election of U.S. senators by popular vote. This was a decisive step, but the support of the great farmers' organizations, especially the Southern Alliance which was the largest, was of such importance that further important action was deferred until the meeting in February 1892.

When the Alliancemen met in St. Louis on February 22, 1892, more than 800 delegates from 22 farm, labor, and reform organizations were given seats. Describing itself as the "first great labor conference in the United States," the convention adopted a platform which anticipated many of the demands for reform that would be made for decades to come. The "St. Louis Platform," as it became known, demanded a "safe, sound, and flexible currency" to be put into the hands of the people without banking corporations through the subtreasury plan of the Farmers' Alliance[90] or its equivalent, free and unlimited coinage of silver at the ratio of 16 to 1, a circulating medium of not less than $50 per capita,[91] a postal savings bank, a graduated income tax, and reclamation of all lands granted to aliens, railroads, and corporations. Further resolutions called for the exclusion of undesirable immigrants, a shorter working day for industrial laborers, the secret ballot, the adoption of the initiative and referendum, direct election of senators, and a single term for the offices of president and vice president.

Before they adjourned the delegates adopted a resolution calling for a nominating convention to meet in Omaha on July 4, 1892, following the Republican and Democratic conventions. There was some hope that those two parties might meet some of the major demands enunciated by the various farmer and labor organizations, particularly those voiced at the St. Louis conference.[92]

The Election of 1892

The Republican Convention, 1892. As the election of 1892 approached, the prospects were grim for the Republicans. They had managed to please only the industrialists and the Civil War pensioners. The tariff-silver compromise of 1890 had proved to be a disaster for them. The owners of silver mines were unhappy with the Sherman Silver Purchase Act because, although the government purchased more silver, its price still went down. Nor did the bankers like the law. In addition, the McKinley tariff was widely unpopular. Harrison had also won the enmity of labor and the farmers by his labor and farm policies.

As the convention approached, President Harrison's coldness prevented an enthusiastic personal following from developing around him. Even Platt and Quay, who cordially disliked Blaine but who also had no desire to spend "four more years in an ice-house," would have preferred, had it been possible, to lure the plumed knight out of political retirement. Blaine, however, although he was only 68 in 1892, was in bad health and he refused to seek the nomination.[93] Even so, many were convinced that he was preparing for a draft when, on June 4, on the eve of the convention, he resigned as secretary of state, making his break with the president complete. Senator Plumb of Kansas expressed a generally held view of Blaine, when he told friends that Blaine "would run if he had to carry his coffin on his back."

The Republican convention opened on June 7, 1892, in Minneapolis on a blistering hot day. "It was a fan-fluttering convention," a young reporter wrote. The selection of the Minnesota city as a convention site was urged on the ground that there had been an increase in the foreign population of the Northwest and that the Democrats and the Farmers' Alliance were gaining support from this element. There was danger, it was asserted, that the Northwest would waver in its loyalty to the Republican standard. A national convention, therefore, held at Minneapolis would be one of the best ways to "restore order in that great region."[94]

On the second day of the convention McKinley (who was now the governor of Ohio), the permanent chairman, moved straight to the point of his address in a ringing endorsement of the protective tariff. "We stand for the protective tariff," he said, "because it represents the American home, the American fireside, the American family, the American girl and the American boy, and the highest possibility of American citizenship. We propose to raise our money to pay public expenses by taxing the products of other nations, rather than by the products of our own." On the chance that McKinley's speech would start a stampede, Marcus Alonzo "Mark" Hanna, his fellow Ohioan, came to the convention with several boxes containing McKinley portraits and badges.[95]

When nominations were in order, McKinley was the first in the field. Senator Edward O. Wolcott of Colorado then nominated Blaine, lauding him for the enrichment and guidance he had given to "two administrations with his sagacity and statesmanship. Blaine, though he has never occupied the office of President, has made many Republican Presidents possible," and should now be called upon to lead the party he had done so much to shape. When he finished, the faithful cheered, "Blaine! Blaine! James G. Blaine!" for nearly half an hour. But, as Howard Morgan points out, it was a farewell, not a rallying call. "That gigantic demonstration was at once a salutation and a requiem. The Republican Party there took leave of their dying leader, and bade him an eternal farewell."[96] Chairman McKinley was finally able to restore order only by warning the delegates that the stamping of feet was imperiling the structure of the building.[97] General Richard W. Thompson placed Harrison in nomination in a very brief statement.

In the end McKinley and Blaine split the opposition vote and Harrison won easily on the first ballot, causing, as Boss Platt put it, "a chattering of the teeth among the warmblooded Republicans of the East." Hanna, ready to push McKinley, was just as happy to wait for a more promising year.

At the insistence of their New York brethren, the delegates substituted for Vice President Morton the name of Whitelaw Reid, the aristocratic editor of the *New York Tribune*. Because of the heat, no roll call was taken. Reid was the first nominee in Republican history to win without a roll call.[98] Although Reid was a man of personal distinction, he had gained the enmity of labor groups by his long-standing opposition to attempts to unionize the *Tribune,* and could not be counted on to add much to the ticket.

The Republican platform was not a distinguished document. The Harrison administration was commended as "the most glorious chapter in the record of the Republican Party." On the foremost question of the day, the platform reaffirmed the "American doctrine of protection" as embodied in the McKinley Tariff. They adopted a straddle plank on the currency by demanding the use of both gold and silver as standard money.

The Democratic Convention, 1892. The Democrats assembled on June 21 in the barely finished "Wigwam," a huge hall on the Chicago waterfront seating nearly 20,000. Tammany's braves arrived with a large paper tiger that growled at Grover Cleveland on command.

As it turned out, Cleveland's chief challenger for the nomination was his personal and political enemy, New York Governor David Bennett Hill, who had the support of Tammany Hall. Hill first came into prominence in New York politics when, running on the Democratic ticket as candidate for the office of lieutenant governor in 1882, he polled some 8,000 votes more than Cleveland, the party's candidate for governor. He had succeeded to the governorship in 1885, upon Cleveland's elevation to the presidency, and had then been elected governor in his own right in 1888, receiving for that office some 18,000 votes more than were given to Cleveland at the same election. His supporters stated the proposition in simple terms: "Hill carried New York in 1888, Cleveland lost it. You can't win without New York. Hill is the man who can surely give you New York's thirty-six electoral votes."[99]

Even so, the delegates realized that, all things considered, former President Cleveland was the logical Democratic candidate and he was nominated on the first ballot. As a sop to the agrarians the delegates then named for their vice presidential nominee Adlai E. Stevenson of Illinois, a friend of the silverites. Stevenson also appealed to spoilsmen, who remembered that "Adlai and his Axe" had "decapitated sixty-five Republican postmasters in two minutes." The platform was a happy blend of expediency and principle. It reaffirmed the party's allegiance to the principles of Jefferson and to the long line of distinguished Democrats who had succeeded him from Madison to Cleveland. The McKinley Act was condemned "as the culminating atrocity of class legislation." A strong civil service plank was included which denounced the Republicans for "the scandalous satire upon free popular institutions" exhibited at the Minneapolis convention, where President Harrison was "renominated by officeholders." In an attempt to gain the allegiance of both the silver producing states of the West and of the financial community of the East, the platform adopted an ambiguous position on the currency question, favoring both metals while denouncing the Sherman Silver Purchase Act as a "cowardly makeshift," but urging "all currency at par with gold."

The Populist Convention, 1892. When the new People's Party assembled for their first national convention in Omaha, Nebraska, on July 4, 1892, there were present the leaders of the Farmers' Alliance, the Knights of Labor, the single-tax people, the nationalists, the Prohibitionists, the antimonopolists, the People's Party, the Reform Party, and the Women's Alliance. The convention was noisy, tumultuous, and full of the excitement of a new party in rebellion.

The death of the popular Leonidas L. Polk of North Carolina just before the convention opened probably deprived the Populists of their strongest candidate. The party's leaders then turned to Judge Walter Q. Gresham (of Indiana) who had been a strong contender for the presidential nomination of the Republican Party in 1884 and 1888. When Gresham notified the convention that he was not available, the new party nominated General James B. Weaver of Iowa, a veteran of many agrarian campaigns who had been the Greenback-Labor candidate for president in 1886, to head their ticket.[100]

Weaver had a great many supporters in the party for he was well known in Western reform circles where he espoused railroad regulation and easy currency. As we have seen, Weaver had previously run for president on the Greenback ticket in 1880, and had alternately represented that party, liberal Democrats, and farmer-laborites in the national House of Representatives between 1879–81 and 1885–89. "General" James B. Field of Virginia, who had lost a leg in the service of the Confederacy, was chosen to be Weaver's running mate.

The Omaha Platform. The highlight of the Omaha convention, however, was the reading of the platform by Ignatius Donnelly.

The Omaha platform, the handiwork of Donnelly, was infused with moral indignation of the oppressed against their oppressors. The nation, the platform proclaimed, has been "brought to the verge of moral, political and material ruin" by the political events of the preceding years. Corruption dominated national life, the people were demoralized, the newspapers were muzzled, labor was impoverished, the people's homes were mortgaged, business was prostrate, and the land itself was controlled by the capitalists: "The fruits of the toil of millions are boldly stolen to build up colossal fortunes for a few . . . and the possessors of these, in turn despise the republic and endanger liberty. From the same prolific womb of governmental injustice we breed the two great classes — tramps and millionaires."

The money power above all the rest was the source of the people's distress. "A vast conspiracy against mankind has been organized on two continents," the conspiracy was "rapidly taking possession of the world," and if it were "not met and overthrown at once," it would produce "terrible social convulsions, the destruction of civilization or the establishment of an absolute despotism."[101]

The Populist antidote to these fearful conditions, as expressed by the Omaha platform was the expansion of federal power. It made a flat demand for government ownership of the railroads and also of the telegraph and telephone systems; they recommended a graduated income tax to reduce the tax burden on the common people; and favored giving the government, rather than the banks and private institutions, the power to issue the circulating medium of the nation.

The Omaha platform endorsed new political machinery to improve the processes of democratic control. Such reforms as the initiative and referendum, popular election of U.S. senators, and the secret ballot would help the people to bypass unresponsive officials and legislators and guarantee that government would listen to the discontented and aggrieved.[102]

An "Expression of Sentiments," which accompanied the platform, sought labor support by proclaiming that the farmer and the city wage earner were allies in the struggle for social and economic justice. It strongly endorsed the rights of labor to organize and called for shorter hours, the eight-hour day on government contracts, and condemned "the maintainence of a large standing army of mercenaries, known as the Pinkerton system."[103]

When the platform was adopted, the 6,000 exultant delegates and spectators exploded into a demonstration which raged for 38 minutes. As they demonstrated, they sang the party's songs: "Good-bye, My Party, Good-bye," "The Hayseed,"[104] and the "People's Hymn" to the consecrated music of the "Battle Hymn of the Republic":

> They have stolen our money, have ravished our homes;
> With the plunder erected to Mammon a throne;
> They have fashioned a god, like the Hebrews of old,
> Then bid us bow down to their image of gold.

General Weaver promised that, God willing, he would carry the fight into every state in the Union. With these calls to action sounding in their ears, the delegates to the first People's Party National Convention voted an adjournment.

The Prohibition Party, 1892. The Prohibition Party met in convention in Cincinnati, Ohio, June 29–30, with 972 delegates and alternatives in attendance. Only Louisiana and South Carolina were not represented. Miss Francis Willard, president of the Women's Christian Temperance Union and delegate at large from Illinois, presided. The delegates nominated former Congressman John Bidwell of California and James B. Cranfill of Texas.

Their platform began and ended with a call for the complete suppression of the manufacture, sale, importation, exportation, and transportation of alcoholic beverages by federal and state legislation. In between they addressed themselves to a variety of social and economic questions, including women's suffrage and equal wages for women, an inflated currency, and the nationalization of railroad, telegraph, and other public corporations. The last resolution, the sixteenth, affirmed that the "prohibition of the liquor traffic has become the dominant issue in national politics." All who "on this one dominant issue . . . with us agree" were invited to "full party fellowship."

The Socialist-Labor Party, 1892. The election of 1892 marked the first appearance of a socialist candidate for the presidency of the United States. The earliest socialist party was sponsored by the United Workers of America, a small trade union, whose members organized the Social Democratic Workingmen's Party at a meeting in New York in 1874. Without altering its makeup or aims, this party changed its name to the Workingmen's Party of the United States in 1876. A year later, stimulated by the depression, this party became the Socialist-Labor Party. There were some initial electoral successes in the wake of the strikes and violence of 1877, but as soon as prosperity returned the voters deserted the SLP.[105]

The Socialist-Labor Party did not engage in the campaign of 1884, either on its own authority or through fusion. Instead, it suggested that Socialists refrain from going to the polls. The attitude of the party was that, because both the Democratic and Republican parties were in equal degree controlled by the capitalist class, "the Presidential elections were nowadays nothing but a humbug and cannot be anything else."[106]

By 1890 the Socialist-Labor Party had fallen under the control of Daniel De Leon, a doctrinaire Marxist, who quickly became its national lecturer and the editor of its newspaper, *The People.* Under De Leon's direction the antipolitical bias disappeared. *The People* openly advocated that the working class should tear itself from the two old parties, keep aloof from the Farmer's Party, and set up its own independent workingmen's party upon a thoroughgoing socialist and labor platform. Independent political action would not only give the laborer candidates for whom he could honestly vote but would also serve as a means of educating the public to socialism.

The Socialist-Labor Party engaged exclusively in local politics until 1892, when a conference of its leaders from Connecticut, Massachusetts, New Jersey, New York, and Pennsylvania met in New York on August 28 at the Labor Lyceum. They picked Simon Wing of Massachusetts, the owner of a photography business, and Charles H. Matchett, a carpenter of Brooklyn, New York, as the SLP presidential and vice presidential candidates. In its platform the party advocated government ownership of public utilities, progressive inheritance and income taxes, universal and equal suffrage, free education, municipal home rule, abolition of child labor, employers' liability legislation, and the secret ballot.

The Campaign of 1892. Allan Nevins, Cleveland's biographer, described the campaign of 1892 as "the cleanest, quietest, and most creditable in the memory of the postwar generation." Other historians, however, merely described it as being incredibly dull. Absent were the torchlight processions and brass bands, the idiotic chants, and personal slurs of recent elections. No scandals were unearthed and no sensational episodes occurred. The president's supporters worked hard (but unsuccessfully) to build enthusiasm for their candidate with the slogan:

> Let every honest fellow from Maine to Oregon
> Let every honest fellow, unless he's a son-of-a-gun
> Let every honest fellow, unless he's a son-of-a-gun
> Be sure and vote for Benjamin Harrison.

When his opponents cried "Grover, Grover, all is over," the Democrats responded:

> Grover, Grover
> Four more years of Grover;
> In we'll go,
> Out they'll go,
> Then we'll be in clover.

Cleveland made it clear that he hoped that "trip taking and speech making" would not be urged upon him. The campaign committee respected his wish and Cleveland made only one or two speeches during the campaign. The burden of personal campaigning fell on Stevenson and various surrogates. When he did speak, Cleveland emphasized tariff reform and avoided the silver question. The Populists, on the other hand, preached the doctrine of free silver with great vigor and enthusiasm. William Jennings Bryan refused to stump for Cleveland and instead spoke for Weaver, the Populist candidate. Henry George, the other prominent radical, supported Cleveland and urged his followers not to vote the Populist ticket.

No matter how hard they tried, the Republicans could not dissociate the Harrison administration from the economic distress of the times. The president's claims that workers were prosperous and happy were undercut by the violent and bloody strike against Carnegie's Homestead plant in the middle of the campaign. Again, the Democratic campaigners effectively "peddled" 25 cent dippers for $1 in the rural areas and blamed the high price on the McKinley Tariff.

What interest there was in the campaign of 1892 was generated by the colorful spellbinders of the Populist Party. "Read your bibles every Sunday and the Omaha platform every day in the week," Field counseled audiences as he gamely limped around the circle. Tom Watson, now a congressman, William A. Peffer, now a senator, and "Sockless Jerry" Simpson were all active in the campaign. Ignatius Donnelly, running for governor of Minnesota made 150 speeches and talked personally with 10,000 voters. Weaver and Mary Ellen Lease toured the South during the campaign where they were pelted with a mixture of threats, epithets, and rotten eggs.

The 1892 Outcome. When the results came in on election day, the results were electrifying. Harrison went down to defeat and Cleveland received a popular plurality for the third successive time, garnering 5,557,000 popular votes to 5,176,000 for Harrison, and an electoral college vote of 277 to Harrison's 145.[107] Congress was safely Democratic in both houses.

As narrow as Cleveland's victory margin was, it was still the first decisive presidential election victory since 1872. Following in the wake of the elections two years previously it was an ominous portent for the Republican Party. For the first time since the Civil War the Democrats were in full control of the national government, so naturally they were jubilant and confident. The party appeared to many observers to have a solid bloc of strength, with support coming from every group in American society. All outward appearances indicated that Cleveland would be the strongest president since the Civil War.[108] Two years later (1894), the Democratic Party was in ruins. Those same forces of protest that swept Cleveland's democracy into office were to prove fickle friends. Despite the massive bloc that the Democrats presented to the nation, the party was sadly divided over the silver and tariff issues. Had economic conditions improved and had party leaders been willing to offer major concessions to groups within the party, factional differences might have been minimized. Instead, divisive influences became so explosive that within one year after Cleveland's inauguration the Democratic Party was on the verge of ruin.

More than 1 million popular votes — nearly 9 percent of the national total — and 22 electoral votes were cast for Weaver and Field.[109] The appeal of the Omaha platform and the People's Party was limited outside the South, the Plains, and the mining states of the Rocky Mountain region. Weaver and Field carried Kansas, Idaho, Colorado, and Nevada, while several Populist electors were also chosen in North Dakota and Oregon. But the Populists claimed few if any votes in the Eastern cities, and in such Western states as Kansas and California the labor planks of the platform attracted relatively few working-class voters.[110]

The voters also sent a dozen avowed Populists and a number of sympathizers to Congress, elected three governors, and hundreds of state legislators. Except for the Republicans in 1856, no third party had done nearly so well in its first appearance on the national scene. The election appeared to confirm that a strong third-party organization had finally risen to challenge the two major ones — a party which had all the elements necessary to compete with its opponents, was founded upon a broad popular basis, and possessed persuasive leaders and experienced organizers.[111] However, the election unmistakably showed that the appeal of Populism was regional not national, and that it did not extend to the East or to the labor groups. Populism had little appeal to labor. Its tone and rhetoric was decidedly agrarian, with a strong soft-money (monetary) emphasis, and few workers were willing to accept monetary answers to their problems. Many wage earners considered the People's Party was a farmer's party, so that populism had little to offer them. In reality, workers had good reason to suspect Populist monetary policy. At the very best it meant that the downward trend of prices would be stopped; at the very worst that falling prices and the falling cost of living would give way to higher prices and a growing struggle to make ends meet.[112]

John Bidwell, the Prohibition Party candidate, finished a poor fourth with 270,000 votes (or 2.25 percent of the total). Simon Wing, the SLP standard-bearer finished last with slightly over 21,000 votes — less than 0.02 percent of the total cast.

Cleveland's Second Administration

The change in 1893 from Harrison and the Republicans to Cleveland and the Democrats was one from tweedledum to tweedledee — so far as the seriously dissatisfied elements in American society were concerned. The Cleveland who took the oath of office on March 4, 1893, in the midst of a driving gale, was the same Cleveland who had left office four years earlier. In his brief inaugural address the bareheaded retread president strongly reaffirmed his devotion to laissez-faire and the gold standard. He pledged his party to economy, honesty, and good government, and declared that it would sustain the currency, revise the tariff without injuring the economy, and avoid "the unwholesome progeny of paternalism."

Cleveland put together a strongly conservative cabinet of Easterners and Southerners who were as completely out of touch with the radical discontent of the country as he was himself. He named the absent-minded Walter Q. Gresham as his secretary of state. (It was said of Gresham that he never forgot a number or remembered a name.) Gresham had been a lifelong Republican who had declined the Populist nomination in 1892 to help Cleveland. The president somehow thought the choice of Gresham would please the low-tariff Republicans. It did, but it angered many more Democrats. John G. Carlisle, an experienced legislator who had been three times Speaker of the House, took the treasury, for the post of attorney general Richard Olney of Boston was selected. William S. Bissell of New York, an old and intimate friend and former law partner, became postmaster general. Bissell would not oppose presidential wishes in handling that department's rich patronage.

Two representatives of the new South served in the cabinet. Hoke Smith, owner of the *Atlanta Journal*, was made secretary of the interior and Hilary A. Herbert of Alabama, a Confederate veteran, secretary of the navy. Herbert was the first former Confederate to be placed in charge of one of the military departments of the government. Cleveland filled the last seat at his cabinet table with J. Sterling Morton of Nebraska in the Agriculture Department. Morton's crowning achievement in office was the invention of Arbor Day. No spokesman for labor gained admittance to the select circle of Cleveland's advisers.

The Panic of 1893. The Cleveland administration was just two months old when the panic of 1893 struck the country.[113] No ordinary panic, it soon broadened into the worst depression in the nation's history. By the end of the first year at least 16,000 businesses had declared bankruptcy, and 500 banks, most of them in the West or in the South, closed their doors. The unemployment rate was over 13 percent of the labor force, a figure representing over 3 million men out of work. In the cities long lines of unemployed waited outside soup kitchens which quickly were dubbed "Cleveland Cafes."

Like most depression presidents before him, Cleveland did not regard the relief of unemployment as a direct responsibility of the government. He insisted that the depression was a business problem which the business community must work out for itself. Blind hatred flared up between the defenders of the gold standard and advocates of free coinage of silver.[114]

Cleveland and his advisers — mostly Eastern businessmen, bankers, and Southern conservatives — were in agreement that the renewal of "confidence" on the part of the business community in the treasury's ability to maintain the gold standard would arrest the depression. The problem, the president concluded, was the Sherman Silver Purchase Act of 1890 which required the government to buy 4.5 million ounces of silver monthly, to be paid for in treasury notes redeemable in gold. By 1893 the treasury was purchasing about $50 million worth of silver certificates a year, while bankers and others were redeeming their silver certificates in gold. Consequently, the treasury had lost about $132 million in gold and gained about $147 million in silver between 1890 and 1893. The situation was particularly acute by the spring of 1893 as large numbers of people rushed in a state of panic to exchange silver certificates for gold, fearing that the treasury's resources would soon be depleted. Cleveland thought it would be only a matter of time before the United States would be forced to abandon gold payments. The panic of 1893, consequently, was accompanied by a run on the gold reserves of the treasury designated for redeeming paper currency. When Cleveland assumed office in 1893, the reserve had shrunk to a little over $100 million (which was generally regarded as an acceptable level).

Cleveland, a sound-money man by conviction, resolved to maintain the gold standard at all costs – that is continue to redeem all U.S. treasury notes in gold. To this end he summoned a special session of Congress in August 1893 for the purpose of obtaining "prompt repeal" of the Sherman silver law and the enactment of legislation which would "put beyond all doubt or mistake the intention and the ability of the government to fulfill its pecuniary obligation in money universally recognized by all civilized countries." Wall Street heaved a sigh of relief.

The president could hardly have thought of a better way to alienate the West and the South, where silver orators were gaining converts every day. When Representative William L. Wilson of West Virginia introduced a bill for the repeal of the silver act, William Jennings Bryan, an eloquent new member from Nebraska, rose to argue and plead the cause of the white metal. Bryan closed with words which were to become the keynote of the great struggle of 1896:

> Today the Democratic Party stands between two great forces, each inviting its support. On the one side stand the corporate interests of the nation, its money institutions, its aggregations of wealth and capital, imperious, arrogant, compassionless. They demand special legislation, favors, privileges, and immunities.... On the other hand, stands that unnumbered throng which gave a name to the Democratic Party and for which it has assumed to speak. Work-worn and dust begrimed, they make their sad appeal.... Although the ones who deserve most the fostering care of government, their cries for help too often beat in vain against the outer wall, while others less deserving find ready access to legislative halls.[115]

Despite the bitter opposition from agrarian inflationists, the repeal bill was adopted by the House of Representatives after only two weeks of debate. In the Senate, however, the silver senators from the West, supported by Populists and Southerners, fought off repeal of the Sherman Silver Purchase Act until the end of October when it finally passed by a very close vote. Thus ended government purchase of silver. The American Bimetallic League immediately announced that it would carry the fight for the free coinage of silver into the next presidential election.

The president had won, but it was a costly victory. When he signed the bill on November 1, his party was shattered. In both houses the Democrats had divided along sectional lines. The Democrats of the agrarian South and West had allied in opposition to repeal; members from the industrial North and East, with rare exceptions, sided with the president. The basis for a new party alignment was clearly evolving.

Much to Cleveland's chagrin, repeal did not restore confidence, bring relief from the depression, stop the drain on the gold reserve, or squelch the demand for free silver. He had staked his reputation on the repeal of silver purchases, but by the end of 1893 the amount of gold in the treasury was down to $68 million (a dangerously low level). Two emergency bond issues sold by the treasury in 1894 brought in more than $117 million in gold. However, this amount was quickly exhausted because of the operation of a so-called "endless chain." The government sold bonds to obtain gold, the public presented paper money for redemption to get gold to buy the bonds, and the government paid out the notes, again to meet its bills. The notes were then presented for redemption, the gold reserves once more declined, and the government had to float a new bond issue.

At the beginning of February 1895 the gold reserves had fallen to less than $42 million. The day of judgment appeared to be at hand. To meet the crisis, the desperate Cleveland borrowed $65 million in gold from the Morgan and Belmont banking syndicate in exchange for 4 percent gold bonds at a figure significantly below the price the issue would have brought on the open market — a politically unwise move. Joseph Pulitzer's *New York World* accused the bankers of having made at least $16 million dollars on the deal (which was a gross exaggeration).

To the silverites of the West and South the bond issue seemed further proof that Cleveland was firmly allied with the money power of Wall Street. Although the president received thousands of letters denouncing him as a traitor and a friend of financial bloodsuckers, he was certain that he had done no wrong. Sarcastically denying that he was "Morgan's errand boy," he confessed "without shame and without repentance" his "share of the guilt."[116]

This deal, while violently and perhaps justly criticized, did serve to restore confidence, and in January 1896 a fourth bond sale — this time by popular subscription — of $100 million brought the gold reserve up to $281 million. With confidence restored, the gold in the government reserve became increasingly plentiful. Cleveland had saved the gold standard, but in doing so he had saddled a debt of $262 million upon the American people, a debt from which only the more affluent investors would profit.

The Wilson-Gorman Tariff, 1894. In his second term Cleveland finally got his tariff revision. Work on the new tariff bill began under the leadership of William L. Wilson of West Virginia, the scholarly chairman of the House Ways and Means Committee. In striking contrast to the object of the McKinley Tariff, the purpose of the new act was to increase the revenue and yet provide adequate protection for domestic producers. The Wilson Bill, a reasonably good bill which removed the duties from many raw materials and reduced those on most manufacturers, easily passed the House on February 1, 1894. However, it encountered bitter resistance in the Senate where it was modified by the protectionists. Directed by Maryland's Arthur P. Gorman and aided by senators from both parties and all parts of the country, more than 600 amendments were added which changed the House bill not only in detail but also in principle. After five months of bitter debate the Senate passed the bill on July 3 by the narrow vote of 39–34. In the final bill, although the overall tariff levels dropped some, the revised rates merely created new injustices. Benefits for the Standard Oil Trust, the National Lead Trust, the coal interests, and many other special interests, were much in evidence. The Sugar Trust alone had inserted benefits worth a sweet $20 million a year. To Cleveland and the tariff reformers, the Wilson-Gorman Act was a bitter disappointment. Cleveland, who had insisted that "a tariff for any other purpose than public revenue is public robbery," denounced it as representing "party perfidy and dishonor" to the glee of the Republicans.[117] However, the president faced a real dilemma. To sign the Wilson-Gorman Bill would be to accept something he did not want; to veto it meant to reinstate the much worse McKinley Act. In the end he grudgingly allowed it to become law in 1894 without his signature. Nevertheless, the Wilson-Gorman Tariff was a defeat for him, for his party, and for the agrarians of the West.[118]

One of the few provisions of the new tariff law that proved popular was a concession to the demand, included in the Populist platform of 1892, for an income tax on the wealthy. As it was finally passed, this measure provided for a 2 percent tax on incomes above $4,000. However, this tax was declared unconstitutional by the U.S. Supreme Court the following year. The case against the tax was argued by the famous corporation lawyer, Joseph H. Choate, who called on the court to stem the "communist march" that he alleged had begun. The outraged tax reformers denounced the decision as a tortured essay in constitutional construction.

By 1894, as the depression deepened, the American mood was growing dangerously sullen, but Cleveland refused to desert his rigid, oft-stated principle – "While the people should patriotically and cheerfully support the government its functions do not include the support of the people." Predictably, the president became a target for all who were riding the tides of discontent. Governor Ben Tillman of South Carolina told a howling audience, "When Judas betrayed Christ, his heart was not blacker than this scoundrel, Cleveland, in deceiving the Democracy. He is an old bag of beef and I am going to Washington with a pitchfork and prod him in his old fat ribs."[119] Alabama's Senator John T. Morgan put it in more simple terms: "I hate the ground the man walks on," and on the Senate floor he referred to Cleveland's supporters as "Cuckoos."[120]

Coxey's Army. Since the government offered no relief to the destitute, agitators (most of whom the public regarded as "crackpots") began to propose their own schemes for solving the problem of unemployment. In some cases there were attempts to use the unemployed in mass demonstrations of protest. In the hope of mitigating their lot, 16 "armies" of the jobless ("petitions in boots") set out for the nation's capital that spring to help the jobless. Only "Coxey's Army" reached it, after weeks of marching.

When this "army" (including one of the leaders, Jacob Coxey, a prosperous businessman with a strong social conscience, his wife, and infant son "Legal Tender") and about 500 followers (plus about another 1,200 marchers), reached their destination on May 1, 1894, several marchers were clubbed, trampled, and arrested for trespassing on the Capitol grounds. The "army" was dispersed, having gained nothing but public attention. The president, who hardly seemed to notice this army of misery, should have paid more attention. As the men left Washington, a marcher threw a verbal clod at the White House, expressing the frustration of all the unemployed: "We are going to our homes where we will continue to do all in our power to condemn the administration of Grover Cleveland."[121]

The Pullman Strike, 1894. As the depression worsened, Cleveland found himself a target for criticism on all sides. His second administration was plagued by some of the worst labor disturbances of American history. Many workers who still had jobs considered themselves little better off than the unemployed, and some 1,400 strikes were called in 1894 alone, affecting almost 700,000 workers.

In April 1894 about 125,000 United Mine Workers' members struck in protest over a cut in wages. The owners broke the strike without difficulty and after eight weeks the miners went back to work. Almost simultaneously, the newly organized American Railway Union, founded by Eugene V. Debs, struck against James J. Hill's Great Northern Railroad for the same reason.

However, the nation's emotional climax came when the nation's railroad system was paralyzed by the Pullman strike, which broke out in 1894.

With the onset of the depression in 1893, the Pullman Palace Car Company of Pullman, Illinois, the nation's chief manufacturer of railroad sleeping cars, laid off more than 3,000 of its 5,800 employees, and cut the wages of those kept on by an average of 25 percent. When the desperate workers formed a grievance committee to speak for them, Pullman responded by discharging all of its members. He refused even to talk to their representatives. After pleas for arbitration failed to move Pullman, the American Railway Union (ARU), headed by the tall, slender Debs, ordered its 150,000 members to stop handling Pullman cars on all roads. Other affiliated unions followed in sympathy and refused to handle trains hauling Pullman cars. Such trains usually contained mail cars also. The boycott spread rapidly over the West and Midwest. By July 1 the 24 railroads operating out of Chicago had shut down, idling thousands of men. As the strike spread, mobs and gangs of hoodlums terrorized their communities by burning, looting, and killing.

When Democratic Governor Altgeld of Illinois (who had pardoned the men who had been sentenced to life imprisonment for participating in the

Haymarket riots) refused to ask for federal troops, President Cleveland, acting on the advice of Attorney General Richard Olney—who despised and feared labor agitators and symphasized with the railroads (he was a director of three railroads)—intervened on his own authority. On July 2 the government secured a "blanket injunction" which forbade Debs, his fellow strike leaders, and "all other persons whomsoever" to interfere in any manner, direct or indirect, with the operation of the railways. When trains began to move under the protection of the troops, angry mobs sought to stop them. The president then declared that there was a reign of terror in the city and on July 3 (1894), sent 2,000 federal soldiers to Chicago to restore order. President Cleveland soon found himself, once again, fighting his own party. The sweeping character of the injunction—"a Gatling gun on paper" as Debs characterized it—and the alliance of government with management hurt labor leaders deeply and turned them against Cleveland.

On July 17 Debs and other ARU officials were arrested for violating the injunction. Deprived of leadership, the strike soon petered out. Released on bail, Debs defied the antistrike injunction and was rearrested a week later, tried, and sentenced to six months in prison.

With the strike smashed, the railroads blacklisted strikers, and the ARU died. But Debs emerged from prison a martyr in the eyes of working men. While serving out his sentence for contempt, Debs studied a number of radical works, including Edward Bellamy's *Looking Backward* and Henry Demerest Lloyd's *Wealth Against Commonwealth.* In the end he concluded that the American working man could not hope to get a fair break within the capitalist system and that socialism was the only real answer to labor's discontent. When Debs emerged from jail he announced his conversion to socialism.[122] With others he founded the Social Democratic Party of America in 1897 which later became the Socialist Party, and in 1900 he became its presidential candidate for the first time.

The Congressional Election of 1894. Revitalized Republicans, singing "The Soup House" and "Times Are Mighty Hard," won the congressional elections in the fall of 1894 in a landslide. The Democrats limped into the House of Representatives with only 105 (down from 218) to the Republican's 284 seats. Eastern, Western, and border states elected Republicans in numbers unprecedented since the days of Grant. It was, in fact, one of the most widespread political realignments in American political history. The Republicans clearly emerged as the majority party (at least they looked like the majority party), leaving the Democrats to wander in the political wilderness for a generation. In 24 states no Democrat won any federal office; in 6 others there was only one Democrat each. "Honey-Fitz" Fitzgerald of Boston (a grandfather of President John F. Kennedy) was the lone Democratic congressman to survive the election in all of New England. Although the Democrats maintained technical control of the Senate, it was tenuous because of the large number of anti-administration Democrats and Populists elected. The results almost emptied Congress of Democratic leaders. William L. Wilson of West Virginia, William M. Springer of Illinois, William D. Bynum of Indiana, and Richard P. Bland of Missouri all went down to defeat.

The most ominous feature of the election was the stunning 1.5 million votes polled by the Populists for their congressional candidates — an increase of 42 percent over their vote in 1892 — and the election of six senators, not counting many others pledged to the farmers' programs (which gave them the balance of power in that body), and seven congressmen, in addition to winning many state offices. Although the Populists had shown no serious working-class support (workers wanted tariff protection and did not trust agrarian rule), the outcome encouraged them to think they had an excellent chance to elect a president in 1896. The Democrats, exulted Ignatius Donnelly, were "buried under the drift a thousand feet deep." He was convinced that ultimately the Democrats would disappear, leaving only the Populists and the Republicans.[123] Tom Watson agreed: "Never since the Wonderful One Hoss Shay went to pieces in one comprehensive, simultaneous and complete smashup . . . has there been such an all-round catastrophe as that which has happened to the Democratic Party."[124] Even many Democrats concurred with the assessment. Tom Reed lamented: "The Democratic mortality will be so great next fall that their dead will be buried in trenches and marked 'unknown.'"

The Cleveland administration attempted to explain "the great switch" away from the Democrats to the Republicans in 1894 as a more or less inevitable result of the severe depression then gripping the nation. The bolters would return, they predicted, when economic conditions improved. However, many observers disagreed. They put the blame directly on the shoulders of Cleveland, who, by refusing to accommodate the members of the party on the silver issue, had alienated not only many leaders of the Democrats but large sectors of the depressed nation as well. In the agrarian West and South it appeared that increasing numbers of anti–Cleveland Democrats were prepared to disentangle themselves from Cleveland and form a new group, possibly in alliance with the Populists. In the East and Northeast thousands of urban workers and immigrants who blamed Cleveland personally for the depression, and who were suspicious of the economic interest and the nativist tinges of farmers, were moving, somewhat illogically, into the ranks of the McKinley Republicans.[125]

On the other hand, the prospects of the Republicans for 1896 seemed rosy. All they had to do was stand aside and watch the Democratic Party commit suicide. They soon were openly boasting that they had only to nominate a "rag baby" or a "yaller dog," and they could put it in the White House.

The Silver Controversy

The depression of 1893 gave a new emphasis to the money question and strengthened the demand for the coinage of silver. In March 1894 Richard P. Bland pushed through the House of Representatives a bill to coin the treasury's seigniorage,[126] hoping to enlarge the currency. The Senate followed suit, and the bill went to the president. Since the number of silver dollars to be minted under the act would not be large and would not provoke inflation, most political observers thought Cleveland would sign it. However, Cleveland refused to yield on what he considered a matter of principle. He simply would not sign any bill that would add silver to the currency. Furthermore, he regarded the silver question as settled by the repeal of the silver purchase law. When Cleveland vetoed the bill on March 29 with a stinging indictment of silver and prevented its repassage, the reaction of the supporters of silver coinage was extreme. Unable to comprehend the president's action, his opponents were convinced that the party was "booked for ruin."[127]

The growing enthusiasm for unlimited coinage displayed many of the elements of a mighty religious revival, and in 1894 the Bible of the new silverite faith appeared — a small and not particularly profound book entitled *Coin's Financial School*, written by William Hope Harvey, a lawyer then living in Chicago.[128]

Harvey's book purported to be a record of a series of classes conducted by the youthful "Professor Coin," an "authority on currency." A number of well-known opponents of silver were said to have attended the lectures, in order to hold Coin up to ridicule. However, the professor easily disposed of all arguments in support of the gold standard and extolled the marvelous restorative qualities of free silver. "It means the reopening of closed factories, the relighting of fires in darkened furnaces; it means hope instead of despair; comfort in place of suffering; life instead of death." Most of his critics went away converted to his views.

By the beginning of 1895 *Coin's Financial School* had become a national best-seller. Hundreds of thousands of people, after reading Harvey's booklet, became convinced that silver inflation was the one thing needed to restore good times.[129]

Silver orators, such as William Jennings Bryan, spread the gospel of free silver far and wide. In thousands of schoolhouses throughout the West and South the people assembled to debate the absorbing question and to rattle the rafters with the free-silver hymn:

> The dollars of our daddies,
> of silver coinage free,
> Will make us rich and happy,
> Will bring prosperity.

Increasingly, the silver issue came to dominate politics. With the Populists demanding unlimited coinage of silver at a ratio of 16 to 1, the major parties found it impossible to continue straddling the money question. As we have seen, the Populists vote had increased by 40 percent in the 1894 congressional elections. Since they were almost certain to make the coinage of silver the main issue of 1896, both Republicans and Democrats were shaking in their boots.

The Election of 1896

Easily the strongest contender for the Republican nomination for president as the election of 1896 approached was William McKinley. As we have already seen, Marcus Hanna had declined to make a strong push for McKinley in 1892, waiting for a year in which victory seemed a little more likely. That year appeared to be 1896 for Hanna.

McKinley was an extremely attractive candidate. Born in 1843 in Niles, Ohio, of Scotch Irish parentage, he had enlisted in the Union Army as a private at the age of 18, emerging as a major. Following his Civil War service he entered politics in his home state of Ohio, where he adroitly worked his way through the chairs of state politics. In 1876 McKinley was elected to Congress and began a long — though not unbroken — tenure in the House of Representatives, where he gained national prominence as the Republicans' most forceful champion of the protective tariff system. In 1890, as we have seen, he was defeated for reelection to the House.

Hanna's efforts and money had facilitated McKinley's election as governor of Ohio in 1891 and reelection in 1893. In 1894 McKinley had proved to be the hero of the Republican victory. He had fueled his presidential boom in 1895 with the highly attractive slogan: "The People Against the Bosses." He also attacked the Cleveland administration for not "doing justice" to silver currency, although he tried not to emphasize the issue. Throughout the preconvention period, McKinley worked to keep the tariff question to the forefront and ignored the currency issue.[130] Like Hanna, he had many friends in organized labor, and his sincerity in presenting the argument that a protective tariff protected the wages of American workers heightened his appeal in shops and factories. His knowledge of public opinion and of the issues was widely admitted, and he was seldom far out of line with majority opinion. Joe Cannon, in fact, once remarked that McKinley had his ear so close to the ground that it was full of grasshoppers.[131]

In 1895 Hanna retired from business and took over the active direction of McKinley's campaign. To give the delegates a chance to become personally acquainted with McKinley, Hanna held a series of house parties in the South and West at which he entertained hordes of politicians white and black, both with McKinley as the guest of honor. By late 1895 the boom for McKinley had developed impressive momentum.

Former President Harrison seemed a possible choice, despite his difficulties with party leaders. However, in February Harrison disclaimed interest in the nomination, and McKinley secured many of his followers in the crucial Midwest. As it turned out, McKinley's only serious rival for the nomination was "Czar" Reed (who summed up his chances: "The Convention could do worse, and probably will"). He was right on both counts. Although Reed had extensive support among the conservatives — he staunchly supported protection and in the view of many was more firmly wedded to the gold standard than McKinley — his well-known cynicism and biting sarcasm made it hard for him to gain a wide following. In any case, by the time Reed entered the race, Hanna had already locked up the nomination for McKinley.

The Republican Convention, 1896. The Republican convention met in overwhelmingly Democratic St. Louis in June 1896. The biggest problem confronting the convention was not the naming of a candidate, because almost everyone took it for granted that McKinley would be the candidate. The biggest problem would be that of writing a platform which would appeal to the voters in very turbulent times. Since the convention contained an aggressive minority, chiefly from the Rocky Mountain region and the South that demanded the free coinage of silver, it was clear that the paramount issue was the money question. It seemed to some observers that the platform had to offer at least a gesture in the direction of bimetallism, especially since McKinley, the leading aspirant for the presidential nomination, had not committed himself to the gold standard.

The money question involved serious difficulties for McKinley. Although he had no deep convictions on the issue, he had, in fact, voted for the Bland-Allison Act and the Sherman Silver Purchase Act. Moreover, his strongest delegate support was from areas friendly to silver. His natural inclination was against fooling around with money. "Good money never made times hard," he often said. Yet Hanna understood the destructive potential for the Republican Party in the money issue. The Western Republicans, he was well aware, were shrieking for free silver. At the same time, the "gold bugs" of the East were insisting on a simple, unequivocal declaration by the party pledging adherence to a single gold standard. Hanna's problem was to conciliate the East while endeavoring to retain the West.

The result was a shrewdly devised plank which read in part: "We are . . . opposed to the free coinage of silver except by international agreement . . . which we pledge ourselves to promote, and until such agreement . . . can be obtained the existing gold standard must be preserved." Since international conferences in 1878, 1881, and 1882 had clearly shown the unwillingness of European countries to depart from the gold standard, the plank was rightly construed by the silverites as a repudiation of free coinage.[132]

When the gold plank was presented to the convention, Senator Henry M. Teller, an original Republican from Colorado speaking for a minority of the Committee on Resolutions, moved to substitute one calling for the "independent coinage of gold and silver at our mints" at the ratio of 16 to 1. Teller was pleading a lost cause and his proposal was overwhelmingly rejected 818.5 to 195.5 and the silver-haired Colorado senator left the hall, accompanied by a grim band of 22 silver delegates including the entire Colorado and Idaho delegations and members of the Montana, South Dakota, and Utah delegations.[133] As the departing men walked up the center aisle toward the main doors at the rear of the hall, frenzied gold delegates shouted, "Go! Go! Go!" and sang, "Goodbye, my Lover, Goodbye." After Teller and his supporters had departed, the remaining delegates adopted the gold plank and the rest of the platform without disagreement.

The finished platform strongly endorsed the policy of protection, and the Wilson tariff was described as "sectional, injurious to the public credit and destructive to business enterprise." It also promised generous pensions to veterans of the Union Army and pledged special support for the civil service law. The last plank called for the admission of women to wider spheres of usefulness and urged their cooperation "in rescuing the country from Democratic and Populist mismanagement and misrule."

McKinley's name was placed in nomination in an eloquent speech by Senator Joseph Foraker, which concentrated on McKinley's qualities of leadership. The Ohio senator closed with the prophetic words: "My countrymen, let not your hearts be troubled; the darkest hour is just before the day. The Twentieth Century will dawn bright and clear; God lives, the Republican Party is coming back to power and William McKinley is to be President of the United States."[134] The demonstration which followed McKinley's nomination on the first ballot (the votes which put him over the top came from Ohio, which pleased McKinley) came as no surprise — but it was far short of sensational.

For McKinley's running mate the convention quickly selected Hanna's choice — Garret A. Hobart, governor of traditionally Democratic New Jersey, and an unwavering supporter of the gold standard. The selection of Hobart, a close friend, as a running mate greatly pleased McKinley. Naturally, Hanna was named chairman of the national committee to manage the campaign.

The Democratic Convention, 1896. When the Democratic national convention assembled at the newly built Chicago Coliseum on July 7, 1896, the political tension was obvious. After the congressional disaster of 1894, and with President Cleveland's popularity declining rapidly as a result of the depression, the party was more divided than at any time since the Civil War. More than two-thirds of the delegates, their silver badges gleaming from their lapels, were already committed to "the free and unlimited coinage of silver at the ratio of sixteen to one."[135] On the second day, when John Peter Altgeld, the colorful host governor, addressed the convention and declared that the Democrats would make "no compromise on the currency issue," the delegates cheered him uproariously. There was little doubt that a free-silver candidate would be nominated. The question was who would it be? "All the Silverites need," wrote the *New York World*, "is a Moses . . . they are wandering in the wilderness like a lot of lost sheep because no one with the courage, the audacity, the magnetism, and the wisdom to be a real leader has yet appeared among them."[136]

Several prospects were available in the radical wing of the Democratic Party. Considering the importance of the silver issue, Richard Parks Bland of Missouri was probably the logical candidate. Bland had devoted most of his energies in politics to fighting for the free coinage of silver. Because of his authorship of the Bland-Allison Silver Purchase Act of 1878 his name had become a household word, and he was known nationally as "Silver Dick" Bland. But Bland had chosen to stay home in Missouri, which may have cost him the nomination. Another possibility was the young and fiery 36-year-old congressman, William Jennings Bryan of Nebraska, who came to the convention as the voice of prairie populism.

The Emergence of William Jennings Bryan. William Jennings Bryan was born in 1860 in Salem, Illinois, in the northeastern portion of "Egypt" — a geographic area of Illinois populated by Southern stock evangelical Protestants who had openly and bitterly opposed the Republican Party and its "unholy crusade" of 1860 — where the early influences of small-town rural Illinois gave him an agrarian focus. His father, Silas L. Bryan, was of Southern Baptist stock; his mother had been reared a Methodist until she joined her husband's Baptist congregation in the 1870s. Silas Bryan had been active in Democratic Party politics, having served six years in the Illinois Senate.[136]

Although Bryan's father had been active in Democratic Party politics, the younger Bryan's most important legacy from his family was not a political one but a religious one — a legacy which made it difficult for him to view issues except in moral terms. It also was to give him, according to his wife, "a source of tremendous strength . . . freedom from doubt."[137] His critics were quick to add that it also made him self-righteous and narrow-minded in his relations with others and intolerant of those who disagreed with him.

In 1887 Bryan moved west to heavily Republican Lincoln, Nebraska, to practice law, where he soon was drawn into Democratic politics. In 1890 he had accepted that party's nomination as a candidate for Congress in a district where no other Democrat was willing to stand, the contest being considered hopeless. However, Bryan made a spirited canvass, and astounded everyone by converting a Republican majority of 3,000 into a

Democratic majority of 7,000. Taking his seat in the House of Representatives, the young Nebraskan worked hard for tariff reform, but he quickly discovered that the voters of Nebraska were more interested in free silver.

In 1892 Bryan had become so partisan to the silver cause that he worked for the nomination by the Democratic Party of Horace Bois, the Iowa silverite, against Grover Cleveland. When the nomination and the election went to Cleveland, Bryan found himself in an awkward position. He could not go along with the president's hard-money policy. In a speech delivered on August 16, 1893, against the repeal of the Sherman Silver Purchase Act, Bryan openly declared war against Cleveland. In retaliation, the president made arrangements to have Bryan manipulated out of renomination at the Nebraska congressional convention of 1894.

Bryan's difficulties with Cleveland did not mean that he could be counted out, however. He spent 1894 and 1895 as editor of the *Omaha World Herald*, a newspaper controlled by the silver interests, and systematically organized a quiet boom for the 1896 nomination. By the time the Democratic National Convention met in 1896 he had become well known throughout the South and West as a champion of the free coinage of silver.

Whether to remain on the gold standard or to return to the bimetallic standard with a 16 to 1 ratio between gold and silver was an extremely complex issue. By 1896 the market ratio of gold to silver had sunk to about 32 to 1; in other words, the world price of silver had dropped so low that the silver needed to make a silver dollar was worth only 52 cents.[138] To adopt bimetallism at 16 to 1 would have pushed the country on to a silver standard when most of the major nations of the world were abandoning the silver standard and going to the gold. In consequence, the prestige of the dollar abroad could be injured, creating many difficulties in carrying on international trade. As we have already seen, the Republicans in 1896 with McKinley as their candidate had declared for gold.

To settle the question, a debate was scheduled at the Democratic convention between the gold and silver advocates. "Pitchfork" Ben Tillman opened the debate for the silver interests with a violent denunciation of the Eastern money power generally and of President Cleveland specifically. The Easterners, Tillman charged, viewed the men of the South and West as "mere hewers of wood and drawers of water, tied in bondage." "We of the South," he said, "have burned our bridges behind us so far as the Eastern Democrats are concerned." The South Carolinian's intemperate language provoked shocked hisses and shouts of protest throughout the hall, even from sympathizers. Even so, Tillman was in no mood to compromise.

David B. Hill, William F. Vilas, and William E. Russell ably defended the Cleveland administration. In pleading for unity, Hill warned of the obvious: no Democrat could win without carrying some of the East. Declarations for an income tax, an assault on Cleveland, and a campaign weighted toward agricultural interests opposing tariff protection would alienate much support. Hill ended his address with an appeal not "to drive old Democrats out of the party who have grown gray in the service, to make room for a lot of Republicans and Populists, and political nondescripts [a not-so-veiled jab at Bryan] who will not vote your ticket at the polls."

Bryan, who, ironically, had not been originally seated as a delegate, closed the debate for the majority. In doing so, he delivered what proved to be one of the most remarkable political orations known to American political history — the famous "Cross of Gold" speech. It was an extraordinary extemporaneous speech (which Bryan had been polishing for two years):

> When you . . . tell us, . . . that we are about to disturb your business interests, we reply that you have disturbed our business interest by your course. We have petitioned, and our petitions have been scorned; we have entreated, and our entreaties have been disregarded; we have begged, and they have mocked when our calamity came. We beg no longer; we entreat no more; we petition no more [a dramatic pause] *we defy them.* . . . [In tones of disdain, with Bryan's whole body thrust suddenly forward] We will answer their demand for a gold standard by saying to them [a hypnotic silence]: *You shall not press down upon the brow of labor this crown of thorns* [a hand raised], *you shall not crucify mankind upon a cross of gold!* [Arms to the side, the very figure of the crucified Christ.]

At the close of the speech there was a long silence, and then 20,000 delegates and spectators went mad; shouting, waving their arms, marching, dancing, crying, and throwing things in the air. Silver had its leader. Covering the convention for the *Emporia (Kansas) Gazette*, William Allen White wrote: "It was a fanaticism like the Crusaders. . . . Indeed the delusion that was working on the convention, and later on the people, took the form of religious frenzy." After Bryan had been uproariously cheered for 35 minutes, the prosilver report was overwhelmingly adopted as the party's platform.

At the conclusion of the "Cross of Gold" speech, Bryan would have been nominated by acclamation if the regular order of business had been disregarded. However, the agenda called for adjournment and adjourn they did. The following day the 36-year-old Bryan was nominated on the fifth ballot, receiving the necessary two-thirds majority, even though more than 162 gold Democrats persistently declined to vote. The second place went to Arthur Sewell, a rich Maine banker and shipowner who for some reason shared Bryan's free silver views.

The platform, from the pen of Altgeld, the friend of the Pullman strikers and the pardoner of the Haymarket anarchists, was a comprehensive program for reform which had the effect of reading President Cleveland out of his own party. It acclaimed free silver as the question "paramount to all others," denounced the Supreme Court for invalidating the income tax law of the previous year, and demanded a reconstruction of the court, so that the burden of taxation could be equally apportioned and wealth forced to bear its due share. In an allusion to Cleveland's action in the Pullman strike, a plank denounced federal interference in labor conflicts. The platform also denounced the McKinley Tariff, which had proved "a prolific breeder of trusts and monopolies" and "enriched the few at the expense of the many." It insisted that labor, which created the wealth of the country, should be protected in all its rights. A gold plank proposed for the platform was rejected 626–303, and even a resolution to commend "the honesty, economy, courage and fidelity" of the Cleveland administration was defeated 564–357. Conservative control of the Democratic Party was at an end.

The older Democrats were affronted and appalled by the nomination of Bryan, and a good many walked out of the convention, just as the silverites had left the Republican convention only weeks before. It was certainly the end of the party, they said, if not the world. Typical was the response of Senator Hill who, when asked if he would quit the party, replied, "I am still a Democrat — very still." Other Democrats did bolt.

The Populist Convention, 1896. Meeting in St. Louis shortly after the Democrats had stolen their chief issue, the Populists were faced with a dilemma. They had to choose whether to sacrifice their own party by endorsing Bryan, the Democratic nominee, or aid the Republicans by running their own candidate and thereby splitting the silver vote. Bryan, as they well knew, was not a Populist in either the formal or ideological sense. He was particularly out of step with Donnelly and the more radical agrarians who wanted to remain separate in order to push a thoroughgoing reform of all aspects of American society.

Many of the Southern Populists also opposed cooperation with the Democrats. In the one-party solid South the enemy had always been the very group that the Populists were now being asked to embrace as a close ally. "The Democratic idea of fusion," Tom Watson, who had refused to attend the convention because of his opposition to and fear of fusion, had complained, is "that we play Jonah, while they play whale." However, the fusionists, led by James Weaver, were ready to follow the Democratic lead by endorsing Bryan and the Democratic platform, which, in fact, did demand most of what the Populists wanted.

In an unusual move the convention determined to nominate the vice presidential candidate first, on the assumption that a Southern Populist would be chosen instead of Sewell who, as a banker and railroad director, was wholly unacceptable to dyed-in-the-wool Populists. The delegates then settled on Watson, who accepted, he later claimed, in the expectation that the Democrats would drop Sewell (which they had no intention of doing).

The vice presidential selection made, General Weaver presented Bryan — "that matchless champion of the people, that intrepid foe of corporate greed, that splendid young statesman" — to the delegates. Following a noisy and prolonged demonstration, the nomination of the golden-voiced young silverite was whooped through.

The delegates then adopted a platform differing only slightly from that of the Chicago Democrats. It declared for a graduated income tax, free silver at 16 to 1, an immediate increase in the volume of money sufficient to meet the "demands of business and population," and the establishment of a postal savings bank. One unique and significant item declared that "in times of great industrial depression, idle labor should be employed on public works as far as practicable." A silver Republican Party hastily organized by Senator Teller, nominated Bryan and Sewell and adopted a silver platform.

John Dobson concludes that, in accepting Bryan and the Democratic platform, the Populists made the decision that effectively destroyed the party's individuality. The two-party system thus survived its most serious challenge since the Civil War.[139]

The Gold Democrats, 1896. In mid-July a group of anti–Bryan Democratic leaders organized what they called the National Democratic Party (which the Bryanites quickly labeled the "Gold Bugs" and "Yellow Bellies") and issued a call for a convention. When gold Democrats from 41 states and 3 territories assembled in Indianapolis on September 2, a platform was adopted which declared that the Democratic platform had attacked "individual freedom, the right of private contract, the independence of the judiciary and the authority of the President to enforce Federal laws." The Cleveland administration was praised, and protection "and its ally, free coinage of silver," were denounced as "schemes for the personal profit of a few at the expense of the masses." It also declared for the gold standard and for "a uniform, safe and elastic bank currency, under governmental supervision, measured in volume by the needs of business."[140]

The gold Democrats also faced a dilemma. They were bolting from the candidate of their party and not the party itself: they sincerely wanted to preserve the Democratic Party. They wanted to defeat Bryan but they did not want to do so at the expense of weakening the party identification of those Democratic voters who opposed the commoner. If they only succeeded in shifting the voters to McKinley that would be dysfunctional to their objectives. To this end, the delegates tried to draft Cleveland. However, when the president declined, they settled for the 80-year-old Senator John M.

Palmer of Illinois — a former Union general — for the presidency and the more than 70-year-old General Simon Buckner of Kentucky — a former Confederate general — for the vice presidency. In accepting the nomination, Palmer made it clear that he was running only to injure Bryan. "Fellow Democrats," he announced, "I will not consider it any great fault if you decide to cast your vote for William McKinley." For the most part, the financing for the gold Democrats' campaign came from the Republicans.[141]

The Prohibition Party, 1896. In 1896 even the Prohibitionists were affected by the silver question, and broke into two parties with different platforms and candidates. The regulars or narrow gaugers, who controlled the convention, were unwilling to sacrifice their party's pristine purity and were opposed to any broadening of the party's program to include reforms other than the control of the liquor traffic or cooperation with the Democrats. Joshua Levering of Maryland and Hale Johnson of Illinois were their candidates. When the national convention endorsed this stand, the broad gaugers, who advocated that the party adopt a program embracing several reforms in addition to prohibition, withdrew and organized a separate "cold water" party, the National Party.

The "broad gaugers" then nominated Charles E. Bentley of Nebraska, and James H. Southgate of North Carolina, on a platform which, besides its statements on prohibition, declared for free silver, women's suffrage, and direct election of the president and vice president. Ridiculed by the narrow gaugers as "Populists with Prohibition tendencies" the National leaders actively promoted fusion between their organization and Bryan's Democrats. With the support of these leaders, as well as that of the state and local Women's Christian Temperance Union organizations, the new party of morality drew voting support from groups that for half a century had condemned the Democrats as the party of "the saloon interests." The split produced irreparable fissures in the state organizations and rendered the Prohibition Party as weak organizationally as it had been in the 1870s.

The Campaign of 1896. The "battle of the standards" between Bryan and McKinley in 1896 was one of the bitterest of all American presidential campaigns. From coast to coast the country was aroused as it had not been since 1860. The campaign opened in August — an unprecedentedly early date — with Bryan leading off and deliberately carrying the war to the "enemy's territory" by formally accepting his nomination at New York's Madison Square Garden. Quoting Lincoln, Jefferson, and Jackson in support, he endorsed and defended the Democratic platform in all its features. He devoted most of his argument to the money question and maintained that free coinage would restore silver to parity with gold at 16 to 1 throughout the world, and that the mint price would control the bullion price, in fact, fix the price, and that there would be no repudiation involved.

Bryan's campaign was almost a one-man show. He was a novelty in

American politics. The "Cross of Gold" speech had made him a popular hero and people clamored to see and hear the "Boy Orator of the Platte."[142] He identified his campaign as a moral crusade in "the cause of humanity." Bryan cut the issue sharply: "Upon which side," he asked, "will the Democratic Party fight; upon the side of the 'idle holders of idle capital' or upon the side of the 'struggling masses'"? Behind McKinley, Bryan charged, stood the entrenched wealth of America. The "Man of Mark" he said, was the tool of the gold bugs and the Trusts.

The Nebraskan traveled over 18,000 miles in 21 states in his railroad car, misnamed the "Idler," in an unprecedented effort to carry his free-silver gospel to every voter in the land. He made over 600 speeches and addressed an estimated 5 million people in every nook and cranny of the country — probably the greatest audience that ever listened to a single human voice before the invention of the radio. In the depression-stricken farm belt, hordes of fanatical free silverites sang for Bryan, "We'll All Have Our Pockets Lined with Silver" and "No Crown of Thorns, No Cross of Gold."[143]

Hanna made no attempt to have McKinley compete with Bryan on the stump. Rather, he had his candidate wage a "front porch" campaign. Several times a day, through the months of September and October, groups representing every corner of the land, occupation, and interest descended upon Canton, Ohio, with the railroads cooperating by cutting fares so low that the trip was "cheaper than staying at home," according to one newspaper man. Each delegation was escorted from the railway station to McKinley's unpretentious frame house by "The Canton Cornets," the local GAR band, playing music appropriate to the section of the country from which the delegation came. Once there the visitors paid their compliments to the candidate and after refreshment (hard or soft depending on whether the delegation was wet or dry), heard him deliver a brief response on the significant issues of the campaign, carefully attuned to the interest of the group of listeners and carefully edited by McKinley's staff to avoid the same sort of political blunder that had hurt James Blaine in 1884.[144] In this way, without moving from his doorstep, McKinley met thousands of people from every section of the country. The major's home almost vanished. The front yard look as if "a herd of Buffalo had passed that way," and pilgrims pried off so much wood that the house almost collapsed. The picket fence was long since gone, and grass went into scrapbooks like pressed flowers.

Hanna, as chairman of the Republican National Committee, spared nothing to defeat Bryan. He sent active campaigners into every doubtful district in the country where they engaged in the free and unlimited coinage of speeches. Former President Benjamin Harrison helped out by speaking frequently in the industrial area of Indiana and New York, where he supplied workers with an easily quotable answer to silver inflation: "The first dirty errand that a dirty dollar does is to cheat the workingman."

In addition, an anthology of McKinley's speeches on the money question was distributed widely in the East where McKinley was being criticized. Over 120 million campaign leaflets were sent out: an especially effective one being *Coin at School in Finance* by G.S. Roberts, a rebuttal of Harvey's famous prosilver classic, *Coin's Financial School.* [145] There were 250 million copies of 275 different pamphlets in English, German, Italian, Greek, Polish, Yiddish, Swedish, and other languages distributed across the nation (or about 5 pamphlets for each voter). More than 500 posters were prepared; the most popular pictured McKinley and Hobart as "The Advance Agents of Prosperity." The Republican Campaign Committee appropriated the American flag as their campaign banner — leaving the Democratic campaign managers in an infuriatingly frustrating position. This move implied that McKinley's patriotism made him a national symbol coequal with the flag. [146] Meanwhile, a trainload of former Union generals was sent to every city, county seat, and rural hamlet to speak for the Republican candidate and his principles.

Denunciation and ridicule were heaped upon Bryan by the press. The *New York Times* accused him of being insane; the *Louisville Courier-Journal* called Bryan "a dishonest dodger . . . a daring adventurer . . . a political faker"; and Whitelaw Reid's *New York Tribune* referred to him as a "wretched, rattle-pated boy." The independent journals and influential weeklies, such as *Harper's Weekly*, the *Nation*, and the *Independent*, were all against him.

Even his own party's press devoted most of its symbolism to the theme that Bryan was not a real Democrat but a Populist and then not so subtly implied that all Populists were anarchists. The implication was that Bryan's election would bring disaster. In New York City only William Randolph Hearst's *New York Journal* supported Bryan (Hearst had inherited a potential fortune in silver from his father). Homer Davenport's cartoons in the *Journal* depicted Hanna as a bloated plutocrat leading the child McKinley by a string. Hanna was also caricatured by opposition newspapers as an obese money bag, marked with dollar signs, lugging a hurdy-gurdy with McKinley as a dejected monkey hitched to his master's wrist. Farm wives allegedly hid their children at the mention of Hanna's name.

Ironically, Bryan was supported by the Populist and Prohibitionist press and that became something of an embarrassment to him. The Populist papers, seeking Prohibitionist support for Bryan, denounced the "saloon power" with which they argued McKinley was identified, and heralded Bryan's candidacy as the beginning of a new "moral crusade." His election, they argued, would guarantee the advent of a "grander civilization," of "the moral society." Where the voting population was preponderantly German, the Bryan Democrats frequently found it necessary to disavow any connection between Bryan and the "Prohibition craze."

Nor did Bryan fare well with the clergy of the mainstream denominations. A conservative clergyman asserted that Bryan's platform was "made in hell." On November 2, the Sunday before the election, congregations throughout the country heard anti–Bryan sermons where they were told that nobody could be a Christian and vote for the Democratic "anarchists."

Hanna collected from the great banking and business interests an election fund of unknown amount, officially about $4 million; a huge sum for the times, and particularly for a lean year.[147] Banks and insurance companies were "assessed" a percentage of their assets and big corporations a share of their receipts. Capitalists throughout the country loosened a flood of money to save the country "from the insanity" of Bryanism, free silver, and repudiation.[148]

As usual, Bryan was severely hampered by lack of funds. Silver mine owners paid much of Bryan's expenses but could not equal Hanna's resources, and only about $650,000 was raised. Some rich Democrats who had supported the party in previous elections became gold Democrats and gave their money to McKinley.

Vachel Lindsay, the poet, caught the essence of Bryan and his movement when he wrote:

> Prairie avenger, mountain lion,
> Bryan, Bryan, Bryan, Bryan,
> Gigantic troubadour, speaking
>   like a siege gun,
> Smashing Plymouth Rock with his boulders
>   from the West.[149]

Bryan's lack of a Civil War record was a decided political handicap. Also Bryan's relative lack of political experience — two terms in the House of Representatives — contrasted unfavorably with McKinley's long service in Congress and as governor of Ohio "the state of presidents." Bryan was also handicapped by lack of support in his own party. President Cleveland and his cabinet supported the gold Democrat ticket but like most of the yellow bellies, as the gold Democrats became known, they preferred McKinley to Bryan and hoped for a Republican victory.

The 1896 Outcome. Election day in 1896 was November 3. The turnout was particularly heavy — some 14 million male citizens, more than in any presidential election, made their way to the designated polling places. When the votes were counted, McKinley had 7,100,000 popular votes; Bryan, 6,500,000, including fusion tickets. Bryan and the Democratic Party had suffered a crushing defeat. McKinley's popular plurality of over 600,000 was the largest any presidential candidate had received since Ulysses Grant trounced Horace Greeley in 1872. Ironically, in losing, Bryan had polled 1 million votes more than Cleveland had received in his victory four years earlier, and more than any victorious candidate had ever before polled. The Ohioan triumphed in the electoral college by 271 to 176. Both houses of Congress were Republican by a safe margin.

When the election was analyzed, it was strikingly evident that the votes of labor had defeated Bryan. The cities, where the industrial workers were concentrated, voted overwhelmingly Republican. Only 12 of the 82 cities with a population of 45,000 or more went for Bryan — and 7 of the 12 were in the Democratic South, while 2 others were located in silver-producing states. It was clear that organized labor favored the Republican protective tariff policy because it bolstered wages and discouraged competition from cheap foreign labor. In reality, labor simply had little in common with Bryan's agrarian interests.

The 1896 result was replete with irony. During a period of widespread depression, urban labor had moved into a party whose primary objective appeared to be that of protecting persons of great wealth. Still more unusual, thousands of urban immigrants had flocked to the party of the American Protective Association. Hollingsworth concludes that, for whatever reason, by the time McKinley entered the White House in 1897, the Democratic Party could boast only of small cliques on the state and local levels, new converts, amateurs, disloyal bolters, and Southerners.[150]

Epilogue

By the turn of the century the American political party system had clearly demonstrated its instability. In fact, the chief characteristic of the political system at this time was a unique period of partisan stalemate. The elections following the Civil War had been marked by competition among the Democrats and the Republicans and several minor parties, principally the Populists, Greenbackers, and Prohibitionists.

For 25 years following the Civil War, the two great parties had fought each other to a national standoff. In northern New England the Republican Party clearly dominated both local and national elections. In the lower South, once Reconstruction ended, the Democrats seldom had to worry about their Republican opponents. But elsewhere in the nation the two parties had waged annual battles for local offices – biennial ones for Congress, and quadrennial ones for the presidency – that neither could regularly count on winning.

In the presidential elections during those years neither party won decisively. The winner's margin – usually the Republican – had been only paper thin. No Republican president from Rutherford B. Hayes to Benjamin Harrison received a clear majority of the popular vote. Only James Garfield secured a popular plurality and his was the smallest in history.

This popular inertia can be clearly seen in the election returns. Though campaigns were marked by religious fervor and high voter turnout, in no election from 1876 to 1896 was the winning side's share of the popular vote more than 51 percent. In two elections, 1876 and 1888, the Republican victor was elected with fewer popular votes than his Democrat opponent. The Democrats only for one brief interval (1893–95) and the Republicans only for two (1881–83, 1889–91) established that simultaneous control of the presidency and both houses of Congress which was essential for positive party achievement.

Ironically, the 1896 results were followed by a sharp decline of voter interest in national and local elections. Although voter turnouts were extremely high in this period – reaching to well over 80 percent of the eligible voters in national elections – the proportion of those voters who actually cast their ballots following the Bryan-McKinley contest dropped to 60 percent or less. Apparently, after 1896 the voters wearied of the predictable Republican majorities and started to stay away from the polls. Finally, the election of 1896 marked the beginning of independent voting on a large scale. Party loyalties declined as more and more people abandoned their fervent attachment to the major parties and began to support reform groups, especially on the local level.

By the turn of the century, however, the American political party system had emerged from the fluctuations and uncertainties of the post–Civil War era and was moving toward relative stability. The minor parties had collapsed and American politics would witness the return of the traditional model of two-party competition between Republicans and Democrats.

The Republican Party After 1896. Following the Civil War, as we have seen, the Republicans dominated the office of president. The GOP had been a minority in 1860 but they had emerged from the civil conflict augmented in numbers and influence. During the period of Reconstruction in the South they were able to count on the support of the new black voters grateful for emancipation and for the civil rights accorded to their race by the party of Abraham Lincoln. It was under their auspices that the Union had been saved, that the perpetuity of the republic had been assured.

Bryan's defeat in 1896 ushered in a generation of Republican ascendancy broken only by Woodrow Wilson's election as a minority president in 1912 when the Bull Moose secession split his opponents, and as a "peace" president in 1916 when war was an imminent threat. Not until 1932 — after massive shifts of population from rural areas to cities had occurred and when the deep social traumas of the worst depression in U.S. history produced a loyal Democratic majority — could the Democrats win again in the North. By the end of the nineteenth century the Republican Party had become the political home of a majority of Americans.

The Democratic Party After 1896. The post–Civil War period was a time of intense political tension within the Democratic Party. Early in the decade of the 1890s Democratic prospects appeared bright. In 1890 the party registered substantial gains in Congress and in 1892 won control of both houses and the presidency. But the depression which began in 1893 brought a dramatic reversal of party fortunes when the electorate returned to the polls in 1894. After that disaster, with economic conditions growing more severe and President Cleveland's popularity declining, the Democratic faithful, in desperation, turned to William Jennings Bryan and free silver. As we have seen, this led to a severe breach between the Eastern gold standard Democrats, led by Cleveland, and the Western and Southern silverites, led by Bryan, which rendered the party helpless and irrelevant until the ascendency of Woodrow Wilson.

Before the Democratic Party could regain its status as a truly national party it had to overcome two major obstacles.

The first was its reputation as the party of traitors. The Democratic Party — discredited in the minds of many by their opposition to the Civil War — survived with its hard core in the South. After the war their opposition to the three great war amendments had put them in the wrong in the eyes of the millions to whom the Union soldier had been a crusader in a holy cause. Beginning with General Grant and ending with Major McKinley, every successful Republican aspirant for the presidency in the 40 years after the Civil War had been a participant in the struggle.

However, the postwar rise in the pulse of the national Democracy was dramatic. By 1871 the Democrats had carried the House of Representatives. Five years after that, in 1876, they outpolled the Republicans in the popular vote for president (but, as we have seen, Hayes defeated Tilden in the famous electoral college deadlock and manipulations) and two years later the Democrats won a majority in the Senate. As the party out of power during the Civil War and Reconstruction periods, Democrats were in no position to employ the resources of the presidency for the reconstruction of the party and they were not able to consolidate national power. Part of the trouble was their inability to win over dissident groups, like the Greenbackers and Populists. But the main difficulty was that the Republicans, riding the wave of a long-term economic boom, were in accord with the main temper of the time.

The second major obstacle which the Democratic Party had to overcome was its lack of leadership. Although defeated in 1896, William Jennings Bryan made himself the full-time titular leader of the party. Between 1897 and 1899 he traveled some 93,000 miles on the lecture circuit, speaking on the topics of money, trusts, and imperialism. Instead of dropping the symbolic issue of silver and facing the concrete problems of the present, Bryan continued to hold the sword of silver over the party's head, with the result that the party failed to come to grips with the current concerns. It had also failed to develop new and effective northern leadership. Though approximately 60 percent of the party's vote was polled in the North, rarely did a new or dynamic face appear on the scene north of the Mason and Dixon Line. The party's national leadership had shifted to the South and West, and there was no one with sufficient prestige or influence to challenge the entrenched position of Bryan. As a result, Bryan remained the dominant figure in the Democratic Party and remained so until the rise of Woodrow Wilson.

After the turn of the century, however, national conditions changed, and the times were propitious for an upturn in Democratic Party fortunes. Business conditions improved, unemployment declined, and income rose. Close upon the footsteps of the Republicans, the Democrats fitted themselves to the big business mood of the postwar period and placed their party in the service of the same economic interests as the Republicans.

The Populist Party After 1896. The Populist Party virtually dissolved during the campaign of 1896. For the next three presidential elections it continued to put tickets in the field, but after 1896 it was never again a serious factor in American politics.

The return of prosperity beginning in 1897 saw most Midwestern Populists return to the Republican Party. Thereafter they sought to gain narrow economic ends by pressure politics, and the farm bloc in Congress became their true symbol. But a sizable minority, mainly from the middle of the road Populists who opposed fusion with the Democrats in 1896, were interested not just in higher prices but also in social reconstruction. Thousands of these voters moved leftward toward socialism.

During the first half of the twentieth century, however, the impact of war, reform movements, and dynamic political leaders returned the control of policy to Washington. As a result, political parties once again assumed a powerful role in the direction of national affairs. Major policy questions were resolved not independently by the business community but by political leaders operating within the party system. Thus the political system reemerged as the focal point of the policymaking process.

Out of these developments came a new political realignment and the foundation for a new party system. Before that realignment could take place (starting around the turn of the century), important adjustments to the American political system would be made: direct primaries to facilitate the nomination of presidential and congressional candidates; the popular election of senators; the direct election of presidential electors; public opinion polling, reporting, analyzing, and projecting by newspaper, radio, and television anchorpersons of the performance of candidates and the most likely outcome of elections; the advent of single-issue pressure groups hoping to influence presidents and members of Congress in the shaping of public policy in their best interest (and when necessary, to pay whatever it cost); and public funding of political campaigns. All these changes would drastically alter the basic rules under which the American two-party system operated and which, more importantly, would substantially change the fundamental nature of the system itself.

Notes

The Whigs

1. Ever since then it has been accepted that on the president's death the vice president succeeds to the title with full powers of the office and the Twenty-Fifth Amendment writes this understanding into the Constitution. On the political career of President John Tyler, see Oliver Perry Chitwood, *John Tyler: Champion of the Old South;* and Robert J. Morgan, *A Whig Embattled: The Presidency Under John Tyler.*

2. See G.R. Poage, *Henry Clay and the Whig Party.*

3. See Chitwood, *John Tyler;* and Morgan, *A Whig Embattled,* which reflects the view that John Tyler betrayed the Whig Party.

4. Eric Foner, *Free Soil, Free Labor, Free Men,* p. 189.

5. Congressional Quarterly, *National Party Conventions 1831-1976,* p. 25.

6. Kirk H. Porter and Donald Bruce Johnson, *National Party Platforms 1840-1964,* p. 9.

7. Arthur M. Schlesinger, Jr., *History of American Presidential Elections 1798-1868,* 2:750.

8. The next would be Champ Clark in the 1912 convention which nominated Woodrow Wilson.

9. The term "dark horse" was borrowed from the racetrack — a candidate who unexpectedly won the nomination was likened to a horse that had not been run hard enough or long enough to "work up a sweat" and thus remained dry and dark. An excellent account of the maneuvering leading to Polk's nomination is found in Charles Sellers, *James K. Polk, Continentalist, 1843-1846,* pp. 67-107.

10. Most people never got it straight about Polk's true age. Although he was not yet 50 years of age, he looked 20 years older by reason of poor health.

11. Joseph Rayback interprets this statement as less a gesture of loyalty than "an obvious indication of his feeling that the Democratic ticket was doomed to failure." See Joseph G. Rayback, *Free Soil: The Election of 1848,* p. 14.

12. Henry Minor, *The Story of the Democratic Party,* p. 210.

13. Howard P. Nash, Jr., *Third Parties in American Politics,* p. 27.

14. William B. Hesseltine, *Third Party Movements in the United States,* pp. 34-35. Also see Theodore C. Smith, *The Liberty and Free Soil Parties in the Northwest.*

15. Frederick J. Blue, *The Free Soilers,* p. 4.

16. Eugene H. Roseboom, *A History of Presidential Elections,* p. 58.

17. On the campaign of 1844 see J.C.N. Paul, *Rift in the Democracy;* and Benjamin Le Fevre, *Campaign of 1844.*

18. Glyndon Van Deusen, *The Life of Henry Clay,* p. 371.

19. Clay set forth his entire campaign philosophy on his campaign button: "Champion of a Protective Tariff." Polk's button called him and his running mate George Dallas the "People's Candidates," and boasted that "Success Will Crown Our Efforts."

20. Minor, *The Story of the Democratic Party*, p. 209.

21. Rayback, *Free Soil*, p. 99.

22. Few American political leaders were so possessed of what modern political analysts call charisma (defined in the dictionaries as a mystically bestowed magnetism) as Henry Clay. Although frustrated repeatedly in his efforts to become president, he nevertheless commanded a legion of loyal supporters. One such was A.B. Norton of Dallas, Texas, a college student in 1844, who vowed he would not shave until Clay was elected president of the United States. True to his pledge, when he died at the age of 80, Norton's beard was 12 feet 9 inches long! It was so long he had to roll it up and keep it tucked in his vest.

23. The usual method of admission of states requires a two-thirds vote in the Senate — which the expansionists clearly did not have.

24. Several excellent histories of President Polk have been published, including Edwin P. Hoyt, *James Knox Polk*; Milton Lomask, *This Slender Reed: A Life of James K. Polk*; C.A. McCoy, *Polk and the Presidency*; James K. Polk, *The Diary of a President, 1845–1849*; Charles Sellers, *James K. Polk: Continentalist, 1843–1846*; and Bill Severn, *Frontier President: James K. Polk*.

25. Rayback, *Free Soil*, p. 261.

26. The first of a long line of slogans which have substantially affected the outcome of a presidential election. However, E.A. Miles, in his "'Fifty-Four Forty or Fight' — An American Political Legend," *Mississippi Valley Historical Review* (September 1957): 291–310, denies the importance of the slogan in the campaign of 1844.

27. *The Works of James Russell Lowell*, Standard Library edition (Boston 1890), 8:46–47.

28. In American political parlance, availability has little to do with a prospective candidate's willingness to accept nomination — acceptance is taken for granted. Availability refers rather to qualities deemed likely to increase the prospective candidate's chances for electoral victory. When politicians discuss availability, they are sizing up a potential candidate to see if he or she possesses the personal, social, and political characteristics the party seeks in its presidential nominee.

29. August 15, 1846.

30. Rayback, *Free Soil*, p. 113.

31. Cass, henceforth, was reviled by his enemies as a "doughface" — a congressman from a Northern state who was not opposed to slavery in the South.

32. Blue, *The Free Soilers*, p. 48.

33. Quoted from Roy Franklin Nichols, *The Invention of the American Political Parties*, p. 374.

34. Rayback, *Free Soil*, p. 191.

35. Blue, *The Free Soilers*, p. 49.

36. Roy F. Nichols, *The Invention of the American Political Parties*, p. 371.

37. Taylor was one of the fewer than 1,800 Americans who owned over 100 slaves.

38. On President Taylor generally, see Brainerd Dyer, *Zachary Taylor*; Holman Hamilton, *Zachary Taylor: Soldier in the White House*; and Edwin P. Hoyt, *Zachary Taylor*.

39. Taylor, who had not attended the convention, was notified of his nomination

by mail. When the letter arrived it had postage due and Taylor refused to pick it up and it was sent to the dead letter office. Weeks later he received a duplicate letter notifying him of his nomination. He then replied with an official acceptance.

40. Malcolm E. Moos and Stephen Hess, *Hats in the Ring*, p. 157.

41. On Fillmore generally, see William Griffis, *Millard Fillmore;* and Robert J. Rayback, *Millard Fillmore.*

42. Frank R. Kent, *The Democratic Party: A History*, p. 156.

43. Blue, *The Free Soilers*, p. 70.

44. Nash, *Third Parties in American Politics*, p. 50. Also see Rayback, *Free Soil*, p. 226.

45. Hesseltine, *Third Party Movements in the United States*, p. 42.

46. Rayback suggests that this was an effort to link Van Buren with Jefferson, who had backed the Northwest Ordinance of 1787, whereby slavery was banished from the land north of the Ohio River and east of the Mississippi. See Rayback, *Free Soil*, p. 229.

47. Alma Lutz, *Created Equal: A Biography of Elizabeth Cady Stanton, 1815–1902.*

48. Only one woman present at Seneca Falls in 1848 would live long enough to vote for president in 1920.

49. Taylor's campaign badge was a real lapel-full. It listed his successful battles — Palo Alto, Resaca de la Palma, Monterrey, and Buena Vista, plus his profile, rank, "Never Surrender," "I Ask No Favors, I Shrink from No Responsibilities," plus assorted shields, draped flags, eagles, and swords.

50. Schlesinger, *History of American Presidential Elections*, 2:889.

51. Sheet music was being increasingly used by candidates for the presidential office because it had an effective and emotional way of stirring the voters.

52. Quoted from Rayback, *Free Soil*, p. 238.

53. *Ibid.*, p. 247.

54. Nash, *Third Parties in American Politics*, p. 51.

55. Blue, *The Free Soilers*, p. 132.

56. Schlesinger, *History of American Presidential Elections*, 2:889.

57. Quoted from Blue, *The Free Soilers*, p. 107.

58. For detailed election data and an analysis, see Rayback, *Free Soil*, pp. 279–302.

59. In Virginia, the only Southern state where Van Buren received any popular votes, he polled a total of 9 votes. But when the Free Soilers cried fraud, one Virginian exclaimed, "Yes fraud! And we're still looking for the son-of-a-bitch who voted nine times." Related in Paul F. Boller, *Presidential Anecdotes*, p. 89.

60. Rayback, *Free Soil*, provides an excellent study of the 1848 Free Soil campaign.

61. On the career and death of President James K. Polk, see Homer F. Cunningham, *The President's Last Years: George Washington to Lyndon B. Johnson*, pp. 77–83.

62. On the political career of Zachary Taylor, see Brainerd Dyer, *Zachary Taylor;* Hamilton, *Zachary Taylor;* and Edwin P. Hoyt, *Zachary Taylor.*

63. Harold U. Faulkner, *American Political and Social History*, p. 311.

64. For the complete text of Daniel Webster's historic Seventh of March speech in support of the Compromise of 1850, see Arthur M. Schlesinger, Jr., *History of U. S. Political Parties*, 1:461–474

65. Quoted in John D. Hicks, *The Federal Union*, p. 543.

66. On Charles Sumner see David Donald, *Charles Sumner and the Coming of the Civil War.*

67. On Fillmore as President see: William Griffis, *Millard Fillmore;* and Robert Rayback, *Millard Fillmore.*

68. The best study of the political history of the Compromise of 1850 is Holman Hamilton, *Prologue to Conflict: The Crisis and Compromise of 1850.* Also see Holman Hamilton, "'The Cave of the Winds' and the Compromise of 1850." For the voting on the Compromise of 1850, see Felice A. Bonadio, ed., *Political Parties in American History: 1828–1890,* pp. 630–31.

69. On the political career of Douglas, see Gerald M. Capers, *Stephen A. Douglas;* and Allen Johnson, *Stephen A. Douglas.*

70. Quoted from John A. Garraty, *The American Nation,* p. 382.

71. Boller recounts that when Pierce heard that he had been nominated he exclaimed: "You are looking at the most surprised man that ever lived." He wasn't the only one. See Paul F. Boller, *Presidential Campaigns,* p. 89.

72. Minor, *The Story of the Democratic Party,* p. 235.

73. Allan Nevins, *The Ordeal of the Union,* 2:21.

74. Chester C. Maxey, *Bipartisanship in the United States,* p. 123.

75. Congressional Quarterly, *National Party Conventions 1831–1976,* p. 31.

76. Thomas A. Bailey, *The American Pageant,* p. 410.

77. A century later this became a booksellers' bonanza.

78. On the 1852 election see Roseboom, *A History of Presidential Elections,* p. 65.

79. Pierce's victory over Scott was the largest electoral victory since that of James Monroe in 1820, before the Democratic Party was born. Pierce was one of the few presidents able to succeed in unifying his party and leading it to victory.

80. President Pierce and his administration can be studied in Roy Nichols, *Franklin Pierce.* Also see Nathaniel Hawthorne, *The Life of Franklin Pierce.*

81. For religious reasons President Pierce "affirmed" rather than swore to the oath of office, the only president to do so.

82. It cost $322 to construct and dismantle the platform in front of the Capitol for Pierce's inauguration. In 1980 construction costs at the Capitol for Ronald Reagan's inauguration were budgeted at $375,000.

83. Schlesinger, *History of American Presidential Elections,* 2:1008. James Pike, the *New York Tribune's* Washington correspondent, wrote: "We expect Mr. Pierce will give us a quiet, moderate, conservative, unexceptionable, good-for-nothing kind of administration, to which nobody will think of making any special objection or opposition."

84. Quoted from Michael Kraus, *The United States to 1865,* p. 449.

85. Bailey, *The American Pageant,* p. 418.

86. The historian James McPherson says that within two years proslavery writers had answered *Uncle Tom's Cabin* with at least 15 novels whose sole thesis was that slaves were better off than free workers in the North. See James McPherson, *Battle Cry of Freedom: The Civil War Era,* p. 90.

87. For a discussion of the origins of the Kansas-Nebraska Act, see David M. Potter, *The Impending Crisis: 1848–1861.*

88. Douglas was the only Northern senator to hold an important Senate committee chairmanship.

89. Quoted from Kraus, *The United States to 1865,* p. 449.

90. For the text of the "Appeal of the Independent Democrats," see Reading No. 1 in Franklin L. Burdette, *The Republican Party: A Short History,* pp. 119–23.

91. See Peter A. Isely, *Horace Greeley and the Republican Party, 1853–1861: A Study of the New York Tribune.*

92. Five of the 9 free-state legislatures (Maine, Massachusetts, Rhode Island, New York, and Wisconsin) passed resolutions of protest against the Kansas-Nebraska Act.

93. Hesseltine, *Third Party Movements in the United States*, pp. 24–25.

94. The Native American Party stated its program as "Anti-Romanism, Anti-Bedinism, Anti-Pope's Toeism, Anti-Nunneryism, Anti-Jesuitism, and Anti–the Whole Sacerdotal-Hierarchism with all its humbugging Mummeries."

95. Nash, *Third Parties in American Politics*, p. 7.

96. Hesseltine, *Third Party Movements in the United States*, p. 27. The secret sign apparently was the third finger laid alongside the nose while the thumb and index finger formed an "O."

97. See Humphrey J. Desmond, *The Know-Nothing Party.* Also see Carleton Beal, *Brass-Knuckle Crusade: The Know-Nothing Conspiracy, 1820–1860.*

The Republicans

1. Franklin L. Burdette, *The Republican Party: A Short History*, p. 9.

2. Howard P. Nash, Jr., *Third Parties in American Politics*, p. 70.

3. Malcolm E. Moos, *The Republicans: A History of Their Party*, p. 11.

4. Republican National Committee, *The History of the Republican Party*, p. 10.

5. Quoted in Michael Kraus, *The United States to 1865*, p. 454.

6. Moos, *The Republicans*, p. 18.

7. On Sumner see David H. Donald, *Charles Sumner and the Coming of the Civil War.*

8. Burdette, *The Republican Party*, p. 14.

9. According to Moos, *The Republicans*, p. 50.

10. Burdette, *The Republican Party*, p. 17.

11. Andrew W. Crandall, *The Early History of the Republican Party, 1854–1856*, describes the different groups that came together between 1854 and 1856 to form the Republican Party.

12. Although he had publicly expressed the opinion that his defeat in the race for governor of New York in 1844 could be attributed to the votes of foreign-born citizens.

13. Eric Foner, *Free Soil, Free Labor, Free Men*, p. 198.

14. Congressional Quarterly, *National Party Conventions 1831–1976*, p. 34.

15. Burdette, *The Republican Party*, p. 19.

16. See George W. Julian, "The First Republican National Convention," *American Historical Review* 4 (1898).

17. Quoted from Burdette, *The Republican Party*, p. 19.

18. Polygamy, practiced in Utah by some of the Mormons, was attracting attention. Under popular sovereignty the territory could decide such matters for itself.

19. Arthur M. Schlesinger, Jr., *History of American Presidential Elections 1798–1868*, 2:1023. For the text of the 1856 Republican platform, see Burdette, *The Republican Party*, reading no. 2, pp. 123–26.

20. Chester C. Maxey, *Bipartisanship in the United States*, p. 172.

21. Quoted from George H. Mayer, *The Republican Party, 1854–1966*, p. 33.

22. Schlesinger, *History of American Presidential Elections*, 2:1024.

23. On the qualifications of John C. Fremont for the presidency, see Ruhl J. Bartlett, *John C. Fremont and the Republican Party;* and Allan Nevins, *Fremont, Pathmarker of the West.*

24. See Fred H. Harrington, "Fremont and the North Americans," pp. 842–48.

25. Maxey, *Bipartisanship in the United States*, p. 164.

26. Roy F. Nichols, *The Stakes of Power, 1845–1877*, p. 37.

27. Crandall, *The Early History of the Republican Party*, p. 215.

28. Burdette, *The Republican Party*, p. 21.

29. Wilfred E. Binkley, *American Political Parties*, p. 219.

30. Paul F. Boller, *Presidential Campaigns*, p. 98.

31. Moos, *The Republicans*, p. 52.

32. Foner, *Free Soil, Free Labor, Free Men*, p. 164.

33. See D.E. Fehrenbacher, *The Dred Scott Case*. Also see E.S. Corwin, "The Dred Scott Decision," *American Historical Review*, 17 (1911): 52–69.

34. Alexander Johnston, *History of American Politics*, pp. 182–83.

35. Quoted from John A. Garraty, *The American Nation*, p. 391.

36. *Ibid.* Garraty suggests that Douglas had little choice but to oppose the president. If he stood aside while Congress admitted Kansas before the people of the territory had an opportunity to vote on its proslavery constitution he would not only be abandoning his cherished belief in popular sovereignty but would also be committing political suicide. Fifty-five of the 56 newspapers in Illinois had declared editorially against the Lecompton Constitution. Douglas knew that if he supported it his defeat for reelection to the Senate in 1858 was certain.

37. A.J. Beveridge, *Abraham Lincoln 1809–1858*, provides an excellent overview of Lincoln's early career.

38. Binkley, *American Political Parties*, p. 225.

39. Quoted from Allan Nevins and Henry Steele Commager, *A Short History of the United States*, p. 225.

40. Quoted from Burdette, *The Republican Party*, p. 12.

41. On the Lincoln-Douglas debates see Harry V. Jaffa, *Crisis of the House Divided*. Also see Paul A. Angle, ed., *Created Equal*, which contains the full texts of the debates. In each debate the opening speaker talked for 1 hour, his opponent responded for 1 hour and 30 minutes, and the first speaker closed for 30 minutes. Douglas and Lincoln alternated as opening speaker, Douglas opening and closing 4 of the debates.

42. Mayer, *The Republican Party, 1854–1966*, p. 4.

43. For a discussion of Douglas's position at Freeport, see reading no. 3 in Burdette, *The Republican Party*, pp. 126–31.

44. In his recent book, David Zarefsky says that "The Freeport debate is remembered most for Lincoln's interrogatories, especially the second question: whether the people of a territory might legally prohibit slavery. Folklore has it that this question placed Douglas in a cruel dilemma: he must lose either his Southern or his Northern support. He might win the Senate seat, but the dilemma would thwart his presidential aspirations. 'I am after bigger game,' Lincoln is widely thought to have said of his maneuver. But virtually every step in the story is false. Lincoln knew how Douglas would respond since the Little Giant had answered substantially the same question for more than one year." David Zarefsky. *Lincoln, Douglas and Slavery: In the Crucible of Public Debate*, p. 57.

45. Paul F. Boller, *Presidential Anecdotes*, p. 132.

46. Kraus, *The United States to 1865*, p. 474.

47. The resolutions were eventually adopted on May 24 after the Democrats had tried and failed to nominate a presidential candidate.

48. Nichols, *The Stakes of Power, 1845–1877*, p. 79.

49. Ralph M. Goldman, *The Democratic Party in American Politics*, p. 55.

50. Quoted from Bruce Catton, *The Coming Fury*, p. 32.

51. Reported in Murat Halstead, *Caucuses of 1860: A History of the National Political Convention of the Current Presidential Campaign (1860)*, pp. 49–50.

52. Cushing's ruling countered precedents established at the 1840 and 1848 Democratic conventions when the nominating majority was based on those present and voting.

53. Nichols, *The Stakes of Power, 1845–1877*, p. 82.

54. Boller, *Presidential Campaigns*, p. 101.

55. Bruce Catton, the Civil War Historian, suggests that it was perhaps "one of the most dangerous fire traps ever built in America." Catton, *The Coming Fury*, p. 49.

56. P. Orman Ray, *The Convention That Nominated Lincoln*, pp. 5–8.

57. On the political career of Chase see Albert B. Hart, *Solomon Portland Chase*.

58. Mayer, *The Republican Party, 1854–1966*, p. 62.

59. Foner, *Free Soil, Free Labor, Free Men*, p. 212.

60. For the text of Lincoln's Cooper Union speech see Burdette, *The Republican Party*, reading no. 4, pp. 132–37.

61. Lincoln stayed at home in Springfield, Illinois, during the Chicago convention, explaining: "I am a little too much a candidate to stay home, . . . and not quite enough a candidate to go." Boller, *Presidential Campaigns*, p. 104.

62. Moos, *The Republicans*, p. 69. For the Republican platform see Burdette, *The Republican Party*, reading no. 5, pp. 138–41.

63. Catton, *The Coming Fury*, p. 63.

64. Gerald Pomper, *Nominating the President: The Politics of Convention Choice*, p. 150.

65. Despite the "no bargains" instruction to his managers, Lincoln eventually made good on the promises. Of the 5 leading contenders on the first ballot, 4 received cabinet posts and the fifth became minister to France. For his part, Judge Davis became later both an associate justice of the U.S. Supreme Court and U.S. Senator.

66. See Glyndon G. Van Deusen, "Thurlow Weed's Analysis of William H. Seward's Defeat in the Republican Convention of 1860," pp. 101–4. Also see Glyndon G. Van Deusen, *Thurlow Weed, Wizard of the Lobby*, pp. 231–54.

67. Proceedings of the National Republican Convention, 1860, p. 39.

68. Several Republican newspapers pointed out that "Honest Abe the Rail Splitter" was a fraud. There was, they insisted, no credible evidence that Lincoln had ever split a rail (except perhaps one or two in his youth). The *New Albany* [Indiana] *Herald* calculated that if Lincoln had split all the rails he was credited with, they would make a 10-foot rail fence reaching from the North to the South Pole. Boller, *Presidential Campaigns*, p. 106.

69. A later version depicted him with a beard. Lincoln reportedly grew a beard during the 1860 campaign after a young girl wrote him that "all the ladies like whiskers."

70. Thomas A. Bailey, *Democrats v. Republicans*, p. 65.

71. If the election went into the House of Representatives Lincoln's chances were probably the best of the candidates, but it was no sure thing. The Republicans

could reasonably count on 15 of the 33 states and needed but 2 more, with Illinois and Oregon offering good prospects, especially if Douglas were eliminated. However, a House deadlock beyond the inauguration date (March 4) might make Lane president, as the Senate was Buchanan-controlled and if Lane were elected vice president by that body in the event no one had a majority, he would then assume the presidency.

72. Binkley, *American Political Parties*, p. 320. Also see Reinhold H. Luthin, *The First Lincoln Campaign*.

73. Boller, *Presidential Campaigns*, p. 110. Vigorous campaigning was frowned on until the advent of primary elections at the turn of the century, which eventually made personal campaigning unavoidable.

74. Burdette, *The Republican Party*, p. 30.

75. For an analysis of the 1860 election see Joseph Shafer, "Who Elected Lincoln?" pp. 51–63. Also see Seymour Lipset, "The Emergence of the One-Party South — The Election of 1860," pp. 344–54.

76. In 1860 South Carolina was the only state in which presidential electors were still chosen by the legislature. Therefore, every 4 years a special session was prescribed for the day before the general November election at which the electors would be named. In 1860 the legislature met as usual but at the request of the governor they stayed over to learn the national result. See Nichols, *The Stakes of Power, 1845–1877*, p. 87.

77. *New York Tribune*, November 9, 1860.

78. Cameron added significantly to the folklore of American politics when he defined an honest politician as one "who when he is bought, stays bought."

80. See Harry J. Carman and Rheinhard H. Luthin, *Lincoln and the Patronage*.

81. Arthur M. Schlesinger, Jr., ed., *History of U.S. Political Parties*, 2:1164.

82. For the Emancipation Proclamation, see Burdette, *The Republican Party*, reading no. 7, pp. 143–44.

83. Quoted from Eugene H. Roseboom, *A History of Presidential Elections*, p. 190.

84. On the elections of 1862 see Burdette, *The Republican Party*, pp. 33–34.

85. Roseboom, *A History of Presidential Elections*, p. 188.

86. A reference to a common practice in farming areas of putting a pumpkin in each end of a burlap bag and thereby making a crude saddlebag which would stay put on a horse's back.

87. Seymour was defeated for reelection in 1864 by Republican Congressman Reuben E. Fenton. See Stewart Mitchell, *Horatio Seymour, of New York*.

88. For an excellent history of the Copperheads see Wood Gray, *The Hidden Civil War: The Story of the Copperheads*. Also see F.L. Klement, *The Copperheads in the Middle West*; and George F. Milton, *Abraham Lincoln and the Fifth Column*.

89. Mayer, *The Republican Party 1854–1966*, p. 115.

90. Moos, *The Republicans*, p. 102.

91. Burdette, *The Republican Party*, p. 35.

92. See W.A. Dunning, "The Second Birth of the Republican Party," *American Historical Review* 16 (1910): 56–63.

93. Nevertheless, a few months later, on the death of Chief Justice Roger Taney, Lincoln unhesitatingly redeemed an outstanding promise to Charles Sumner to make Chase the chief justice of the United States. But this was not until after the election, and after Chase had done his duty in the campaign. If Lincoln thought that

he could cure Chase's advanced case of "Potomac fever" by isolating him from politics on the Supreme Court, he was mistaken. As chief justice, Chase's old desire persisted and even seemed to grow with the years and opportunity.

94. See Stephen W. Sears, *George B. McClellan: The Young Napoleon*.

95. The strange case of Vallandigham inspired Edward Everett Hale to write his moving story of Philip Nolan, *The Man Without a Country* (1863) which was immensely popular in the North and which helped stimulate devotion to the Union. See Thomas A. Bailey, *The American Pageant*, p. 479.

96. Quoted from Binkley, *American Political Parties*, p. 270.

97. Roseboom, *A History of Presidential Elections*, p. 201.

98. *Ibid.*, p. 198.

99. Bailey, *The American Pageant*, p. 481.

100. Roseboom, *A History of Presidential Elections*, p. 200.

101. Boller, *Presidential Campaigns*, p. 122.

102. For the text of the Homestead Act see Burdette, *The Republican Party*, reading no. 8, 145–46.

103. This was increased in 1862 and 1865 until incomes between $600 and $5,000 were taxed at 5 percent and those over $5,000 at 10 percent.

104. See Irwin Unger, *The Greenback Era: A Social and Political History of American Finance, 1865–1879*.

The Radical Republicans

1. Quoted in Claude Bowers, *The Tragic Era: The Revolution After Lincoln*, p. 6.

2. On the political career of Andrew Johnson, see Howard K. Beale, *The Critical Year: A Study of Andrew Johnson and Reconstruction*; Edwin P. Hoyt, *Andrew Johnson*; James S. Jones, *Andrew Johnson: Seventh President of the United States*; Eric L. McKitrick, *Andrew Johnson and Reconstruction*; Eric L. McKitrick, ed., *Andrew Johnson: A Profile*; George F. Milton, *The Age of Hate: Andrew Johnson and the Radicals*; Lloyd P. Stryker, *Andrew Johnson: A Study in Courage*; Lately Thomas, *The First President Johnson*; and Robert W. Winston, *Andrew Johnson: Plebian and Patriot*.

3. Roy F. Nichols, *The Stakes of Power, 1845–1877*, p. 165.

4. Quoted from Lloyd Robinson, *The Stolen Election*, p. 19.

5. Nichols, *The Stakes of Power, 1845–1877*, p. 165.

6. George H. Mayer, *The Republican Party, 1854–1966*, p. 145.

7. And, for the most part, they did. Only 32 votes were cast for ratification in all the Southern legislatures.

8. Thomas A. Bailey recounts that at one dinner party in South Carolina the guest list included a distinguished group of exgovernors, excongressmen, and exjudges. The only voter in the room was the black servant who served the meal. See Thomas A. Bailey, *The American Pageant*, p. 502.

9. The U.S. Supreme Court so ruled in 1926.

10. Franklin L. Burdette, *The Republican Party: A Short History*, p. 41.

11. Louis W. Koenig, *The Chief Executive*, p. 64.

12. Malcolm E. Moos, *The Republicans: A History of Their Party*, p. 127.

13. Arthur M. Schlesinger, Jr., *Political and Social Growth of the American People 1865–1940*, p. 18.

14. When Stevens died in August 1868, conservative white Southerners

rejoiced. "The prayers of the righteous have at last removed the Congressional curse!" wrote one Southern editor. "May his new ironworks wean him from earth and the fires of his new furnaces never go out." Quoted from Kenneth Stampp, "Triumph of the Conservatives," in Felice A. Bonadio, ed., *Political Parties in American History 1828–1890*, p. 790.

15. Somewhat ironically, when Grant left the White House he was bankrupt. For a stirring account of how Grant paid off his many debts see Homer F. Cunningham, *The Presidents' Last Years: George Washington to Lyndon B. Johnson*, pp. 131–42.

16. *New York Tribune*, November 9, 1867.

17. Since only 10 Northern states had admitted blacks to the franchise, Southerners naturally concluded that the radicals were being more than a little hypocritical in insisting that the blacks in the South be allowed to vote. This hypocrisy was expressed in a derisive jingle:

> To every Southern River
> Shall Negro Suffrage come;
> But not to fair New England,
> For that's too close to hum.

18. Moos, *The Republicans*, p. 131.

19. Charles H. Coleman, *The Election of 1868*, p. 161.

20. Seymour's nomination in 1868 was the first genuine draft of a presidential candidate in American politics and the last until 1952 when Adlai Stevenson was also drafted by the Democrats. Because of his reluctance to accept the nomination, Seymour quickly was dubbed "The Great Decliner" by the Republicans.

21. Boller, *Presidential Campaigns*, p. 126.

22. The "bloody shirt" expression is said to have originated in a speech in Congress by Representative Benjamin F. Butler, who actually waved before the House the bloodstained shirt of a carpetbagger flogged in Mississippi. See Bailey, *The American Pageant*, p. 513.

23. Boller, *Presidential Campaigns*, p. 124.

24. Coleman, *The Election of 1868*, p. 256.

25. Vallandigham remained active in Democratic Party politics until 1872 when he was killed in a freak accident—defending an accused murderer. While making a point in the courtroom, he placed a pistol he thought was unloaded to his head, pulled the trigger, and sent a bullet into his brain.

26. Coleman, *The Election of 1868*, p. 265.

27. *Ibid.*, p. 268.

28. Mayer, *The Republican Party 1854–1966*, p. 170.

29. William S. Myers, *The Republican Party: A History*, pp. 178–88.

30. On the Ku Klux Klan in American politics. See John M. Mecklin, *The Ku Klux Klan; A Study of the American Mind.*

31. William B. Hesseltine, *Ulysses S. Grant, Politician.*

32. In making appointments to his personal staff, President Grant appointed so many old army friends and family that one wit was prompted to comment: "No President ever 'got in the family way' so soon after inauguration." Senator Charles Sumner told the Senate that Grant appointed so many old friends to office that the country was suffering from "a dropsical nepotism swollen to elphantiasis." Quoted from Dixon Wecter, *The Hero in America*, p. 329.

33. On Tweed see Seymour J. Mandelbaum, *Boss Tweed's New York*; and Alexander B. Callow, Jr., *The Tweed Ring.*

34. Quoted in Gustavus Myers, *The History of Tammany Hall*, p. 239.

35. Quoted from, Eric Goldman, *Rendezvous with Destiny*, p. 13.

36. See Earle Dudley Ross, *The Liberal Republican Movement*.

37. Susan B. Anthony appeared at the convention to plead the cause of votes for women but was refused permission to speak.

38. Reporting the choice of Greeley, a reporter covering the convention suggested that there had been "too much brains and not enough whiskey" at the Cincinnati convention.

39. For the liberal Republican platform see Burdette, *The Republican Party*, reading no. 9, pp. 146–48.

40. On Horace Greeley see William H. Hale, *Horace Greeley: Voice of the People*; Don C. Seitz, *Horace Greeley*; Peter Isely, *Horace Greeley and the Republican Party, 1853-1861: A Study of the New York Tribune*; and Henry L. Stoddard, *Horace Greeley, Printer, Editor, Crusader*.

41. *New York Times*, July 11, 1872.

42. Howard P. Nash, Jr., *Third Parties in American Politics*, p. 119.

43. *New York Times*, June 4, 1872.

44. Quoted in Chester C. Maxey, *Bipartisanship in the United States*, p. 218.

45. Arthur M. Schlesinger, Jr., ed., *History of U.S. Political Parties*, 2:1571.

46. Victoria Woodhull knew there was very little chance that she would be elected. Therefore, it made little difference to her or the party that she would not be constitutionally eligible because of her age (34) until September 1873.

47. Quoted in Henry Minor, *The Story of the Democratic Party*, p. 308.

48. When pressed for an explanation of an earlier remark that all Democrats were saloonkeepers, Greeley explained: "I never said all Democrats were saloonkeepers. What I said was that all saloonkeepers were Democrats."

49. Quoted from Harold U. Faulkner, *American Political and Social History*, p. 395.

50. Schlesinger, *Political and Social Growth of the American People 1865-1940*, p. 81.

51. O'Conor, the "Straight-Out" candidate, received about 30,000 votes, mostly in the South and Midwest. The Prohibition Party polled only 5,588 votes — a meager 0.09 percent of the national vote. Victoria Woodhull, the Equal Rights candidate, actually received a few thousand votes — cast, of course, by men. Her own husband could not have voted for her, had he been so inclined, since he was in jail.

52. Mayer, *The Republican Party, 1854-1966*, pp. 184–85.

53. For the effects of the depression of 1873, see Allan Nevins, *The Emergence of Modern America 1865-1878*.

54. See Irwin Unger, *The Greenback Era: A Social and Political History of American Finance, 1865-1879*.

55. Mayer, *The Republican Party, 1854-1966*, p. 187.

56. Moos, *The Republicans*, p. 145.

57. In 1883 in the civil rights cases, the Supreme Court declared invalid those parts of the Civil Rights Act of 1875 designed to secure social equality. The court also ruled that, although the Fourteenth Amendment forbade the invasion of civil rights by the states, it did not prohibit the invasion of civil rights by individuals unaided by state authority. Blacks might be driven from the polls or otherwise abused by individuals, and the federal government would have no power to intervene.

58. On the disputed election of 1876, see P.L. Haworth, *The Haves-Tilden Disputed Presidential Election of 1886;* Lloyd Robinson, *The Stolen Election — Hayes versus Tilden 1876;* and Keith Ian Polakoff, *The Politics of Inertia: The Election of 1876 and the End of Reconstruction.*

59. Nineteen years later Conkling, a tall, muscular, good-looking man with curly red hair, got even. Asked to help Blaine in his bid for the presidency, he replied: "I can't. I've retired from criminal practice." Conkling's unwillingness to support Blaine may have cost him the nomination.

60. Robinson, *The Stolen Election,* pp. 49–50.

61. See E. Bruce Thompson, "The Bristow Presidential Boom of 1876."

62. On the early political career of Rutherford B. Hayes, see Harry Barnard, *Rutherford B. Hayes and His America;* H.J. Eckenrode, *Rutherford B. Hayes: Stateman of Reunion;* H. Wayne Morgan, *From Hayes to McKinley: National Party Politics 1877–1896;* William O. Stoddard, *Lives of Presidents Rutherford B. Hayes, James A. Garfield and Chester A. Arthur;* and C.R. Williams *The Life of Rutherford B. Hayes.*

63. Robinson, *The Stolen Election,* p. 60.

64. *Ibid.,* pp. 60–61.

65. Ingersoll's speech nominating Blaine can be read in Burdette, *The Republican Party,* reading no. 11, pp. 150–52.

66. In the course of the proceedings the convention abandoned the unit rule for voting. Thereafter, no delegate would be bound to vote on the floor on the basis of a decision by the majority of delegates from his state.

67. Quoted from Robinson, *The Stolen Election,* p. 64.

68. On the early political career of Tilden, see Alexander C. Flick, *Samuel Jones Tilden: A Study in Political Sagacity.*

69. The Prohibitionists nominated Green Clay Smith of Kentucky and Gideon Tabor Stewart of Ohio. The American National Party nominated James B. Walker of Illinois and Donald Kirkpatrick of New York on a platform declaring God the author of civil government and favoring Sabbath observance, Prohibition, forfeiture of all charters granted to secret societies, the Bible in schools, and direct vote for the president.

70. In 1876 the Democratic campaign badge showed the party symbol as the cock — the future symbol of the donkey had not come into common usage yet. The Grand March was played wherever Democrats assembled as a means of getting out the vote.

71. Robinson, *The Stolen Election,* p. 115.

72. Robinson, *The Stolen Election,* p. 112.

73. Hayes would become the winner if Congress accepted the commission's findings. Congressional acceptance, however, was not certain. Democrats controlled the House and had the power to filibuster to block action on the vote.

74. Morgan, *From Hayes to McKinley,* p. 3.

75. C. Vann Woodward, in his book *Reunion and Reaction,* sets forth the reasons for the Democratic Party's acquiescence in the decision of the electoral commission. For the salient points of the compromise of 1877 see Morgan, *From Hayes to McKinley,* p. 18.

76. Haworth, *The Hayes-Tilden Disputed Presidential Election of 1876,* p. 341.

77. Moos, *The Republicans,* p. 152.

78. Morgan, *From Hayes to McKinley,* p. 4.

79. Nor from outside his party for that matter. His administration soon

became known as the "cold water regime" because the first lady, a strong temperance advocate, served only nonalcoholic beverages at the White House (earning for herself the epithet: "Lemonade Lucy"). As one dry-mouthed guest newspaperman remarked, "The water flowed like wine."

80. Morgan, *From Hayes to McKinley*, p. 12.

81. Robinson, *The Stolen Election*, p. 214.

82. Quoted from Morgan, *From Hayes to McKinley*, p. 37. For an account of the civil service reform movement, see F.M. Stewart, *The National Civil Service Reform League*. See also Ari Hoogenboom, *Outlawing the Spoils*; and Dorothy G. Fowler, "Precursors of the Hatch Act," pp. 247–62.

83. Schlesinger, *Political and Social Growth of the American People 1865 1940*, p. 100.

84. Wilfred E. Binkley, *American Political Parties: The Natural History*, p. 309.

85. Moos, *The Republicans*, p. 158.

86. See Stanley P. Hirshon, *Farewell to the Bloody Shirt: Northern Republicans and the Southern Negro, 1877–1893* (which describes the declining attention Northern Republicans gave to the lot of Southern blacks after 1877). Vincent P. De Santis, *Republicans Face the Southern Question: The New Departure Years, 1877–1897* (has a different emphasis but the same conclusion as Hirshon).

87. For President Hayes's veto message, see Burdette, *The Republican Party*, reading no. 12, p. 153.

Mugwumps, Populists and Others

1. For an incisive study of the economic and social ideology of the post–Civil War period, see Richard Hofstadter, *Social Darwinism in American Thought, 1860–1915*.

2. Ray Ginger, *The Age of Excess: The United States from 1877 to 1914*, p. 32.

3. Foster Rhae Dulles, *Labor in America*, p. 101.

4. Howard P. Nash, Jr., *Third Parties in American Politics*, p. 149.

5. On the Granger movement, see Fred A. Shannon, *American Farmer's Movements*. Also see Nathan L. Fine, *Labor and Farmer Parties in the United States, 1828–1928*; and Murray S. Stedman, Jr., and Susan Stedman, *Discontent at the Polls: A Study of Farmer and Labor Parties, 1827–1948*.

6. Shannon, *American Farmer's Movements*, p. 55.

7. On Donnelly see Martin Ridge, *Ignatius Donnelly: Portrait of a Politician*.

8. See Chapter 3 of this book, pp. 149–50.

9. Recounted from Herbert J. Clancy, *The Presidential Election of 1880*, p. 92.

10. *Ibid.*, p. 98.

11. Quoted from Henry L. Stoddard, *Presidential Sweepstakes*, p. 81.

12. Clancy, *The Presidential Election of 1880*, p. 101.

13. One of the Stalwarts who stood by Grant to the end had medals struck for the "Faithful 306" bearing the legend, "The Old Guard for Ulysses S. Grant for President," thereby coining a new name for Republican regulars.

14. Garfield was the last of the presidents to go from a log cabin to the White House. Horatio Alger soon chronicled Garfield's career in one of his thrilling books for boys: *From Canal Boy to President, or the Boyhood and Manhood of James A. Garfield.*

15. On the early political career of Garfield, see Robert G. Caldwell, *James A.*

Garfield: Party Chieftain; Justus D. Doenecke, *The Presidencies of James A. Garfield and Chester A. Arthur*; Edwin P. Hoyt, *James A. Garfield*; Allan Peskin, *Garfield*; John Clark Ridpath, *The Life and Work of James A. Garfield and the Tragic Story of His Death*; William O. Stoddard, *Lives of Presidents Rutherford B. Hayes, James A. Garfield and Chester A. Arthur*; and J.M. Taylor, *Garfield of Ohio: The Available Man*.

16. Clancy, *The Presidential Election of 1880*, p. 96.

17. H. Wayne Morgan, *From Hayes to McKinley: National Party Politics 1877–1896*, p. 98.

18. Clancy, *The Presidential Election of 1880*, p. 149n.

19. Morgan, *From Hayes to McKinley*, p. 117.

20. For an excellent assessment of the political character of Hancock, see Glenn Tucker, *Hancock the Superb*.

21. Paul F. Boller, *Presidential Anecdotes*, p. 169.

22. On the effort to elect Hancock, see Leonard Dinnerstein, "Election of 1880," in Arthur M. Schlesinger, *History of American Presidential Elections 1798–1868*.

23. This was the last election in which this source could be legally tapped. The Civil Service Reform Act of 1883 protected federal workers against the demands of the parties for tribute money. See Herbert E. Alexander, *Political Financing*, 1972), p. 20.

24. Conkling would also lose the services of some 200 Federal employees at the New York Custom House who did nothing but perform services for his machine. See John M. Dobson, *Politics in the Gilded Age: A New Perspective on Reform*, p. 59.

25. At his trial Guiteau went so far as to ask all those who had benefited politically by Garfield's assassination to contribute to his defense fund. He was found guilty of murder and hanged, although apparently insane. See Thomas A. Bailey, *The American Pageant*, p. 537.

26. *New York Evening Telegraph*, July 2, 1881, cited in Boller, *Presidential Anecdotes*, p. 171.

27. Platt's withdrawal came soon after a group of Half-Breeds, peering through a transom into Platt's room in an Albany hotel, found him locked in the embrace of "an unspeakable female." See Ginger, *The Age of Excess*, p. 102.

28. On the political career of Arthur, see Justus D. Doenecke, *The Presidencies of James A. Garfield and Chester A. Arthur*; George F. Howe, *Chester A. Arthur: A Quarter Century of Machine Politics*; Thomas C. Reeves, *Gentleman Boss: The Life of Chester Alan Arthur*; and William O. Stoddard, *Lives of Presidents Rutherford B. Hayes, James A. Garfield and Chester A. Arthur*.

29. Quoted from Ginger, *The Age of Excess*, p. 105.

30. On the final vote in the Senate many of the Republicans voted in favor of the Civil Service Reform Bill because its tenure provisions would protect Republicans already in office; otherwise the Democrats would turn them out if they won the presidency. In the House nearly all the opponents were Democrats from the South or the old Northwest. See Ginger, *The Age of Excess*, p. 104.

31. President Arthur's support of civil service reform may have resulted from his realization (as a former spoilsman) that patronage reform was inevitable and that when it came it would drastically enhance the power of the president vis-à-vis Congress by restoring to him greater control over appointments. Although, theoretically, one of the most important holds the chief executive had over congressmen and senators was his ability to grant or withhold patronage, in reality,

large numbers of federal offices, such as postmasters, tax collectors, customs inspectors, and the like, were dispensed by local bosses who stood behind and controlled most congressmen — the president simply rubber-stamped his selections. As a result, political parties were decentralized, sectional, and irresponsible. Abolition of spoils would thus enhance the power of the chief executive by producing a party more accountable to the president.

32. Ginger, *The Age of Excess*, p. 70. Also see Ari Hoogenboom, *Outlawing the Spoils: A History of the Civil Service Reform Movement, 1865–1883*.

33. In anticipation of the presidential election of 1884, the Republican Congress enacted a reduction in the postage rates. Every citizen who licked a stamp would praise Arthur for a penny saved. The party even put out a pamphlet titled: "The Great Postal Triumph."

34. Quoted from Howe, *Chester A. Arthur*, p. 254.

35. Arthur would not have survived a full term in office. He died on November 18, 1866, of Bright's Disease, a kidney ailment.

36. For the first time the call for the Republican National Convention included specific directions for the selection of delegates; those at-large delegates by state conventions, and others by conventions in districts or by caucus in district sections of state conventions.

37. As Gerald Pomper points out, the Republican convention of 1884, which rejected Chester Arthur, was the last to deny renomination to an incumbent president if he wanted to be renominated. See Gerald Pomper, *Nominating the President: The Politics of Convention Choice*, p. 25.

38. By 1853 Blaine was a member of the House of Representatives and he decided that his work in the House would be a more valuable contribution to the war effort than any he could make on the battlefield. A faulty decision, as it turned out, for anyone who wished to become president of the United States in the post–Civil War era.

39. Harry Thurston Peck, *Democrats and Republicans*, p. 43.

40. Dobson, *Politics in the Gilded Age*, p. 105.

41. *Ibid.* Another, more popular definition of a Mugwump was that he was a man who straddled the fence with his "mug" on one side and his "wump" on the other: which Dobson suggests was a rather accurate description since they had stopped participating in one party before they decided what to do with themselves.

42. Geoffery T. Blodgett, "The Mind of the Boston Mugwumps," pp. 614–34, identifies the character of the Boston area Mugwumps and discusses the substance of their political thought.

43. On the political career of Grover Cleveland see, Henry Jones Ford, *The Cleveland Era*; J.R. Hollingsworth, *The Whirling of Politics: The Democracy of Cleveland and Bryan*; Dennis Tilden Lynch, *Grover Cleveland: A Man Foresquare*; Robert McElroy, *Grover Cleveland: The Man and the Statesman*; and Horace S. Merrill, *Bourbon Leader: Grover Cleveland and the Democratic Party*.

44. Nash, *Third Parties in American Politics*, p. 145.

45. Dobson, *Politics in the Gilded Age*, p. 148.

46. Due to the mother's misconduct, the child was placed in an orphanage, from which he was later adopted. He then faded from the public scene.

47. Quoted from: Allan Nevins, *Grover Cleveland: A Study in Courage*, p. 177.

48. Peck, *Democrats and Republicans*, p. 40. Trade or advertising cards promoting Cleveland were given away with the purchase of various kinds of commodities. One, given away with cigarettes by W. Duke Sons and Company of

Durham, North Carolina, in addition to listing the numerous virtues of Cleveland, pridefully pointed out: "Our average sales are over two million per day."

49. Dobson, *Politics in the Gilded Age,* p. 156.

50. Cleveland's popular vote was 4.9 million votes to Blaine's 4.8 million votes. So close was the election that several days passed before the result could be known.

51. Quoted form Ginger, *The Age of Excess,* p. 107.

52. Harrison C. Thomas, *The Return of the Democratic Party to Power in 1884.*

53. Quoted in Morgan, *From Hayes to McKinley,* p. 232.

54. Quoted from Ginger, *The Age of Excess,* p. 108.

55. When a vexed senator criticized Cleveland for not appointing Democrats fast enough, the president reportedly responded with the query whether he ought to "appoint two horse-thieves a day," instead of one.

56. On a single day the Senate passed 400 of these bills, and the House had regular evening sessions set aside for the claims of veterans.

57. Quoted from Bess Furman, *White House Profile,* p. 239.

58. Twenty years later Republican President Theodore Roosevelt signed a bill passed by a Republican Congress providing for the return of these very same flags, and there was not a ripple of protest.

59. On Henry George see Charles A. Barker, *Henry George.*

60. There is considerable evidence that George was actually counted out. See John R. Commons, *History of Labour in the United States* 2:453; and Anna DeMille, *Henry George,* p. 152.

61. S.E. Bowman, *The Year 2000: A Critical Biography of Edward Bellamy.*

62. Pomper, *Nominating the President,* p. 102.

63. Robert D. Marcus, *Grand Old Party: Political Structure in the Gilded Age, 1880–1896,* p. 124.

64. Thomas B. ("Czar") Reed, who would be, most likely, the Speaker of the House if Harrison won, was invited to "board the Harrison bandwagon" just before the nomination but declined, declaring: "You should say ice-wagon," and added, "I never ride in an ice-cart." (Related in Harry J. Sievers, *Benjamin Harrison: Hoosier President,* p. 215.)

65. William B. Hesseltine, *Third Party Movements in the United States,* p. 56.

66. Probably an allusion to Edgar Allen Poe's poem, "The Raven."

67. In 1888, 400,000 votes were cast for minor party candidates. The Union Labor ticket polled 147,000 votes, 1.29 percent of the total; the United Labor Party got 2,800 votes, or less than 0.5 percent of the total; the Prohibition Party received 250,000 or 2.2 percent; and others 8,500.

68. In several key states Cleveland also suffered from a division in the Democratic Party. In New York, for example, Harrison's plurality was 13,000 votes; but the Democratic candidate of Tammany Hall was elected governor by a margin of 1,500. However, the Democrats of New York later charged that the outcome in that state was due to electoral fraud when the Republican National Committee arranged for the "movement" of 50,000 Republican "floaters" to the empire state.

69. Harold U. Faulkner, *Politics: Reform and Expansion, 1890–1990,* p. 94.

70. Quoted in Harry J. Sievers, *Benjamin Harrison: Hoosier Statesman, 1865–1888,* pp. 426–27. Also quoted in Ginger, *Age of Excess,* p. 117.

71. Republican Senator Joseph R. Hawley of Connecticut, in a note to President-elect Harrison, injected some wry cheer into the cabinet selection process: "choosing a Cabinet is like dying — it is something that nobody can do for you."

72. George H. Mayer, *The Republican Party, 1854–1966*, p. 222.

73. Ginger, *The Age of Excess*, p. 121.

74. William A. Robinson, *Thomas B. Reed, Parliamentarian*.

75. Quoted from David C. Whitney, *The American Presidents*, p. 203.

76. Widows would receive $8 a month with $2 for each child.

77. Quoted form John A. Garraty, *The American Nation*, p. 607.

78. Under the Bland-Allison Act and the Sherman Silver Purchase Act the currency had been expanded by some $450 million.

79. Dulles, *Labor in America*, p. 147.

80. Paul W. Glad, *McKinley, Bryan and the People*, p. 53.

81. See Elizabeth N. Barr, "The Populist Uprising," in William E. Connelly, ed., *A Standard History of Kansas and Kansans*, 2:1148–49.

82. Several commentators remarked that there seemed to be a close relationship between hair and populism.

83. See Ridge, *Ignatius Donnelly*. Also see John D. Hicks, "The Political Career of Ignatius Donnelly," pp. 80–132.

84. On the political career of Tom Watson, see C. Vann Woodward, *Tom Watson: Agrarian Rebel*.

85. Though he was blind in one eye, unattractive in appearance, irascible in disposition, careless in manners, and rasping in speech, the people of South Carolina loved Tillman. Placing himself at the head of the underprivileged farmers, Tillman won the governorship from the conservative Wade Hampton and pushed a series of agrarian reforms through the palmetto state legislature. See Francis B. Simkins, *Pitchfork Ben Tillman*; and Francis B. Simkins, *The Tillman Movement in South Carolina*.

86. Russel B. Nye, *Midwestern Progressive Politics*, p. 61. Excited audiences often filled her ever-present laundry basket with loose change and, in better times, silver dollars.

87. Quoted in Solon Buck, *The Agrarian Crusade*, p. 135.

88. Related from Malcolm E. Moos, *The Republicans: A History of Their Party*, p. 183. A more likely explanation for McKinley's defeat was that the Democratic Ohio legislature had gerrymandered his district against him for the third time by adding heavily German, heavily rural, and strongly Democratic Holmes County to it.

89. For an excellent general history of Populism, see John D. Hicks, *The Populist Revolt: A History of the Farmer's Alliance and the People's Party*.

90. A plan for government warehouses where farmers could deposit nonperishable crops and receive greenbacks for up to 80 percent of the market value of the crops deposited. The loan was to be secured by the deposited crops and repaid when crops were sold, thus enabling the farmer to hold the produce for a favorable market. Some components of the subtreasury idea, though not the essential feature of popular control over the currency, were embodied in the New Deal measure of 1933 creating the Commodity Credit Corporation.

91. The amount of money in circulation per capita had declined from $30.35 in 1865 to $17.51 in 1876. After that, there was a gradual increase to about $22.81 in 1890.

92. George Harmon Knoles, *The Presidential Campaign and Election of 1892*, pp. 99–100.

93. He died one year later, on January 27, 1893.

94. Knoles, *The Presidential Campaign and Election of 1892*, p. 49.

95. Mayer, *The Republican Party*, p. 233.

96. Morgan, *From Hayes to McKinley*, p. 414.

97. Moos, *The Republicans*, p. 190.

98. Franklin L. Burdette, *The Republican Party: A Short History*, p. 53.

99. Peck, *Democrats and Republicans*, p. 249.

100. On Weaver see Frederick E.H. Haynes, *James Baird Weaver*.

101. Irwin and Debi Unger, *The Vulnerable Years: The United States, 1896–1917*, p. 19.

102. *Ibid.*

103. Ginger, *The Age of Excess*, p. 127.

104. Sung to the tune of "Save a Poor Sinner, Like Me": "The Railroads and old party bosses together did sweetly agree" to deceive and exploit "a hayseed like me."

105. On the history of Socialism in America, see David A. Shannon, *The Socialist Party of America: A History*; Howard Quint, *The Forging of American Socialism*; and Henry Kuhn and O.M. Johnson, *The Socialist-Labor Party During Four Decades, 1890–1930*.

106. Knoles, *The Presidential Campaign and Election of 1892*, p. 116.

107. The election of 1892 was the first presidential election in which all the states used the Australian (or secret) ballot, a ballot printed at public expense by public authorities, which lists all candidates for office on a single, consolidated form. It is distributed only at the polling places and only to qualified voters who then marked it in the seclusion of a closed voting both.

108. On the election of 1892, see Knoles, *The Presidential Campaign and Election of 1892*.

109. A significant figure, since in those days, 1 million votes was considered the threshhold which any group had to cross before it could be considered a real political party.

110. Unger and Unger, *The Vulnerable Years*, p. 20.

111. Dobson, *Politics in the Gilded Age*, p. 174.

112. On Populism generally, see Hicks, *The Populist Revolt*; and Norman Pollack, *The Populist Response to Industrial America*.

113. On the causes of the panic of 1893 see W. Jelt Lanck, *The Causes of the Panic of 1893*.

114. Ginger, *The Age of Excess*, p. 158.

115. *Congressional Record*, 53d Congress, 1st session, 1893, pp. 410–11.

116. Nevins, *Grover Cleveland*, pp. 649–76.

117. *Congressional Record*, 53d Congress, 2d session, 1894, pp. 7712–13.

118. For an analysis of the Wilson-Gorman Tariff, see John R. Lambert, *Arthur P. Gorman*, pp. 200–38; and Festus P. Summers, *William L. Wilson and Tariff Reform*, pp. 152–208.

119. Quoted in Simkins, *Pitchfork Ben Tillman*, p. 315.

120. Nevins, *Grover Cleveland*, pp. 543–68.

121. The best account of Coxey's march is D.L. McMurry, *Coxey's Army*. Also see Henry Vincent, *The Story of the Commonweal*, pp. 56–124.

122. Ginger, *The Bending Cross: A Biography of Eugene Victor Debs*, p. 193.

123. Fred E. Haynes, *Third Party Movements Since the Civil War*, pp. 280–81.

124. Quoted in Woodward, *Tom Watson*, p. 244.

125. See J. Rogers Hollingsworth, "The Cuckoos Create a Storm," in Felice A. Bonadio, ed., *Political Parties in American History: 1828–1890*, pp. 911–13. Also see Samuel P. Hays, *Response to Industrialism*.

126. Seigniorage is the gain to the government resulting from the purchase of

bullion at a price less than the value stamped on the metal when it is coined. It is the difference between the dollar's worth in raw silver and a silver dollar.

127. Hollingsworth, "The Cuckoos Create a Storm," p. 929.

128. William H. Harvey, *Coin's Financial School.*

129. Hundreds of writers disagreed with Harvey. One of the best was Horace White, a gold standard supporter, who replied to Harvey with a pamphlet titled, *Coin's Financial Fool,* which charged *Coin's Financial* with being a senseless fabrication. Some 300,000 copies of White's pamphlet were distributed.

130. Marcus, *Grand Old Party,* p. 198.

131. Moos, *The Republicans,* p. 208.

132. *Ibid.,* p. 212.

133. See Elmer Ellis, "The Silver Republicans in the Election of 1896," pp. 525–57.

134. Quoted in Mayer, *The Republican Party,* p. 249.

135. Quoted in Allan Nevins and Henry Steele Commager, *A Short History of the United States,* p. 383.

136. On the life and political career of William Jennings Bryan, see Paolo E. Coletta, *William Jennings Bryan: Political Evangelist, 1860–1908,* vol. 1; Paul W. Glad, *The Trumpet Soundeth: William Jennings Bryan and His Democracy 1896–1912;* Paul Glad, *McKinley, Bryan and the People;* Paxton Hibben, *The Peerless Leader: William Jennings Bryan;* Richard D. Hofstadter, *The Age of Reform: From Bryan to F.D.R.;* J. Roger Hollingsworth, *The Whirligig of Politics;* Louis W. Koenig, *Bryan: A Political Biography of William Jennings Bryan;* John C. Long, *Bryan, the Great Commoner;* and Wayne C. Williams, *William Jennings Bryan.*

137. Quoted in Faulkner, *Politics, Reform and Expansion, 1890–1900,* p. 201.

138. In view of the low world price for silver and the relatively high world price for gold, if the government purchased all the silver presented to it at a price fixed at 16 to 1 it is conceivable that the entire world supply of silver would end up in the U.S. treasury and eventually minted into coins, with results which could not be completely anticipated.

139. Dobson, *Politics in the Gilded Age,* 181.

140. Stanley L. Jones, *The Presidential Election of 1896,* p. 271.

141. Mayer, *The Republican Party,* p. 251.

142. Ohioan Senator Joseph Foraker, campaigning for McKinley, delighted in reminding audiences he was addressing that the Platte River was "six inches deep and six miles wide at the mouth."

143. See George F. Whicher, ed., *William Jennings Bryan and the Campaign of 1896.*

144. Eugene H. Roseboom, *A History of Presidential Elections,* p. 314.

145. Mayer, *The Republican Party,* p. 253.

146. Jones, *The Presidential Election of 1896,* p. 291.

147. Democratic estimates of the amount collected and spent by the Republicans went as high as $16 million.

148. For other less regular methods used to ensure the defeat of Bryan, see Gilbert C. Fite, "Republican Strategy and the Farm Vote in the Presidential Campaign of 1896," pp. 787–806. Also see James A. Barnes, "Myths of the Bryan Campaign," pp. 399–400.

149. Vachel Lindsay, "Bryan, Bryan, Bryan, Bryan," in *Collected Poems.* (New York: Macmillan, 1925).

150. J. Rogers Hollingsworth, "The Whirligig of Politics," in Paul L. Murphy, ed., *Political Parties in American History, 1890–Present,* p. 997.

Bibliography

Books

Alexander, Herbert. *Political Financing*. Minneapolis, Minn.: Burgess, 1972.

Alexander, Holmes. *The American Tallyrand: Martin Van Buren*. New York: Harper and Brothers, 1935.

Angle, Paul A., ed. *Created Equal? The Complete Lincoln-Douglas Debates of 1858*. Chicago: University of Chicago Press, 1858.

Bailey, Thomas. *Democrats vs Republicans: The Continuing Clash*. Des Moines, Iowa: Meredith, 1968.

_____, and David Kennedy. *The American Pageant: A History of the Republic*. Sixth edition. Boston: Heath, 1979.

Banner, Lois W. *Elizabeth Cady Stanton: A Radical for Woman's Rights*. New York: Little, Brown, 1980.

Barker, Charles A. *Henry George*. Westport, Conn.: Greenwood Press, 1974.

Barnard, Harry. *Eagle Forgotten: The Life of John Peter Altgeld*. Indianapolis: Bobbs-Merrill, 1938.

_____. *Rutherford B. Hayes and His America*. Indianapolis: Bobbs-Merrill, 1954.

Bartlett, Ruhl, J. *John C. Fremont and the Republican Party*. Columbus: Ohio State University Press, 1931.

Beal, Carleton. *Brass-Knuckle Crusade: The Know-Nothing Conspiracy 1820–1860*. Mamaroneck, N.Y.: Hastings House, 1960.

Beale, Howard K. *The Critical Year: A Study of Andrew Johnson and Reconstruction*. New York: Frederick Unger, 1958.

Bellamy, Edward. *Looking Backward*. New York: Harper, 1959.

Beveridge, Albert J. *Abraham Lincoln 1809-1858*. Two volumes. Boston: Houghton, Mifflin, 1928.

Binkley, Wilfred E. *American Political Parties: Their Natural History*. Fourth edition. New York: Alfred A. Knopf, 1962.

Bishop, Joseph B. *Presidential Nominations and Elections, National Campaigns, Inaugurations and Campaign Caricature, with Numerous Illustrations*. New York: Charles Scribner's Sons, 1916.

Blue, Frederick J. *The Free Soilers: Third Party Politics 1848-1854*. Urbana: University of Illinois Press, 1973.

Boller, Paul F., Jr. *Presidential Anecdotes*. New York: Oxford University Press, 1981.

_____. *Presidential Campaigns*. New York: Oxford University Press, 1984.

Bonadio, Felice A., ed. *Political Parties in American History: 1828-1890*. New York: G.P. Putnam's Sons, 1974.

Bowers, Claude G. *The Tragic Era: The Revolution After Lincoln.* Boston: Houghton, Mifflin, 1929.

Bowman, Sylvia E. *The Year 2000; A Critical Biography of Edward Bellamy.* New York: Octagon Books, 1979.

Bruce, Robert V. *1877: A Year of Violence.* Indianapolis: Bobbs-Merrill, 1959.

Bryan, William Jennings. *The First Battle. A Story of the Campaign of 1896.* Chicago: W.B. Conkey, 1896.

Buck, Paul H. *The Road to Reunion: 1865–1900.* New York: Little, Brown. 1937.

Buck, Solon J. *The Agrarian Crusade.* New Haven, Conn.: Yale University Press, 1920.

_____. *The Granger Movement: A Study of Agricultural Organization and Its Political, Economic and Social Manifestations 1870–1880.* Lincoln: University of Nebraska Press, 1963.

Burdette, Franklin L. *The Republican Party: A Short History.* Princeton, N.J.: Van Nostrand, 1968.

Burnham, Walter Dean. *Presidential Ballots 1836–1892.* Baltimore: Johns Hopkins University Press, 1955.

Caldwell, Robert G. *James A. Garfield: Party Chieftain.* New York: Dodd, Mead, 1931.

Callow, Alexander B., Jr. *The Tweed Ring.* New York: Oxford University Press, 1965.

Capers, Gerald M. *Stephen A. Douglas, Defender of the Union.* New York: Little, Brown, 1959.

Carman, Harry J., and Reinhard H. Luthin. *Lincoln and the Patronage.* New York: Columbia University Press, 1943.

Carroll, E. M. *Origins of the Whig Party.* Durham, N.C.: Duke University Press, 1925.

Catton, Bruce. *The Coming Fury.* Garden City, N.Y.: Doubleday, 1961.

Chidsey, Donald B. *The Gentleman From New York: A Life of Roscoe Conkling.* New Haven, Conn.: Yale University Press, 1935.

Chitwood, Oliver P. *John Tyler: Champion of the Old South.* New York: Russell and Russell, 1964.

Clancy, Herbert J. *The Presidential Election of 1880.* Chicago: Loyola University Press, 1958.

Cole, Donald B. *Martin Van Buren and the American Political System.* Princeton, N.J.: Princeton University Press, 1984.

Coleman, Charles H. *The Election of 1868: The Democratic Effort to Regain Control.* New York: Columbia University Press, 1933.

Coletta, Paolo E. *William Jennings Bryan: Political Evangelist, 1860–1908.* Three volumes. Lincoln: University of Nebraska Press, 1964–1969.

Commons, John R. *History of Labour in the United States.* Four volumes. New York: Macmillan, 1918–1935.

Congressional Quarterly, *National Party Conventions 1831–1976.* Washington, D.C.: Congressional Quarterly, Inc., 1979.

Coolidge, Louis A. *Ulysses S. Grant.* Boston: Houghton, Mifflin, 1922.

Crandall, Andrew W. *The Early History of the Republican Party, 1854–1856.* Reprint. Gloucester, Mass.: Peter Smith, 1960.

Crenshaw, Ollinger. *The Slave States in the Presidential Election of 1860.* Baltimore: Johns Hopkins University Press, 1946.

Cunningham, Homer F. *The Presidents' Last Years: George Washington to Lyndon Johnson.* Jefferson, N.C., McFarland: 1989.

Current, Richard N. *Daniel Webster and the Rise of National Conservatism.* New York: Little, Brown, 1955.

Curtis, Francis. *The Republican Party, 1854–1904.* Two volumes. New York: G.P. Putnam's Sons, 1904.

Darden, Robert F. *The Climax of Populism: The Election of 1896.* Lexington: University Press of Kentucky, 1965.

David, Henry. *The History of the Haymarket Affair: A Study in the American Social-Revolutionary and Labor Movements.* New York: Farrar and Rinehart, 1936.

Davis, James W. *Presidential Primaries: The Road to the White House.* New York: Thomas Y. Crowell, 1967.

DeMille, Anna. *Henry George.* Chapel Hill: University of North Carolina Press, 1950.

DeSantis, Vincent P. *Republicans Face the Southern Question: The New Departure Years, 1877–1897.* Baltimore: Johns Hopkins University Press, 1959.

Desmond, Humphrey J. *The Know-Nothing Party.* Washington, D.C.: New Century, 1905.

Dobson, John M. *Politics in the Gilded Age: A New Perspective on Reform.* New York: Praeger, 1972.

Doenecke, Justus D. *The Presidencies of James A. Garfield and Chester A. Arthur.* Lawrence: University Press of Kansas, 1981.

_____. *The Politics of Reconstruction, 1863–1867.* Baton Rouge: Louisiana State University Press, 1965.

Donald, David H. *Charles Sumner and the Coming of the Civil War.* New York: Fawcett/Ballantine Books, 1960.

Donovan, Herbert D. A. *The Barnburners: A Study of the Internal Movements in the Political History of New York State and of the Resulting Changes in Political Affiliation, 1830–1852.* New York: The New York University Press, 1925.

Duberman, Martin B. *Charles Francis Adams, 1807–1886.* Boston: Houghton, Mifflin, 1961.

Dulles, Foster Rhae. *Labor in America.* New York: Thomas Y. Crowell, 1949.

Dunn, Arthur W. *From Harrison to Harding, A Personal Narrative Covering a Third of a Century, 1888–1921.* Two volumes. New York: G.P. Putnam's Sons, 1922.

Dyer, Brainerd. *Zachary Taylor.* Baton Rouge: Louisiana State University Press, 1946.

Eaton, Clement. *Henry Clay and the Art of American Politics.* New York: Little, Brown, 1957.

Eckenrode, H.J. *Rutherford B. Hayes: Statesman of Reunion.* Port Washington, N.Y.: Kennikat, 1963.

Ewing, Cortez A. M. *Presidential Elections from Abraham Lincoln to Franklin D. Roosevelt.* Norman: University of Oklahoma Press, 1940.

Faulkner, Harold U. *American Political and Social History.* New York: F.S. Crofts, 1943.

_____. *Politics, Reform, and Expansion, 1890–1900.* New York: Harper and Row, 1959.

_____. *The Quest for Social Justice, 1898–1914.* New York: Macmillan, 1931.

Fehrenbacher, Don E. *The Dred Scott Case, Its Significance in American Law and Politics.* New York: Oxford University Press, 1978.

_____. *The Era of Expansion, 1800–1848.* New York: Wiley, 1968.

_____. *Prelude to Greatness: Lincoln in the 1850's.* Stanford, Calif.: Stanford University Press, 1964.

Filler, Louis. *Crusaders for American Liberalism.* New York: Antioch Press, 1961.

Fine, Nathan L. *Labor and Farmer Parties in the United States, 1828–1928.* New York: Russell and Russell, 1961.

Fite, Emerson D. *The Presidential Campaign of 1860.* New York: Macmillan, 1911.

Fladeland, Betty. *James Gillespie Birney: Slaveholder to Abolitionist.* Ithaca, N.Y.: Cornell University Press, 1955.

Flick, Alexander C. *Samuel Jones Tilden: A Study in Political Sagacity.* New York: Dodd, Mead, 1939.

Foner, Eric. *Free Soil, Free Labor, Free Men: The Ideology of the Republican Party Before the Civil War.* New York: New York University Press, 1970.

Ford, Henry Jones. *The Cleveland Era: A Chronicle of the New Order in Politics.* New Haven, Conn.: Yale University Press, 1919.

Fuess, Claude M. *Daniel Webster.* New York: Little, Brown, 1930.

Furman, Bess. *White House Profile: A Social History of the White House, Its Occupants and Its Festivities.* Indianapolis: Bobbs-Merrill, 1951.

Garland, Hamlin. *Ulysses S. Grant: His Life and Character.* New York: Doubleday and McClure, 1898.

Garraty, John A. *The American Nation.* Third edition. New York: Harper and Row, 1974.

Ginger, Ray. *The Age of Excess: The United States from 1877 to 1914.* New York: Macmillan, 1965.

————. *The Bending Cross; A Biography of Eugene Victor Debs.* New Brunswick, N.J.: Rutgers University Press, 1949.

Glad, Paul W. *McKinley, Bryan and the People.* Philadelphia: J.B. Lippincott, 1964.

————. *The Trumpet Soundeth: William Jennings Bryan and His Democracy, 1896–1912.* Lincoln: University of Nebraska Press, 1960.

Goldman, Eric F. *Rendezvous with Destiny: A History of Modern American Reform.* New York: Alfred A. Knopf, 1952.

Goldman, Ralph M. *The Democratic Party in American Politics.* New York: Macmillan, 1966.

————. *The Search for Consensus: The Story of the Democratic Party.* Philadelphia: Temple University Press, 1979.

Gosnell, Harold. *Boss Platt and His New York Machine.* Chicago: University of Chicago Press, 1924.

Graebner, Norman A., ed. *Politics and the Crisis of 1860.* Urbana: University of Illinois Press, 1961.

Gray, Wood. *The Hidden Civil War: The Story of the Copperheads.* New York: Viking Press, 1942.

Greenstone, J. David. *Labor in American Politics.* New York: Alfred A. Knopf, 1969.

Griffis, William E. *Millard Fillmore, Constructive Statesman, Defender of the Constitution, President of the United States.* Ithaca, N.Y.: Andrus and Church, 1915.

Hale, William Harlan. *Horace Greeley, Voice of the People.* New York: Harper, 1950.

Halstead, Murat. *Caucuses of 1860: A History of the National Political Convention of the Current Presidential Campaign (1860).* Columbus: Ohio State University Press, 1860.

Hamilton, Holman. *Prologue to Conflict: The Crisis and Compromise of 1850.* Lexington: University Press of Kentucky, 1964.

_____. *Zachary Taylor: Soldier in the White House.* Indianapolis: Bobbs-Merrill, 1951.

Hammond, Bray. *Banks and Politics in America from the Revolution to the Civil War.* Princeton, N.J.: Princeton University Press, 1957.

Harper, Ida Husted. *The History of Woman Suffrage.* New York: National American Woman Suffrage Association, 1922.

Harvey, William H. *Coin's Financial School.* Cambridge, Mass.: Harvard University Press, 1963.

Haworth, Paul L. *The Hayes-Tilden Disputed Presidential Election of 1876.* New York: Russell and Russell, 1966.

Hawthorne, Nathaniel. *The Life of Franklin Pierce.* New York: Garrett, 1970.

Haynes, Frederick E. *James Baird Weaver.* Iowa City: State Historical Society of Iowa, 1919. (Iowa Biographical Series.)

_____. *Third Party Movements Since the Civil War.* Iowa City: State Historical Society of Iowa, 1916.

Hays, Samuel P. *Response to Industrialism.* Chicago: University of Chicago Press, 1957.

Hesseltine, William B. *The Rise and Fall of Third Parties; From Anti-Masonry to Wallace.* Washington, D.C.: Public Affairs Press, 1948.

_____. *Third Party Movements in the United States.* New York: Van Nostrand, 1962.

_____. *Ulysses S. Grant, Politician.* New York: Dodd, Mead, 1935.

_____, and Rex G. Fisher, eds. *Trimmers, Trucklers and Temporizers; Notes of Murat Halstead from the Political Conventions of 1856.* Madison: State Historical Society of Wisconsin, 1961.

Hibben, Paxton. *The Fearless Leader, William Jennings Bryan.* New York: Farrar and Rinehart, 1929.

Hicks, John D. *The Federal Union: A History of the United States to 1865.* Third edition. Boston: Houghton, Mifflin, 1957.

_____. *The Populist Revolt: A History of the Farmer's Alliance and the People's Party.* Minneapolis: University of Minnesota Press, 1931.

Higham, John. *Strangers in the Land: Patterns of American Nativism 1860–1925.* New Brunswick, N.J.: Rutgers University Press, 1955.

Hirshon, Stanley P. *Farewell to the Bloody Shirt: Northern Republicans and the Southern Negro, 1877–1893.* Bloomington: Indiana University Press, 1962.

Hofstadter, Richard. *The Age of Reform: From Bryan to F.D.R.* New York: Random House, 1955.

_____. *The American Political Tradition.* New York: Alfred A. Knopf, 1948.

_____. *Social Darwinism in American Thought, 1860–1915.* Boston: Beacon, 1963.

Hollingsworth, J. Roger. *The Whirligig of Politics: The Democracy of Cleveland and Bryan.* Chicago: University of Chicago Press, 1963.

Hoogenboom, Ari A. *Outlawing the Spoils: A History of the Civil Service Movement, 1865–1883.* Urbana: University of Illinois Press, 1961.

Horner, Harland H. *Lincoln and Greeley.* Urbana: University of Illinois Press, 1953.

Howe, George F. *Chester A. Arthur: A Quarter Century of Machine Politics.* New York: Dodd, Mead, 1934.

Hoyt, Edwin P. *Andrew Johnson*. Chicago: Reilly and Lee, 1965.
—————. *James A. Garfield*. Chicago: Reilly and Lee, 1964.
—————. *James Buchanan*. Chicago: Reilly and Lee, 1966.
—————. *James Knox Polk*. Chicago: Reilly and Lee, 1965.
—————. *Zachary Taylor*. Chicago: Reilly and Lee, 1965.
Isely, Peter A. *Horace Greeley and the Republican Party, 1853–1861: A Study of the New York Tribune*. Princeton, N.J.: Princeton University Press, 1947.
Jaffa, Harry V. *Crisis of the House Divided: An Interpretation of the Issues in the Lincoln-Douglas Debates*. Seattle: University of Washington Press, 1973.
Johnson, Allen. *Stephen A. Douglas: A Study in American Politics*. New York: Macmillan, 1908.
Johnston, Alexander. *History of American Politics*. Revised edition. New York: Holt, 1910.
Jones, Charles O. *The Republican Party in American Politics*. New York: Macmillan, 1965.
Jones, James S. *Andrew Johnson: Seventeenth President of the United States*. Greenville: East Tennessee Publishing, 1901.
Jones, Stanley L. *The Presidential Election of 1896*. Madison: University of Wisconsin Press, 1964.
Josephson, Matthew. *The Politicos, 1865–1896*. New York: Harcourt, Brace, 1938.
Kent, Frank R. *The Democratic Party: A History*. New York: Century, 1928.
Kleeberg, Gordon S. *The Formation of the Republican Party as a National Political Organization*. New York: Columbia University Press, 1911.
Klein, Philip Shriver. *President James Buchanan*. University Park: Pennsylvania State University Press, 1962.
Klement, Frank L. *The Copperheads in the Middle West*. Chicago: University of Chicago Press, 1960.
Kleppner, Paul. *The Cross of Culture: A Social Analysis of Midwestern Politics, 1850–1900*. New York: Free Press, 1970.
Knoles, George Harmon. *The Presidential Campaign and Election of 1892*. Stanford, Calif.: Stanford University Press, 1942.
Koenig, Louis W. *Bryan: A Political Biography of William Jennings Bryan*. New York: G.P. Putnam's Sons, 1971.
—————. *The Chief Executive*. Third edition. New York: Harcourt Brace Jovanovich, 1975.
Kohlsaat, Herman H. *From McKinley to Harding: Personal Recollections of Our Presidents*. New York: Charles Scribner's Sons, 1923.
Korngold, Ralph. *Thaddeus Stevens: A Being Darkly Wise and Rudely Great*. New York: Harcourt, Brace, 1955.
Kraus, Michael. *The United States to 1865*. Ann Arbor: University of Michigan Press, 1959.
Kuhn, Henry, and O.M. Johnson. *The Socialist-Labor Party During Four Decades, 1890–1930*. New York: New York Labor News Company, 1931.
Lambert, John R. *Arthur P. Gorman*. Baton Rouge: Louisiana State University Press, 1953.
Lanck, W. Jelt. *The Causes of the Panic of 1893*. Boston: Houghton-Mifflin, 1907.
Laughlin, James Laurence. *The History of Bimetallism in the United States*. Fourth edition. Westport, Conn.: Greenwood Press, 1968.
Leech, Margaret. *In the Days of McKinley*. New York: Harper and Brothers, 1959.
LeFervre, Benjamin. *Campaign of 1884*. Chicago: Baird and Dillon, 1894.

Lindsey, Almont. *The Pullman Strike: The Story of a Unique Experience and of a Great Labor Upheaval.* Chicago: University of Chicago Press, 1942.
Litwack, Leon. *The American Labor Movement.* Englewood Cliffs, N.J.: Prentice-Hall, 1962.
Lomask, Milton. *This Slender Reed: A Life of James K. Polk.* New York: Farrar, Straus and Giroux, 1966.
Long, John C. *Bryan, The Great Commoner.* New York: Appleton, 1928.
Luebke, Frederick C., ed. *Ethnic Voters and the Election of Lincoln.* Lincoln: University of Nebraska Press, 1971.
Luthin, Reinhard H. *The First Lincoln Campaign.* Cambridge, Mass.: Harvard University Press, 1944.
Lutz, Alma. *Created Equal: A Biography of Elizabeth Cady Stanton, 1815–1902.* New York: John Day, 1940.
Lynch, Dennis T. *Grover Cleveland: A Man Foresquare.* New York: Horace, Liveright, 1932.
McCarthy, Charles. *The Anti-Masonic Party: A Study of Political Anti-Masonry in the United States, 1827–1840.* American Historical Association, *Annual Report.* 1902, 1: 367-574.
McCoy, Charles Allan. *Polk and the Presidency.* Austin: University of Texas Press, 1960.
McElroy, Robert. *Grover Cleveland: The Man and the Statesman.* New York: Harper and Brothers, 1923.
McFarland, Gerald W. *Mugwumps, Morals and Politics, 1884–1920.* Amherst, Mass.: University of Massachusetts Press, 1960.
McKitrick, Eric L. *Andrew Johnson and Reconstruction.* Chicago: University of Chicago Press, 1960.
————, ed. *Andrew Johnson: A Profile.* New York: Hill and Wang, 1969.
McMurry, D.L. *Coxey's Army.* New York: Little, Brown, 1929.
McPherson, James M. *Battle Cry of Freedom: The Civil War Era.* New York: Oxford University Press, 1988.
Macy, Jesse. *Political Parties in the United States, 1846–1861.* New York: Macmillan, 1900.
Mandelbaum, Seymour J. *Boss Tweed's New York.* New York: Wiley, 1965.
Marcus, Robert D. *Grand Old Party: Political Structure in the Gilded Age, 1880–1896.* New York: Oxford University Press, 1971.
Martin, Ralph. *Ballots and Bandwagons.* Skokie, Ill.: Rand-McNally, 1964.
Maxey, Chester C. *Bipartisanship in the United States.* Caldwell, Idaho: Caxton, 1965.
Mayer, George H. *The Republican Party, 1854–1966.* Second edition. New York: Oxford University Press, 1967.
Mayo, Bernard. *Henry Clay, Spokesman of the New West.* Boston: Houghton, Mifflin, 1937.
Mecklin, John M. *The Ku Klux Klan: A Study of the American Mind.* New York: Harcourt, Brace, 1924.
Merrill, Horace S. *Bourbon Leader: Grover Cleveland and the Democratic Party.* New York: Little, Brown, 1957.
Milton, George F. *Abraham Lincoln and the Fifth Column.* New York: Vanguard Press, 1942.
————. *The Age of Hate: Andrew Johnson and the Radicals.* New York: G.P. Putnam's Sons, 1930.
Minor, Henry. *The Story of the Democratic Party.* New York, Macmillan, 1928.

Mitchell, Stewart. *Horatio Seymour of New York.* Cambridge, Mass.: Harvard University Press, 1938.

Mitchell, Wesley C. *A History of the Greenbacks; With Special Reference to the Economic Consequences of Their Issue.* Chicago: University of Chicago Press, 1903.

Moos, Malcolm E. *The Republicans: A History of Their Party.* New York: Random House, 1956.

————, and Stephen Hess. *Hats in the Ring.* New York: Random House, 1960.

Morgan, H. Wayne. *From Hayes to McKinley: National Party Politics 1877–1896.* Syracuse, N.Y.: Syracuse University Press, 1969.

————. *The Gilded Age: A Reappraisal.* Syracuse, N.Y.: Syracuse University Press, 1970.

————. *William McKinley and His America.* Syracuse, N.Y.: Syracuse University Press, 1963.

Morgan, Robert J. *A Whig Embattled: The Presidency Under John Tyler.* Lincoln: University of Nebraska Press, 1954.

Morrison, Chaplain W. *Democratic Politics and Sectionalism: The Wilmot Proviso Controversy.* Chapel Hill: University of North Carolina Press, 1967.

Muzzey, David S. *James G. Blaine; A Political Idol of Other Days.* New York: Dodd, Mead, 1934.

Myers, Gustavus. *The History of Tammany Hall.* Second edition. New York: Boni and Liveright, 1917.

Myers, William Starr. *The Republican Party, A History.* New York: Appleton-Century Crofts, 1931.

Nash, Howard P., Jr. *Third Parties in American Politics.* Washington, D.C.: Public Affairs Press, 1959.

National Republican Committee. *Proceedings of the National Republican Convention, 1860.* Washington, D.C., 1861.

Nevins, Allan. *The Emergence of Modern America 1865–1878.* New York: Macmillan, 1927.

————. *Fremont, Pathmarker of the West.* New York: Appleton, Century, 1939.

————. *Grover Cleveland: A Study in Courage:* New York: Dodd, Mead, 1947.

————. *Ordeal of the Union.* Two volumes. New York: Charles Scribner's Sons, 1947.

———— and Henry Steele Commager. *A Short History of the United States.* New York: Modern Library, 1942.

Nichols, Roy F. *The Democratic Machine 1850–1854.* New York: Columbia University Press, 1923.

————. *Franklin Pierce, Young Hickory of the Granite Hills.* Philadelphia: University of Pennsylvania Press, 1931.

————. *The Invention of the American Political Parties.* New York: Macmillan, 1967.

————. *The Stakes of Power, 1845–1877.* New York: Hill and Wang, 1961.

Niven, John. *Martin Van Buren.* New York: Oxford University Press, 1983

Nye, Russel B. *Midwestern Progressive Politics: A Historical Study of Its Origins and Development, 1870–1950.* East Lansing: Michigan State University Press, 1959.

O'Connor, Thomas H. *The Disunited States: The Era of Civil War and Reconstruction.* New York: Dodd, Mead, 1972.

————. *Lords of the Loom: The Cotton Whigs and the Coming of the Civil War.* New York: Charles Scribner's Sons, 1968.

Olcott, Charles S. *The Life of William McKinley.* Two volumes. Boston: Houghton, Mifflin, 1916.

Ormsby, Robert M. *A History of the Whig Party, or Some of the Main Features with a Hurried Glance at the Formation of Parties in the United States, and the Outlines of the History of the Principal Parties of the Country to the Present Time, Etc., Etc.* Boston: Crosby, Nichols, 1859.

Overdyke, W. Darrell. *The Know-Nothing Party in the South.* Baton Rouge: Louisiana State University Press, 1950.

Paul, James C.N. *Rift in the Democracy.* Philadelphia: University of Pennsylvania Press, 1961.

Peck, Harry Thurston. *Democrats and Republicans: Ten Years of the Republic.* Toms River, N.J.: Capricorn Books, 1964.

Peskin, Allan. *Garfield.* Kent, Ohio: Kent State University Press, 1978.

Poage, George R. *Henry Clay and the Whig Party.* Chapel Hill: University of North Carolina Press, 1936.

Polakoff, Keith Ian. *The Politics of Inertia: The Election of 1876 and the End of Reconstruction.* Baton Rouge: Louisiana State University Press, 1973.

Polk, James K. *The Diary of a President, 1845-1849.* Edited by Allan Nevins. New York: Longmans, Green, 1952.

Pollack, Norman. *The Populist Response to Industrial America: Midwestern Political Thought.* Cambridge, Mass.: Harvard University Press, 1962.

Pomper, Gerald. *Nominating the President: The Politics of Convention Choice.* New York: W.W. Norton, 1966.

Porter, Kirk H., and Donald Bruce Johnson. *National Party Platforms 1840-1964.* Urbana: University of Illinois Press, 1966.

Potter, David M. *The Impending Crisis, 1848-1861.* New York: Harper and Row, 1976.

Pringle, Henry F. *Theodore Roosevelt: A Biography.* New York: Harcourt, Brace, 1931.

Quint, Howard. *The Forging of American Socialism.* New York: Columbia University Press, 1952.

Randall, James G., and David Donald. *The Civil War and Reconstruction.* Revised edition. New York: Little, Brown, 1969.

Ratner, Lorman. *Antimasonry: The Crusade and the Party.* Englewood Heights, N.J.: Prentice-Hall, 1969.

Ray, P. Orman. *The Convention That Nominated Lincoln: An Address Delivered Before the Chicago Historical Society on May 18, 1916, the Fifty-sixth Anniversary of Lincoln's Nomination for the Presidency.* Chicago: University of Chicago Press, 1916.

Rayback, Joseph G. *Free Soil: The Election of 1848.* Lexington: University Press of Kentucky, 1970.

Rayback, Robert J. *Millard Fillmore: Biography of a President.* Buffalo, N.Y.: Henry Stewart, 1959.

Reeves, Thomas C. *Gentleman Boss: The Life of Chester Alan Arthur.* New York: Alfred A. Knopf, 1975.

Remini, Robert Vincent. *Martin Van Buren and the Making of the Democratic Party.* New York: Columbia University Press, 1959.

Republican National Committee. *The History of the Republican Party.* Washington, D.C.: Republican National Committee, 1962.

Rice, Arnold S. *The Ku Klux Klan in American Politics.* Washington, D.C.: Public Affairs Press, 1962.

Rice, Stuart A. *Farmers and Workers in American Politics.* New York: Columbia University Press, 1924.

Ridge, Martin. *Ignatius Donnelly: Portrait of a Politician.* Chicago: University of Chicago Press, 1962.

Ridpath, John Clark. *The Life and Work of James A. Garfield and the Tragic Story of His Death.* Cincinnati: Jones Brothers, 1881.

Riegel, Robert E. *American Feminists.* Lawrence: University Press of Kansas, 1968.

Robinson, Lloyd. *The Stolen Election — Hayes versus Tilden 1876.* New York: Doubleday, 1968.

Robinson, William A. *Thomas B. Reed, Parliamentarian.* New York: Dodd, Mead, 1930.

Roseboom, Eugene H. *A History of Presidential Elections.* Second edition. New York: Macmillan, 1964.

Ross, Earle Dudley. *The Liberal Republican Movement.* Seattle: University of Washington Press, 1970.

Rutland, Robert A. *The Democrats: From Jefferson to Carter.* Baton Rouge: Louisiana State University Press, 1982.

Saloutos, Theodore. *Farmer Movements in the South, 1865-1933.* Berkeley: University of California Press, 1960.

Schlesinger, Arthur Meier, Jr., *Political and Social Growth of the American People 1865-1940.* Third edition. New York: Macmillan, 1941.

_____, ed. *History of American Presidential Elections 1798-1968.* Four volumes. New York: Chelsea House, 1971.

_____, ed. *History of U.S. Political Parties.* Four volumes. New York: Chelsea House, 1973.

Sears, Stephen W. *George B. McClellan: The Young Napoleon.* New York: Ticknor and Fields, 1988.

Seitz, Don C. *Horace Greeley.* Indianapolis: Bobbs-Merrill, 1926.

Sellers, Charles. *James K. Polk: Continentalist, 1843-1846.* Princeton, N.J.: Princeton University Press, 1966.

Severn, Bill. *Frontier President: James K. Polk.* New York: Ives Washburn, 1965.

Shannon, David A. *The Socialist Party of America: A History.* Second edition. Chicago: Quadrangle Books, 1967.

Shannon, Fred A. *American Farmer's Movements.* New York: Van Nostrand, 1957.

Shepard, Edward M. *Martin Van Buren.* Boston: Houghton, Mifflin, 1972.

Sievers, Harry J. *Benjamin Harrison: Hoosier President.* Indianapolis: Bobbs-Merrill, 1968.

_____. *Benjamin Harrison: Hoosier Statesman 1865-1888.* New York: University Publishers, 1959.

Simkins, Francis B. *Pitchfork Ben Tillman: South Carolinian.* Baton Rouge: Louisiana State University Press, 1944.

_____. *The Tillman Movement in South Carolina.* Durham, N.C.: Duke University Press, 1926.

Sinclair, Andrew. *The Age of Excess: A Social History of the Prohibition Movement.* New York: Harper, 1964.

Sloan, Irving J., ed. *James Buchanan, 1791-1868.* Dobbs-Ferry, N.Y.: Oceana, 1968.

Smith, Elbert B. *The Presidency of James Buchanan.* Lawrence: University Press of Kansas, 1975.

Smith, Theodore Clarke. *The Liberty and Free Soil Parties in the Northwest.* New York: Longmans, Green, 1897.

_____. *The Life and Letters of James Abram Garfield.* New Haven, Conn.: Yale University Press, 1925.

Sproat, John. *The Best Men: Liberal Reformers in the Gilded Age.* Oxford: Oxford University Press, 1968.

Stampp, Kenneth. *The Era of Reconstruction, 1865–1877.* New York: Alfred A. Knopf, 1956.

Stanwood, Edward. *American Tariff Controversies in the Nineteenth Century.* Two volumes. Boston: Houghton, Mifflin, 1903.

_____. *A History of the Presidency from 1788 to 1897.* Boston: Houghton, Mifflin, 1928.

Stedman, Murray S., Jr., and Susan Stedman. *Discontent at the Polls: A Study of Farmer and Labor Parties, 1827–1948.* New York: Columbia University Press, 1950.

Stewart, F.M. *The National Civil Service Reform League.* Austin: University of Texas Press, 1929.

Stoddard, Henry L. *Horace Greeley, Printer, Editor, Crusader.* New York: G.P. Putnam's Sons, 1946.

_____. *Presidential Sweepstakes: The Story of Political Conventions and Campaigns.* New York: G.P. Putnam's Sons, 1948.

Stoddard, William O. *Lives of Presidents Rutherford B. Hayes, James A. Garfield and Chester A. Arthur.* New York: F.A. Stokes and Brothers, 1889.

Stryker, Lloyd P. *Andrew Johnson: A Study in Courage.* New York: Macmillan, 1929.

Summers, Festus P. *William L. McKinley and Tariff Reform.* New Brunswick, N.J.: Rutgers University Press, 1953.

Taussig, Frank W. *The Tariff History of the United States.* Eighth edition. New York: G.P. Putnam's Sons, 1931.

Taylor, John M. *Garfield of Ohio: The Available Man.* New York: Norton, 1970.

Thomas, Harrison C. *The Return of the Democratic Party to Power in 1884.* New York: Columbia University Press, 1919.

Thomas, Lately. *The First President Johnson.* New York: William Morrow, 1968.

Trefousse, Hans L. *The Radical Republicans: Lincoln's Vanguard for Racial Justice.* New York: Alfred A. Knopf, 1969.

Tucker, Glenn. *Hancock the Superb.* Indianapolis: Bobbs-Merrill, 1960.

Unger, Irwin. *The Greenback Era: A Social and Political History of American Finance, 1865–1879.* Princeton, N.J.: Princeton University Press, 1964.

_____, and Debra Unger. *The Vulnerable Years, The United States, 1896–1917.* Hinsdale, Ill.: Dryden Press, 1977.

Vale, Vivian. *Labor in American Politics.* Totowa, N.J.: Rowan and Littlefield, 1971.

Van Deusen, Glyndon G. *The Life of Henry Clay.* New York: Little, Brown, 1937.

_____. *Thurlow Weed, Wizard of the Lobby.* New York: Little, Brown, 1947.

Van Riper, Paul P. *History of the United States Civil Service.* New York: Row, Peterson, 1958.

Vincent, Henry. *The Story of the Commonweal.* Salem, N.H.: Arno Press, 1969.

Wecter, Dixon. *The Hero in America: A Chronicle of Hero-Worship.* New York: Charles Scribner's Sons, 1941.

Weston, Florence. *The Presidential Election of 1828.* Washington, D.C.: Ruddick, 1938.

Whicher, George F., ed. *William Jennings Bryan and the Campaign of 1896.* Boston: Heath, 1953.

White, Leonard D. *The Republican Era, 1869-1901: A Study in Administrative History.* New York: Macmillan, 1958.

Whitney, David C. *The American Presidents.* Garden City, N.Y.: Doubleday, 1967.

Wiebe, Robert H. *The Search for Order 1877-1920.* New York: Hill and Wang, 1967.

Williams, Charles R. *The Life of Rutherford Birchard Hayes, Nineteenth President of the United States.* Two volumes. Boston: Houghton, Mifflin, 1914.

Wiliams, T. Harry. *Lincoln and the Radicals.* Madison: University of Wisconsin Press, 1941.

Williams, Wayne C. *William Jennings Bryan.* New York: G.P. Putnam's Sons, 1936.

Winston, Robert W. *Andrew Johnson: Plebian and Patriot.* New York: Henry Holt, 1928.

Woodward, C. Vann. *Reunion and Reaction: The Compromise of 1877 and the End of Reconstruction.* New York: Little, Brown, 1951.

_____. *The Strange Career of Jim Crow.* Revised Edition. New York: Oxford University Press, 1957.

_____. *Tom Watson: Agrarian Rebel.* New York: Macmillan, 1938.

Zarefsky, David. *Lincoln, Douglas and Slavery: In the Crucible of Public Debate.* Chicago: University of Chicago Press, 1990.

Zornow, William. *Lincoln and the Party Divided.* Norman: University of Oklahoma Press, 1954.

Articles

Barnes, James A. "Myths of the Bryan Campaign." *Mississippi Valley Historical Review* 34 (1947-48): 367-404.

Barr, Elizabeth N. "The Populist Uprising," in William E. Connellly, ed., *A Standard History of Kansas and Kansans.* Chicago: Lewis Publishing Co., 1918-1919, 2:1115-1195.

Blodgett, Geoffery T. "The Mind of the Boston Mugwumps." *Mississippi Valley Historical Review* 48 (March 1962): 614-34.

Commons, J.R. "Horace Greeley and the Working Class Origins of the Republican Party." *Political Science Quarterly* 24 (September 1909): 468-489.

Corwin, E.S., "The Dred Scott Decision," *American Historical Review* 17 (1911) 52-69.

Cravens, Avery. "The 1840s and the Democratic Process." *Journal of Southern History* 16 (1950): 161-76.

Degler, Carl. "American Political Parties and the Rise of the City." *Journal of American History* 51 (June 1964): 41-59.

Dinnerstein, Leonard. "Election of 1880," in Arthur M. Schlesinger, Jr., ed., *History of American Presidential Elections 1798-1968,* 2:1491-1516.

Donald, David H. "The Republican Party 1864-1876," in Arthur M. Schlesinger, Jr., ed., *History of U.S. Political Parties.* New York: Chelsea House, 1973, 2:1281-1289.

Downey, Matthew T. "Horace Greeley and the Politicians: The Liberal Republican Convention in 1872." *The Journal of American History,* 53 (1967): 727-750.

Dudley, Harold M. "The Election of 1864," *Mississippi Valley Historical Review* 18 (March 1932): 500-18.

Dunning, W.A. "The Second Birth of the Republican Party." *American Historical Review* 16 (1910): 56–63.

Ellis, Elmer. "The Silver Republicans in the Election of 1896." *Mississippi Valley Historical Review* 18 (March 1932): 525–57.

Fite, Gilbert, C. "Republican Strategy and the Farm Vote in the Presidential Campaign of 1896." *American Historical Review* 65 (1959-60): 787–806.

Fowler, Dorothy G. "Precursors of the Hatch Acts." *Mississippi Valley Historical Review* 47 (1960-61): 247–62.

Hamilton, Holman. "'The Cave of the Winds' and the Compromise of 1850." *Journal of Southern History* 23 (August 1957): 331–53.

Harrington, Fred H. "Fremont and the North Americans." *American Historical Review* 44 (1939): 842–48.

Hicks, John D. "The Political Career of Ignatius Donnelly." *Mississippi Valley Historical Review* 8 (June-September 1921): 80–132.

_____. "The Third Party Tradition in American Politics." *Mississippi Valley Historical Review* 19 (June 1933): 27–28.

Hollingsworth, J. Roger. "The Cuckoos Create a Storm," in Felice A. Bonadio, ed., *Political Parties in American History: 1828-1890*. New York: G.P. Putnam's Sons, 1974, 911–13.

_____. "The Whirligig of Politics," in Paul L. Murphy, ed., *Political Parties in American History: 1890-Present*. New York: G.P. Putnam's Sons, 1974, 995–1000.

Holt, Michael F. "The Antimasonic and Know Nothing Parties," in Arthur M. Schlesinger, Jr., ed., *History of U.S. Political Parties*. New York: Chelsea House, 1973, 2:575–620.

Julian, George W., "The First Republican Convention." *American Historical Review* 4 (1898): 313–322.

Lipset, Seymour M. "The Emergence of the One-Party South—The Election of 1860." In *Political Man: The Social Basis of Politics*. New York: Doubleday, 1960, pp. 344–54.

Luthin, Reinhard. "Abraham Lincoln Becomes a Republican." *Political Science Quarterly* 59 (1944): 420–38.

McFarland, Gerald W. "The New York Mugwumps of 1884: A Profile." *Political Science Quarterly* 78 (March 1963): 40–58.

Miles, E.A. "'Fifty-four Forty or Fight'—An American Political Legend." *Mississippi Valley Historical Review* (September 1957): 291–310.

Nichols, Jeannette. "The Monetary Problems of William McKinley." *Ohio History* 72 (October 1963): 263–92.

Nichols, Roy F. "Some Problems of the First Republican Campaign." *American Historical Reviews* 28 (1922): 492–96.

Schafer, Joseph. "Who Elected Lincoln?" *American Historical Review* 47 (1941): 51–63.

Sellers, Charles G., Jr. "Who Were the Southern Whigs?" *American Historical Review*, 59 (1954): 335–46.

Stampp, Kenneth. "Triumph of the Conservatives," in Felice A. Bonadio, ed., *Political Parties in American History: 1828-1890*. New York: G.P. Putnam's Sons, 1974, 788–809.

Thompson, E. Bruce. "The Bristow Presidential Boom of 1876." *Mississippi Valley Historical Review* 32 (June 1945): 3–32.

Van Deusen, Glyndon G. "Thurlow Weed's Analysis of William H. Seward's Defeat in the Republican Convention of 1860." *Mississippi Valley Historical Review* 34 (1947): 101–4.

————. "The Whig Party," in Arthur M. Schlesinger, Jr., ed., *History of U.S. Political Parties*. New York: Chelsea House, 1973, 1:333–63.
Woods, Gordon S. "The Massachusetts Mugwumps." *New England Quarterly* 33 (December 1960): 435–51.

Index